Mirror of Medicine

Mirror of Medicine

A History of the *British Medical Journal*

P. W. J. BARTRIP
Wolfson College, Oxford

BRITISH MEDICAL JOURNAL
AND
CLARENDON PRESS · OXFORD
1990

Oxford University Press, Walton Street, Oxford OX2 6DP
Oxford New York Toronto
Delhi Bombay Calcutta Madras Karachi
Petaling Jaya Singapore Hong Kong Tokyo
Nairobi Dar es Salaam Cape Town
Melbourne Auckland
and associated companies in
Berlin Ibadan

Published in the United States
by Oxford University Press, New York

British Library Cataloguing in Publication Data
Bartrip, P. W. J. (Peter W. J.)
Mirror of medicine : the BMJ, 1840–1990
1. Great Britain. Medicine, history
I. Title
610.941
ISBN 0–19–261844–X

Library of Congress Cataloging in Publication Data
Bartrip, P. W. J. (Peter W. J.)
Mirror of medicine : the BMJ 1840–1990 / Peter Bartrip.
p. cm. —(Oxford medical publications)
1. British medical journal—History. 2. British Medical Association—History. 3. Medicine—Great Britain—History.
I. Title. II. Series.
[DNLM: 1. British medical journal. 2. History of Medicine,—19th Cent.—Great Britain. 3. History of Medicine,—20th Cent.—Great Britain. 4. Periodicals—history—Great Britain. PN 4784.M4 B294m]
R487.B37 1990 610′.5—dc20 90–7100
ISBN 0–19–261844–X

Typeset by
Latimer Trend & Co. Ltd

Printed in Great Britain by
Courier International Ltd
Tiptree, Essex

Foreword

D. J. Weatherall, FRS

I was absolutely delighted when Stephen Lock invited me to write a short preface to Peter Bartrip's account of the first 150 years of the *British Medical Journal.* I have had a soft spot for the *BMJ* ever since 1960 when, in a moment of uncharacteristic editorial carelessness, it published my first paper. As a young national serviceman working in the military hospital in Singapore I had discovered that the child of a Gurkha serjeant had an inherited disorder of the blood, at that time thought to be restricted to the Mediterranean region. Realizing that it was vital that the world heard about this breakthrough my first thought was the *BMJ.* After an interminable wait, all of six months as I recall it, the issue of the journal carrying my masterpiece arrived in Singapore. My elation was short-lived, however. A few days later I was hauled in front of the Director-General of Medical Services for the Far East Land Forces and told that the publication of information about military personnel without permission from the War Office was an offence which could lead to a court martial. In the event both the Editor of the *BMJ* and I survived, though I often wonder if the British Medical Association know that its esteemed journal was once guilty of breaking the Official Secrets Act.

Many scientific journals are no more than a collection of articles describing original work in their particular fields. There are a few exceptions, however. Broadly based science journals like *Nature* and *Science*, and medical journals such as the *BMJ,* the *Lancet*, and the *New England Journal of Medicine* attempt to do much more. In essence they combine the role of a scientific journal with that of a weekly newspaper. As well as articles describing new research they carry editorials on a wide spectrum of topics ranging from the state of the art of particular areas of science to current political issues, gossip columns on the goings on in the scientific or medical worlds, extensive and occasionally vituperative correspondence sections, obituaries of various shades of improbability, and reviews of books on every aspect of science or medicine. For the last 150 years the *BMJ* has been the prime example of this genre.

It follows, therefore, that a general journal of the type to which the *BMJ* has always aspired, if it speaks with an independent voice and is well edited, has the potential to be a valuable historical document, reflecting not just the scientific development of its field but also many of the social and political changes that have occurred over its lifetime.

The first 150 years of the life of the *BMJ* has been a period of remarkable change and development for medical practice. At the time of the first issue there was little to offer patients except kindness and support together with injudicious blood-letting. A browse through the pages of the journal enables the reader to follow the extraordinary panorama of discoveries on which modern clinical practice is based: antiseptic surgery; anaesthesia; the identification of infectious agents; the control of communicable disease with public health measures, vaccines, and antibiotics; the gradual emergence of clinical science; the symptomatic control of many of the major killers of western society; the realization that environmental agents such as tobacco, rich food, alcohol, and the other good things of life may be major players in the generation of heart disease and cancer; and, last but not least, the recent evolution of medical research from studies of whole patients to their individual cells and genes. The story is interspersed from time to time with those rare papers that change medical thinking overnight and which open up completely new vistas; Rennie on plaque, Manson and Ross on malaria, Simpson on chloroform and painless childbirth, and so on.

It is clear that the pace of change has often been too much for a particularly conservative profession and its journal. Innovators have never had an easy ride and controversies have abounded. Witness the long period of deep suspicion about the early development of anaesthesia, with its gloomy editorial prognostications. Even today the pages of the journal sometimes reflect this unease with anything new; its rather guarded views on the value of supporting research in molecular and cell biology as compared with more immediate public-health-related activities for example. Perhaps this recurring theme is a reflection of the profession's continual difficulties in maintaining a balance between the increasing reductionism that results from rapid scientific advance and those holistic attitudes essential for good patient care.

But the story of the *BMJ* is much more than a catalogue of the trials and tribulations of advances in medical practice. It is also a fascinating window of social and political change, particularly society's attitudes to poverty and sickness. It gives us some unique insights into how the medical world and the country as a whole survived two world wars, and, in particular, how a highly individualistic generation of doctors coped with the social reforms that began after 1945, and moved uneasily towards that unique British institution, the National Health Service. It is too early to put into true perspective the relationship between changes in medical practice over the last 40 years and the social climate that has brought them about. The motives for the continual governmental tinkering with the National Health Service which has gone on over this period will have to be evaluated by the historian who tackles the next 150 years of the life of the *BMJ*. But it is only necessary to reflect on the fundamental reorganization that is occurring within the National Health

Service at the time that this book is going to press, and the way that it reflects new attitudes and divisions in British society, to appreciate the enormous potential of a journal like the *BMJ* as a social document.

The broad range of institutions and customs that have been the subject of comment in the pages of the journal over the years also tells us much about ourselves as a nation and helps to put some of our current social ills into perspective. Those who pine for our virtuous Victorian past, and hold that the recent spate of violence in our football grounds is a reflection of the moral dissolution of our society combined with the evils of an uncaring government, may be surprised to read an editorial attack on soccer hooliganism, written in 1884 and ending with the statement that it is distasteful to see somebody kicked to death, 'even in a friendly way.' And as they shake their heads about the increasing problem of drink they may be equally taken aback to read that, in 1864, a study of over four thousand souls at the London Hospital revealed that in the previous year they had consumed 1558 gallons of wine, 359 gallons of beer, and 77 gallons of gin. Decadent we may be, but at least we are consistent.

One difficulty for the historian who tries to assess the value of the *BMJ* as a mirror of social climate is that, for most of its lifetime, it has been the official mouthpiece of the British Medical Association, a body that has never been over-endowed with angry young men. Hence its value in this context has always relied on the independence of mind of its editors. Happily, for at least some of its lifetime the *BMJ* seems to have been blessed with editors with strong personalities, as evidenced by their differences of opinion, not just with the Association but with government, the Royal Colleges, the General Medical Council, and, at one time or another, with most of the British establishment. Thus, although it is inevitable that its willingness to speak freely has varied over the years, at its best the journal has been a valuable voice for criticism and change of some of the rather ossified bodies that have governed British medical practice.

So how well does the *BMJ* stand up to a close scrutiny of its first 150 years? The fact that it has survived at all over such a long and turbulent period suggests that it must be in reasonable health. The current editor has often quoted the journal's low rating in citation indexes as evidence that somehow he has not got it quite right. But I wonder if he has done himself justice. A general journal of this type has to be of immediate interest to doctors ranging from general practitioners through health administrators to specialists and clinical scientists in increasingly narrow fields. At a time when many of the most exciting developments in medical science are appearing in top rating scientific journals like *Nature* and *Cell*, and when their contents is often totally incomprehensible to practising doctors, the *BMJ* cannot hope to head the citation lists. But does this matter? If, through its editorial columns, it can make some of these advances intelligible to the medical world at large, and continue to keep its readers informed about the broader aspects of medical care in their social context, it will have succeeded in its purpose. And if, at the same time, it can reflect the enormous satisfaction and fun of medical practice, so much the better.

As I write, the *BMJ* of 3 February 1990 is lying on my desk. A glance through the index reveals an editorial review about a new haemopoietic growth factor; a general section warning about the effect of the Government White Paper on academic medicine together with a tirade on the paucity of women in the top places in professions in the UK; original scientific articles on the epidemiology of blood pressure and monitoring for fetal abnormality; a catholic series of 'middle articles' which include accounts of fertile flukes in Brazil and housing for people with special needs; a correspondence column with letters ranging from the inadvertent use of superglue in eyedrops to screening for breast cancer; and a final 'personal view' section which consists of a *crie du coeur* from a cyclist who claims that the government's national transport policy, as it relates to riding a bicycle for health, is akin to rearranging the deckchairs on the Titanic. The journal is obviously in fine form, and is anticipating the next 150 years with a good heart.

Oxford
March 1990

Acknowledgements

Many people have helped and encouraged me in this project. First, I would like to thank the editor of the *British Medical Journal*, Stephen Lock, for commissioning me to write this history and for imposing no constraints on my freedom of expression—even when it showed the *Journal* in a less than flattering light. The staff of the *BMJ* between 1987 and 1989 were unfailingly courteous and helpful in responding to my frequent queries and requests for assistance. I welcome this opportunity to express my gratitude to them. I would particularly like to thank Jane Smith, who removed numerous obstacles. She and her colleagues, Tony Delamothe and Richard Smith, offered much valuable comment, advice, and encouragement.

No request was too much trouble for Leslie Moore and I thank him and the staff of the *Journal*'s general office for their many kindnesses. Ruth Holland and Sharon Davies helped to carry a flagging historian through the final traumas of authorship, while the staff of the BMA's library and registry provided much needed guidance. I am particularly grateful to Derek Wright, the Association's former librarian, and the registry supervisor, Alison Muhr, both of whom gave generously of their time and steered me towards vital source material.

Beyond Tavistock Square I have benefited incalculably from the advice and erudition of Bill Bynum and Roy Porter of the Wellcome Institute for the History of Medicine. Without them this would have been an immeasurably poorer book. In preparing this history I have also profited by giving papers at the seminar on newspaper and periodical history (at the Institute of Historical Research in the University of London), at the Centre for the History of Science, Technology and Medicine in the University of Manchester, and at the 1989 conference of the Society for the Social History of Medicine.

No historian would be able to function without libraries and archives; I acknowledge my profound debt to the Bodleian Library, the British Library, the British Newspaper Library, the library of the Royal College of Surgeons, the Wellcome Institute Library, the library of Wellcome's Oxford Unit for the History of Medicine, and the library of Wolfson College, Oxford. I wish also to express my gratitude to the ESRC Centre for Socio-Legal Studies at Wolfson College for providing me with such a congenial and stimulating academic base.

The following individuals have helped me in a variety of ways: Virginia Berridge, Betty Bostetter, Robert Dingwall, David Hamilton, Bob Hayzen, Godlieve van Heteren, Irvine Loudon, Jean Loudon, Charlotte Mackenzie,

Richard Palmer, Ruth Richardson, Caroline Richmond, Zuzanna Shonfield, Douglas Swinscow, Anne Summers, and John Thwaites. Finally, I wish to thank Pamela Bartrip, who helped not only with reading and criticizing drafts but also in tolerating a project which involved extended household storage for some two tons of *BMJ*s.

Stanton Harcourt, Oxford P. W. J. B.
November 1989

Contents

List of Plates

1
Introduction

Politics and society in 1840

The *Provincial Medical and Surgical Journal* (*PMSJ*), which became the *BMJ*, was first published on Saturday 3 October 1840. Its appearance, not surprisingly, went unnoticed in the national press. *The Times* of that day came out with each column of its first news page bordered in black, though this had nothing to do with the appearance of another medical periodical: it was a mark of respect for Princess Augusta Sophia, aunt of the young Queen Victoria, who, on the previous day, had been interred at Frogmore. *The Times* provided extensive coverage of the funeral. Its other leading news stories included reports of troubles in Ireland, the election of the Lord Mayor of the City of London, voting in which still had several more days to run, and a case of arson in HM Dockyard at Sheerness.

In fact, the Frogmore funeral was but one instalment in a series of Royal news stories, 1840 being a momentous year for the Royal Family. In February the 20-year-old Victoria had married Prince Albert. Four months after her marriage she survived the first of the several assassination attempts made upon her in the course of her reign, and on 21 November 1840 she gave birth to her first child.[1]

Politically, 1840 was a relatively quiet year. In 1839 some parts of the country had been rocked by Chartist violence. Most notably, miners led by John Frost had attacked the town of Newport, Monmouthshire. At Frost's trial in January 1840 he and others were sentenced to be hanged, beheaded, and quartered, though these sentences were subsequently commuted to transportation for life. Chartism was a central feature of the early Victorian social and political landscape. It was organized around the six political demands incorporated in the 'People's Charter': universal male suffrage, secret ballot, equal electoral districts, payment of MPs, abolition of a property qualification for MPs, and annual parliamentary elections. Its main activity was the compilation of huge petitions in support of these ends. But Chartism was more than a movement for political reform; it was an expression of working-class disaffection nurtured by economic hardship (1837–42 were years of serious agricultural and industrial depression), the imposition of the new Poor Law, and the terms of the Reform Act of 1832, which had slammed the door shut against enfranchisement of the working man.

[1] Elizabeth Longford, *Victoria R.I.* (London: Pan, 1966 edn), pp.188–9.

The prevalence of violent protest movements between 1815 and 1848 has led some historians to conclude that Britain was poised on a knife edge of bloody revolution, escaping only by virtue of a skilful blend of repression and concession on the part of the ruling class. Such a view, however, is overly dramatic. Notwithstanding the strains of rapid industrialization and urbanization, serious unrest was mostly sporadic and short-lived, posing few genuine threats to the prevailing social and political order. Great Britain, unlike some of her continental neighbours experienced evolutionary rather than revolutionary change.

By 1840 there was a middle-class analogue to Chartism in the form of the Anti-Corn Law League (founded 1839). Its aim was repeal of the Corn Laws, dating from 1815, which kept the price of wheat artificially high in order to protect agricultural and hence aristocratic interests. Like Chartism the League owed its existence mainly to poor trade and bad harvests, but its chief motive was to promote free trade, to the advantage of industrial and mercantile interests.

In 1840 Lord Melbourne was Prime Minister of a Whig–Liberal government. The Great Reform Act had brought the well-to-do middle classes into the electoral system but had left political power in the hands of the landed classes. The Whigs, authors of the Reform Act, had gained much from the enlarged franchise and had held power ever since, first under Earl Grey's premiership and, from 1834, under Melbourne. However, in the General Election of July 1841 the Tories gained 40 seats and by August Sir Robert Peel was Prime Minister—the first whose wealth and position were derived from industry.

Other notable developments in 1840 were the introduction of the penny post and the beginning of rebuilding work on the Houses of Parliament, which, in 1834, had been destroyed by fire. Kew Gardens were opened and plans for erecting a Nelson monument and creating a Trafalgar Square in front of the National Gallery were well advanced. Dickens, still in his 20s, published *The Old Curiosity Shop* and was at work on *Barnaby Rudge*. Abroad, Britain fought the Opium War and claimed sovereignty over New Zealand, while Upper and Lower Canada were unified under the terms of the Durham Report.

The population of the United Kingdom in 1841 (a census year) was around 26.75 million. It was on a sharply upward curve, though one effect of the Irish famine of 1845–7 was to impose a temporary brake on the rate of increase. Population growth in the period 1801–45 has been estimated at over 75 per cent. By the standards of the later twentieth century, though not of earlier centuries, the United Kingdom had a very young population; around 70 per cent of those alive in 1840 were below the age of 35. In England the fastest growth was occurring in the industrial and commercial regions of London, the north-west, and the north-east.

Manufacturing and extractive industry had already transformed large tracts of the British countryside. Thus, in 1830 William Cobbett could write that 'all the way along from Leeds to Sheffield it is coal and iron, and iron and coal.'[2] Foreign visitors were mightily impressed by the huge cotton factories in Manchester and massive coal-mining operations in the Midlands and north-east. The 1840s were, more than any other, the decade of the railway boom. Between 1838 and 1841 London was linked with Birmingham, Brighton, Bristol, Manchester, Liverpool, Southampton, and York. The advent of the Victorian railway network did much for the economy, laying the basis for the great advance in prosperity from the mid-1840s. It also facilitated BMA annual meetings (as they were known throughout the nineteenth century) in most of the principal towns of the United Kingdom, thereby allowing the Provincial Medical and Surgical Association to become a truly British Medical Association. But in 1840 all this was for the future. For the moment, notwithstanding the spread of industry and the spectacular growth of towns like Bradford, Merthyr Tydfil, and Glasgow, Britain remained predominantly a nation of agriculture and craft industries, of villages and small market towns. Farming, domestic service, and the building trades were still the three largest sources of employment, while the horse and the canal continued to provide the chief means of inland transport.

Population and urban growth had gone far enough, however, to give rise to a serious public health problem. Inadequate facilities for supplying households with clean water and disposing of the foul meant widespread intestinal disease. The cholera epidemic of 1831–3 which, from its point of entry in Sunderland, had spread rapidly throughout the kingdom, was a recent memory. The outbreak had accounted for more than 30 000 lives, but it had spawned little in the way of preventive measures. The challenge of urbanization and industrialization was one with which, as the pages of the *BMJ* testify, medicine was intimately concerned. To say that medical science was unprepared for the challenge would be to oversimplify, but in 1840 it had comparatively few comforts and little hope to offer to the sick, being, in the words of one historian, in a 'feeble state'.[3]

Medicine and the medical profession

A major medical advance had been made at the end of the eighteenth century when Edward Jenner published *An Inquiry into the Causes and Effects of Variolae Vaccinae* (1798), a book which showed that the prevention, indeed, the elimination of smallpox was feasible through vaccination. Since smallpox

[2] Quoted in N. Gash, *Aristocracy and People. Britain 1815–1865* (London: Edward Arnold, 1979), p. 10.

[3] A. J. Youngson, *The Scientific Revolution in Victorian Medicine* (London: Croom Helm, 1979), p. 12.

was a major killer, his discovery is well described as one of medicine's 'greatest practical triumphs'.[4] By 1840 vaccination against smallpox was reducing the incidence of disease, death, and disfigurement. But 'aside from this signal instance of improved practice, medicine as it affected the vast majority of the population was not very different in 1840 from what it had been in 1740.'[5]

Some new 'tools of the trade'—for example, the stethoscope, pulse watches, and clinical thermometers—had been invented in the eighteenth and early nineteenth centuries. These were all to have a major impact on medical practice, but in 1840 their value was imperfectly understood by general practitioners and they were not in widespread use. For the rest, surgery was undertaken without the benefits of anaesthetics or aseptic technique while some common treatments, using toxic substances such as lead and mercury, were guaranteed further to damage health rather than repair it. Blood-letting, for hundreds of years the doctor's standby, remained a standard response to all manner of ailments. In 1876 Henry Moon informed the BMA's East Sussex branch that during his apprenticeship in London

> my chief employment from day to day was to bleed and cup those patients who had been seen by the physicians and surgeons. Blood-letting was then used as a remedy whenever there was an increase of the temperature and a quickening of the pulse; and, doubtless, this indiscriminate irrational application of so bold a remedy destroyed thousands of lives annually.[6]

When Peel suffered a riding accident in 1850 he was liberally bled and died soon afterwards.

The most important functions of the eighteenth-century practitioner were to provide a comforting presence, diagnosis, and prognosis. Only four of his remedies—quinine, digitalis, fresh fruit and vegetables, and opium—have proved of lasting value.[7] The treatments at his disposal were strictly limited, but, within these limitations, his efforts should not be underrated. A similar verdict is appropriate on the voluntary hospitals, many of which date from the eighteenth century. Until recently these possessed a fearsome reputation as hotbeds of disease and neglect from which few patients were likely to emerge in good health. However, Woodward's reassessment concludes that

> the miserable reputation that they have endured has little foundation. The voluntary hospitals may not have been the most hygienic or the most pleasant of institutions by the standards of today; nor may the standard of medical care have been very high; but

[4] *Ibid.*, p. 11.

[5] *Ibid.*, p. 12.

[6] *Journal*, 15 Jan. 1876, 68–9; 31 May 1873, 617–18.

[7] I. Loudon, *Medical Care and the General Practitioner, 1750–1850* (Oxford: Oxford University Press, 1986), pp. 62–3. See also John M. T. Ford, *A Medical Student at St. Thomas's Hospital, 1801–1802. The Weekes Family Letters* (London: Wellcome Institute for the History of Medicine, 1987), p. 10.

they provided a service for a section of the population which had previously been neglected with some degree of success . . . .[8]

So much for the practice of medicine; as far as its organization is concerned, the medical profession of the eighteenth and early nineteenth centuries, once thought to have been neatly differentiated into a tripartite division, was in fact far more amorphous, not to say chaotic.[9] Ostensibly, the three medical corporations or colleges (in England and Wales) controlled the practice of physicians, surgeons, and apothecaries, who were sharply divided by income, social status, and professional activity. However, while the tripartite division was an institutional, social, and legal reality, it did not, except in London, correspond to the actual practice of medicine, for the second half of the eighteenth century saw the emergence of general practitioners concerned with two or more of the four main categories of orthodox medicine: physic, surgery, pharmacy, and midwifery. Many of these general practitioners, especially those in the provinces, were, formally, physicians or surgeons. When the select committee on medical education sat in 1834, many witnesses pointed out that the clear distinction between medical and surgical practice no longer applied. The term 'general practitioner', in the sense of one who practised across the spectrum of orthodox medicine, was current from the first decade of the nineteenth century and in common usage by 1840. The Apothecaries Act 1815, once considered so important in establishing the GP, improving medical education, and outlawing quacks, was of very limited significance.[10]

By 1840 the real distinction within the medical profession was between consultants and general practitioners—that is, between those who held hospital appointments, whether as physicians or surgeons, and others. These others constituted the majority of the profession, providing at least nine-tenths of the nation's medical care. Although many hospital consultancies were honorary positions, they opened the way for those who held them to secure large incomes from teaching fees and lucrative private practice among wealthy clients. Since consultants dominated the Royal Colleges, they also monopolized power and influence within the profession. General practice, however, became rather less lucrative in the first half of the nineteenth century.[11] The typical general practitioner lacked money, status, power, and

[8] John Woodward, *To Do the Sick No Harm. A Study of the British Voluntary Hospital System to 1875* (London: Routledge and Kegan Paul, 1974), p. 146.

[9] In compiling this summary I have relied upon I. Loudon, *Medical Care and the General Practitioner, 1750–1850* (note 7); Ivan Waddington, *The Medical Profession in the Industrial Revolution (Dublin: Gill & Macmillan, 1984); M. Jeanne Peterson, The Medical Profession in Mid-Victorian London* (Los Angeles and London: University of California Press, 1978).

[10] S. W. F. Holloway, 'The Apothecaries' Act, 1815: A Reinterpretation', *Medical History* (1966) **10**, 107–29, 221–36; I. Loudon, *Medical Care and the General Practitioner, 1750–1850* p. 171 (note 7).

[11] *Ibid.*, p. 259.

influence. The only thing of which he had the lion's share was workload. The gulf that existed between privileged consultants and deprived GPs did much to promote the medical reform movement in the pre- and early Victorian period. This movement, which originated in the eighteenth century, was well underway when the *PMSJ* appeared; its legislative phase was to dominate the *Journal*'s first 18 years of existence.

Medical societies and medical journalism

For most of its existence the *Journal* has been linked with the British Medical Association, formerly the Provincial Medical and Surgical Association (PMSA), as 'the organ of the Association'. This institutional link has distinguished it from other general medical journals to which it otherwise bore marked similarities.[12] As background to the history of the *Journal* we therefore need to look at the origins of the Association.

The nineteenth century was the great age of the medical society; few societies may be traced back further than the mid-eighteenth century.[13] Many were principally social gatherings for which the consumption of food and drink by like-minded friends amid convivial surroundings was the true *raison d'être*. Some placed more emphasis upon discussing professional matters, whether relating to the economics of practice or details of interesting cases. These might have run a small library or originated as a circulating book club. Bodies such as the Association of Apothecaries and Surgeon Apothecaries (founded 1812), or Thomas Wakley's London College of Medicine (1830) had political goals among their aims.[14] Wakley, for example, sought the eradication of rank in the profession; others aspired to advance the standing of general practice. Many such efforts at association were short-lived and disappeared leaving little or no trace behind them.

The PMSA was founded in Worcester in July 1832 by a local physician, Charles Hastings, and a group of some 50 colleagues. It made no distinction between general practitioners and consultants. It was intended that the society should foster social and scientific intercourse and also promote the interests of non-metropolitan practitioners. During its early years, and from time to time much later, members disagreed about which of these objects should have priority. Some felt that politics intruded too much and thereby compromised the PMSA's role as a social club or scientific society. The same

[12] W. R. Lefanu, *British Periodicals of Medicine 1640–1899* (Oxford: Wellcome Unit for the History of Medicine, 1984 edn), p. 2.

[13] Sir D'Arcy Power (ed.), *British Medical Societies* (London: Medical Press and Circular, 1939), p. vii.

[14] I. Loudon, *Medical Care and the General Practitioner, 1750–1850* pp. 174, 279–80 (note 7); W. H. McMenemey, 'The Influence of Medical Societies on the Development of Medical Practice in Nineteenth-Century Britain', in F. N. L. Poynter (ed.), *The Evolution of Medical Practice in Britain* (London: Pitman, 1961), p. 68. See M. J. Peterson, *The Medical Profession in Mid-Victorian London*, p. 18 (note 9).

arguments were later to be made in respect of the *Journal*'s content, which was sometimes seen as being too controversial.

The word 'provincial' in the PMSA's title was important, for the association was conceived as a counterweight to the dominant position of London in British medicine. Many other regional medical associations were formed at around the same time,[15] but these represented particular localities. The PMSA, the 'most successful of all the medical societies',[16] was different in that it sought to include all medical men outside London. To help bind them together it held annual meetings in towns up and down the country and published regular *Transactions*. At first Wakley was enthusiastic about the PMSA, seeing in it the possibility of a truly national medical society.[17] But—although he himself was a provincial by birth—its determined provincialism and moderation soon aroused his contempt. He began to assert that no organization based outside London stood any chance of success, and dismissed the PMSA as a 'disgraceful abortion' comprising 'general practitioners who have allowed themselves to be made the dupes and puppets of the migratory showmen'.[18] Wakley tried, with only limited success, to encourage rival societies to fill a need which, he felt, the PMSA had so signally failed to meet. But, despite the *Lancet*'s scorn, the Association flourished. By 1840 its membership was almost 1200. Even Wakley relented and joined the Association himself in 1854.

The PMSA's inspiration may have been the Royal Medical Society of Edinburgh by way of the Worcestershire Medical and Surgical Society.[19] But its immediate forebear was the *Midland Medical and Surgical Reporter* (*MMSR*), a quarterly journal which Hastings and friends had started in 1828 with a view to recording pathological observations made in provincial hospitals and other aspects of medicine and medical practice in the Midlands. Hastings had realized that medical journalism could do much to further professional interests. But existing journals were based in London, Edinburgh, and Dublin and failed to represent adequately provincial interests and opinion. By 1832, 16 numbers of the *MMSR* had been issued. The success of the venture convinced Hastings and his colleagues that there was scope for something more than the *Reporter*, and the outcome was the foundation of the PMSA. The *MMSR* was replaced by an annual volume of *Transactions of*

[15] I. Loudon, *Medical Care and the General Practitioner, 1750–1850*, p. 281 (note 7); M. J. Peterson, *The Medical Profession in Mid-Victorian London*, p. 23 (note 9); Philip Swan, 'A Brief Summary of their Role and Position of Medical Societies in the Early Nineteenth Century Medical Profession', *Journal of Local Studies* (1982) **2**: 43–7.

[16] I. Loudon, *Medical Care and the General Practitioner, 1750–1850*, p. 280 (note 7).

[17] E. M. Little, *History of the BMA* (London: British Medical Association, n.d., 1932?), p. 24.

[18] Paul Vaughan, *Doctors' Commons. A Short History of the British Medical Association* (London: Heinemann, 1959), p. 1; W. H. McMenemey, 'The Influence of Medical Societies on the Development of Medical Practice in Nineteenth-Century Britain', pp. 69 72 (note 14).

[19] William H. McMenemey, *The Life and Times of Sir Charles Hastings* (Edinburgh and London: Livingstone, 1959), pp. 40–1.

the Provincial Medical and Surgical Association, which was published between 1833 and 1853.

That Hastings was not alone in identifying the potential market for medical journalism is indicated by the growing number of medical journals. LeFanu's *British Periodicals of Medicine, 1640–1899*, shows that just as medical societies and associations mushroomed during the early nineteenth century, so too did the number of medical journals.[20] LeFanu gives 38 entries for the 160 years to the end of the eighteenth century. In the early nineteenth century, between 1801 and 1840 inclusive, 107 new titles were launched. Although most of these were short-lived, some proved durable. The *Edinburgh Medical and Surgical Journal*, for example, survived under the same name for 50 years (1805–55), during which time it was among the leading medical quarterlies in Britain.[21]

Why were so many medical journals launched in the nineteenth century? This is not an easy question to answer without falling into the trap of vapid generalization, to the effect that a growing sense of professional maturity generated 'the need to satisfy . . . [a] . . . natural tendency toward inquiry and expression'.[22] It is important to recognize that after 1800 growth was not a new trend but the acceleration of an existing one. The twentieth century has also seen a vast output of new medical periodicals, largely because of the growth of specialisms. Specialization began to take off in the Victorian period and accounts for a good many of the journals launched at that time. Fads such as mesmerism, herbalism, and homoeopathy also gave rise to journals, as did regional centres of learning. In the eighteenth century most journals were linked to societies and concerned themselves with the reporting of proceedings. The growing number of these societies after 1800 spawned a corresponding increase in the number of such journals. The *Transactions of the PMSA* falls into this category. The onset of the medical reform question also stimulated the launch of journals to report it and represent particular viewpoints.

At any event, in the nineteenth century medical knowledge expanded rapidly, so there was more to be communicated. The only practical way of reaching a wide and far-flung readership regularly was by means of a periodical. Without a medical journal, country practitioners and others remote 'from the head quarters, as it were, of scientific knowledge' were, as

[20] See also Samuel J. Rogal, 'A Checklist of Medical Journals Published in England during the Seventeenth, Eighteenth, and Nineteenth Centuries', *British Studies Monitor* (1980): **IX**, 3–25. As LeFanu (note 12) points out, there are problems in defining precisely what is meant by a medical periodical. For our purposes, it includes anything listed by LeFanu.

[21] In 1855 it amalgamated with the *Monthly Journal of Medicine* to become the *Edinburgh Medical Journal*. In 1955 it combined with the *Glasgow Medical Journal* to form the *Scottish Medical Journal*. See W. R. Lefanu, *British Periodicals of Medicine 1640–1899* (note 12).

[22] S. J. Rogal, 'A Checklist of Medical Journals Published in England during the Seventeenth, Eighteenth, and Nineteenth Centuries', p. 3 (note 20).

Thomas Wakley said when launching the *Lancet*, 'almost without the means of ascertaining its progress'.[23] Not only was there more science to cover, there were more meetings, more ideas, more politics, and more means.

The transport revolution and postal reform aided the expansion of medical journalism by facilitating rapid distribution. This was particularly important for the weeklies, which could hardly have existed in earlier centuries. It is no mere coincidence that the *PMSJ* was founded in the year of the penny post and on the eve of huge railway construction projects. The effect of these developments was to allow prompt distribution of weeklies throughout the UK and even further afield. But in 1840 the 'golden age' of the national weekly had yet to arrive.

Among the most influential of the early nineteenth century medical journals was the *London Medical and Physical Journal* (*LMPJ*), which dated back, under its earlier titles, to 1781. It has been termed 'a decent monthly magazine of some 90 pages, with no particular reason for its existence'. Most of its articles consisted of translations from foreign journals and long extracts from scientific books. It first ignored, then criticized, and finally imitated the *Lancet*.[24] The *LMPJ*, which became in turn the *Medical Quarterly Review* (1833–5) and the *British and Foreign Medical Review* (1836–47), aspired to be a quarterly journal of practical medicine and surgery. As the *BFMR* it was edited and owned by John Forbes, under whose guidance it acquired a sound reputation. In 1848 it combined with the *Medico-Chirurgical Review* to become the *British and Foreign Medico-Chirurgical Review*, in which guise it survived until 1877.

Towering above the competition was the *Lancet*, the first medical weekly and 'the oldest English medical journal running in unbroken series'.[25] The pre-*Lancet* medical press was 'tame, but . . . not ill-informed'.[26] The *Lancet* introduced a new type of medical journalism which was not only crusading, controversial, and combative but also personally abusive towards opponents. Its success had important implications for new and existing titles; they might criticize it, but they could not long ignore it. None emulated its bitter invective and forthright literary style, but many followed its format of reaching out to the profession at large with a varied diet of news, opinion, and information which became the stock-in-trade of the medical weeklies.

The *London Medical Gazette* was the second weekly, though others were soon to follow. The *Gazette* was founded by Sir Benjamin Brodie, John Abernethy, and other hospital surgeons who hated Wakley as a direct challenge to the *Lancet*.[27] But, with its assumption of quality and high

[23] *Lancet*, 5 Oct. 1823, p. 1.

[24] S. Squire Sprigge, *The Life and Times of Thomas Wakley* (London: Longmans, 1897), pp. 157–8.

[25] W. R. Lefanu, *British Periodicals of Medicine 1640–1899*, p. 2 (note 12).

[26] J. F. Clarke, *Autobiographical Recollections* (London: Churchill, 1874), p. 67.

[27] S. S. Sprigge, *The Life and Times of Thomas Wakley*, pp. 165–6 (note 24).

breeding, it was a very different publication, one commentator referring to its 'tameness and milk and water contents'.[28] Many other weeklies were launched between 1829 and 1840. Of one of them, the *New Doctor* (1836–7), Victor Plarr wrote in the *BMJ* in 1925, 'Practice and domestic medicine in 1837 were necessarily more primitive than now, but we should hardly have imagined them to be as nearly mediaeval as appears from ... "The New Doctor".'[29]

Few of the new titles lasted long, for few could match the quality and interest of the *Lancet*. In 1852 two of the more successful combined to form the *Medical Times and Gazette*. This survived until 1885, up to which time it provided the *Lancet* and the *BMJ* with some of their main competition. Their other leading competitor was the *Medical Press and Circular*, which was formed, in 1866, by another amalgamation. It survived until comparatively recently, closing only in 1961.[30]

The *BMJ*'s main competitor was, of course, the *Lancet*, which Wakley founded in 1823 as a 28-year-old general practitioner in London. In 1820 he had survived a brutal assault in his own house during the course of which his home had been destroyed by fire. He then became embroiled in a court case (which he finally won) with his insurers who refused to meet his claim for loss of property. After these traumas Wakley was casting around for a new 'enterprise into which he could throw all his energies'.[31] He was 'intolerant to the contemporary medical press' which, he felt, 'was written to please the eminent few rather than the profession at large'.[32] Encouraged and financially aided by an American doctor who shared his passion for medical reform, Wakley quit medical practice in favour of medical journalism.

Wakley set out his aims in a preface to his first number, dated 5 October 1823.

> It has long been a subject of surprise and regret, that in this extensive and intelligent community there has not hitherto existed a work that would convey to the Public, and to distant Practitioners as well as to Students in Medicine and Surgery, reports of the Metropolitan Hospital Lectures.

As well as reproducing lectures, starting with those of Sir Astley Cooper—

[28] J. F. Clarke, *Autobiographical Recollections*, pp. 134-6, 153 (note 26).

[29] *Journal*, 13 June 1925, 1101.

[30] From 1947 to 1961 it reverted to the title, the *Medical Press*. A centenary history was published by R. J. Rowlette, *The Medical Press and Circular, 1839–1939: a Hundred Years in the Life of a Medical Journal* (London: Medical Press and Circular, 1939); *Medical Press and Circular* (1939): **201**: 71–83; *Journal*, 4 Feb. 1939, 233–4. On its demise see *Journal*, 7 Oct. 1961, 949.

[31] Mary Bostetter, 'The Journalism of Thomas Wakley' in Joel H. Wiener (ed.), *Innovators and Preachers. The Role of the Editor in Victorian England* (Westport, Connecticut: Greenwood Press, 1985). On Wakley and the *Lancet* see also S. S. Sprigge, *The Life and Times of Thomas Wakley* (note 24) and Charles Brook, *Battling Surgeon* (Glasgow: Strickland Press, 1945). Mary Bostetter is writing a new biography.

[32] S. S. Sprigge, *The Life and Times of Thomas Wakley*, pp. 76–7, 80 (note 24).

'easily the most competent and professionally knowledgeable' London surgeon—Wakley planned to provide, in plain English, medical news, case descriptions, and non-medical articles which would entertain and instruct the general public as well as medical practitioners.[33]

Before long the *Lancet* was involved in all manner of controversy as its pugnacious editor and proprietor launched fierce attacks upon nepotism, incompetence, quackery, and malpractice; published lectures and the proceedings of medical societies without obtaining permission; and vilified the state of the teaching hospitals, medical education in general and the medical corporations. These and other campaigns, conducted in Wakley's unrestrained journalistic style, which spared no effort to give offence, made the *Lancet* the scourge of the London medical establishment and all charlatans. They rapidly brought it commercial success, with a circulation of several thousand by the end of 1825, but also notoriety and a string of libel actions—'plenty as blackberries'—to defend and, less often, prosecute.[34]

Wakley was a political radical who wished to use the *Lancet* 'to *in*form and *re*form'. His main aim was to disseminate medical information, though he intended also 'to make war upon the family intrigues and foolish nepotism that swayed the elections to lucrative posts in the metropolitan hospitals and medical corporations'.[35] As a result the *Lancet* was, for its first decade, 'a duelling ground for a series of fierce encounters between the editor and the members of the privileged classes in medicine'.[36] Thereafter, while it remained a champion of reform, its tone and content became somewhat less vitriolic.

The early *Lancet* did much to expose the abuses in British medicine. There have, however, been conflicting opinions as to its achievement in securing remedies. Sprigge, who in 1908 became the first non-Wakley to edit the *Lancet*, acknowledges that some of its early numbers contained 'certain errors of taste and judgment', but argues that it made important contributions not only to medical reform but also to the elevation of professional competence and status.[37] Others suggest that Wakley's heavy-handed satire, name-calling, and intemperate language were counter-productive in that they diminished professional dignity and gave the impression that all medical men were incompetent. There is some truth in both these viewpoints. The state of British medicine demanded vigorous criticism, but the *Lancet* might have

[33] *Lancet*, 5 Oct. 1923, 1–2; M. Bostetter, 'The Journalism of Thomas Wakley', p. 276 (note 31).

[34] J. F. Clarke, *Autobiographical Recollections*, p. 153 (note 26). Sprigge gives the *Lancet*'s circulation for this period as over 4000; see Thomas Wakley, p. 102 (note 24). Bostetter referring to the same year mentions 8000 subscribers. 'The Journalism of Thomas Wakley', p. 280 (note 31).

[35] S. S. Sprigge, *The Life and Times of Thomas Wakley*, pp. 76–7, 80 (note 24).

[36] *Ibid.*, p. 81.

[37] *Ibid.*, pp. 77, 235–6. See also M. Bostetter, 'The Journalism of Thomas Wakley' (note 31).

achieved its objectives more quickly and more completely if Wakley had employed greater discretion and moderated his tone. In later life he came to recognize this himself for, according to James Fernandez Clarke, who had worked on the early *Lancet*, Wakley subsequently regretted some of his early editorial conduct.[38]

When the *PMSJ* was launched, medical journalism was in a vibrant phase which reflected the lively state of the medical reform question. By this time the *Lancet* was well established. But it is a mistake to think of the *Lancet* and the *BMJ* as sole representatives of nineteenth-century British medical journalism. They were two among very many, most of which failed, or at least succeeded only briefly. There was nothing inevitable about their success. Indeed, as far as the *PMSJ*/*BMJ* is concerned, for over 25 years its very existence, let alone its success, was in doubt.

[38] J. F. Clarke, *Autobiographical Recollections*, pp. 67–71, 134–6 (note 26); I. Loudon, *Medical Care and the General Practitioner, 1750–1850*, p. 321 (note 7).

2
The battle for survival, 1840–1867

Introduction

The *Journal*'s first editors were Dr P. Hennis Green, lecturer on the diseases of children at the Hunterian School of Medicine, who was also its founder, and Dr Robert Streeten of Worcester, a member of the PMSA Council.[1] It was published by William Ball of Paternoster Row in the City of London, and printed by Richard Clay of Newmarket Terrace, Cambridge Heath, Middlesex. Inclusive of stamp duty it cost 7d, a price which remained unchanged till March 1844.[2]

The first number was 16 pages long and contained three simple woodcut illustrations, though no more were included till the fourth issue and no others that year. The longest items were the editors' introductory address and a report of the annual meeting and dinner of the PMSA's Eastern branch. Other pages contained a condensed version of Henry Warburton's medical reform bill, book reviews (Charles Waller's *Practical Treatise on the Function and Diseases of the Unimpregnated Womb* was dismissed as '200 scanty pages of commonplace professional twaddle'), clinical papers, and case notes. There were 2½ columns of advertisements. In their leading article Green and Streeten noted that they had '*received as many advertisements (in proportion to the quantity of letter press) for our first number, as the most popular Medical Journal of the present day,* [the *Lancet*] *after seventeen years of existence*. This is a circumstance, we believe, unparalleled in the history of periodical publications [emphasis in original].'[3] William Greenhill, in his brief history of the *Journal* published in 1856, observes that in its early years

[1] *Journal*, 14 Aug. 1844, 312.

[2] Stamp duty on newspapers and periodicals was one of the so-called 'taxes on knowledge', the others being advertisement and paper duty, import duty on paper and foreign books, and a pamphlet and almanac duty. In 1836 newspaper stamp duty was cut from 4d to 1d following a campaign of opposition in which Thomas Wakley played a prominent part. It was abolished in 1855. Advertisement duty, 'a major obstacle to the unfettered development of the press', was cut in 1833 and abolished in 1853. Excise duty on paper remained till 1861. See Joel H. Wiener, *The War of the Unstamped. The Movement to Repeal the British Newspaper Tax, 1830–1836* (Ithaca and London: Cornell University Press, 1969); Donald Read, *Press and People, 1790–1850: Opinion in Three English Cities* (London: Edward Arnold, 1961), pp. 67–8; W. H. Brock and A. J. Meadows, *The Lamp of Learning: Taylor and Francis and the Development of Science Publishing* (London and Philadelphia: Taylor & Francis, 1984), pp. 93–4.

[3] *Journal*, 3 Oct. 1840, 4.

the *PMSJ* 'was not, externally, inferior to the other medical periodicals, with which it competed respectably, if not successfully.'[4]

Although its title suggests that the *Journal* began life as the organ of the PMSA, this was not altogether the case. It was launched as an independent commercial speculation, the success of which depended upon sales and advertising revenue. However, from the start it was aimed at PMSA members, of whom there were, in 1840, some 1220:

> ... Green determined on publishing a weekly periodical journal which he was desirous to connect with the Provincial Association, and he declared his intention to advocate all those objects for which the Association was formed, and to demonstrate the possibility of aiding the efforts of the scattered members of the profession.[5]

In order to further his endeavours Green asked for a member of the PMSA's Council to join him as editor. Streeten had written for both the *Midland Medical and Surgical Reporter* and the Association's *Transactions*. Consequently, the PMSA's Council chose Dr Streeten as the coadjutor of Dr. Green 'with the understanding that all endeavours should be used to insure continuance to the new work by the members of the society'.[6] Until 1844 Green was the 'responsible Editor'; Streeten had little to do with management—'he only wrote the leading articles'.[7]

In their first number Green and Streeten promised to promote PMSA interests, emphasizing that the goals of the *PMSJ* were those of the Association. Clearly Green identified in provincial practitioners an important and little exploited market for medical journalism and set out to capture it. Between 1840 and 1844 the link between the Association and the *Journal* became gradually closer. From 1842 the PMSA obtained the *Journal* at a discount and supplied it as a benefit of membership to all who were not in arrears with subscriptions (but see note 5). This has been the basis of distribution to Association members ever since. In 1843, when Hastings became PMSA president, Streeten succeeded him as secretary, thereby strengthening the Association's link with the *Journal*. What the Association did not possess, until 1844, was proprietorship and full editorial control.

Until 1844 the *Journal* seems to have been generally admired by PMSA members. Afterwards, and intermittently for some 20 years, there was

[4] *Ibid.*, 5 Jan. 1856, 13.

[5] PMSA membership figures have to be treated with caution. At best they represent a 'snapshot' of membership on a particular day. Numbers changed constantly as individuals joined, resigned, died, or lapsed. Provision of the *Journal* was ostensibly restricted to those members who had actually paid their dues, but in practice subscriptions could be three years in arrears before membership lapsed. There were sometimes dozens, even hundreds, who had not paid and had no intention of paying their subscriptions, yet remained on the membership list. See *Journal*, 19 Aug. 1853, 731; 1 Sept. 1854, 775–6. Henry Ancell described membership figures as a 'fiction', *ibid.*, 15 Dec. 1854, 1129–30.

[6] *Ibid.*, 13 June 1849, 319.

[7] *Ibid.*

regular criticism of it, and frequent demands for its abolition on the grounds that the Association's slender resources were being squandered upon an inferior publication. Until the mid-1860s no editor could feel wholly secure in his position. Indeed, William Ranking (1849–52) and John Rose Cormack (1853–6) resigned because of virulent criticism of their regimes. Ranking's co-editor, John Walsh (1849–52) was, in effect, 'sacked'.

Honeymoon

In their introductory address and subsequent statements Green and Streeten outlined 'the main objects for the promotion of which the PROVINCIAL MEDICAL AND SURGICAL JOURNAL is established'. Two clear objectives emerge: the advancement of the profession, especially in the provinces, and dissemination of medical knowledge.[8] Green and Streeten expressed an interest in promoting public well-being, while at the same time maintaining 'medical practitioners, as a class in that rank of society which, by their intellectual acquirements, by their general moral character, and by the importance of the duties entrusted to them, they are justly entitled to hold'. This was to be the standard line of the *Journal* over many years. It won immediate support from the PMSA.

As early as October 1840, at a meeting of the Association's Taunton and Bridgewater branch, Mr West of Shepton Mallet called upon his colleagues 'to take this opportunity of *strongly expressing their satisfaction that the* PROVINCIAL MEDICAL AND SURGICAL JOURNAL *has been established, and pledge themselves to give their cordial support to the Editors in their truly laudable undertaking* [emphasis in original].'[9] Charles Hastings, an indefatigable attender of branch meetings and, until 1852, an enthusiast for the *Journal*, 'gave his full approbation' to West's motion.[10]

The following August (1841) at the PMSA's ninth anniversary meeting at York, Hastings, having praised the Association's *Transactions* as an ideal vehicle for the publication of essays which would build into a medical history of England, remarked that

> it would be desirable to have a quicker means of communication than is supplied by an annual volume. This consideration has for some time been present to your Council and they have long been of opinion that a weekly periodical journal, in connexion with the association, would form an appropriate vehicle for these communications. The expense incident to such an undertaking has been the great obstacle to making this attempt, although its manifold advantages were strongly felt by the Council. They could not conceal the fact, that a periodical publication which would bring the members of the association into weekly communication, and afford a powerful organ

[8] *Ibid.*, 3 Oct. 1840, 1; see 13 Feb. 1841, 336; 2 Oct. 1841, 10–11.
[9] *Ibid.*, 13 Feb. 1841, 336.
[10] *Ibid.*, 31 Oct. 1840, 92.

through which their opinions might be heard when occasion required, would be highly advantageous, by combining their exertions and concentrating their opinions. The Council, therefore, have much gratification in announcing to the members, that they have been for some time engaged in endeavouring to mature a plan by which every member of the association, whose subscription is not in arrear, will receive every week, without any addition to the guinea which has been annually paid, a copy of the Provincial Journal.[11]

If the members approved this proposal, publication would be 'under the sanction and control of the Council, and the communications sent to the Council will be published in the *Journal*, unless they are such as to require coloured drawings for their illustration, or are, from their nature and extent, inappropriate to a weekly journal; in which event they will, as heretofore, appear in the transactions, as will, also the future memoirs on medical topography.' In November 1841 the *Journal* noted that it had been 'established under the patronage' of the PMSA.[12]

What Council had done was to reach a bulk purchase agreement with Henry Renshaw, the *Journal*'s publisher, by which the Association would be supplied with sufficient copies of the *Journal* to supply all of its members at a cost equivalent to 2d per copy.[13] Clearly, the *Journal* had, in less than a year, gone a long way towards establishing itself upon a secure basis with a list of some 1250 (by 1841) guaranteed subscribers. In a leading article commemorating the *Journal*'s first anniversary Green and Streeten could reflect with satisfaction on their accomplishment.

The experience of the period which has just expired ... has fully confirmed the anticipations which we were induced to form, that a work similar to the Provincial Medical and Surgical Journal was called for as a medium for the expression of the opinions of provincial practitioners ... Perhaps the best evidence which we can adduce of the estimation in which the information conveyed through the medium of the Provincial *Journal* is held, is to be found in the frequent use—sometimes we regret to say, without acknowledgement—made of it by other periodical publications.[14]

PMSA members seem to have shared their enthusiasm. The president of the Association's southern branch, for example, referred to 'this excellent weekly Journal'.[15] At the Association's anniversary meeting in Leeds (1843), Council attributed the large increase in PMSA membership, which by this time officially totalled 1628, to the provision of the *Journal*. Dr Chadwick estimated that the *Journal* connection had added 500 PMSA members.[16] Charles Hastings in an after-dinner speech at Leeds said:

[11] BMA mss. Proceedings of the PMSA at the Ninth Anniversary Meeting (York, 1841). Report of Council.

[12] *Journal*, 20 Nov. 1841, 164.

[13] *Ibid.*, 26 May 1854, 450; 5 Jan. 1856, 13; see *Transactions* (1842) 357.

[14] *Journal*, 2 Oct. 1841, 10; see 25 June 1842, 242.

[15] *Ibid.*, 16 July 1842, 288; see 25 June 1842, 236–7; 9 July 1842, 277.

[16] *Ibid.*, 5 Aug. 1843, 379.

. . . he thought they had now placed that *Journal* on such a footing and connected it so closely with the Association, that it must become more and more the organ of the body, be more and more acceptable to the members, and be more and more fruitful in communicating the knowledge which they were daily and weekly acquiring.[17]

The Association takes over

Following the Leeds meeting, the PMSA Council reached agreement with the *Journal*'s proprietors on terms for maintaining the bond between the Association and the *Journal*. But it soon received a request for revised terms, for the 'advance on the sum formerly paid was considered insufficient by the acting Proprietor, not merely to afford any profit or adequate remuneration for his trouble but to enable him to make those arrangements which were considered essential for conducting the *Journal* in an efficient and satisfactory manner.' Council refused to comply. Instead, it

came to the conclusion that the then existing arrangements between the Association and Proprietors of the *Journal* could no longer be carried out with advantage and satisfaction to either party, and that the objects of the Association could be best attained, and its interests consulted, by having a weekly periodical entirely under their own management. According to the statements which the Council from time to time received, the Proprietors of the *Journal*, on the one hand, appear to derive no profit, and no sufficient remuneration was allowed to those who had the management of it; on the other hand, the Association, though contributing the greatest part, if not the whole, of the funds necessary for carrying on the concern, had not, and could not have that entire controul [sic] over it which was desirable . . . .[18]

In effect, Council 'hijacked' the *Journal*, transferring publication from London to Worcester, where it would be edited by Streeten alone and placed under the sole control of the PMSA.[19] The PMSA did not undertake its own printing, but entrusted this to a commercial printer in Worcester. Paper and print from 3 April (the first PMSA number) were of poorer quality.[20] Editorial content, on the other hand, changed little, though PMSA affairs began to be more fully reported. With these developments the price of the *Journal* was cut from 6d (stamped edition 7d) to 4d (5d), though the average number of pages also fell. Standard length before the PMSA takeover was 20 pages, whereas afterwards it varied between 12 and 20. Obviously, the above prices applied to individual subscribers; members of the Association continued to receive the *Journal* as a benefit of membership.

Between April 1842 and February 1844 the *Journal* had been published by Henry Renshaw of 356 the Strand. He provides us with his version of events:

[17] *Ibid.*, 381.

[18] BMA mss. Proceedings of the PMSA at the Twelfth Anniversary Meeting (Northampton, 1844). Report of Council. See *Journal*, 26 May 1854, 450.

[19] *Ibid.*, 3 April 1844, 11.

[20] *Ibid.*, 5 Jan. 1856, 13.

> ... the transfer of this Journal to Worcester was adopted ... in consequence of an application by Mr. Renshaw, as one of the proprietors of the *Journal*, for such an increase on the price paid, namely 2½d per number, stamped, as would make it remunerative, and enable him to give gentlemen of talent a proper recompense for their labors [sic] in the editorial department, and to compete successfully with the exertions of other medical journals ... Mr. Renshaw suggests that he could not be expected to neglect his own profitable affairs for a *Journal* which had thus virtually passed out of his hands (it being only continued by him until other arrangements were made), which had been supplied to the Association considerably under cost price, during the period of his connection with it, and in other respects had been anything but profitable.[21]

Renshaw's reference to editorial remuneration brings us to the subject of editorial salaries. No information survives as to what these were until 1846–7, for which year PMSA accounts show a payment of £200 for 'editing'. In the next few years varying sums, up to £268 p.a., were paid to the editor. Ranking and Walsh, joint editors between 1849 and 1852, each received £125 p.a. Their successor, John Rose Cormack, was paid £250 p.a., though he received a further £100 for his work as Association secretary. Andrew Wynter, editor from 1855 to 1860, also received £250 p.a., but the salary of his successor, William Markham was only £200 p.a.[22]

Honeymoon over

No sooner had the PMSA taken control of the *Journal* than its members, hitherto so appreciative, began to express reservations about its value. These reservations stemmed partly from economic considerations—the *Journal* was felt to be too expensive—and partly from doubts about its quality. In more general terms, members became far more sensitive about, and critical of, a publication which was unambiguously the Association's than they had been towards virtually the same publication when it had gone to PMSA members as a part of their membership and yet was not an Association publication.

A notable critic was the epidemiologist, William Budd. He felt that there were already too many medical periodicals and that, far from assisting the profession, they were 'an obstacle ... and quite a task to get through, in the many interruptions of a professional life'.[23] Citing the example of the British Association, he suggested that a body which met annually had no need of a weekly journal. Although conceding that the *Journal* had included 'valuable contributions' and had provided a useful medium for Council to publish its proceedings, he judged it to be of 'inferior character' and of little value in representing the Association. Its inferiority, he felt, stemmed not from poor management, but from members' lack of enthusiasm and its provincial

[21] *Ibid.*, 23 March 1844, 489.
[22] It was estimated in 1842 that a moderate practice in London should bring in £300–£400 p.a.
[23] *Journal*, 14 Aug. 1844, 311.

location. Budd suggested two possible courses of action—abolition or less frequent publication—but he made it clear that he favoured abolition and use of the large savings which would result for charitable purposes.

Charles Hastings, however, emphasized that immediate withdrawal was not possible because provision of a journal was an Association rule, alteration of which would be impossible before the 1845 anniversary meeting. With this information Budd proposed: 'That a Committee be appointed to take into consideration whether it be expedient for the Association to continue the publication of a weekly medical periodical, and that such Committee be requested to report the result of their inquiry to the next anniversary meeting.' In the ensuing debate Charles Cowan of Reading suggested that arrangements might be made for an existing London-based journal to take over as the organ of the Association. Dr Forbes claimed that a good general journal could not be maintained by the PMSA alone. He suggested that, if the Association wished to publish its own journal, such a publication should be confined to reports of official business with the possible addition of observations and treatises submitted by members. Although some members praised the *Journal*, the meeting decided to appoint a committee of inquiry.

The criticism to which he was subjected in the course of the debate prompted Streeten to offer his resignation. He was, however, shouted down, and with a vote of thanks for his efficient editorship—which was surely hard for him to swallow—the debate on the future of the *Journal* was concluded.

Much of the disquiet about the *Journal* was born of concern over the PMSA's growing financial commitment to it. As Table 2.1 shows, during the 1840s the Association spent up to 60 per cent of its income from subscriptions upon producing and supplying the *Journal*.[24] With heavy expenditure

Table 2.1. PMSA income and *PMSJ* expenditure, 1841–7

Year	Income (£)*	Expenditure (£)*	Expenditure as percentage of income
1841–2	1085	476	44
1842–3	1489	698	47
1843–4	2135	879	41
1844–5	1842	1115	61
1845–6	1713	926	54
1846–7	1304	635	49

Source: Council Minute Book and *Journal*.
* to nearest £.

[24] By the 1850s the *Journal* was regularly consuming over 80 per cent of the Association's annual income.

on the lavishly illustrated *Transactions*, little of the PMSA's income was left for the benevolent fund, prizes, educational purposes, and other causes which some members held dear. During 1844–5 finances were further drained by a compensation award to Hennis Green.

Green claimed compensation on the grounds that the *Journal*'s 'establishment had cost him much labour and expense, and then the Association had stepped in and appropriated the benefit of his exertions.' A committee appointed to investigate the matter found in Green's favour and recommended a payment of £516 11s 4d. Although faced with the problem of raising a sum exceeding 25 per cent of its annual income, the Association's 1845 anniversary meeting accepted the verdict. Council proposed and the membership agreed that 'the amount be raised by the members, by a voluntary subscription of from five shillings and upwards.'[25] But the amount subscribed fell far short of the figure awarded to Green. 'Nearly the whole' of the award became 'chargeable on the ordinary revenue of the Association'. As a result the Association's 1846–7 accounts showed a deficit of over £22 10s.[26]

The extent of the PMSA's financial obligations to Green was explained to the 1845 meeting before discussion turned to the *Journal*'s future. The journal committee appointed 12 months earlier had little to report, because the committee members lived so far apart that there had never been a meeting of the full committee. Charles Hastings then interceded to move that 'it is expedient to continue the publication of the *Transactions* and of the *Journal* for the next year, but it is necessary to lessen the expense of the same, on which account for the future, the size of the *Journal* shall not exceed sixteen pages weekly ... .'[27] Although this motion was carried unanimously, unanimity may indicate the esteem in which members held Hastings rather than universal respect for the *Journal*, for the debate which preceded the vote had indicated some dissatisfaction with its quality and costs. Streeten offered a trenchant defence, claiming that 'it would bear comparison with any other journal in the kingdom', while a Mr Daniell predicted that withdrawal of the *Journal* would mean the loss of 'many members'. Dr Jeffreys inquired:

> What was the reason that that Association was unprecedented in its extent, and also in its success? It was not to be attributed simply to their meetings; but that they had resources within themselves—the advantages which they enjoyed, and the information which they conveyed by the publication of their *Journal*; and so long as their prosperity existed, why were some gentlemen so anxious for the discontinuance of those means to which they, in great measure, owed it ... Many of them who could spare half an hour would receive information which they would neither know nor hear of, but for that publication.[28]

[25] *Journal*, 6 Aug. 1845, 504–5.

[26] BMA mss. Proceedings of the PMSA at the Fifteenth Anniversary Meeting (Derby, 1847). Report of Council. See *Journal*, 11 Aug. 1847, 427; 26 May 1854, 450.

[27] *Journal*, 6 Aug. 1845, 505.

[28] *Ibid.*, 507; 29 July 1846, 353–4.

The journal committee never produced a report.

The *London Medical Gazette*, one of the leading medical periodicals of the time, expressed its pleasure that the *Journal* was to survive: 'The *Journal* may not contain so much matter as some of its cotemporaries [sic], but it is less infected with politics and personalities, and we hope long to see it continue its quiet and even course.'[29] A *Journal* correspondent agreed: 'I cannot help saying that if the question be put at every annual meeting—'Shall the *Journal* be discontinued?' it will be but poor encouragement to the members.'[30]

But debate upon the *Journal*'s future did continue. George Kelson referring to the coverage of medical politics inquired: 'Is it equitable towards your subscribers to fill the pages of this *Journal* with such trash?'[31] A Bath and Bristol branch resolution criticized both the *Journal* and *Transactions* for providing 'a very inadequate return for the large sum of money expended upon them.' It called for termination of the *Transactions* or, at least, a change from annual to occasional publication with concentration upon 'important original researches', and fortnightly or even monthly publication of the *Journal*. The money which would be saved might then be spent on grants for original investigations, prizes for essays on medical subjects, or other objects approved by the Council. The general meeting of the East Yorkshire branch of the PMSA simply called for termination of the *Journal* and higher expenditure on the benevolent fund.

In the light of these criticisms the Association appointed another committee, which included Hastings and Budd, to examine the future of the Association's publications.[32] The committee concluded its inquiry well ahead of schedule, producing an interim report on the *Journal*'s format and frequency before the end of 1846. The committee considered that enlargement or improvement of PMSA publications could be effected only if savings on current expenditure were achieved. At the same time it was resolutely opposed to scrapping the *Journal*. This, it suggested, would be

> ... a most unwise proceeding, and highly prejudicial to the interests of the Society, comprising as it does so large a proportion of Provincial Practitioners in Medicine and Surgery, whose means of obtaining practical information is very great, and whose ability to make that information available to the general body of subscribers is undoubted; your Committee consider, that the Society should not only publish a Journal, but that it should hold a position not inferior to any other similar publication in the United Kingdom.[33]

The question which the committee faced, therefore, was that of determining the most appropriate format for the *Journal*. The range of possibilities was circumscribed by the requirement for postal dispatch throughout the

[29] *London Medical Gazette*, 15 Aug. 1845, reprinted in the *Journal*, 27 Aug. 1845, 548.

[30] *Journal*, 24 Sept. 1845, 593.

[31] *Ibid.*, 10 Dec. 1845, 727–8.

[32] *Ibid.*, 26 Aug. 1846, 397.

[33] *Ibid.*, 12 Aug. 1846, 372–3; 13 Jan. 1847, 1–2.

UK, including to 'the most remote rural districts'. This ruled out the otherwise desirable possibility of a monthly or quarterly journal, since such a publication could be issued only through London booksellers or local secretaries, thereby entailing either additional expense or the unacceptable imposition of additional duties upon Association officials. It would also mean losing regularity of delivery 'which is *so important a feature* in periodical literature'.[34] The committee therefore decided in favour of publishing the *Journal* fortnightly at twice its current size and retaining postal transmission. Such a solution, it judged, would save £200 p.a. in postage; this was a significant sum in the context of PMSA finances. As far as the *Transactions* was concerned, the committee decided that it had largely outlived its usefulness and that, while it might continue to be issued on an occasional basis, annual publication was no longer warranted. Finally, the Committee recommended that 'the most active and energetic measures be adopted to raise the character of the Journal as a medium of conveying PRACTICAL and USEFUL information, and that as one means of attaining this object, a Sub-Editor, with a commensurate salary be appointed.'[35] Council accepted the committee's recommendations and fortnightly publication began in 1847. The appointment of a sub-editor was held over, with Council expressing its 'full confidence' that Streeten would 'in the meantime make such arrangements for its [the *Journal*'s] improvement as circumstances seem to call for'.

Critics of the *Journal* had generally been at pains to stress that they did not hold the editor responsible for its poor quality. The problem, they usually stated, lay in the resources devoted to it. It would, however, have required an extraordinarily tolerant, not to say insensitive, man to accept such statements at face value and not be hurt by attacks on the publication for which he was responsible. How Streeten reacted in private is unknown. In the pages of the *Journal* he merely stated that he would make 'every effort' to carry out Council's wishes and 'to render the *Journal* under its increased size, a record of the progress of Medical Science and Practice, giving special prominence to the provincial districts and to all subjects of interest to, or connected with, the Provincial Association'.[36]

The first fortnightly issue, priced at 9d for non-members of the PMSA, appeared on 13 January 1847. It contained a new section, or rather the resurrection of an old one, the 'General Retrospect', which consisted of excerpts from foreign periodicals. The new volume contained more clinical material than hitherto. Individual issues were 28 pages long; this represented rather less than the proposed doubling of size, for in 1846 the *Journal* had often been published in issues of 20 pages.

The journal committee submitted a second report to the anniversary

[34] *Ibid.* [35] *Ibid.* [36] *Ibid.*, 17.

meeting held at Derby in 1847. This recommended the appointment of an additional editor with responsibility for the *Journal*'s foreign department, though it seems that William Harcourt Ranking was already filling this role in at least an unofficial capacity as he had, for six months, been assisting Streeten by compiling the 'General Retrospect'.[37]

The new-look *Journal* was praised by Dr Barham, president of the PMSA's south-west branch. He told a branch meeting that 'its improvement in quality has been more than proportionate to the lessened frequency of its publication' and expressed his hope 'that yet greater strength may be thrown into this organ, which I will call the lungs of our Association.'[38] Others agreed. For example, in 1848 the PMSA's president, George Newman, suggested that 'conducted as it now is, by its talented Editors, on the plan recommended by the Committee, it not only answers the expectations of the Association, but forms a valuable addition to the medical press.'[39] By 1848 the *Journal* seemed finally to have established itself upon a firm basis, warmly regarded by PMSA members and respected by its rivals. This, however, was a false dawn; it was to be some years before the *Journal* gained complete security, and there were to be several more threats to its existence.

New editors

The *Journal* was struck a severe blow in May 1849 when Streeten died aged 48. When Council discussed the question of his successor it decided that the positions of secretary and editor were too demanding to be held by the same man and recommended James Sheppard for the secretaryship. A selection committee was charged with finding a new editor in time for his appointment to be confirmed at the 1850 anniversary meeting.

The committee reached a rapid decision. In September the *Journal* announced that William Harcourt Ranking of Norwich and John Walsh of Worcester would act as joint editors. Ranking, former physician to Suffolk General Hospital, had been assisting Streeten for some while and was, at the time of his appointment, running the *Journal*'s foreign department. He was 36 in 1850. Walsh had had 'superintendence' of the *Journal* since spring 1849 during Streeten's illness. Born in 1810, Walsh had become FRCS in 1844. At the time of his appointment as editor he was in private practice in Worcester.[40] The appointments promised, therefore, to maintain continuity in publication. They also reinforced the provincial and especially the Worcester locus of the Association. According to Greenhill, the appointment of

[37] *Ibid.*, 5 Jan. 1856, 14.

[38] *Ibid.*, 25 Aug. 1847, 466.

[39] *Ibid*, 23 Feb. 1848, 107; 23 Aug. 1848, 451.

[40] *Ibid.*, 13 June 1849, 321; R. N. Rose, *The Field 1853–1953. A Centenary History* (London: Michael Joseph, 1953), p. 73.

Ranking and Walsh was followed by 'a marked improvement ... in the whole external appearance of the Journal, which has ever since [1856] continued as clean and neat-looking as any Journal need be'.[41] The 1850 anniversary meeting duly endorsed the appointments.

In May 1852 Charles Cowan gave notice that he intended to propose at that summer's anniversary meeting in Oxford that the *Journal* should revert to being edited and published weekly in London. The editors objected, claiming that the proposal was both impractical, since the cost of metropolitan production was so much higher than provincial, and undesirable, as the *Journal* was the organ of provincial practitioners and would lose its distinctive character if transferred to the capital.[42]

Cowan sent details of his proposal to the Association's various regional branches, which, traditionally, held their annual meetings immediately before the anniversary meeting. A North Wales member, James Edwards, expressed enthusiasm for a move to London, believing that it would improve the *Journal*'s quality and make it 'what it ought to be as their recognised organ'.[43]He contended that its poor quality had had an adverse effect upon the Association's standing. But some other members agreed with Ranking and Walsh that transferring to London would destroy the *Journal*'s distinctive character and make it merely another inferior London journal. The North Wales branch president thought that the important issue was not place of publication, but editorial quality, and he felt there was widespread agreement that this was poor.[44]

Council's report for 1851–2, read at the Oxford meeting, claimed that members were 'generally of opinion' that Ranking and Walsh had improved the *Journal.* It nevertheless conceded that there were differences of opinion on this question and observed that in the course of the year it had received suggestions for changing the Association's publications. In what was evidently an attempt to avoid acrimonious discussion on Cowan's proposal, Council, suggesting that the matter 'cannot with advantage be discussed in a General Meeting,' proposed the appointment of (yet another) committee 'to take into consideration any suggestions that may be made for improving the publications, and especially as to the Editorship of the *Journal*'.[45]

Cowan, however, was not to be denied and brought his proposal before the members. He attributed the recent decline in Association membership to the 'defective' quality of the *Journal* and argued that by moving it to London under the control of a single editor and making it '*the* best medical periodical in the kingdom' they would soon induce the medical profession to join the

[41] *Journal*, 5 Jan. 1856, 14.
[42] *Ibid.*, 9 June 1852, 297–8; see 23 June 1852, 312–13; 7 July 1852, 338–9.
[43] *Ibid.*, 7 July 1852, 346.
[44] *Ibid.*, 21 July 1852, 368.
[45] *Ibid.*, 4 Aug. 1852, 391.

PMSA in their 'thousands'. On the question of cost, Cowan believed that the Association 'might bring out a first-rate professional literary weekly publication for about the same or rather a less sum than they were now paying for bringing out fortnightly a journal which did not give satisfaction'.[46] At the end of a robust and eloquent speech in support of his proposal, Cowan 'resumed his seat amidst much applause'.

In the debate on the motion Mr Lord of Hampstead called the *Journal* '*effete* ... stale, flat and unprofitable'; the question which faced the meeting, he averred, was 'whether they would continue to have a journal supplied to them, backward in intelligence and torpid in delivery, or such an efficient organ as that proposed by Dr. Cowan'. Thomas Nunneley of Leeds then took up the Council's suggestion that a committee be appointed to consider the question. A show of hands on Nunneley's amendment yielded an indecisive result. Accordingly, members were requested to move to the left or right of the chair depending on whether they supported or rejected the amendment. The undecided were asked to clear the room. Of the 120 members who stayed, 61 voted for the amendment. The announcement of this result 'was received with much applause, and an exciting scene ensued, and in the midst of the confusion attendant on this, the President declared the *original motion (which had not been formally put to the meeting)* carried' [emphasis in original]. What happened next is unclear. Cowan signified his acceptance of the committee nominated by Nunneley and moved for its appointment with an instruction that it superintend future *Journal* production in London. But most of those whom Nunneley had nominated withdrew their names. According to the *Journal*'s account, compiled by a Council reporter, 'a Committee consisting of eight or nine gentlemen was understood to be appointed, though the proceedings here were extremely confused, and the appointment, if made at all, was done in a most irregular manner.'[47]

Cowan, who was appointed chairman of the new committee, assured Ranking and Walsh that they might remain as editors for the remainder of the year, but Ranking had had enough and resigned. Walsh was inclined to do likewise but, fearing that the *Journal* might be irreparably damaged by the sudden departure of both editors, agreed to stay on. During August and September Walsh, in a series of editorials, sought to establish that nothing had been achieved at the Oxford meeting because Cowan had given insufficient notice of his motion and because the chairman had followed incorrect procedure. But, at a meeting held in September, Council 'having ascertained from many influential members of the Association, that the *general* feeling is in favour of the validity of the resolution passed at Oxford, with regard to the *Journal*, are of opinion that it is not desirable further to insist upon the informality of Dr. Cowan's proposition'.[48]

[46] *Ibid.*, 395. [47] *Ibid.*, 397–9. [48] *Ibid.*, 15 Sept. 1852, 489.

Meanwhile, the journal committee pressed ahead with its deliberations. At a meeting held as early as 5 August, it was decided to offer the editorship to John Rose Cormack of Putney. The committee could hardly have made a better choice, for at the age of 37 Cormack already had behind him a distinguished career in medicine and medical journalism. He was born at Stow, Midlothian, in 1815, and had graduated MD at Edinburgh in 1837, having been awarded a gold medal for his dissertation on the presence of air in the organs of circulation. After graduating he had studied in Paris before starting to practise in Edinburgh, where he was also physician to the Royal Infirmary and Fever Hospital. In 1843 Cormack published a volume on epidemic fever in Edinburgh and other towns, a work which had been enthusiastically reviewed in the *Journal*.[49] In 1841 he had founded the *Edinburgh Monthly Journal of Medical Science*, which he edited until he moved to London in 1847. In 1849 he established the *London Journal of Medicine* which amalgamated with the *PMSJ* soon after Cormack became editor of the latter, to form the *Association Medical Journal*.[50]

On 10 August Cormack notified the journal committee of his acceptance of the *Journal*'s editorship, though, as he later revealed, he feared—with good reason—that the dispute over the *Journal*'s future would leave him with a legacy of hostility.[51] In notifying the committee of his acceptance of the editorship he let it be known that there were two things with which he was less than satisfied; one was his remuneration. This was to be at the same rate which had applied when the *Journal* was published fortnightly. Cormack thought that '£250 per annum is not a sufficient encouragement to any one to embark in this enterprise with the needful toil and determination.' He made it clear that as membership, advertising, and sales revenue increased he expected his salary to be raised. Cormack's second point was that a good *Journal* had to be the work of several hands and heads. 'It is, therefore, obvious that, as soon as circumstances permit, a certain sum of money ought to be placed annually at the disposal of the editor for the payment of contributors.' He had promises of unpaid help, but warned the committee that it should not rely upon 'a long continuance of unremunerated labour'.

In response to Cormack's statement, the committee decided to place at his disposal a sum of up to £50 per quarter for payment of literary and artistic contributors.[52] This allowed Cormack to employ a full-time 'literary assistant' (Dr Alexander Henry) at a salary of £85 p.a.[53] During the first half of 1853 a total of 14 guineas was paid to other contributors. The Committee

[49] J. R. Cormack, *Natural History, Pathology, and Treatment of the Epidemic Fever at Present Prevailing in Edinburgh and other Towns; illustrated by Cases and Dissections* (London: Churchill, 1843); *Journal*, 27 Jan. 1844, 328–36.

[50] *Dictionary of National Biography* (London: Smith, Elder, 1908); *Journal*, 20 May 1882, 761.

[51] *Ibid.*, 30 Dec. 1853, 1145.

[52] *Ibid.*, 19 Aug. 1853, 728.

[53] *Ibid.*, 729.

made no immediate move, however, to increase Cormack's salary, and, in fact, this remained static throughout his 33-month tenure of office. Cormack took up his duties in January 1853, Walsh having continued in post for the remainder of 1852, during which time he missed no opportunity to criticize Cowan and the new *Journal* plans.[54]

Securing an editor was but one of the journal committee's priorities. Another was finding a London printer. They invited tenders and, at a meeting held on 29 September, decided to accept the quotation of Thomas Richards of 37 Great Queen Street, Lincoln's Inn Fields. Perhaps as attractive as the price quoted by Richards was his offer of business accommodation, for the Association had no London premises from which to conduct the *Journal*'s commercial and editorial activities.[55]

In September 1852 Cowan's journal committee submitted a scheme of publication for the consideration of Association members. The remodelled *Journal*, it said, with a measure of exaggeration, was to have a 'greatly augmented' staff of London and provincial contributors. The committee's goal was to produce a high-quality weekly at the lowest possible cost. More specifically, it planned to publish 'a faithful digest of medical literature and science, as well as an attractive summary of professional news'. It hoped that the result would be such as to 'render the purchase of any other periodical a matter of choice rather than of necessity'. The proposed list of contents was as follows:

1 Leading articles
2 Original communications
3 Book reviews

[54] *Ibid.*, 29 Sept. 1852, 512–13. On vacating the editorial chair Walsh gave up his Worcester practice and moved to London where he was soon to find his vocation as editor of the recently established *Field* magazine. Walsh had vigorously pursued his love of field sports in the Worcestershire countryside. He lost a finger and a thumb on his left hand in a shooting accident. 'The Great Walsh', as he became known, was a triumphantly successful editor of the *Field* for 30 years, during which time he contributed to the development of 'the shotgun as we know it today'. R. N. Rose, *The Field 1853–1953. A Centenary History*, pp. 73–84, 111 (note 40). Ranking's subsequent career was less successful. In 1865 he was admitted to Ticehurst Asylum in Sussex with symptoms that suggest he may have suffered a stroke. After 5½ months he was transferred to another asylum. His last listing in the *Medical Register* is for 1867. See Wellcome Institute for the History of Medicine. Ticehurst Asylum, casebook no. 10, 1964–5. I am grateful to Charlotte Mackenzie for steering me towards this reference.

[55] *Journal*, 19 Aug. 1853, 728. The *Journal* retained these offices till 1878 when, along with the BMA, it moved to the Strand. In 1872 the General Secretary of the BMA and manager of the *Journal*, Francis Fowke, moved into one of the rooms in Great Queen Street. Two years later the BMA, hitherto without business premises, took accommodation in an adjoining shop. In 1853 the Great Queen Street office was open six days a week from 9. 00 a. m. till 7. 00 p. m. Cormack, however, did most of his editorial work at his Putney home, confining his office appearances to 75 minutes per week 'when not unavoidably prevented by other duties'. *Journal*, 24 Nov. 1852, unnumbered page; 4 Nov. 1871, 536; Paul Vaughan, *Doctors' Commons. A Short History of the British Medical Association* (London: Heinemann, 1959), p. 161.

4 'Periscopic Review'—i.e. summaries of important topics in British and foreign periodicals
5 Reports of societies ('faithful, succinct and early')
6 Association news
7 Topics of the day
8 Obituaries
9 Appointments
10 Letters
11 Advertisements

In seeking members' support Cowan explained the importance to the Association of a successful re-launch of the *Journal*: 'It may with perfect truth be asserted, that on the success of our journal depends the retrogression, stagnancy, or the prosperity of our Association . . . .'[56] That this view was accepted by senior PMSA figures is indicated by the fact that in 1853 the *Journal*'s new editor was permitted to treat as his budget all but £305 of the Association's total annual subscription income.[57]

At the core of the debate on the *Journal* which Cowan initiated at Oxford in 1852 was the question: what kind of publication should the *Journal* be? Should it be a narrow record of Association business, seasoned with a smattering of original articles from members and excerpts from other journals, aimed at some 2000 provincial practitioners?[58] Or should it possess a more assertive, proselytizing character, take on the best of the commercial journals, seek a nationwide readership by paying for and publishing the best available work, and thereby attempt to make the PMSA an institution of national importance?[59] In appointing Cormack, remodelling the *Journal*, and moving it to London, the PMSA appeared to have chosen the second option. Association and *Journal* were seemingly intent upon establishing themselves at the centre of the profession, and thereby gaining more influence. The days of provincial insularity were apparently over.[60]

However, a sizeable section of the Association's membership, including Hastings, was implacably opposed to the PMSA losing its provincial character and becoming a metropolitan organization. Hence the decisions taken at Oxford did not so much mark the opening of a new chapter in the PMSA's progress, but rather initiated a kind of civil war between London expansionists and provincial conservatives. As George Webster, founder of the first British Medical Association, pointed out some two years later that

[56] *Journal*, 29 Sept. 1852, 513–14.

[57] *Ibid*., 19 Aug. 1853, 728.

[58] *Ibid*., 29 Sept. 1852, 514.

[59] *Ibid*., Cowan's speech on the launch of the metropolitan branch of the PMSA, 14 Jan. 1853, 44.

[60] *Ibid*., 7 Jan. 1853, 1–3; 14 Jan. 1853, 44. See 14 July 1854, 628–9; 21 July 1854, 652–3; 28 July 1854, 685–6.

the 'Executive Council and their President, so far from immediately acquiescing in and cheerfully carrying out the Oxford decision, for months pertinaciously opposed and frivolously and vexatiously thwarted the proceedings of the Journal Committee.'[61] The divisions created at Oxford eventually led to Cormack's resignation, and, indeed, were to threaten the Association's very existence.

From Oxford to Manchester

Cormack proved to be an able editor, certainly the best that the *Journal* had hitherto possessed. In a short time he transformed it from a somewhat dull publication carrying little high-quality journalism or clinical material into a stimulating, well-presented compendium of medical news and knowledge. Although his tenure of office was brief and today he is but little remembered, he did much to set the *Journal* on a more secure footing.

The re-modelled *Journal* was favourably received by PMSA members.[62] During the first half of 1853 membership of the Association rose by over 400. Whether this was in response to the improved quality of the *Journal* is debatable, but George Webster, who, admittedly, was a member of the journal committee, observed that everyone with whom he had had 'professional communication' in the first half of 1853, felt

> that the manner in which the JOURNAL was conducted gave universal satisfaction. His opinion coincided with that of an eminent physician, whom he had that day met, viz., that the ASSOCIATION JOURNAL was not only an excellent medical journal, but the best medical journal . . . he (Dr. Webster) knew that the vast majority of the four hundred and odd members who had recently joined the Association, had been attracted chiefly by its excellence; and many old members had remained members, who would have resigned, had the Oxford decision not been carried out.[63]

The journal committee agreed that the move to London 'has been the means of causing a great increase of Members to the Association, including a very large number of the most respected and influential members of the profession both in town and country, in Scotland as well as in England.'[64] The PMSA Council, on the other hand, was ambivalent, not to say antipathetic towards Cormack's *Journal*, and seriously concerned that it could prove a drain upon Association resources. This attitude was indicative of the continuing tension within the PMSA between metropolitans and provincials. Hastings sat in the latter camp. Speaking at the 1853 anniversary meeting at Swansea, he said that

[61] *Ibid.*, 26 Oct. 1855, 981; see 9 Nov. 1855, 1019; 16 Nov. 1855, 1037.
[62] *Ibid.*, 8 July 1853, 600; 15 July 1853, 615.
[63] *Ibid.*, 22 July 1853, 655; 23 Dec. 1853, 1136.
[64] *Ibid.*, 19 Aug. 1853, 730.

As to the great accession of new members, he could not ascribe this to the *Journal.* Some might have joined on that account: but in Swansea and its neighbourhood, for example, the increase of the Association was owing to the establishment of a new Branch; and in Manchester, the influx was owing to the prospect of the anniversary being held there next year.[65]

At the 1854 anniversary meeting in Manchester Jonas Malden, a member of the Worcester branch, moved for expenditure on the *Journal* to be 'considerably reduced'.[66] Council supported the motion stating that Cormack had run the *Journal* 'at an expense so large, that, in the present state of the finances of the Association, it becomes a question for very careful consideration whether our resources will be adequate for the maintenance of the *Journal* in its present form'.[67] Cowan feared that success for Malden's motion would destroy 'at one blow the *Journal* system now being gradually and laboriously built up'.[68] Consequently, the journal committee, which he dominated, compiled a lengthy report congratulating Cormack on the 'very able' manner in which he had conducted the *Journal*'s literary and financial business, and calling for increases in his salary, starting with an extra £100 p.a. from 1 January 1855. In addition, the committee called for the appointment of a business manager, pending which Cormack, aided by a commercial assistant, would continue to manage the *Journal*'s commercial affairs.

Clearly the journal committee planned to fight fire with fire. Indeed, its proposals were even more inflammatory than would first appear, for it sought to take advantage of the recent death of the PMSA's secretary, James Sheppard, to locate the *Journal*'s business department entirely in London. Philip Williams had been appointed his successor, but the appointment had to be confirmed by members at the anniversary meeting.[69] Before this could be done, Charles Cowan proposed

That in consequence of the transference of the publication of the *Journal* from Worcester to London, a paid Secretary at Worcester is no longer desirable; and that the duties of the office be in future discharged by the Editor of the *Journal*, in conjunction with a salaried commercial assistant, who shall keep all the Association accounts, collect the subscriptions of members and assist in the commercial department of the Journal.[70]

A Bath member objected strongly. 'We are,' he protested, 'a 'provincial association': but if we send up this commercial assistant to Dr Cormack in London, he will be to all intents and purposes Secretary to the Association, and the next thing will be the transfer of the Central Council of the Association to London.' He feared that, if accepted, Cowan's plan would lead to the Metropolitan Counties branch 'swallowing' the PMSA—'I

[65] *Ibid.*, 731–2.
[66] *Ibid.*, 11 Aug. 1854, 728.
[67] *Ibid.*, 22 Sept. 1854, 851–2.
[68] *Ibid.*, 854.
[69] *Ibid.*, 10 March 1854, 232.
[70] *Ibid.*, 22 Sept. 1854, 856.

foresee eventually ... [it] ... will be *the* Association ... [emphasis in original].'[71] Cowan, however, 'utterly' rejected the metropolitan/provincial distinction observing that we 'are a united body, and the *Journal* is just as much for the interests of the metropolitan practitioner as for the provincial.'[72] When Cowan's proposal was put to the vote it was carried on a show of hands by 'a large majority', with over 100 in favour and only 15 or 16 against. Hastings was dismayed by a verdict 'so opposed to the views I hold' and offered his resignation as treasurer and President of the Council. This, however, was refused and another potential crisis was averted.[73]

The provinces fight back

Hastings's disenchantment was soon heightened, for in October 1854 he was obliged to tell PMSA members that profligate expenditure on the *Journal* had forced suspension of the *Transactions*. In announcing this Hastings made no secret of his disappointment that the *Journal*'s 'more ephemeral pages' would continue, while the *Transactions*—a publication which he believed had made a profound contribution to the development of medical science—should cease publication.[74]

The PMSA's 1855 anniversary meeting was held at York. On the second day of the meeting William Husband, later a president and treasurer of the BMA, moved that the offices of General Secretary and Editor of the *Journal* should not be held by one person. Hastings spoke enthusiastically in support of the motion, reminding the assembly that he had been prompted to tender his resignation once on this question, and that he would do so again (and not withdraw it) if Husband's motion failed. Cormack, for his part, promised that he would resign all his official posts within the Association if he were to be stripped of any one of them. The members were therefore faced with a clear choice between the PMSA's founder, who was virtually an institution within the institution, and the *Journal*'s editor. There was no real choice; Hastings was supported. The meeting also decided that the name of the *Journal* should revert to the original *Provincial Medical and Surgical Journal* (from *Association Medical Journal*), the proposal to change the Association's name to the British Medical Association having failed.[75]

Cormack promptly announced that, while he was willing to continue in post for a further week or month, publication of the *Journal* would soon be interrupted unless a new editor was appointed. Several members suggested

[71] *Ibid.*, 857.

[72] *Ibid.*, 862.

[73] *Ibid.*, 863. See also 5 Jan. 1855, 23.

[74] *Ibid.*, 27 Oct. 1854, 973–4.

[75] By 50 votes to 31. A similar proposal had failed in 1854. The change of name was agreed at a special meeting in Birmingham in November 1855. *Ibid.*, 786–93. See E. M. Little, *History of the BMA* (London: British Medical Association, n.d. 1932?), pp. 73–7.

that Cormack's resignation should be refused. Even Hastings, who had done much to prompt Cormack's resignation, urged that he should stay on. But Cormack denied that the Association had any claim upon him 'either in law, equity, or honour. The ... contract is absolutely dissolved by your own act, and no new bargain has been made.' He felt deeply aggrieved that, having worked long and hard in the service of Association and *Journal*, for a small reward, he had been peremptorily cast aside. He viewed the *Journal*'s future with grave misgivings:

I look upon much that has been done and said as utterly ruinous to the JOURNAL, and as fraught with disaster to the Association. You have in my opinion sown the seeds of disease which must terminate in early dissolution. You have taken your stand upon an exclusive provincialism. The *Journal* will be ruined by the proceedings of this meeting: of that I have no doubt. The cognate power of editor and secretary must lead to dispeace. In a commercial point of view the reassumption of the old name of "Provincial Medical and Surgical Journal" is equivalent to throwing away several hundred pounds a year in the revenue from advertisements ... the name "Provincial" is at all times fatal to the success of any literary undertaking.[76]

Cormack had no doubt that the decisions arrived at in York constituted a retreat to provincialism and a rebuttal of the London members. 'The London members,' he said, 'were treated as intruders by various speakers.' There was a good deal of truth in these observations, though, as we now know, Cormack's prediction of catastrophe was wide of the mark. Only a small minority of PMSA members attended the York meeting; the views expressed there were not necessarily representative of PMSA feeling as a whole. There is a hint of this in the discussion on the last item on the meeting's agenda. This concerned a memorial addressed to the meeting by 453 members who were unable to attend. The document called, among other things, for adoption of the title British Medical Association and massive expansion of the Association both at home and overseas, and it warmly endorsed the conduct of the *Journal* under Cormack:

... the funds of the Association cannot be better employed than in the support of a *Journal* ... the existing *Journal* has, under the management of the present Editor, been greatly improved, and has been conducted by him in accordance with the spirit and objects of the Association, ... this is indicated by the increased number and increasing influence of the Association.[77]

When John Propert, a Londoner, observed that the memorial should have been the *first* item on the agenda, Cormack responded that, 'So thought some members of Council; but in arranging the order of business last night, it was decided to make it last.' Hastings maintained that this was 'Simply because it was the last in coming into the Secretary's hands'.[78] This may have been the

[76] *Journal*, 24 Aug. 1855, 798–9. See also 773.
[77] *Ibid.*, 799–800.
[78] *Ibid.*; see 14 Sept. 1855, 860.

literal truth, but it seems likely that the memorial was also held back for tactical reasons.

Several of the decisions made at York were soon to be reversed. Within months the name British Medical Association was adopted. As a consequence the *PMSJ* became the *BMJ* in 1857. These were more than semantic changes, for they underlined the Association's national constituency. The *Journal*, which Cormack had done so much to improve, did not slip back into provincial insularity after his departure but remained of comparable quality to its commercial competitors and a worthy standard for the Association. Cormack, a figure little remembered today compared with Charles Hastings, achieved much in his short term of office by improving the quality of the *Journal*, thereby increasing Association membership. Greenhill stated that 'Probably all persons will admit (in general terms) that the *Journal* was improved under Dr. Cormack's management, while it is incontestable that his exertions, both as Secretary and as Editor, considerably reduced the amount of arrears of subscriptions, and added several hundred members of the Association.'[79] Charles Williams, who refers to Cormack's 'long life chequered with many chapters', asserts, perhaps too harshly, that Cormack was 'an amiable man of enterprising and industrious disposition . . . [who] . . . wanted firmness and strength of character necessary to ensure success'. However, his contribution deserves more recognition than it has hitherto received. Neither should it be forgotten that Hastings was ambivalent about the *Journal* and harboured great reservations about the PMSA becoming more than a small-scale provincial organization.[80]

In the last quarter of 1855 the *Journal*'s pages were full of letters from leading figures within the PMSA blaming each other for bringing the Association to the brink of disaster.[81] Wisely, the Association moved quickly to appoint Cormack's successor. The vacancy was advertised in *The Times* and each of the London medical periodicals. Fourteen applications were

[79] *Ibid.*, 12 Jan. 1856, 35.

[80] Charles Williams, *Memoirs of Life and Work* (London: Smith Elder, 1884), p. 411; P. Vaughan, *Doctors' Commons*, pp. 72, 130 (note 55). Cormack's contribution was formally recognized in the *Journal* after his departure: 'The great prosperity of the Association, before the late troubles, was, in fact, mainly due to the improved character of the *Journal*.' 26 Oct. 1855, 977; see 5 Jan. 1856, 35; 2 Feb. 1856, 95.

[81] After stepping down as editor, Cormack remained a member of the Association and continued to practise medicine in London. In 1858 he was an unsuccessful candidate for the position of Secretary to the General Medical Council. In 1866 ill-health prompted him to settle in Orleans. In 1869 he moved to Paris to take up the position of physician to the British Embassy. He was also appointed physician to the Hertford British Hospital in the same city. During the Franco–Prussian War he acted as the *Journal*'s Paris correspondent. During the war and subsequent 'commune' he provided a hospital service in Paris. Cormack received the Chevalier Legion d'Honneur in 1871 and a knighthood in 1872. He died in Paris in 1882. *Dictionary of National Biography* (note 50); *Journal*, 6 Nov. 1858, 933; 5 June 1869, 517; 17 Dec. 1870, 664; 28 Jan. 1871, 102; 18 Nov. 1871, 588; 20 Jan. 1872, 76; 17 Feb. 1877, 201–10; 20 May 1882, 761.

received and in October Andrew Wynter, of London, was appointed at a salary of £250 p.a.

Wynter, who was not, at the time of his appointment, a member of the Association, was born in Bristol in 1819. He had studied medicine in London at St George's Hospital and graduated MD at St Andrews in 1853. He had been a contributor to the *Medical Times and Gazette* and the *Quarterly Review*. His main medical interest was in the treatment of the insane.[82] Under Wynter's supervision, the *Journal* maintained the high standards set by Cormack, but in 1859 its future was again called into question when John Dix of Hull attacked the *Journal*'s content and costliness. 'Let us, then,' he said at the BMA's annual meeting in Liverpool, 'use our united endeavours to cast off this millstone from about our necks.' He suggested, as others had done before him, that the *Journal* should be little more than a record of Association business. The meeting passed two motions calling for alteration in the format and frequency of publication.[83] At the 1860 meeting in Torquay, Council and some members expressed misgivings about the *Journal*'s quality. In addition, Wynter was criticized for being inaccessible and out of touch with recent developments in medical science.[84]

It may have been this constant carping which prompted Wynter to resign in October 1860, though it is also possible that he was 'pushed' and made a scapegoat for the Association's static or falling membership figures.[85] Wynter may also have wished to devote more time to his literary career, for he wrote widely on non-medical subjects and was a regular contributor to the *Edinburgh Review*, the *Quarterly Review*, and *Once a Week*. He went on to publish six books in the 15 years between his leaving the *Journal* and his death.[86]

The *Journal* established

Wynter's successor as editor was William Orlando Markham (1818–91), who had joined the Association, as a member of the Middlesex branch only in 1859. He remained with the *BMJ* for five years till the end of 1866, at which point he resigned to take up a position as Poor Law Inspector for the metropolitan district.[87] Like Cormack and Streeten, he was a graduate of

[82] *Dictionary of National Biography* (note 50).

[83] *Journal*, 8 Oct. 1859, 819–21; see 6 Aug. 1859, 628–9. 15 Oct. 1859, 841–2; 22 Oct. 1859, 859–64; 29 Oct. 1859, 879–80; 5 Nov. 1859, 900; 12 Nov. 1859, 948–50; 17 Dec. 1859, 1026–7; 31 March 1860, 255; 23 June 1860, 481; 30 June 1860, 495.

[84] *Ibid.*, 11 Aug 1860, 621–4.

[85] *Ibid.*, 7 Jan. 1865, 14.

[86] *Dictionary of National Biography* (note 50); *Journal*, 20 May 1876, 637–8; 15 July 1876, 84.

[87] According to Joseph Rogers, Markham, at the time of his appointment, 'had been the editor of what was at this time an obscure journal. He was not known to have ever been associated with any sanitary work, nor to have seen the inside of a workhouse in his life'. Joseph Rogers, *Reminiscences of a Workhouse Medical Officer* (London: Fisher Unwin, 1889), p. 57.

Edinburgh University, where he qualified MD in 1840. His later book on heart disease was based upon a dissertation for which he had been awarded a gold medal at Edinburgh. This was *Diseases of the Heart; their Pathology, Diagnosis and Treatment* (1856), the second edition of which was warmly reviewed by the *BMJ* in September 1860. It must have been very soon after the appearance of this review that the BMA Council selected him to replace Wynter. His salary as editor was £200 p.a., £50 less than Cormack and Wynter had received.

From November 1841 to June 1842 Markham had been house surgeon at Charing Cross Hospital. Thereafter he was elected FRCP, was physician to St Mary's Hospital and lecturer in physiology and pathology at St Mary's Medical School. He was a regular contributor to the medical press, including the *Lancet*, the *Medical Times and Gazette*, and the *British and Foreign Medical-Chirurgical Review*. Before becoming editor of the *BMJ* he had contributed frequently to its pages. In 1859 and 1860 he published papers in the *Journal* on 'The Uses of Bleeding in Diseases' and a long multi-part essay on cardiac disease.[88]

Markham made few changes to the *Journal*. His formula seems to have given satisfaction to members, the numbers of whom began to rise again after a rather stagnant period.[89] During his editorship expenditure on the *Journal* ran at even higher levels than in the 1850s—that is, 80–90 per cent and more of Association income. At the BMA's 1865 annual meeting in Leamington, Robert Carter of Stroud moved a resolution in favour of a more limited, less expensive *Journal*. This, however, was resoundingly defeated, for most members had come to recognize the value to the Association of a high-quality, wide-ranging *Journal*.[90] Never again was the *BMJ*'s existence seriously questioned. The matter, as a leading article later stated, was 'fairly and decisively' resolved by the 'distinct and unmistakeable' vote of BMA members at Leamington 'to have and maintain a journal'.[91] After a full quarter of a century the *Journal*'s struggle for survival, as Markham recognized, was over:

[88] Markham's book, *Bleeding and Change in Type of Disease* was published in 1864. He translated and wrote several other books and was Gulstonian lecturer in 1864. See *Journal*, 9 April 1859, 284–7; 16 April 1859, 307–8; 20 Aug. 1859, 667–8; 10 Sept. 1859, 740–1; 15 Oct. 1859, 828–30; 18 Feb 1860, 125–7; 19 Jan. 1867, 47; 14 Dec. 1867, 551; 7 Feb. 1891, 323. For more information on Markham's life and career see F. Boase, *Modern English Biography* (London: Frank Cass, 2nd impression, 1965); *London and Provincial Medical Directory* (London: Churchill, 1866).

[89] *Journal*, 8 July 1865, 2, 13, 15, 17, 22; 15 July 1865, 45, 51–3; 26 Aug. 1865, 226. After his resignation Markham was presented with a bound volume containing the signatures of over 1500 Association members and an 'address', written by Sir Thomas Watson, thanking him for his service in 'that difficult and invidious office'. Some BMA members believed 'a more substantial testimony' should have been offered. See *Journal*, 2 March 1867, 237; 9 March 1867, 270; 23 March 1867, 328.

[90] *Ibid.*, 12 Aug. 1865, 160–1.

[91] *Ibid.*, 2 Sept. 1865, 236–8.

> ... we may remind our readers of the struggles for its very existence which the *Journal* has had to maintain; or rather, we should say, of the many and constant efforts which have been made by ill-judging friends and open enemies to bring it to a close. This struggle, happily, is now at an end. Friends have become convinced of the error of their intentions, and enemies of the inutility of their attacks; and no one now ventures either to question or to doubt the propriety of its existence. Its special object and usefulness are now accepted facts.[92]

The year 1866 saw the death of Charles Hastings, the man who had dominated the Association for over 30 years, and also the appointment as *Journal* editor of Ernest Hart, the man who was to dominate it for the next 32. It may truly be said, therefore, that this year marked the end of one era and the beginning of another.

There are several questions arising from this account of the *Journal*'s early tribulations which demand answers. Why did the *BMJ* not go the way of most of its competitors, but survive in the face of a barrage of criticism from within the PMSA/BMA, including from some of those at the helm? It is clear that one interest group, which might be characterized as metropolitan and expansionist, prevailed at the expense of the provincial retrenchers. But why did the expansionists succeed and what did they perceive as the value of the *Journal*? In fact, most Association members recognized the benefits of a journal even if they complained about the format, content, and cost of the one they had. Some sort of regular publication was vital as a means of holding together a federal institution which otherwise was linked by little more than a perambulating annual meeting. But a high-calibre *Journal* could do more than help bind the Association together: it could assist medical men outside the London élite to advance their professional interests. These included not only matters of status and income but broader questions of public health and therapeutics. A quality *Journal* could recruit Association members and help establish medicine as a responsible and reputable profession. If such objectives were to be realized much would depend on the standard of its contents; a newsletter restricted to Association business would appeal only to those who were already members. So if we are fully to comprehend how the *Journal* survived we must consider the topics it covered and its treatment of them.

[92] *Ibid.*, 29 Dec. 1866, 720.

3
The *Journal* in the age of medical reform

Medical reform

In its first two decades the *Journal* aired no subject more often or at greater length than that of medical reform. Indeed, its very first issue contained a summary of Henry Warburton's 'Bill for the registration of medical practitioners, and for establishing a college of medicine'.[1] As a question of major concern to the profession, medical reform had never really gone away after the passing of the Apothecaries Act, 1815, though in terms of parliamentary activity, it was resurrected only in 1840, the year of the *Journal*'s launch. That year saw the first of a succession of parliamentary bills, 17 altogether, which sought to transform medical education, qualification, and professional organization.

The *Journal*'s preoccupation with medical reform is understandable, for the PMSA 'acted as a spokesman for provincial practitioners in the long and complicated activities of the profession in the search for medical reform'.[2] It is hard to discern a distinctive *Journal*, as against Association, position on the question. Both held the same views, with the *Journal* minimizing its role as against that of the Association. Hence, in 1858, when reporting William Cowper's (ultimately successful) bill, an editorial said, 'we abstain from comment, this properly being the duty of the Medical Reform Committee of the Association.'[3] Some weeks later, a leading article reviewing the role of the medical press in the reform process noted that 'Journals could do no more than point out the path of Reform ... it was the Association alone which could and *did* act.'[4] Although largely true, this assessment ignored the importance of the medical press in disseminating information and maintaining solidarity within particular factions of the profession. In these respects the *Journal* played a key role as the mouthpiece of the PMSA. Because of its propaganda value the Association was willing to spend heavily on it, notwithstanding its other alleged inadequacies.

The repeated failure of attempts at reform in the 1840s and 1850s

[1] *Journal*, 3 Oct. 1840, 13–15. See *Parliamentary Papers* (1840) **III**: pp. 17–50.

[2] M. J. Peterson, *The Medical Profession in Mid-Victorian London* (Los Angeles and London: University of California Press, 1978), p. 24.

[3] *Journal*, 3 April 1858, 268.

[4] *Ibid.*, 24 July 1858, 603.

underlines the divisions within the mid-nineteenth century medical profession, particularly between the London élite and rank and file practitioners. In general the latter sought reform that would increase their power, status, and remuneration at the expense both of quacks—by confining practice to qualified and registered men—and of the London medical corporations—by eroding their privileges. General practitioners were not united in their hostility to the corporations; some of the more moderate among them, including the GP-dominated PMSA, were willing to see them survive, albeit within a more democratic context.[5] The priority of the PMSA and *PMSJ* was action to put down the quacks who were making a living at the expense of their members and readers. They were far less concerned than the London-based Wakley about their position in relation to the medical corporations, because outside London the colleges were remote compared with the threat of the quack.

From the beginning the *Journal* was an enthusiastic advocate of reform: 'The prospect of a speedy reform in medical affairs is a pleasing repast for the mind.'[6] Like the PMSA, it favoured a uniform test of qualification—instead of the notorious 19 distinct portals of entry—conferring an equal right to practise throughout the kingdom, a register of those qualified, and the use of a representative system in the formation of a governing body. It believed not in abolition of the colleges, but in reform so that their doors were open to those of sufficient merit.[7] With these aims in mind the *Journal* dismissed Warburton's bill as 'quite inadequate'. It was, indeed, vague on such details as how the unqualified were to be prevented from practising. Benjamin Hawes' bill, 'to amend the Laws relating to the Medical Profession', published in 1841, was adjudged 'greatly preferable' but 'too cumbrous and complicated'.[8]

In 1844 Sir James Graham, Home Secretary in Peel's government, introduced a bill proposing a single register and a 'Council of Health and Medical Education' to govern the profession. Newman terms it 'a much more serious contribution than its predecessors'.[9] However, the *Journal* disliked it because it failed to tackle the problem of quackery, imposed the costs of registration upon practitioners, and failed to give the rank and file of the profession any voice on the regulatory body. Graham's bill rejected prohibition of irregular practice on *laissez-faire* grounds—that is, that the

[5] I. Waddington, *The Medical Profession in the Industrial Revolution* (Dublin: Gill & Macmillan, 1984), p. 91. *Journal*, 21 Jan. 1852, 37. See 23 Oct. 1858, 888. This edition of the *Journal* stated that 95 per cent of BMA members were general practitioners.

[6] *Ibid.*, 17 Oct. 1840, 43.

[7] *Ibid.*, 24 Oct. 1840, 64–7; 22 Jan. 1842, 333–5; 2 April 1842, 532–3; 21 Jan. 1852, 51.

[8] Charles Newman, *The Evolution of Medical Education in the Nineteenth Century* (London: Oxford University Press, 1957), pp. 155–6; *Journal*, 14 Nov. 1840, 120–1; 2 Jan. 1841, 230–2. See *Parliamentary Papers* (1841) **II**: p. 577.

[9] C. Newman, *The Evolution of Medical Education in the Nineteenth Century*, p. 160 (note 8).

public should be free to choose its medical treatment from whomsoever it wished. Its only concession towards suppression of the unqualified was a proposed bar on their appointment to public positions, such as army medical surgeons or Poor Law medical officers. This was not enough for the *Journal*, which described Graham's proposals as a 'tissue of mystification and humbug'. Nevertheless, it was less hostile than the *Lancet*, which characterized 'this extraordinary measure' as 'poison'.[10]

Graham's bill was withdrawn at the end of the 1844 parliamentary session but re-introduced, with amendments, in the following year. While the PMSA saw the amended bill as an improvement, it was far from satisfied. For its part, the *Journal* was no more than lukewarm in its appraisal of a 'still . . . defective and unequal measure'.[11] The bill was also opposed by the colleges.[12] By the time Graham had further revised it to meet these objections, it was too late in the parliamentary session for progress to be made. Frustrated by his experiences, Graham told the House in January 1846 that he had finished with medical reform.[13]

In these circumstances a *Journal* editorial called for the passing of a limited measure upon the terms of which the profession could agree.[14] When Wakley and Warburton introduced a Medical Registration Bill in 1846, the PMSA Council supported it as an interim measure. But this too generated controversy because the Royal Colleges rejected a single register which lumped all practitioners together without distinction. It got as far as committee stage before being dropped.[15]

The 1850s saw a quickening of the pace with a steady stream of bills brought before Parliament, and the Association heavily involved in trying to secure the passage of a measure fulfilling its objectives. But by the time that Lord Derby took over as prime minister of a Tory administration in February 1858, little real progress had been made. In March the *Journal* announced that 'the prospects of medical reform are for a time obscured'.[16] This was ironic, for over the years the *BMJ* had often said that reform was imminent; when it was only months away, the *Journal* predicted that it was a distant prospect.

W. F. Cowper, who had been President of the Board of Health in Palmerston's government, undaunted by the prospect of securing legislation

[10] *Journal*, 26 Feb. 1842, 434–5; 9 July 1842, 274–6; 28 Aug. 1844, 338; 4 Sept. 1844, 354–5; 2 Oct. 1844, 416; 16 Oct. 1844; 11 Dec. 1844, 576–7; 12 Feb. 1845, 102–3. *Lancet*, 17 Aug. 1844, 641, 645-7.

[11] *Journal*, 19 March 1845, 181; see 26 March 1845, 200–1; 9 April 1845, 230–2; 16 April 1845, 246–7; 4 June 1845, 358; 30 July 1845, 496–7.

[12] M. J. Peterson, *The Medical Profession in Mid-Victorian London*, pp. 32–3 (note 2).

[13] *Journal*, 4 Feb. 1846, 52–3.

[14] *Ibid.*

[15] C. Newman, *The Evolution of Medical Education in the Nineteenth Century*, pp. 169–70 (note 8).

[16] *Journal*, 13 March 1858, 215.

from the opposition back benches, introduced a medical reform bill in 1858. It had been drafted largely by John Simon, no friend of the colleges, whom Cowper had appointed as Medical Officer of Health to the Board of Health in 1855.[17] It proposed to leave the colleges intact, but to remove their control over education and examination by transferring it to a General Council of Medical Education and Registration. There would also be a single medical register, another change which the colleges opposed. With a few reservations, which Cowper agreed to deal with, the BMA's medical reform committee approved Cowper's proposals, as did the *Lancet*.[18]

On 2 June 1858 Cowper's bill received a second reading. But the colleges then put pressure upon the government and persuaded the Home Secretary, Spencer Walpole, that the proposed powers of the Council were too extensive. Walpole suggested that Cowper should modify his bill on this crucial point. Since Cowper needed government support if his bill were to succeed, he had little option but to make several changes, the most important of which was to remove completely the Council's control over medical education and to replace it with a clause giving it authority only to require information concerning courses and examinations.[19]

Waddington notes that the excision of clause IV 'removed the heart from the bill' and took away the chief feature which had caused the BMA to support it.[20] In fact, when the *Journal* came to consider the revised bill it noted that the 'expunging' of clause IV was the most important modification, but it registered no great objection. Indeed, an editorial in July noted that there were no amendments 'to which a positive objection can be raised', and 'several which will meet with the special approbation of the profession'.[21] One of the main objectives of Cowper and Simon had been that practitioners should be qualified in medicine *and* surgery rather than in one branch of the profession alone. In the original bill this was to be achieved by empowering the Council to require examining bodies to conduct joint examinations. Although this became impossible with the loss of clause IV, a new clause (XVI) specified that no one who qualified after 1 September 1858 would be eligible for registration unless qualified in both medicine and surgery. But this was lost in committee. Notwithstanding this and two other significant changes introduced in committee—namely, that physicians could renounce their right to recover fees by legal action (thereby preserving their separation from the rest of the profession) and another modifying the composition of the Council—the *Journal* remained enthusiastic about the bill.[22]

[17] Sir John Simon, *English Sanitary Institutions* (London: Cassell, 1897), pp. 272–3.

[18] *Journal*, 10 April 1858, 294–5; 1 May 1858, 351; 17 Aug. 1858, 314; *Lancet*, 10 April 1858, 368; 17 April, 390; 24 April, 416.

[19] *Journal*, 5 June 1858, 455.

[20] I. Waddington, *The Medical Profession in the Industrial Revolution*, pp. 119–20 (note 5).

[21] *Journal*, 3 July 1858, 534.

[22] *Ibid.*, 10 July 1858, 561.

During the hot, dry summer of 1858, the bill continued its passage through Parliament, receiving the Royal Assent in August. The reaction of most reformers to the Medical Act was 'relatively muted'.[23] The *BMJ* acknowledged that the measure was flawed: 'The corporations have nibbled holes here and there, which undoubtedly make the measure less perfect than we would have wished.'[24] The BMA saw two serious defects. Firstly, the absence of a uniform education and qualification, which would mean that legally qualified practitioners might, in fact, have no knowledge of a branch of medicine in which they could be called upon to give treatment. Secondly, the absence of a clause requiring proof of general education on the part of persons intent on entering the profession.[25] But the *Journal* was not despondent, for it believed the establishment of registration, a General Medical Council, reciprocity of practice (i. e. that a qualification achieved in one part of the kingdom would allow its possessor to practise in all other parts), and prohibition of the assumption of medical titles by unqualified persons were important gains. Like the *Lancet*, it saw the Act as a first instalment of reform.[26] Moreover, it believed that the Association, by steadfastly carrying the torch of reform for 25 years, was chiefly responsible for the passing of the Act: 'Had there been no Association, there would have been no Medical Bill; of this there can be no doubt whatever.'[27]

Quackery and fringe medicine

The popular notion of a quack is 'of an ignorant and unscrupulous pretender, often itinerant, who preyed upon a credulous public for profit; a confidence trickster . . .'.[28] Modern historiography, however, is more equivocal and tends to avoid use of the word quack, preferring neutral descriptions such as unorthodox or irregular practitioner. There are good reasons for using less pejorative terms when referring to the early nineteenth or previous centuries. At a time when there was no formal and uniform system of medical education, registration, or licensing, there existed a degree of uncertainty as to whether certain practitioners were orthodox regulars or unorthodox quacks. It is also true that alternative or fringe treatments such as hydropathy and homoeopathy were used by both regular and irregular practitioners, thereby further blurring distinctions.[29]

23 I. Waddington, *The Medical Profession in the Industrial Revolution*, pp. 127–8 (note 5).

24 *Journal*, 24 July 1858, 603; see 7 Aug. 1858, 654–7.

25 *Ibid.*, 655.

26 *Lancet*, 14 Aug. 1858, 175; 21 Aug. 205.

27 *Journal*, 24 July 1858, 603.

28 I. Loudon, *Medical Care and the General Practitioner, 1750–1850* (Oxford: Oxford University Press, 1986), p. 14.

29 *Ibid.*, p. 13; *Journal*, 5 Aug. 1843, 393. See Hilary Marland, *Medicine and Society in Huddersfield and Wakefield* (Cambridge: Cambridge University Press, 1987), p. 245; W. F. Bynum and Roy Porter (eds.), *Medical Fringe and Medical Orthodoxy, 1750–1850* (Beckenham: Croom Helm, 1987), p. 1.

Both the PMSA and the *Journal* sought the suppression of 'empiricists', as they often termed irregulars, as one of their prime objectives. According to their rhetoric, they pursued the goal with the sole aim of protecting the public from those who defrauded, injured, or killed the sick. An alternative view is that they sought to monopolize practice for selfish reasons, and that this led them to castigate not only dangerous cheats but alternative practitioners who might be cheaper than regulars and who were, at least in the eyes of their supporters, intellectually and scientifically respectable as well as being comparatively safe. A third view is that public and private interest went hand in hand, in other words, that the regular practitioner sought to benefit the public as well as himself, and that only the cynical or the naïve will give precedence to one motive over the other. We can judge the *Journal*'s attitude by its treatment of the three alternative systems of mesmerism, hydropathy, and homoeopathy, which it once characterized respectively as 'absolute folly', 'dangerous activity', and 'elegant inertness'.[30]

Mesmerism, or animal magnetism as it was often called, was based upon the theories and practice of the German physician Franz Mesmer (1734–1815).[31] In the 1830s and 1840s it excited considerable interest as mesmerizers toured the country with demonstrations which played to large audiences. Although many of these amounted to little more than tawdry entertainments, the claims of some mesmerizers for their 'science' were bound to attract medical attention. Mesmerizers claimed not only to be able to put subjects into a profound sleep, but that while in such a state the mesmerized could perform extraordinary feats such as seeing out of the back of their heads and playing musical instruments even when they had no musical ability. This, of course, was the stuff of entertainment. Performing mesmerists often employed phrenology in conjunction with mesmerism and prevailed upon 'volunteers', whose phrenological organs had been appropriately excited, to demonstrate a range of emotions from veneration to destructiveness. More seriously, some maintained that surgery could be painlessly performed upon the mesmerized and that mesmerism could cure such bodily disorders as 'rheumatism, scrofula, deafness, epileptic fits and most nervous diseases'.[32]

John Elliotson, who held a chair at University College Hospital, was 'the first scientist of undoubted ability' to espouse mesmerism. But the hostility of

[30] *Journal*, 9 Sept. 1843, p. 491.

[31] On mesmerism generally see T. M. Parssinen, 'Professional Deviants and the History of Medicine: Medical Mesmerists in Victorian Britain', in Roy Wallis (ed.), *On the Margins of Science: the Social Construction of Rejected Knowledge* (Keele: University of Keele/Sociological Review, 1979), pp. 103–20; Roger Cooter, 'The History of Mesmerism in Britain: Poverty and Promise', in Heinz Schott (ed.), *Franz Anton Mesmer und die Geschichte des Mesmerismus* (Stuttgart: Franz Steiner, 1985), pp. 152–62.

[32] *Journal*, 9 Sept. 1843, 490–2.

his hospital governors forced him to resign his chair.[33] In 1838 Wakley, with Hennis Green—the future founder of the *PMSJ*—among the witnesses, tested Elliotson's claims. A leading article in the *Lancet* concluded that 'Careful examination and a consideration of all the experiments have convinced us that the phenomena are not real, and that animal magnetism is a delusion.'[34]

For its part, the *PMSJ* believed that 'mesmerism has frequently been weighed in the balance of scientific investigation and found wanting'. It opposed the involvement of medical practitioners with the 'charlatans, fools, or designing philosophers . . . [who] . . . extract money from the pockets of the public, under pretence of pursuit of truth'.[35] For sometimes medical men, including some eminent in the profession, attended these performances in an invigilating role. The *Journal* was concerned that orthodox practitioners should not compromise themselves by associating with questionable characters and theories, and called upon 'every true member' of the profession to dissociate himself from such proceedings.[36] Referring to one 'mesmero-phrenologist' a leading article regretted that the 'impudent humbug' was not in a House of Correction where 'some of his organs might very advantageously be excited by a cat-o'-nine-tails'.[37]

But the *Journal* was less blinkered in its opposition to mesmerism than the *Lancet* or *British and Foreign Medical Review*. It was open-minded enough in 1845 to accord considerable space to a debate on animal magnetism and, in particular, allowed William Newnham, a respected member of the Association and regular contributor to the *Journal*, to contribute 15 lengthy letters advancing the case for mesmerism.[38] Since mesmerists probably encouraged the discovery of inhalational anaesthetics and provided the basis for clinical application of hypnotism, this was to its credit.[39]

[33] Charles Singer and E. A. Underwood, *A Short History of Medicine* (Oxford: Clarendon Press, 1962), pp. 507–9.

[34] *Lancet*, 8 Sept. 1838, 834–6; 15 Sept. 1838, 873–7; S. Squire Sprigge, *The Life and Times of Thomas Wakley* (London: Longmans, 1897), 444–49. See J. Palfreman, 'Mesmerism and the English Medical Profession: A Study of Conflict', *Ethics in Science and Medicine* (1977) **4**: 51–66; Fred Kaplan (ed.), *John Elliotson on Mesmerism* (New York: Da Capo, 1982); Jonathan Miller, 'A Gower Street Scandal', *Journal of the Royal College of Physicians* (1983) **17**: 181–91; George Rosen, 'Mesmerism and Surgery. A Strange Chapter in the History of Anaesthesia', *Journal of the History of Medicine* (1947) **I**: 527–50. As Rosen points out, Wakley's test did not destroy the case for mesmerism, but merely cast doubt upon the influence of magnets upon human behaviour.

[35] *Journal*, 10 Dec. 1842, 213.

[36] *Ibid.*, 18 Feb. 1843, 398–402; see 4 March, 458; 15 July 303–8; 31 July, 417; 5 Aug. 393–5; 12 June 1844, 159–61; 31 July 1844, 269–70.

[37] *Ibid.*, 4 Nov. 1843, 102.

[38] See W. Newnham, *Human Magnetism* (London, 1845).

[39] P. S. Brown, 'Social Context and Medical Theory in the Demarcation of Nineteenth Century Boundaries', in W. F. Bynum and K. Porter (eds.), *Medical Fringe and Medical Orthodoxy*, p. 228 (note 29).

Hydropathy, entailing the internal and external use of cold water to prevent or cure disease, was popular with the British middle and upper classes between about 1840 and 1870. Like mesmerism, this 'heresy' had German origins, owing much to the ideas and practices of the 'Silesian peasant', Vincent Priessnitz (1799–1851). Its rise in popularity generated professional controversy between those who saw it as a threat to conventional medicine (and the fees earned by conventional practitioners) and those who regarded it as a safe and natural treatment. The *Lancet* fought a 10-year 'war' against the hydropaths between 1842 and 1852; the *British and Foreign Medical Review*, on the other hand, though strongly opposed to mesmerism, was keen on hydropathy.[40]

What was the *Journal*'s position in this debate? In 1842 and 1843 it published articles by Charles Hastings casting doubts upon Priessnitz's cures and those of his disciple in Malvern, Dr James Wilson. 'It may well be doubted,' Hastings suggested, 'whether there is any country on the face of the earth in which quackery is so successfully followed as in rich and credulous England.' Resident in the same county as Wilson, Hastings was well placed to monitor the efficacy of his treatments. He rejected 'the monstrous doctrine of the hydropathists, that water should become a *substitute* for all other remedies'.[41] In two editorials, which were probably written by Streeten, the *Journal* categorized hydropathy with mesmerism and homoeopathy as forms of quackery and regretted that regular if unsuccessful practitioners should espouse it.[42] The *Journal* accepted that temperance, a spare diet, and walks in the Malvern Hills could effect '*wonderful* cures' of gout and indigestion, but, like Hastings, questioned the efficacy of the water system in the treatment of many other conditions, fearing that it could be a positive danger.[43] Some 15 years later, however, the *Journal*, then edited by Markham, took a rather different line, regretting that the profession had dismissed water cure as a quackery instead of 'extracting the good' from it.[44]

Homoeopathy is another medical 'heresy' of German origin, having been elaborated by Samuel Hahnemann (1755–1843), a German physician who studied medicine at Leipzig and Vienna.[45] Its basis is treatment with minute quantitities of drugs capable of producing the symptoms of the disease treated. Today homoeopathy is often regarded as being 'among the more respectable systems of fringe medicine'. In the nineteenth century it 'represented a reaction to medical authority—both to unsatisfactory allopathic therapeutics and to the allopathic establishment'. A *Journal* correspondent,

[40] Robin Price, 'Hydropathy in England, 1840–1870', *Medical History* (1981) **25**: 274, 278.

[41] *Journal*, 24 Sept. 1842, 491–2; 29 July 1843, 347.

[42] *Ibid.*, 15 Oct. 1842, 49–50; 5 Aug. 1843, 393–5. See 5 May 1847, 237–8.

[43] 17 June 1846, 279–81; *Lancet*, 13 June 1846, 666–7; 27 June 1846, 707–8; R. Price, 'Hydropathy in England, 1840–1870', 274 (note 40).

[44] *Journal*, 9 Nov. 1861, 505–7.

[45] Hahnemann built on the work of others, notably Paracelsus.

for example, saw the rise of homoeopathy as a reaction to over-drugging by the regular profession.[46] In the 1850s and 1860s the *Journal* evinced considerable hostility towards homoeopaths, whom it regarded as merely another species of quack, although many of them were regularly qualified. Dr Hahnemann, for instance, whom it referred to as a 'Saxon peasant' and 'German trickster', was better educated and qualified than most *Journal* readers.[47] This hostility can be explained in terms of a desire to protect the public; hence the *Journal* repeatedly insisted that: 'the profession . . . have no reason to oppose homoeopathy, except from the knowledge of its utter inutility . . . *we* have no interest in the matter, except, as we all have, to arrive at the truth.'[48] But undoubtedly there was also concern about losing patients and revenue.

The *Journal*'s attacks on homoeopathy began in 1850, by which time the system had enjoyed a decade of expansion, and continued regularly for many years.[49] In October 1850 news of a proposal to open a homoeopathic hospital called forth the *Journal*'s scorn against the 'monstrous absurdity' and 'perniciousness' of 'a practice ... opposed to reason and common sense'.[50] The suggestion was that the government should jettison the *laissez-faire* ideology which permitted the individual 'to be done to death in any way he may think proper'. In 1851 a leading article expressed concern that St Andrews University should have awarded a degree of MD to a gentleman practising in Norwich as a professed homoeopath.[51]

Much of the *Journal*'s invective was reserved for well-to-do dupes, such as aristocrats and clergymen, who provided homoeopathy with a spurious respectability by patronizing its practitioners.[52] But it was also concerned that regular practitioners should not dignify the homoeopaths by entering into consultation with them. It held the view that a firm division should be maintained between orthodox practitioners and homoeopaths. It therefore rejected the notion that homoeopathy was an addition to orthodox medicine rather than an alternative to it.

In 1851 Cormack, soon to succeed to editorship of the *Journal*, called upon the PMSA to exclude from membership all homoeopaths and those who had

[46] Phillip Nicholls, *Homoeopathy and the Medical Profession* (London: Croom Helm, 1988); *Concise Medical Dictionary* (Oxford: Oxford University Press, 1987), p. 242; P. S. Brown, 'Social Context (note 39)', p. 227; A. J. Youngson, *The Scientific Revolution in Victorian Medicine* (London: Croom Helm, 1979), p. 19; *Journal*, 11 March 1853, 222; 30 April 1851, 238.

[47] *Ibid.*, 2 Oct. 1850, 548.

[48] *Ibid.*, 3 Sept. 1851, 491–2.

[49] The *British Journal of Homoeopathy* was founded in 1843, the Homoeopathic Society in 1844, and the London Homoeopathic Hospital in 1849. P. Nicholls, *Homoeopathy and the Medical Profession*, p. 103 (note 46); *Encyclopaedia Britannica* (11th. edn Cambridge: Cambridge University Press, 1910).

[50] *Journal*, 2 Oct. 1850, 547–8.

[51] *Ibid.*, 11 June 1851, 324–5.

[52] *Ibid.*, 25 Dec. 1850, 708–9; 20 Aug. 1851, p. 460.

professional dealings with them. When the Association adopted the proposal, the *Journal* expressed its approval.[53] A year later, at the annual meeting in Oxford, Cormack announced, somewhat optimistically, that there were 'no longer any respectable members of the profession who would maintain intercourse with homoeopathic professors'.[54] In fact, for at least another decade the *Journal* was full of complaints about homoeopaths and the regular practitioners who demeaned the profession by conferring with them. The 1858 Medical Act in not proscribing irregular practice, as the *Journal* had long desired, or establishing a monopoly for qualified men added to the frustration. In the event, homoeopathy proved remarkably resilient, though it did go into long-term decline from around 1900.

Why did fringe medicine generate so much hostility from the regular profession? It may be, as the pages of the *Journal* indicate, that it was because mesmerism, hydropathy, and homoeopathy were seen as dangerous quackeries; hence the regular listing of the fatalities which endorsed such a view. Roger Cooter has suggested an alternative interpretation. Although referring specifically only to mesmerism, Cooter's argument is valid in respect of the other heresies. He states that in the 1830s and 1840s the profession was claiming greater status by virtue of its access to scientific knowledge and that 'Mesmerism seemed only to mock these social aspirations: by diagnosing internal ailments through mere somnambulistic glances and by abolishing pain at literally, a few strokes, mesmeric medicine could be seen to beat orthodox medicine at its own game.'[55] By the same token if mere water or 'trace' medicines could cure the sick, how could doctors advance themselves by playing the scientific 'card'?

Army medicine

Conditions of service for the rank and file of the British army were, till the late nineteenth century, nasty, brutish, and long.[56] Pay was appallingly low and 'radically improved' only in 1902. Barrack room accommodation was usually overcrowded, unventilated, and lacking in facilities for washing and cooking. It could, indeed, be inferior to that provided for paupers by the Poor Law authorities. Substandard living conditions contributed to a high incidence of respiratory disease and a mortality which, in the pre-Crimean

[53] *Ibid.*, 11 June 1851, 324–5; 25 June 1851, 351; 9 July 1851, 374–5; 6 Aug. 1851, 444–6; 3 Sept. 1851, 491; 17 Sept. 1851, 516–17.

[54] *Ibid.*, 4 Aug. 1852, 399; see P. Nicholls, *Homoeopathy and the Medical Profession*, p. 137 (note 46).

[55] R. Cooter, 'The History of Mesmerism in Britain: Poverty and Promise', p. 155 (note 31).

[56] For conditions in the Victorian army see E. M. Spiers, *The Army and Society, 1815–1914* (London: Longman, 1980), A. R. Skelley, *The Victorian Army at Home* (London: Croom Helm, 1977); M. Trustram, *Women of the Regiment: Marriage and the Victorian Army* (Cambridge: Cambridge University Press, 1984); H. F. A. Strachan, *Wellington's Legacy: The Reform of the British Army, 1830–1854* (Manchester: Manchester University Press, 1984).

army was far higher than for civilian men of like age. Drunkenness and venereal disease were increased by tedium and the restriction of marriage 'on the strength' to a mere six per cent of recruits. Pre-Crimean soldiers received a daily allowance of 1.5 lbs of bread and 0.75 lbs of meat (including bone, fat, and gristle). Such abysmal conditions tended to attract only those from the lowest social class; not surprisingly, the respectable working classes viewed military service with disdain.

The *Journal* paid considerable attention to army and navy medicine. This was particularly true of the second half of the nineteenth century when, with many military and naval surgeons BMA members, the Association took a keen interest in their (initially deplorable) terms and conditions of service. It regularly argued the case for improvements in their rank, status, and remuneration, for they were not only poorly paid in comparison with combatant officers, but denied many of the privileges of rank to which, the *Journal* argued, their education and social standing entitled them. When, in 1851, the *Journal* first drew attention to the army's practice of branding deserters with the letter 'D', on the promulgation of an order requiring a medical man to be present during the operation, it did so less out of concern for the deserter than out of dismay as to what it would do to the social and professional standing of medical men:

> This disgusting order is indeed the climax of Government insults, and must have the effect of opening the eyes of the blindest medical officer to the position in which he is regarded. It is manifestly impossible that any medical *gentleman* can remain army surgeon ... ; for although the honourable office of deputy executioner will only devolve upon the prison surgeon, the stigma will cling equally to every medical officer in the service.[57]

The *Journal* paid close attention to medical aspects of the Crimean War. Soon after the declaration of war it announced that 'notices of the hygienic conditions of the troops, and of medical and surgical practice at the seats of the war, will always be acceptable contributions to the ASSOCIATION MEDICAL JOURNAL.'[58] The Crimean War was, in fact, the first to be fought under the penetrating gaze not only of the general press but of the medical press too.

In the 1840s the *Journal* had noted how much military medicine and hygiene had improved: 'far more attention is paid to the sanitary condition of the soldiers and sailors; military and naval hospitals are under more efficient regulations, and the whole medical force of these departments is placed on a

[57] *Journal*, 15 Oct. 1851, 574; see 12 Jan. 1861, 47; 9 Feb. 1861, 148, 155. 'Branding' was performed not with a hot iron, but with a set of needles. It was, therefore, akin to tattooing. The letter was positioned below the left armpit. R. L. Blanco, 'Attempts to abolish branding and flogging in the army of Victorian England before 1881', *Journal of the Society for Army Historical Research* (1968) **xlvi**: 137–45; P. Burroughs, 'Crime and Punishment in the British Army, 1815–1870', *English Historical Review* (1985) **100**: 545–71.

[58] *Journal*, 7 April 1854, 306.

better footing.'[59] Not everyone agreed. On the eve of the Crimean War, George Guthrie, President of the Royal College of Surgeons, believed that sweeping reform was vital if a débâcle in Russia were to be avoided. Frustrated by his inability to cut through the red tape at the War Office, he wrote to *The Times* with his doubts.[60]

According to Guthrie the maladministration which had prevailed during the greater part of Wellington's Peninsular Campaign (which Guthrie had witnessed at first hand as a regimental surgeon) was still in evidence during the Sikh Wars (1845–6 and 1848–9). He quoted from a letter written by a surgeon after the battles of Mudki and Firozshah (1845) which he had earlier been persuaded to keep secret lest it should excite public alarm. This described how the surgeon had been surrounded by 175 wounded men begging for assistance. 'I have no time to do any thing satisfactorily,' he had written. 'I have, however, managed to do some amputations today, and dressed the greater number of the serious cases, including two amputations I brought off the field, and am quite weary of the bloody work.' There had been an inadequate number of litters and insufficient water; the field hospital had been unprotected. When the litter carriers had attempted to move the wounded under cover of darkness they wandered too near to the Sikh camp, 'threw down their loads, and left many of the wounded to be murdered by the enemy in cold blood'.

In a leading article the *Journal*, then under Cormack's direction, agreed with Guthrie that additional senior appointments should be made, but it was confident that with changes since introduced and with the progress of medical science, the Crimean War would be distinguished by much improved standards of treatment of the sick and wounded.[61] The over-optimism of this assessment was soon grimly revealed in southern Russia, where nearly 1000 lives were lost before a shot was fired and where the army suffered more casualties in hospitals than on battlefields.[62]

The unpreparedness of the British government and army to fight a powerful foe in hostile terrain many hundreds of miles from home, where the winter weather was extreme, is legendary. The common soldier suffered mightily from cold, squalor, disease, and hunger.[63] In truth, his lot, miserable as it undoubtedly was, was probably no worse than that of his predecessors in any number of campaigns fought over the centuries. But the communications revolution meant that the public learnt about the horrors of the

[59] *Ibid.*, 8 April 1846, 159.

[60] *The Times*, 17 Feb. 1854; see N. Cantlie, *A History of the Army Medical Department* (Edinburgh and London: Churchill Livingstone, 1974) Vol. I, pp. 481–7.

[61] *Journal*, 7 April 1854, 304–6

[62] Anne Summers, *Angels and Citizens: British Women as Military Nurses, 1854–1914* (London: Routledge and Kegan Paul, 1988), p. 30; Judith Walkowitz, *Prostitution and Victorian Society* (Cambridge: Cambridge University Press, 1980) p. 74.

[63] N. Cantlie, *A History of the Army Medical Department*, Vol. II, pp. 6–7 (note 60).

Crimea, by letters and newspaper reports, more fully and more quickly than it had learnt of any earlier campaign. The high command had yet to discover the benefits of censorship. Skilled in journalistic technique, newspaper correspondents like Russell of *The Times* produced brilliant despatches for an eager readership at home:

> It was to them that the home-circle looked for information concerning the deeds of fathers and sons, of brothers, and husbands, and lovers engaged in the war; and it was not a vain search. Never has there been more brilliant writing, more vivid descriptions of battlefields and martial achievements, than the newspapers of London contained in the closing months of 1854; and when misery followed in the train of glory, when a deplorable winter closed a warlike autumn, still did the journalists furnish the only full and truthful tale. ... There never before was a period in the history of the newspaper press in England, in which the public so generally trusted the journalists in preference to the holders of office, in all that concerned news from the seat of war.[64]

The *Journal* contained little news or comment on events in Russia until October 1854, when the conflicting press reports on the medical care given to those wounded in the previous month's Battle of the Alma were reviewed. *The Times*, Cormack noted, had given details of the treatment of the wounded in the hospital at Scutari 'which, if at all true, would show the medical staff to be most wofully [sic] defective in number, and medical necessities to have been supplied in far from sufficient quantities'.[65] At this point the *Journal*, though concerned, was not alarmed: 'we can scarcely think matters to be so bad as the Times would make them appear.' But Russell's despatches and a mass of supporting evidence soon convinced Cormack otherwise. It rapidly emerged that the army was ill-equipped with surgeons, surgical equipment, medicines, ambulances, and comforts. As soon as the troops were landed, fever and cholera prostrated them in their hundreds. The sick were shipped off in non-hospital ships across the turbulent Black Sea to Scutari at the far end of the Bosphorus. Few surgeons could be spared for these crossings, which frequently saw sick men lying on nothing more than bare boards. In October, after the Battle of the Alma, diarrhoea was thinning the ranks at a rate of about 100 men per day. An army surgeon wrote in January 1855:

> I often look back at the misery and wretchedness I have witnessed in England in my attendance on the sick poor; but, on comparing these with my present everyday experience, their condition was Elysium itself; for when I tell you that the sick in this place have no other couch than the bare ground, itself saturated with wet, and adripping canvas only between themselves and the clouds, you will perfectly comprehend that the veriest hovel would be a palace in comparison.

Mismanagement was not the monopoly of the medical service; there was

[64] *Pictorial History of the Russian War 1854–5–6* (London: Chambers, 1856), p. 390.
[65] *Journal*, 20 Oct. 1854, 956.

hardly a department above criticism. As an officer of the light division wrote: 'There is nothing to eat, nothing to drink, no commissariat, no medicine, no clothes, no management, nothing abundant but cholera.'[66]

That the army medical service was in a mess could not be doubted; the question was whether responsibility lay with incompetent and negligent surgeons or with mismanagement at a higher level. Some newspapers and a court of inquiry held in Lord Raglan's headquarters blamed the medical officers themselves for the failure, but in a series of leading articles published in 1855, Cormack made clear his belief that, so far as inadequate care of the sick and wounded was concerned, blame rested with the 'deplorable mismanagement' of the Army Medical Department, 'from which has resulted the destruction of the finest army that ever left the shores of Great Britain'.[67] The medical officers themselves, though young and inexperienced owing to the inflexible regulation which imposed an age limit of 24 on their recruitment, 'have done their duty, under heart-breaking difficulty'. Cormack, pointed the finger of blame not at Lord Aberdeen's Secretary for War, the Duke of Newcastle, as some, including the *Medical Times and Gazette*, were inclined to do, but at Dr Andrew Smith, the Director General of the Army Medical Department.[68]

Cormack, who in 1855 was fighting his own battles in the PMSA's civil war, unmercifully attacked Smith in the course of 10 leading articles published between February and June under the title 'Our Army Medical System'. Simultaneously, the *Journal*'s 'News and Topics of the Day' section maintained a commentary upon Crimean developments by reprinting newspaper reports, mainly from *The Times*, and publishing letters from army surgeons. In fact, Cormack was probably too hard on Smith who was little criticized by the official inquiry into the state of the army before Sebastopol.[69] The ultimate failure was at the very highest level, hence Lord Aberdeen's resignation in January 1855.[70]

The impassioned Cormack quit the editorial chair in the following September and when Wynter took over, in January 1856, a more generous view was taken of Smith's performance.[71] Wynter, however, continued to praise the work of the surgeons and to urge, as Cormack had, the improvement of their status within the army. At the same time, he insisted that 'an entire remodelling of the Army Medical Department must take place.'[72] Reform, however, was slow in coming. A year after the Treaty of Paris

[66] *Pictorial History of the Russian War 1854–5–6*, pp. 297–8 (note 64). On medical services in the Crimea see N. Cantlie, *A History of the Army Medical Department*, Vol. II, chaps. 1–3 (note 60).

[67] *Journal*, 2 Feb. 1855, 95.

[68] *Ibid.*, 9 Feb. 1855, 116–17.

[69] *Parliamentary Papers* (1854–5) **IX**.

[70] E. M. Spiers, *The Army and Society, 1815–1914*, pp. 157–8 (note 56).

[71] *Journal*, 26 Jan. 1856, 72–3.

[72] *Ibid.*, see e.g. 7 Dec. 1855, 1094–5; 4 April 1857, 280–1.

terminated the Crimean War (on 30 March 1856) a Royal Commission on the Army Medical Department had still to hold its first meeting.

When the Commission reported, it highlighted soldiers' lamentable living conditions and produced important recommendations for change, including the establishment of an army medical school, two general hospitals, a hospital corps of stretcher-bearers and orderlies to replace the Medical Staff Corps, and improved sanitation for barracks. Most of these recommendations were implemented, though improvement of barracks did not attract the sustained commitment of the authorities. The government also promised to change the Army Medical Department, from which Smith had retired at the beginning of the year, and to improve the status and pay of army medical officers. The question of salary and status was very important for the *Journal*. When the new warrant on the rank of army surgeons was issued in October 1858, medical men were placed, with two exceptions, on a position of equality with combatant officers. The *Journal*, while disappointed that there should be any exception, was delighted by the reform and claimed that the medical press had contributed to it.[73]

Poor Law medicine

The Poor Law had existed since the sixteenth century to provide a 'safety net' for the destitute. The main cause of poverty was inability to work, sickness being one of the prime reasons for such inability. From the late eighteenth century, particularly in the poorer areas of the country such as the southern and eastern counties, a rudimentary Poor Law medical service was developed. This usually consisted of a medical officer appointed by the overseers to attend the sick of the parish. In some urban parishes an infirmary was provided either as a ward of the workhouse or as a separate building.

Before the passing of the Poor Law Amendment Act, 1834, Poor Law medicine was relatively generous and effective.[74] Indeed, the Poor Law was reformed because the old system was seen as being expensive and an inducement to indolence. The reformed system was based upon two cardinal principles, the 'workhouse test' and 'less eligibility'. The idea was to force the able-bodied to receive relief in the workhouse or not at all, and to provide assistance at the most basic, uncongenial level. The anticipated consequence was that only the truly destitute would seek relief. In practice these principles

[73] *Journal*, 23 Oct. 1858. The exceptions were that a combatant officer would always preside over courts martial and that garrison and regimental guards would not be required to salute the surgeon.

[74] M. W. Flinn, 'Medical Services under the New Poor Law', in Derek Fraser (ed.), *The New Poor Law in the Nineteenth Century* (London: Macmillan, 1976), p. 47; H. Marland, *Medicine and Society in Huddersfield and Wakefield*, p. 70 (note 29).

were often applied to those who could not work (the sick) as well as to those who would not.

After the passing of the 1834 Act almost all of the newly established boards of guardians appointed district medical officers, of whom there were 2800 in 1844. These appointments, often allocated under a system of tender, were taken by local practitioners on a part-time basis. Their pay was meagre, the more so as they were expected to provide their own medicines and dressings and to bear other expenses. The attentions of the relieving officer, who had to authorize medical care, and of other lay officials, were a constant source of frustration, while the work, especially in large rural areas where much travelling was required, could be hard.[75] Neither was there any security of tenure, for until 1842 appointments were made only on an annual basis. On the other hand, salaries could provide a small regular income for practitioners, many of whom were, in the mid-nineteenth century, struggling to make a living in an over-crowded profession.

Notwithstanding the principles of the 1834 Act, fit paupers were increasingly given outdoor relief while the incapacitated were treated in the workhouses, which more and more became public hospitals. Furthermore, the distinction between those unable to afford doctors' fees and the pauper was gradually blurred as both were commonly treated by a medical officer. In 1852 the Poor Law Board formalized the situation when it authorized provision of medical relief even in cases where the head of the family was in work and therefore not destitute. From 1840 the Vaccination Act—according to the *Journal*, 'the most beneficial legislative measure that our profession has ever obtained from Parliament'—made use of the Poor Law medical officer as a public vaccinator, thereby extending the role of the state in health provision. The *Journal* 'entertained considerable doubts' about entrusting responsibility for vaccination to the Poor Law Commissioners, but, initially, was pleased with the way in which they accepted it.[76] Misgivings were, however, soon to set in.

In 1841 Parliament confirmed that vaccination by the medical officer did not pauperize the recipient (i. e. they would not lose their rights as citizens), though it was easier to make such a statement than to persuade people to accept it.[77] Compulsory vaccination of infants began in 1853. The *Journal* opposed Lord Lyttelton's bill for compulsory vaccination partly because it objected in principle to compulsion, and partly because the bill failed to provide adequate remuneration, or freedom from the control of lay guar-

[75] *Journal*, 19 Feb. 1842, 412–14; 14 May, 108–9.

[76] *Ibid.*, 3 Oct. 1840, 1–2.

[77] In 1853 a *Journal* correspondent wrote that 'People will not bring their children to be vaccinated at the beck of the Poor Law Commissioners; there is something revolting in an Englishman's mind to having his children pauperized', 11 March, 224.

dians, for the vaccinators.[78] These developments in public vaccination and Poor Law medical relief have been described as forming the basis of a patchy national health service, though as late as 1871 expenditure on medical relief amounted to only a small proportion of total Poor Law relief.[79]

The *Journal*, though keen to see better terms and conditions for medical officers and more influence for medical men in administration, was not solely concerned with the impact of the Poor Law on its members and potential members.[80] In a leading article published on Christmas Day 1841, it was highly critical of it as a means of aiding the poor:

The test of destitution adopted as the ground of relief; the mode in which such relief is administered, whether in sickness or in health; the difficulties thrown in the way of obtaining it; the rough, and often inhuman reception which the applicants for assistance, with their spirits already broken down by distress and poverty, often borne to the verge of starvation, meet with; the contumely and disgrace attempted to be thrown upon such as become the recipients of the relief so afforded; the breaking up of family ties; the outrage to domestic affections; the personal restraint; the imprisonment; the stripes, &c., with which the unwilling bestowal of food and lodging is often accompanied, and the insufficient amount and innutritious quality of the former, and the wretched nature of the latter, form a catalogue of misery, which none but a professed cold-blooded disciple of Malthus could contemplate unmoved.[81]

The *Journal* regretted that the real object of the Poor Law was not the relief of destitution, but diminution of the rates, and that this was being accomplished by medical officers subsidizing the system out of their own pockets: '. . . the so-called guardians of the poor are but too often only deserving of

[78] *Journal*, 25 March 1853, 248–9; 15 April 1853, 313–4; 22 Aug 1853, 697; 30 March 1855, 289–90.

[79] D. Fraser, *The New Poor Law in the Nineteenth Century*, p. 4 (note 74); M. W. Flinn, 'Medical Services under the New Poor Law', p. 51 (note 74). *Journal*, 5 Feb. 1842, 381–2; 19 Feb. 1842, 412–13. A letter in the *Journal* (27 Nov. 1841) illustrates the difficulties of the medical profession under the poor law. The correspondent quoted an advertisement for a medical officer to take charge of eight parishes with a combined population in excess of 3500. The appointee's duties would be: 'To attend all poor persons under the care of the directors and acting guardians in all cases of sickness, imbecility of mind, hurts, fractures, accidents, and difficult labours, whether such persons belong to any parish within the hundred or not; and also to find and provide all proper drugs, medicines, and dressings for such patients, &c. &c. without any charge in any of the said cases beyond his respective salary'. The advertisement attracted tenders of £32, £20, and £16 p.a., the lowest of which was accepted. The previous incumbent had received £40 p.a.

[80] *Ibid.*, 20 Jan. 1844, 311–13.

[81] *Ibid.*, 25 Dec. 1841, 255–6. For similar attacks see 5 Feb. 1842, 374–6 and 19 Feb. 1842, 412–14. On the severity of the Poor Law see David Roberts, 'How Cruel was the Victorian Poor Law?', *Historical Journal* (1963) **iv** and U. R. Q. Henriques, 'How Cruel was the Victorian Poor Law?', *Historical Journal* (1968) **xi**. Fraser rejects the proposition that the Poor Law authorities sought to crush the poor. Although there were individual scandals, indoor paupers generally fared better in terms of housing, food, and care than the poor outside the workhouse. But he accepts, in much the same language as the *Journal*, that in 'day-to-day life in the workhouse there was much psychological cruelty'. D. Fraser, *The Evolution of the British Welfare State* (London: Macmillan, 1984 edn) pp. 54–5.

the name of guardians of the pockets of the rate-payers.'[82] On this analysis, the doctors and the destitute were twin, if unequal, victims of the law; both were being exploited in the interests of political economy. Hence the *Journal*'s reference to 'the unfortunate union surgeon and his unfortunate cattle'.[83]

In March 1842 the Poor Law Commissioners in Somerset House issued their first General Medical Order. The *Journal*, which welcomed the 'meagre' and tardy 'concessions', attributed 'any beneficial changes that have been made to the zealous efforts of the Provincial and other associations, and the powerful co-operation of the public press'.[84] The most important changes made by the order were that it abolished the tender system; limited the area and population of districts; provided additional payments for operations and midwifery; made permanent rather than annual appointments, these appointments being restricted to those with qualifications in medicine and surgery; and established a permanent pauper list (i.e. a list of people who could receive treatment without the need of application to the relieving officer on each separate occasion).

The *Journal*'s main fear was that medical officers would benefit little.[85] Indeed, the order made no provision for one of the reformers' main demands, adequate payment. The restriction of appointments to qualified practitioners was a welcome development, but those with Scottish or Irish qualifications were unfairly discriminated against. In the event, the Poor Law unions often ignored or twisted the new regulations anyway.[86] Four years later the *Journal* could still speak of 'miserably paid' medical officers and 'incompetent' guardians.[87]

As it did on behalf of army surgeons, the *Journal* constantly sought, through its leading articles, improved terms and conditions for Poor Law medical officers.[88] Its efforts in this respect were acknowledged by 'Philo' in a letter to the editors: 'Your constant efforts to ameliorate the conditions imposed on medical officers of poor law unions has, I know, called forth the warmest commendations of our brethren in this neighbourhood [Yorkshire] . . . .'[89] In the late 1850s and 1860s the *Journal* encouraged Richard Griffin, Medical Officer of the Weymouth Union, in his efforts to improve the

[82] *Journal*, 16 Dec. 1843, 206–7.

[83] *Ibid.*, 16 April 1842, 30.

[84] *Ibid.*, 9 April 1842, 13; see M. W. Flinn, 'Medical Services under the New Poor Law', pp. 59–60 (note 74).

[85] *Journal*, See 14 May 1842, 115–17.

[86] M. W. Flinn, 'Medical Services under the New Poor Law', p. 61 (note 74). See *Journal*, 5 Aug. 1843, 370. Guardians, a *Journal* correspondent alleged, evaded the provision abolishing the tender system 'by fixing the lowest sum ever accepted by tender, and advertising and threatening until someone is found to accept it'. 12 Aug. 1846, 375–6.

[87] *Ibid.*, 11 Feb. 1846, 66. See 9 Aug. 1848, 434–5; 19 May 1854, 432.

[88] See e.g. 22 July 1846, 336–7.

[89] *Ibid.*, 24 Feb. 1844, 41. See 3 Nov. 1847, 612 for a similar tribute.

position of Poor Law medical officers. Griffin made frequent use of the *Journal*'s pages to address his fellow officers and to air their grievances. But he achieved little and by 'the mid-1860s, after thirty years of campaigning', the reform movement had 'produced only the most trifling of gains'.[90]

In the mid-1860s demands for reform were spurred on by two deaths from neglect in workhouse infirmaries. Individuals such as Edwin Chadwick and Florence Nightingale became powerful voices for change. In 1865 the *Lancet* set up its special commission to inquire into London workhouse infirmaries. Ernest Hart, soon to be the *Journal*'s editor, but then on the *Lancet*'s staff, was one of three commissioners.[91] Indeed, according to Gwendoline Ayers, it was he who persuaded the *Lancet*'s proprietor to appoint the commission. During 1866 he was at the forefront of the movement to plan a scheme of reform and mobilize opinion to support it. He published two influential articles in the *Fortnightly Review* and helped establish the Association for the Improvement of Workhouse Infirmaries, of which such luminaries as Charles Dickens and John Stuart Mill were members.[92]

All this activity encouraged Lord Derby's Conservative government to pass the Metropolitan Asylums Act. This important measure is regarded by many 'as the starting-point for an official state medical service'.[93] Its terms were based in part on Hart's ideas; its most important provision was to separate hospitals and workhouses.[94] The Act demonstrated recognition by the authorities that the state was in duty bound to provide infirmaries for the poor. A building programme was instituted in London and later in the provinces. The sick poor were no longer treated according to the principles of less eligibility; trained nurses replaced able-bodied pauper women; and the stigma of receiving treatment from a publicly-funded institution began slowly to diminish. On the other hand, outdoor medical relief and the position of the medical officer changed little.

Public health

When the *Journal* was launched there was no effective lobby for public health

[90] M. W. Flinn, 'Medical Services under the New Poor Law', p. 63 (note 74).

[91] *Journal*, 10 March 1866, 257–8; 24 March, 313–14; 4 April, 393.

[92] 'The Condition of Our State Hospitals', *Fortnightly Review* (1865) **3**: 218–21; 'Metropolitan Infirmaries for the Pauper Sick', *Fortnightly Review* (1866) **4**: 460–2; Gwendoline Ayers, *England's First State Hospitals and the Metropolitan Asylums Board, 1867–1930* (London: Wellcome Institute, 1971), pp. 7–8; see J. Rogers, *Reminiscences of a Workhouse Medical Officer* (London: T. Fisher Unwin, 1889), pp. 50–3; Ruth Hodgkinson, *The Origins of the National Health Service. The Medical Services of the New Poor Law* (London: Wellcome Historical Medicine Library, 1967), pp. 430, 441, 471, 486.

[93] D. Fraser, *The Evolution of the British Welfare State*, p. 92 (note 81).

[94] Geoffrey Rivett, *The Development of the London Hospital System, 1823–1982* (Oxford: Oxford University Press, 1986), p. 74; G. Ayers, *England's First State Hospitals and the Metropolitan Asylums Board, 1867–1930*, p. 31 *et seq* (note 92); R. Hodgkinson, *The Origins of the National Health Service*, pp. 462, 556 (note 92).

legislation. However, Edwin Chadwick, who was secretary to the Poor Law Commission, was at work on his ground-breaking inquiry into the 'Sanitary Condition of the Labouring Population of Great Britain'. Chadwick produced what has been called 'perhaps the greatest of the nineteenth-century Blue Books'.[95] When the report was published in 1842 it 'conclusively established the incontrovertible link between environment and disease'.[96] Although historians now tend to see Chadwick as the man who got the public health movement going, the *Journal*'s first comment on the report was one of surprise that 'so difficult and complex an investigation was entrusted to a gentleman completely ignorant of the subject [i.e. public health] submitted to his inquiry'. The consequence, it claimed, was a report which lacked clarity and method and also overlooked some important causes of disease such as malnutrition.[97] The *Journal* evidently felt that the inquiry should have been undertaken by a medical man, though it conceded that the report 'is creditable to the industry of its author', and that 'a mass of highly important and useful information has been collected.' Indeed, one leading article pointed out (correctly) that much of the report's value was attributable to the evidence provided by the Poor Law Commission's unpaid medical correspondents.[98]

In November 1842 the *Journal* carried a leading article drawing on that part of Chadwick's report which showed the correlation between social class, life expectancy, and place of domicile. Whereas a professional man, a gentleman, or the family of such living in Bath or Rutland could expect to live into their 50s, their counterparts in Liverpool could expect to die at 35. Labourers and their families in Liverpool could anticipate no more than 15 years of life. The *Journal* believed that the causes of premature death were largely preventable and called on politicians 'to correct . . . that fatal apathy which closes its eyes while nations are committing suicide'.[99]

In December the *Journal* returned to the subject, this time concentrating on bad housing and calling for 'the enactment of some general provision by which the habitations of the poor may be rendered as far as practicable free from all extraneous sources of disease, and the rendering of the poor-law protective of their interests rather than oppressive to them in their calamities'. It urged a re-allocation of government expenditure: money being spent in upholding British honour in Syria, Canada, Afghanistan, and China could, it was suggested, 'be at least equally well bestowed in improving the

[95] D. Fraser, *The Evolution of the British Welfare State*, p. 64 (note 81).

[96] *Ibid.*, p. 63; see M. W. Flinn's 'Introduction' to the Edinburgh University Press reprint of the report (Edinburgh, 1965), pp. 1–73.

[97] *Journal*, 19 Nov. 1842, 152.

[98] *Ibid.*, 3 Dec. 1842, 192. The *Journal* was aggrieved that Chadwick's report accorded so little importance to the role of medical men in improving public health. See *Journal*, 7 Jan. 1843, 292–3. Chadwick was often seen as being hostile to the medical profession. See M. W. Flinn, 'Introduction', pp. 60–1 (note 96).

[99] *Journal*, 26 Nov. 1842, 172–4.

'Water! Water! Everywhere': from *Punch*. Source: Bodleian Library, Oxford.

condition and adding to the comforts of the artisan and laborer [sic] among our home population'.[100]

Chadwick's public health aspirations were thwarted by technological, ideological, financial, and political barriers. These included lack of engineering expertise, concern that local autonomy should not fall victim to centralization, and the Irish famine and Corn Law crises. But in 1846 and 1847 some Nuisance Removal and other acts, including local measures such as the Liverpool Sanitary Act, 1846, under the terms of which the country's first medical officer of health was appointed, became law.[101] From 1844, Dr Thomas Southwood Smith's Health of Towns' Association was at the forefront of the movement for public health reform. It diffused information by tracts and lectures on public health questions. There was, the *Journal*

[100] *Ibid.*, 3 Dec. 1842, 191–4. See 16 Dec. 1843, 207.
[101] *Ibid.*, 6 May 1846, 207–8.

believed, no society 'more deserving of support', and it announced its intention of assisting in the propagation of the HTA's views.[102]

The Public Health Act 1848, the culmination of the first stage of the public health movement and 'a great landmark in social reform', established a General Board of Health and empowered local authorities to set up local boards to regulate sewerage, water supply, refuse disposal, slaughter-houses, gas works, nuisances, cellar dwellings, and slums.[103] These local authorities were also given powers to provide parks, recreation areas, burial grounds, and public baths, and to levy rates and buy land for these purposes. The *Journal*'s main misgiving about the Act was that it set up a General Board on which medical men were poorly represented.[104] In any event, because the Act was permissive it was largely ineffective in the short term. By 1858 only 103 local boards had been created.

Poverty, along with inadequate preventive medicine and public health, gave rise to a heavy incidence of water-borne disease. Nineteenth-century Britain experienced four great cholera epidemics: 1831–2, 1848–9, 1853–4, and 1866–7. Of these, the second, when some 62 000 people died, was the most virulent. The total number of deaths from the four outbreaks was probably under 130 000. In contrast with mortality figures for the major endemic diseases, particularly tuberculosis, these figures were low. Moreover, several other epidemic diseases also claimed more lives.[105] But the dramatic first appearance of cholera and its fearfully anticipated recurrences, coupled with the speed and unpleasantness with which it carried off its victims, gave it an importance which far outweighed its statistical significance.[106]

Cholera, a disease of the gut endemic in India, is mainly caused by consumption of water contaminated with faeces containing the bacterium *Vibrio cholerae*. The disease spreads rapidly where sanitation is poor. After a short incubation period the symptoms of violent abdominal pains, vomiting, diarrhoea, dehydration, and collapse commence. Death comes quickly, sometimes within hours of the first appearance of symptoms; in untreated cases the mortality can be as high as 60 per cent of those attacked. In the nineteenth century there was no cure. Treatment varied greatly; saline injection was employed as early as the first outbreak, though with mixed results.

[102] *Ibid.*, 17 Dec. 1845, 736–7.

[103] Anthony S. Wohl, *Endangered Lives: Public Health in Victorian Britain* (London: Methuen, 1983), p. 149; D. Fraser, *The Evolution of the British Welfare State*, p. 70 (note 81).

[104] *Journal*, 10 Jan. 1849, 17–19; 24 Jan. 1849, 45–7.

[105] Margaret Pelling, *Cholera, Fever and English Medicine, 1825–1865* (Oxford: Oxford University Press, 1978), p. 4.

[106] My summary of cholera in Britain is based largely on A. S. Wohl, *Endangered Lives: Public Health in Victorian Britain*, pp. 118–25 (note 103); F. B. Smith, *The People's Health, 1830–1910* (London: Croom Helm, 1979), pp. 229–38; Norman Longmate, *King Cholera* (London: Hamish Hamilton, 1966).

During the 1840s and 1850s opinion varied as to how cholera was caused and spread. There was vigorous debate among miasmitists, contagionists, and others, including those who saw it as divine punishment or the consequence of a dissolute life. In view of such differing opinions on the cause of cholera, it is not surprising that there was also controversy about how it might be controlled, prevented, and treated. When, in 1849, John Snow and William Budd claimed that the disease was spread by ingestion of a living organism present in water, their hypotheses were initially treated with scepticism by the medical establishment. The *Journal* reviewed neither Snow's *On the Mode of Communication of Cholera* nor Budd's *Malignant Cholera*. The idea that cholera was water-borne did not become dominant till 1866.[107] How was the subject treated in the *Journal*?

The cholera 'visitation' of 1848 came as no surprise. It had, in fact, been anxiously awaited since it had broken out in Asia some two years before. As the disease progressed westward towards Britain, the pages of the *Journal* rapidly filled with papers and correspondence on the subject. Memories of the previous outbreak were recalled and re-analysed in an effort to draw conclusions which might throw light upon its causes and the best means of prevention and treatment. For prevention, Edward Blackmore of Bath recommended 'regular hours for *sleep* and *meals*', generous consumption of meat and wine, '*warm clothing*, particularly flannel around the abdomen, the celebrated "*anti-cholera belt*", and putting on warm silk, or fine worsted stockings, towards evening;—and . . . *moral courage*'. While such advice was no doubt excellent for those who could afford to take it, it offered no guarantee against contracting cholera. Blackmore concluded, rather lamely, that 'whatever maintained the best state of the general health, and gave mental confidence and cheerfulness, was found to be the best preservative.'[108]

Meanwhile, the aetiological debate raged on. The year 1849 saw the cholera–fungus controversy, which centred on whether the disease was caused by a fungus. The *Journal* speedily recanted its initial enthusiasm for fungoid theory when cold-water was thrown on the concept by William Baly and William Gull, who, together, formed the cholera subcommittee of the RCP.[109] Practitioners were anxious to draw lessons from their personal experience of the disease. The PMSA favoured a 'consensus-enquiry' as a means of achieving agreement on clinical and other questions.[110]

In 1850 Philip Williams, physician to the Worcester Infirmary, who later

[107] Koch is traditionally regarded as having isolated the cholera bacillus in 1883, but discovery of the bacillus is now attributed to Pacini, while Koch is thought merely to have refined the work of his teacher, Henle. See M. Pelling, *Cholera, Fever and English Medicine, 1825–1865*, p. 3 (note 105).

[108] *Journal*, 6 Feb. 1848, 482–3.

[109] *Ibid.*, 17 Oct. 1849, 571–2; 31 Oct. 1849, 600–3; 14 Nov. 1849, 631, 643. On the fungus controversy see M. Pelling, *Cholera Fever and English Medicine, 1825–1865*, pp. 146–202 (note 105).

[110] *Ibid.*, pp. 162–3.

became the PMSA's secretary, delivered a 'Report on Cholera' to the anniversary meeting at Hull. Based on the pooled experiences of 48 PMSA members, the report, which was published in the *Journal* in September, indicates that, notwithstanding the work of Budd and Snow, practitioners had learnt little of importance from the 1848–9 outbreak.[111] Consensus was conspicuous only by its absence. Practitioners were still stumbling in the dark. Williams had experienced considerable difficulty even in compiling a report, such was the amount of contradictory evidence he received. As far as treatment was concerned, for example, he pointed out that:

> According to the evidence submitted for consideration *every* method was successful, and *every* method failed. Venesection and brandy; croton oil and gallic acid; opium and ammonia; sulphate of magnesia and acetate of lead; capsicum and ice; calomel and strychnia; scammony and starch; antimony and quinine; blisters and cider; nitrate of silver and gruel; venous transfusion and cupping; gallons of salines and total abstinence from fluids; carbon and oxygen; hot fomentations and cold sheets; in short, *every*thing and nothing has been *in*valuable.[112]

As Williams freely admitted, 'very little new information has been gleaned.' On the eve of the third cholera epidemic a leading article in the *Journal* could still warn against

> . . . the breeze which comes laden with pestilence-miasm, gathered in its way from the straw pallet of the neglected and famishing wretch who occupies one of the rich man's cots, which, through the jalousied and rich man's window, shall bear to the loved and tenderly nursed inmates the message of the angel of death.[113]

It is illustrative of the doubt and confusion which existed on the question of transmission that within weeks of issuing this warning the *Journal*, in another leading article, announced that the 'manner in which cholera is propagated remains to be discovered'.[114] It might be thought that John Snow had in fact demonstrated that the disease was spread through contaminated water (even though the precise nature of the contamination remained in doubt). But an 1866 editorial showed that the *Journal* did not accept this. 'The famous Broad Street pump cases proved nothing . . . . They indicated [only] that water contaminated with sewage or other impurities will bring the body into such a state as to render it an easy prey to cholera.'[115]

Ignorance about propagation did not, however, preclude identification of appropriate remedies. Thus, a *Journal* editorial of December 1853 noted that 'our best hope of diminishing the mortality, is in keeping our towns and habitations well drained, supplied with abundance of water and scrupulously

[111] *Journal*, 18 Sept. 1850, 505–10.

[112] *Ibid.*, 508.

[113] *Ibid.*, 30 Sept. 1853, 846. See also 25 Aug. 1854, 749–50. Budd believed that there was atmospheric, as well as water, transmission. *Ibid.*, 13 Oct. 1854, 928.

[114] *Ibid.*, 18 Nov. 1853, 1007.

[115] *Ibid.*, 15 Sept. 1866, 309–10.

clean'; though it is worth pointing out that the same article also suggested that abstinence from alcohol, tobacco, and 'other sensual excesses' would also do much to reduce the incidence of cholera.[116]

As late as 1866 appropriate treatment remained problematic. Anticipating the fourth epidemic, a leading article in the *Journal* stated pessimistically that 'in the all important matter of treatment, we are very much where we were when the disease first visited Europe.'[117] But the last cholera visitation was relatively short—about six months—and led to fewer deaths than the other three—about 14 000. Improvements in public health and the establishment of an efficient system of state medicine, instituted before the true nature of the disease was fully understood, were largely responsible for terminating its regular occurrence. By the end of the century cholera could be regarded as an 'exotic disease'.[118]

One voice among many

During its first three decades the *Journal*, alongside many other medical periodicals and societies, was mainly concerned with questions of professional status, income, and respectability. Its concentration on these matters made its outlook predominantly introspective and its content largely a record of professional affairs. Until the 1870s its main function was as a propagandist of the BMA in the struggle for professional advancement. This explains why the Association was prepared to pour money into it—and also some of the difficulties which arose in the relationship when the BMA felt that its organ was failing adequately to represent it. Even in its coverage of subjects of broader interest, such as military and Poor Law medicine or public health, the *Journal* was often preoccupied with conditions of service for the practitioners employed therein. It was seldom innovative and exciting, tending to follow trends rather than to set them, to be reactive rather than proactive, and to publish largely second-rate scientific and clinical material.

Cormack, Wynter, and Markham raised standards and attacked parochialism, but it was only during the editorship of Ernest Hart that the *Journal* began to acquire a more independent voice, regularly to publish high-quality subject matter, and consistently to turn its attention to subjects beyond the narrow confines of Association business and professional affairs. In its first three decades the *Journal* had little significant influence on public policy, clinical medicine, or scientific discovery. It is hard to point to an example of a campaign, such as the *Lancet*'s on metropolitan workhouses, which made a political impact. At most the *Journal*'s was one voice among many calling for

116 *Ibid.*, 2 Dec. 1853, 1049.

117 *Ibid.*, 27 Jan. 1866, 100; see also 7 April 1866, 363; 19 May 1866, 526.

118 Sir John Simon, *English Sanitary Institutions*, pp. 314–15 (note 17); A. S. Wohl, *Endangered Lives: Public Health in Victorian Britain*, p. 124 (note 103).

reform. The *Journal* was not necessarily consistently radical in the views which it espoused; its consistency lay in its support of change which would enhance the pay and status of medical men. Occasionally it also showed real concern about the health care and medical attention available to the poor and underprivileged. However, only under Ernest Hart's editorship did it begin to be an effective campaigning periodical.

4
A gigantic national institution

Ernest Hart and Co.

Ernest Hart became editor of the *British Medical Journal* in January 1867 at the age of 31. He remained in the position for more than three decades—including an interruption of 12 months in 1869–70, when he was replaced by Jonathan Hutchinson—and was still editor when he died in January 1898. The distinction of having been the *Journal*'s longest-serving editor belongs to his successor, Dawson Williams (1898–1928), but undoubtedly Hart has been the most controversial, powerful, and influential of the *Journal*'s editors.

For Hart the editorship was 'a labour of love . . . and one that he felt to be the most interesting work of his life. For this work [he continued] he had readily sacrificed other opportunities of professional usefulness and advancement.'[1] He clung tenaciously to the position he loved, and, although out of office for a time and in danger of being permanently ousted on several occasions, he always survived. Hart used to tell the story that, when he was appointed, one of the greatest of editors, Delane of *The Times*, told him that no man could expect to remain more than 10 years at the helm of a journal in whose direction every BMA member claimed a voice. 'Yet,' he said after some 20 years in charge, 'here I am and here I mean to stay.'[2]

A controversial figure in his day, Hart remains something of an enigma. Myth, rumour, and scandal surround both his private life and editorial career.[3] In 1888 he was censured by the BMA Council for his conduct in the Morell Mackenzie/Emperor Frederick affair (recounted later in this chapter). He has been accused of pocketing money intended for *Journal* contributors. It has also been suggested that he behaved unethically in allowing the advertising in the *Journal* of Apollinaris, a German mineral water in which he had a large financial stake.[4] As for his personal life, there have been

[1] *Journal*, 21 Aug. 1875, 237.

[2] *Practitioner* (Feb. 1898) **LX**: 118. As late as April 1897, at which time Hart had only months to live, Council, irritated by his efforts to appoint his unqualified nephew to the *Journal* staff, set up a committee to 'consider the course most desirable to take with the object of facilitating the resignation of Mr. Hart'. BMA mss. Minutes of Council and Sub-Committees, VIII, Journal and Finance Committee, 14 April 1897, 3673–4.

[3] *Practitioner* (Feb. 1898) **LX**: 117–18.

[4] P. Vaughan, *Doctors' Commons. A Short History of the British Medical Association* (London: Heinemann, 1959), p. 141; R. Scott Stevenson, *Goodbye Harley Street* (London: Christopher Johnson, 1954), pp. 85–6.

allegations that Hart was responsible, either by negligence or design, for the death of his first wife.

These rumours and accusations show that Hart possessed many enemies. Almost all the obituaries mention opponents, critics, and foes. At his memorial service his brother-in-law, Canon Barnett, said: 'He made some enemies and some mistakes.'[5] He certainly made some enemies, if not mistakes, at the *Lancet*, for in 1866 his contract there, 'was suddenly severed . . . for reasons of a purely private nature . . . and it would be idle to pretend that relations for some time afterwards between him and the proprietors of THE LANCET were otherwise than hostile'.[6] In fact, 'James Wakley [the *Lancet*'s second editor] and Ernest Hart lived for a considerable period on terms of open hatred which were not softened by Hart's description of himself as late "co-editor" of THE LANCET. There were constant rumours of libel and even threats of violence.'[7] The rift seems to have been caused by Hart's driving ambition and James Wakley's refusal to satisfy it by making him joint editor. One obituary refers to an 'angry altercation' between the two men.[8] It is probable that they came to blows for Wakley had 'an extremely warm temper, and the editorial room of THE LANCET was more than once the scene of a personal fracas'. If so, there can be little doubt about who prevailed for Hart was a diminutive chain smoker, whereas the burly Wakley was 'a notable boxer'.[9]

In several letters he wrote to the historian of the BMA, Edward Muirhead Little, the retired surgeon F. R. Fisher, who had not known Hart personally, but knew men who had, called Hart a 'scoundrel', 'swine', 'rascal', 'beast', and 'skunk'. R. Scott Stevenson knew of him as 'an odd, rather unscrupulous, but brilliant editor'.[10] The *Practitioner*'s obituary, which refers to 'bitter personal enemies', suggests one reason why Hart aroused so much hostility: 'Of his cleverness there could be no question; of the ways he showed it there might often be some difference of opinion. A man so "pushful" could not fail to have many enemies.'[11] Undoubtedly, some of the antagonism towards Hart was pure anti-semitism. Charles Adams, a leading antivivisectionist, and therefore a natural opponent, once suggested that

5 *Journal*, 15 Jan. 1898, 186. Barnett was married to the sister of Hart's second wife. He was a pioneer of university settlements and the first warden of Toynbee Hall. See H. O. Barnett, *Canon Barnett His Life, Work and Friends* (London: John Murray, 1918); *Dictionary of National Biography (1912–1921)* (London: Oxford University Press, 1927); Asa Briggs and Anne Macartney, *Toynbee Hall. The First Hundred Years* (London: Routledge, 1984); *Practitioner* (Feb. 1898) **LX**: 117–18.

6 *Lancet*, 15 Jan. 1898, 193.

7 *Ibid.*, 6 Oct. 1923, 723; *Jewish Chronicle*, 14 Jan. 1898.

8 *Medical Press and Circular*, 12 Jan. 1898, 40.

9 *Lancet*, 6 Oct. 1923, 723.; R. S. Stevenson, *Goodbye Harley Street*, p. 86 (note 4).

10 *BMJ* mss. Ernest Hart File. Letters from F. R. Fisher to E. M. Little, dated 18 April 1929, 28 May 1929, 21 June 1929; see R. S. Stevenson, *Goodbye Harley Street*, p. 85 (note 4).

11 *Practitioner*, (Feb. 1898) **LX**: 117–18.

To have pushed such a paper [the *BMJ*] into such a position is a feat of which any press-man might well be proud, a feat which would hardly have been within the compass of any who had not in his veins the blood of that pre-eminently pushing race, his connection with which Mr. Hart would seem to be so curiously anxious to ignore.[12]

Adams usually referred to Hart as E. Abraham Hart. Certainly, any assessment of Hart's achievement should pay due attention to the barriers he had to overcome as a Jew.

Even those who liked and admired Hart had their reservations. Robert Farquharson, who succeeded him as chairman of the BMA's Parliamentary Bills Committee, described him as 'a wonderful man, who would have come to the top in any position, and who, I think, deserved to be called a genius'.[13] But he admitted that Hart had been unpopular and felt that the reason was his habit of claiming the credit for everything that went right. Henrietta Barnett produced a sympathetic pen portrait of Hart in her biography of her husband. But she too gives glimpses of the 'prickly' character which made Hart such an effective journalist, but, in the eyes of some, such an unloved person. He 'pursued truth', we are told, 'with a reckless disregard of consequences'; he loved 'argumentative fighting, and enjoyed nothing better than to riddle loosely-held theories by the guns of well-planted scientific facts'; he was scornful of his brother-in-law's non-scientific religion and lack of worldly ambition.[14]

For his part, Hart revelled in personal conflict, accepting enemies not only as an occupational hazard of journalism but as a mark of journalistic credibility. He held strong opinions and did not shrink from expressing them, regardless of the possible consequences. As he told an American audience in 1893, 'An editor needs and must have, many enemies; he cannot do without them. Woe be unto the journalist of whom all men say good things.'[15]

After Hart's death his second wife, Alice, promised a biography. Unfortunately no such volume ever appeared. He certainly merits the attention of a biographer for, whatever his personal failings, he was an outstanding medical journalist—'one of the greatest' according to the *Practitioner*—a brilliantly successful editor of the *Journal*, a hugely influential figure within the BMA, and a personality of major stature in the nineteenth-century medical world.[16] His editorial achievement was greatly to increase the *Journal*'s circulation,

[12] Quoted in Richard D. French, *Vivisection and Medical Science in Victorian Society* (Princeton: Princeton University Press, 1975), p. 347.

[13] Robert Farquharson, *In and Out of Parliament* (London: Williams and Norgate, 1911), pp. 116–17.

[14] H. O. Barnett, *Canon Barnett, His Life, Work and Friends* Vol. I, p. 148 (note 5).

[15] *Journal*, 1 July 1893, 20; Wellcome Institute, Hart Papers, undated letter (1875) to Thomas Madden Stone; R. Farquharson, *In and Out of Parliament*, p. 117 (note 13).

[16] *Practitioner* (Feb. 1898) **LX**: 117–18. The *Medical Magazine* called him 'unquestionably the foremost public man of his day . . . in the modern science of Preventive Medicine'. Jan. 1898, 34–5.

and by so doing to help an impecunious Association towards financial security. More than anyone else he transformed the *Journal* from a minor weekly into 'a gigantic National Institution'; indeed, the world's most successful (at least in terms of circulation) medical journal, as well as one truly international in outlook, concerned as much with public health in Asia, or the West Indies as a health resort, as with football injuries in the West Midlands or workhouse infirmaries in County Clare.[17]

As well as being editor of the *Journal*, Hart dominated the BMA for 25 years, during which he chaired its most important committee, that dealing with parliamentary bills. He also sat on many other committees and founded the BMA's library, serving as honorary librarian and, for a time, donating most of the books. Outside the Association he was at various times chairman of the National Health Society, founder and first chairman of the Medical Sickness, Annuity and Life Association Society, president of the Harveian Society, executive member of the metropolitan branch of the Medical Defence Union, a member of the board of management of the British Lying-in Hospital, Lambeth, a member of the committee of the Society for the Prevention of Hydrophobia and Reform of the Dog Laws, and, towards the end of his life, a council member of the State Children's Aid Association. He stood, unsuccessfully, for Parliament in 1885 and gave evidence to parliamentary select committees on the Protection of Infant Life (1871) and the Medical Act (1879). In 1894 he was a witness before the Departmental Committee on Poor Law Schools. In addition, he was active in the Metropolitan Public Gardens Association, and in the cremation, smoke abatement, and temperance movements (though this last involvement did not prevent his proposing the 13th toast at the BMA's 1876 annual meeting).[18] Hart was also an indefatigable traveller—a little too indefatigable in the eyes of some BMA members.[19] In the course of his editorship he visited Ireland, Spain, Gibraltar, France, Germany, Italy, Canada, the United States, Hong Kong, India, Japan, Burma, North Africa, Madeira, Malta, and the Middle East, contributing articles to the *Journal* from many of these places and generally doing much to spread the BMA's name and fame.

Hart had few recreations. His consuming pastime was the study and collection of ancient Japanese art, on which he was an authority. His sister-in-law wrote of him as 'a man with a great love of beauty, a keen appreciation of art, and an unashamed enjoyment of luxury'. More surprisingly, he was an animal lover, active in dog and pigeon breeding. Until his

[17] C. Williams, *Memoirs of Life and Work* (London: Smith Elder, 1884), p. 411; R. Farquharson, *In and Out of Parliament*, p. 116 (note 13). The circulation of the *Journal of the American Medical Association* did not surpass that of the *BMJ* until the twentieth century.

[18] On Hart's activities in smoke abatement see the *Builder*, 22 July 1882, 105–6; Peter Brimblecombe, *The Big Smoke* (London: Routledge, 1987).

[19] In 1893 a member questioned whether the services of a 'peripatetic editor' were required. *Journal*, 5 Aug. 1893, 321.

health deteriorated, he enjoyed exploring the countryside with his wife: 'Directly publishing day was passed, and the JOURNAL, which was the pride of his life, was out, he and his wife quitted London, according to an invariable custom, passing the time either riding on horseback or on the river.'[20]

Ernest Abraham Hart was born in Knightsbridge, London, on 26 June 1835.[21] His father, Septimus, was a dentist in West London and his younger brother followed the same profession. Between the ages of 13 and 17 he was educated at the City of London School, where he had a triumphant academic career.[22] The University Test Acts prevented Hart, as a Jew, from taking up a scholarship at Queens' College, Cambridge. Instead, he chose to study medicine at St George's Hospital and Samuel Lane's school of medicine in Grosvenor Place.[23]

Hart won many prizes at medical school, where his career was as brilliant as it had been at the City of London. As a medical student he was instrumental in forming a student society to agitate—which it did with some success—for improved conditions for juniors in the Naval Medical Service. In 1856 he became a member of the Royal College of Surgeons and, briefly, a house surgeon at St Mary's Hospital. In 1857 he was appointed demonstrator in anatomy and registrar at St George's, but his association with St Mary's was renewed in the 1860s, when he held appointments as ophthalmic surgeon (1861–8), aural surgeon (1865–8), and dean of the medical school (1863–9). In 1861 Hart was one of the leading lights in the formation of the Junior Medical Society of London, a body which sought to encourage discussion of medical subjects by students and the newly qualified.[24]

Hart had contributed articles to periodicals 'as a boy' and published a paper on British Jews in *Fraser's Magazine* while still a student.[25] He became active in medical journalism at the age of 23, when, having been introduced

[20] *Ibid.*, 15 Jan. 1898, 184; H. O. Barnett, *Canon Barnett, His Life, Work and Friends*, Vol. I, p. 148 (note 5).

[21] The *Practitioner*'s anonymous obituary writer, who claimed to have made Hart's acquaintance as a student in the 1860s (when Hart was dean of St Mary's Medical School), states there was doubt about Hart's date of birth and that he was really older than was indicated by other obituaries, (Feb. 1898) **LX**: 117–18. *Who Was Who* gives June 1836 as Hart's month of birth.

[22] In 1856 the *Jewish Chronicle* described the City of London School as 'the only public school of acknowledged merit ... which receives members of *all* religions on equal terms and acknowledges no distinctions save those of merit'. 30 May 1856.

[23] *BMJ* mss. Ernest Hart file. Unpublished paper of E. M. Little, Read at a Meeting of the Osler Club, 1 Nov. 1929; *The Jewish Chronicle 1841–1941. A Century of Newspaper History* (London: Jewish Chronicle, 1949); *Jewish Chronicle*, 2 Aug. 1850; 1 Aug. 1851; 5 March 1852; 14 May 1852; 6 Aug. 1852; 9 June 1854.

[24] *Ibid.*, 12 May 1854; 9 June 1854; 18 May 1855; 14 Dec. 1857; 2 July 1858; 26 Dec. 1862; 2 Oct. 1863; *Lancet*, 2 Feb. 1861, 121–2; 16 Feb. 1861, 174; 23 Feb. 1861, 190; 2 March 1861, 226; 16 March 1861, 271–2, 274–5; *Medical Times and Gazette*, 16 March 1861, 281.

[25] *Dictionary of National Biography* (London: Smith Elder, 1909), Supplement; *Jewish Chronicle*, 10 March 1854. An 1856 lecture was published in Charles Dickens's *Household Words*.

to Wakley as 'the cleverest youngster in London', he joined the staff of the *Lancet*. His testimonials included one from his headmaster stating that Hart was the 'the most capable lad whom he had ever educated'. His duties at the *Lancet* were to write leading articles to order, to write in the editorial style on topics selected by himself but subject to the editor's approval, and to take charge of the column devoted to medico-parliamentary affairs. When James Wakley took over the editorship of the *Lancet* from his father, Hart was employed in reading and correcting proofs and 'assisting in the literary departments'.[26] Throughout this time Hart was, of course, building a private practice and holding his hospital appointments. In 1865 he was involved in the *Lancet*'s inquiry into workhouse infirmaries (p. 55) and also in its investigation of the cholera outbreak at Theydon Bois in Essex. Of Hart's appointment as the *BMJ*'s editor the *Medical Press and Circular* later said that the BMA Council 'had caught the editorial *leprechaun*, actually bought up the life and soul of the opposition establishment'.[27]

Hart was the *Journal*'s dominating personality for the last third of the nineteenth century. He was not, however, the longest-serving member of the editorial staff in that period. This distinction belongs to Alexander Henry. As a medical student Henry had lodged with John Rose Cormack at Putney. After qualification he acted as Cormack's assistant; and when Cormack was appointed editor of the *Journal* Henry followed him as sub-editor. In the event Henry, who retired in 1886 after 34 years' service, outlasted not only Cormack, but Wynter, Markham, and Hutchinson too. Henry, who was honorary secretary of the BMA's Metropolitan Counties branch for 26 years, also sat on the Parliamentary Bills Committee. He attended and reported all the Association's annual meetings from 1852 to 1885, and compiled the celebratory sketches of the BMA which were published in the *Journal* in 1882. During Hart's absences he was the *Journal*'s acting editor. He was an applicant for the editorship in 1869, when Hutchinson was appointed, and again in 1870, when Hart was re-appointed.[28] Henry was a shy and unassuming man. A gifted linguist who spoke 15 languages, he was reputed seldom to have said much in any one of them. But he was methodical, industrious, and conscientious; in fact, the ideal foil for the mercurial Hart. He undertook much of the routine labour, which won few plaudits but was vital if the *Journal* was to make its regular weekly appearance.[29] Other members of Hart's editorial staff were John Murray,

[26] *Lancet*, 15 Jan. 1898, 193.

[27] *Medical Press and Circular*, 5 May 1869, 375; *Journal*, 15 Jan. 1898, 184; *Jewish Chronicle*, 14 Jan. 1898.

[28] BMA mss. Committee of Council Minute Book (1868–1875), 24 Aug. 1869, 86; 9 Aug. 1870, 139.

[29] C. Williams, *Memoirs of Life and Work*, p. 411 (note 17).

George Eastes, Fancourt Barnes, Alban Doran, Charles Taylor, and Dawson Williams.[30]

Format, circulation, and finance

When Hart became editor he stressed that the *Journal* would 'be conducted in the spirit which has already won for it a well deserved success'.[31] But, while he paid lip service to the maintenance of continuity, he immediately began to introduce the changes which quickly distinguished his *Journal* from that of his predecessors. He drastically reduced the space allocated to Association business, placing more emphasis upon 'original communications', scientific and clinical material, and medical news including reports from overseas. He also sought to increase the *Journal*'s appeal to special interest groups such as army and navy surgeons, Poor Law medical officers, and regional practitioners in Ireland and Scotland, all of whom had their own columns.[32] In later years hospital and asylum management, medico-legal, and medico-ethical sections were added.

Another significant development dated from Hart's very first issue, the title page of which announced that the *Journal* was to commence a series of reports on hygiene and preventable disease in the merchant navy. This was the first of many socio-medical investigations which became the hallmark of Hart's *BMJ*. The second volume for 1867 contained a series on industrial disease in various industries, and this at a time when occupational health was attracting little serious attention. Before long the *Journal* had lost all vestige of being an Association newsletter.

There were also new publishers and changes in the *Journal*'s appearance and dimensions. Honeyman, who had published the *Journal* since 1853, was replaced by Robert Hardwick of Piccadilly; then from July 1870 Thomas Richards of 37 Great Queen Street, who had been the *Journal*'s printer and landlord since 1853, took over as publisher. The arrangement with Richards continued till 1878, when *Journal* and Association moved to new premises at

[30] *Journal*, 18 Oct. 1873, 476–7; 25 Oct. 1873, 505; 10 June 1882, 888. 16 Dec. 1899; 29 Feb. 1908, 541; BMA mss. CCMB (1868–75) 9 June 1869, 67; 4 Feb. 1874, n.p.; MCSC, I, Journal and Finance Committee, 8 Jan. 1874, 2; 16 April 1879, 308; III, 20 Oct. 1886, 1295–6; Barnes, son of the eminent obstetrician, Robert, was author of the popular *Manual for Midwives* and physician to the British Lying-in Hospital. He later edited the *British Gynaecological Journal*. Eastes later served on several BMA committees, including the *Journal* and Finance Committee. He also became president of the Association's Metropolitan Counties branch. During Hart's early years his elder sister, Charlotte, acted as his 'most devoted assistant and ammanuensis'.

[31] *Journal*, 5 Jan. 1867, 11.

[32] An Irish column commenced in October 1868 and a Scottish one in November. In the same year a 'Poor Law Medical Science' department was established under the control of Joseph Rogers, who was President of the Council of the Poor Law Medical Officers' Association. The Army and Navy section began in 1873, while a Cottage Hospital department was started in 1877. See *ibid.*, 10 June 1882, 887.

161A Strand. From July 1867 the *Journal* began to appear in quarto, instead of octavo, size, thereby increasing its dimensions by the equivalent of eight pages. From the same month it was printed on better quality paper with a new typeface.[33] In 1886 the first photographs made their appearance, though in all probability readers preferred the old woodcuts, which continued for some years, for the quality of photographic reproduction was poor and remained so for some time.[34] In January 1868 the number of pages was increased to 40 a week, though the more usual number in the 1870s was between 31 and 37. Thereafter the *Journal* grew steadily larger as it dealt with an increasingly broad range of subjects. The 763 pages of Hart's first six-monthly volume was less than half the number of pages of the *Journal* 30 years later. By 1887 Hart could claim that his *Journal* was more voluminous than any other medical periodical. Indeed, the second volume of that year, it was proudly announced, was 'the largest semi-annual volume of any medical periodical ever published' (at 1460 pages of text).[35]

All these developments must have called for much re-organization in the way in which the *Journal* obtained editorial material. We have little information about how the early editors secured articles, but apart from the ubiquitous Association news they seem to have relied upon unsolicited items from Association members, such as letters and case notes; reprinting the reports, lectures, and transactions of institutions, societies, individuals, and periodicals; and writing many of their own leading articles. This, as critics often pointed out, did not make for a very exciting publication. The richly diverse and far larger *Journal* put out by Hart had to be compiled in a different manner. Instead of relying on a permanent full-time staff of what he called 'writers of all work', which Hart indicated was the practice of his competitors, he gradually assembled a large number of contributors on whom he could call for regular or occasional articles. In 1875 the *Journal* had its own part-time reporters in Edinburgh, Dublin, Liverpool, 'and other great cities'. It also employed three men simply to cover the meetings of the London medical societies.[36] Hart and Cormack reported on the Franco-

[33] Other changes, such as further improving paper quality and issuing the *Journal* with 'cut' pages followed.

[34] *Journal*, 16 Oct. 1886, 710.

[35] Although a source of pride, the *Journal*'s size also became something of a problem with contributors being constantly reminded of the need for brevity. Hart admitted that issues were too large by 1890. The launch of the 'Epitome of Medical Literature' supplement had to be accompanied by a four page reduction in *Journal* size. MCSC, V, Journal and Finance Committee, 16 July 1890, 1633–5. In 1891 the Journal and Finance Committee agreed that there should be a limit of 58 pages of editorial matter, but this was not always adhered to. In 1894 the Journal's Reference Committee requested that the maximum weekly size be increased by four pages. The Journal and Finance Committee sanctioned an extra two pages for a one-year period. *Ibid*, 20 Oct. 1891, 1875; *ibid.*, VII, 17 Jan. 1894, 2571–6. See *ibid.*, VIII, 8 July 1896, 3301–3 and Special Meeting of Journal and Finance Committee, 31 July 1896, 3307–11; *Journal*, 8 Jan. 1887, 76–7; 7 Jan. 1888, 29.

[36] *Ibid.*, 9 Jan. 1875, 67; 4 Jan. 1896, 36.

Prussian War, 1870–1; other correspondents covered the 1877–8 Russo-Turkish War. By 1889 there were 'upwards of 140 members of the editorial staff', of whom between 30 and 40 contributed to any one issue.[37] By the end of 1892, the number of regular contributors totalled 250.[38]

Hart's changes elicited generally favourable responses, though a speaker at the Association's south-eastern branch meeting in 1869 complained that, while the *Journal* had 'of late vastly improved in every respect', reports of provincial meetings were being allocated insufficient space. It was not, he suggested, 'the chief intention of the promoters of the JOURNAL' that it should be filled with reports from London, Edinburgh, and Dublin. Similar complaints were still being made in 1896.[39] But in general Hart's changes were warmly welcomed by individual members, the branches, and the BMA's General Council. At any rate, BMA membership rose, as did *Journal* circulation, sales, and advertising revenue.[40]

Although circulation figures are not entirely reliable, it is evident that circulation increased in the course of Hart's editorship from around 2500 in 1867 to 20 500 by the end of 1897. This was an impressive achievement, especially as the medical profession began to increase its numbers only from the 1880s.[41] By the 1870s the *Journal* was disputing (literally) with the *Lancet* the distinction of being the largest circulating medical periodical. In 1878 it claimed a circulation 'some thousands in excess of that of any other British or foreign medical journal'. By 1884 it could claim that its circulation exceeded that of all its rivals combined, and by 1886 that in the course of a year it exceeded the sales of its nearest rival by over $\frac{1}{4}$ million.[42]

[37] *Ibid.*, 4 May 1889, 1025. In 1895 the number of anonymous contributors per issue averaged 50. *Ibid.*, 4 Jan. 1896, 36.

[38] *Ibid.*, 3 Dec. 1892, 1243.

[39] *Ibid.*, 3 July 1869, 19. Complaints about insufficient concentration upon branch business also surfaced in 1882. See 8 July, 74; 15 July, 114; 22 July, 152; 1 Feb. 1896, 305. The changed appearance of the *Journal* was opposed by some members at the BMA's 1867 annual meeting. See *Journal*, 17 Aug. 1867, 134–5.

[40] *Ibid.*, 22 June 1867, 755; 3 Aug. 1867, 96; 10 Aug. 1867, 112; 9 May 1868, 461,464; 11 July 1868, 44; 25 July 1868, 93; 20 July 1872, 60, 72. In 1880 the *Journal* received high praise from the president of the American Medical Association. See *ibid.*, 18 June, 941.

[41] I. Loudon, *Medical Care and the General Practitioner, 1750–1850* (Oxford: Oxford University Press, 1986), p. 309. The number in the profession in 1881 was smaller than in 1841.

[42] *Journal*, 14 Dec. 1878, 881; 1 Jan. 1887, 22. These figures were small in comparison with daily newspapers or popular weeklies. Even *The Times* had a daily sale of around 37 000 in 1897. On the other hand, the largest circulation monthly or quarterly review, the *Nineteenth Century*, sold only around 10 000 copies per issue. On nineteenth century newspaper and periodical circulations see Richard D. Altick, *The English Common Reader. A Social History of the Mass Reading Public, 1800–1900* (Chicago: University of Chicago Press, 1957), p. 391; Diana Dixon, 'Children and the Press, 1866–1914' in Michael Harris and Alan Lee (eds.), *The Press in English Society from the Seventeenth to Nineteenth Centuries* (London: Associated University Presses, 1986), p. 142; Terry Nevett, 'Advertising and Editorial Integrity in the Nineteenth Century' in *ibid.*, p. 153; A. P. Wadsworth, 'Newpaper Circulations, 1800–1954', *Transactions of the Manchester Statistical Society* (1955) **4**: 1–41; John Mason, 'Monthly and Quarterly Reviews, 1865–1914' in George Boyce *et* al (eds.), *Newspaper History from the Seventeenth Century to the Present Day* (London: Acton Society, 1978).

Increased circulation meant increased revenue for the Association through additional membership, advertising, and sales. In 1866, the year before Hart became editor, BMA accounts showed a deficit of £883. Income from subscriptions amounted to £2138 and income from advertising and sales to £582; on the other hand, the expenses of the *Journal* alone were £3251. Within a year this potentially disastrous position had been turned around. In 1867 subscriptions were up by almost £600, while income from advertising and sales was over £700 more. One of the few years after 1866 in which the Association suffered financial loss was 1869, the year in which Hart was out of office. In 1892 some 25 per cent of *Journal* circulation was through sales rather than BMA membership.[43] By the mid-1890s *Journal* advertisements and sales were, in some years, providing a larger share of the Association's income than were subscriptions (e.g. in 1895 £18 519 as against £17 272).

It would be simplistic to attribute the *Journal*'s success to Hart alone—the expansion of the profession and the constitutional link with the Association were more fundamental factors—but he did produce a publication of consistently high standard and broad interest which, in consequence, was well placed to capture a large slice of a market hungry for medical journalism. The *Journal* was not merely the beneficiary of the Association's success. Indeed, it can be argued, as it was from time to time by Hart himself, that the reverse was the case. *Journal* subscribers were recruited by the BMA because membership of the Association was less expensive than the annual subscription to the *Journal* (21s in 1867 as against 26s for the *Journal* without membership). Hence it was in the financial interests of those who wanted the *Journal* but were unattracted by membership of the BMA nevertheless to join the Association.[44]

From 1866 the *Journal* was actively employed to recruit BMA members, subscribers being offered a rebate if they converted their subscriptions into membership.[45] Annually, in December, a free copy of the *Journal* containing an indication of its forthcoming contents was sent to registered practitioners who were neither BMA members nor *Journal* subscribers. Hence, it was justly stated that the *Journal* 'began to be employed systematically as a recruiting agent'.[46] In 1868 the BMA's General Council acknowledged that 'the character of the JOURNAL under the editorship of that gentleman [Hart] has been greatly instrumental in adding to the numbers and influence of the Association.'[47] Hart evidently agreed, for he published a letter in which

[43] *Journal*, 3 Dec. 1892, 1243.

[44] By 1875 the differential had widened with the cost of membership held at one guinea but subscription to the *Journal* raised to 28s. This made membership still more attractive than mere subscription. See *Ibid.*, 25 Dec. 1875, 807.

[45] *Ibid.*, 4 Jan. 1896, 33. In 1872 the *Journal* noted that 'those who begin by subscribing to the JOURNAL, generally end by getting their papers duly signed and becoming also members of the Association'. 24 Feb. 1872, 216.

[46] *Ibid.*, 5 Jan. 1884, 21; 1 Aug. 1885, 215–16; 12 Dec. 1885, 1121–2; 3 Dec. 1892, 1243.

[47] *Ibid.*, 8 Aug. 1868, 147; 4 Aug. 1888, 259.

the writer declared himself 'perfectly convinced that nothing has contributed so much to the present position of the Association, and to the pleasure and improvement of the members, as your management of the JOURNAL'.[48]

There was, nevertheless, disquiet in some quarters of the Association about the BMA's spiralling expenditure. Concern focused particularly upon the cost of editing the *Journal*. Henry Butlin, the Association's Treasurer, prepared a report on the question in 1890. Although concluding that the increased expenditure on the *Journal* was justifiable, he was concerned by the 'astonishing fact' that 'the cost of Editing, apart from Contributions, Engraving and Reporting has steadily risen from £6 5s. per page in 1872 to £41 10s. per page in 1889, while the work has scarcely more than doubled during the same period'.[49] These conclusions provided ammunition for those such as Lawson Tait who, disregarding the income generated by the *Journal*, were critical of the sums spent on it.[50]

Success brought other problems. Most BMA business, including editing and publication of the *Journal*, took place in London, but the Association's secretary lived in Birmingham. Watkin Williams, who was appointed part-time secretary in 1863, allowed business affairs to get into a terrible mess. He failed to take minutes of Council meetings, ignored important business resolutions passed by Council, and let subscription arrears rise alarmingly. The *Journal*'s business transactions, which involved large sums of money, were undertaken by two clerks at Great Queen Street, who worked largely unsupervised. Although it was no part of his duties, Hart attempted, after his re-appointment in 1870, to introduce more order. However, in the prevailing chaos, the clerk responsible for advertising, Mr Powle, absconded with about £300.[51] In these circumstances Council decided that the Secretary should henceforward be based in London and assume responsibility for managing the *Journal* office.[52] There were protests that the Association was becoming even more London-based, and also:

a great joint-stock enterprise for the publication of a weekly journal, which absorbs nearly the whole of the Association's income ... if the Secretary is to be reduced practically to the position of a paid clerk residing in London, and charged with the business management of the *Journal* office, as well as of the Association, he must be subordinate to the Editor, or, in business matters, be co-ordinate with him in authority; the latter alternative would be incompatible with good government, while

[48] *Ibid.*, 23 May 1868, 522; see 8 Jan. 1887, 76–7.

[49] BMA mss. MCSC (1890–1891) V, Special Report by the Treasurer, 12 Nov. 1890, 1876–81.

[50] See e. g. *ibid.*, (1894–95) VII, Minutes of Council, 11 July 1894, 2517; VIII, 15 April 1896, 3024.

[51] BMA mss. CCMB (1868–75) Journal Sub-Committee, 14 Feb. 1871, 154; 14 March 1871, 163.

[52] *Journal*, 12 Aug. 1871, 190. See letter of G. F. Hodgson, Hon. Sec. BMA south eastern branch, *ibid.*, 29 July, 1871, 137; BMA mss. CCMB (1868–75) Journal Sub-Committee, 14 Feb. 1871, 154–5.

the former would inevitably lead to such a centralisation of power in the Editor of the *Journal* as to render him practically . . . the Master of the Association.[53]

Nevertheless, Council's proposals went through. In November 1871 Francis Fowke was appointed General Secretary of the Association and manager of the *Journal* office. When he took up his appointment at the beginning of the following year he moved into one of the *Journal*'s rooms in Great Queen Street.[54] In 1874 the Association acquired offices next door.

Pressure of space and increasing prosperity soon prompted the Association and *Journal* to leave Great Queen Street and sign a lease on premises in the Strand at a rent of £320 p.a. The BMA Council anticipated that relocation of the *Journal* in more prestigious offices would enhance its reputation and lead to further gains in advertising revenue. In 1871 Hart had compiled a report recommending that the *Journal* should be printed by the Association itself. By 1878, with a balance of £5000 at its disposal, Council decided to go ahead with this recommendation, believing that it would lead to savings in the production of the *Journal.*

Several members objected that decisions on premises and printing had been taken without consulting the membership.[55] They also bridled at the proposal to spend some £2000 of Association money on improving the building and purchasing office furniture, fittings, and printing equipment. At an Extraordinary General Meeting in April 1878, William Grigg, honorary secretary of the Metropolitan Counties branch, led the attack against the proposed changes, arguing that advertisers were influenced solely by circulation: 'if the *Journal* were to . . . go back to its former standard of circulation of two thousand copies, you might take Buckingham Palace as an office, and that would not prevent its income from advertisements from falling off.'[56] He also feared that the Association was about to become 'a mere appendage of the *Journal*, located in a converted upholstery store surrounded by shops and eating houses'.[57] Here, in fact was the true basis of Grigg's misgivings. He and his supporters opposed any change which might compromise the Association's dignity and taint it with connotations of 'trade'. Yet the Association was intending to enter the printing business and force its visitors to approach its offices through a shop selling copies of the *Journal* to passers-by. However, when a vote was taken the decision of Council was supported overwhelmingly.[58]

In a letter written in 1880 the BMA's Treasurer, W. D. Husband, reflected

[53] *Journal*, 1 July 1871, 20.
[54] *Ibid.*, 4 Nov. 1871.
[55] *Ibid.*, 16 Feb. 1878, 243; 10 Aug. 1878, 219; BMA mss. MCSC, I, Premises Committee, 9 July 1878, 200.
[56] *Journal*, 6 April 1878, 504.
[57] *Ibid.*, 504–5.
[58] *Ibid.*, 505–6.

on the wisdom of the recent changes. The financial position, he wrote, was 'most satisfactory': 'The amount received for advertisements and sales over the counter has so much increased this last year beyond the experience of any former year, that I cannot think it can be doubted, that the anticipations that such would be the result of removal of the office to a better business locality have been fully realised.'[59]

The Association remained at 161A Strand until 1887, in which year it moved (without protest from members) along the road to the more spacious surroundings of no. 429, with additional accommodation in adjacent Agar Street.[60] The 1887 move was not, however, devoid of controversy. The allocation of rooms placed the *Journal*'s editorial department on the second floor, below the printing room and above the rooms reserved for members and for Council. The basement and ground floor were reserved for conduct of the business affairs of the *Journal* and Association. Hart was not a party to these decisions and when he visited the new offices he was furious with what he had been assigned. He refused to accept any office on the second floor because the windows were so high up the wall as to give him no view. He demanded to be given the members' room, suggesting that they could share the Council Chamber. Hart also made clear that it would be 'impossible' for him to remain as editor unless provided with his own private entrance from Agar Street.

The Premises Committee was in a quandary. It approached the Association's architect to see whether it would be possible to enlarge Hart's windows in order to provide the required view. Apparently, this was not possible and, in any case, the landlord objected to interference with his walls. Hart failed to get his hands on the Council Chamber, but he did obtain a private entrance complete with plaque reading: 'BRITISH MEDICAL JOURNAL, Editor'.[61]

Scandal

Apart from the costs of printing and postage, the largest recurring item of expenditure in the *Journal* accounts was for payment of contributors. In 1865 they received over £230; in the following year this figure had risen slightly, to almost £240.[62] Neither the identities of contributors nor the size of individual payments were ever revealed. We can only assume that the money went to the *Journal*'s 'special correspondents' and to those commissioned to write

[59] BMA mss. MCSC, I, Journal and Finance Committee, 14 Jan. 1880, 371–2.

[60] The BMA had to search long and hard before finding suitable premises at an affordable price. The survey on no. 429 was not promising: 'It is quite unfit for occupation by a Society, many of whose members have been instrumental in pressing the sanitary condition of houses and public buildings upon the attention of the legislature . . . .' *Ibid.*, III, Premises Committee, 12 Nov. 1886, 1301

[61] *Ibid.*, 1 Feb. 1887, 1451.

[62] *Journal*, 14 April 1866, 395; 8 June 1867, 681.

original papers or leading articles. Included among these would almost certainly have been the editor himself.

When Hart became editor the amount paid to contributors immediately increased. In 1867 the figure exceeded £598, while in the following year contributors received over £800. If these figures came as a surprise to members, they should not have surprised the BMA's Council, for when he took over as editor Hart had made it clear that the existing £600 available for literary and editorial purposes, was 'entirely inadequate'. He emphasized that, notwithstanding the Association's financial difficulties, he intended to spend his way to success and, in consequence, solvency.[63]

The Association's 1868 accounts were published in the *Journal* in April 1869. The annual meeting, as ever, provided the opportunity to discuss the financial statement. Some time after 17 April the Rev. Dr Bell gave notice of his intention to call attention at the Leeds meeting in July to the subject of the *Journal*'s income and expenditure. By June Hart had resigned.[64] The assumption has been that his resignation was connected with disquiet over *Journal* finances, though it has also been suggested that Hart had fled abroad in order to avoid being brought to trial for murdering his wife.[65]

The known facts of Hart's resignation are few. At the BMA's annual meeting at Leeds in 1869 the report of the General Council contained the following announcement:

> The Council have to regret the resignation of the very able editor of the JOURNAL. Arrangements have been made for carrying on the business of the JOURNAL until the appointment of his successor, which it will be the duty of the new Committee of Council to decide on at their first meeting.[66]

No official reason for the resignation was given at the time or subsequently.[67] Neither do the unpublished minutes of the BMA's Council or *Journal* and Finance Committee provide any hint. Council's inability to announce a successor suggests that resignation was sudden.

Journal finances were debated at the Leeds meeting, but the discussion was reported only briefly and rather uninformatively in the *Journal*. Several speakers believed the £802 paid to contributors to be much too high. There were also complaints that, while these large sums were being spent on contributions, members' papers, for which no fee was solicited, were being

[63] BMA mss. CCMB (1868–75) Copy of letter from Ernest Hart, dated 20 June 1868, pp. 8–13.

[64] *Ibid.*, 9 June 1869, 67. See *Journal*, 3 July 1869, 19.

[65] E. M. Little, *History of the BMA* (London: British Medical Association, n.d., 1932?), p. 181 (note 4); P. Vaughan, *Doctors' Commons*, p. 138 (note 4); Stephen Lock, unpublished transcript of 'Paper read to the Osler Club Meeting on Medical Journalism held at BMA House on 21. 3. '74'.

[66] *Journal*, 31 July 1869, 127.

[67] At the BMA's south-eastern branch meeting held on 17 June 1869 there was a reference to 'the late editor of our Journal'. See *Journal*, 3 July 1869, 19.

rejected.[68] Drs Seaton and Davey wondered whether the BMA's Treasurer knew to whom the payments had been made and if particulars could be announced. Dr Lingen observed that 'the Editor of the *Journal* was placed in a very delicate position by this large expenditure.'[69] The BMA Treasurer, Dr Falconer, explained that the practice had been for the editor to have access to Association funds with which to pay contributors, but that, in future, contributors would be paid by cheque issued by the treasurer. Dr Stewart came to Hart's defence, remarking that 'If an Editor is appointed, he must be trusted thoroughly.' Somewhat cryptically, he stated that the 'interests of the Association demanded the large expenditure', but questioned whether it should be continued. The meeting agreed that the names of *Journal* contributors should not be disclosed.[70]

In all this there is no evidence that Hart was lining his own pockets with BMA funds. Neither is there any indication that Hart resigned over the issue. So what are the possibilities? First, Hart may simply have been stealing from the Association, listing his ill-gotten gains as payments to contributors. When the prospect of exposure arose, he offered to resign, and Council accepted because it was as anxious as Hart to avoid scandal. The main problem with this scenario is that it makes it impossible to believe that Hart would have been re-appointed as editor only one year later. On this basis alone it can be rejected.

On the other hand, Hart, who clearly was ambitious to improve the *Journal*, may have been offering greatly increased sums to eminent contributors; it is also possible that a substantial proportion of the £802 found its way into his pocket in payment for articles which he actually wrote. If Hart was doubling or trebling his salary in this way, it is perfectly conceivable that he resigned in order to avoid public exposure. His re-appointment as editor, while surprising, does not undermine this explanation, for Hart's record as editor was otherwise excellent; he may have been deemed to have suffered his punishment, and the *Journal*, as was stated later, was thought to have 'languished' under his successor.[71]

The third possibility is that his resignation was wholly unconnected with financial irregularity but was submitted because of the impending prospect of being tried for the murder of his wife. Such an explanation is supported by the absence of any explicit indication, even in confidential Association records, that Hart's resignation was related to malfeasance, and also because it removes the difficulty of explaining why Hart was re-appointed *Journal*

[68] BMA members sometimes assumed that their membership entitled them to expect automatic inclusion of their contributions to the *Journal*. Complaints about the rejection of articles were therefore fairly regular occurrences. See for example 29 April 1871, 460.

[69] *Journal*, 31 July 1869, 127.

[70] *Ibid.*

[71] *Ibid.*, 12 Jan. 1898, 40.

editor, for if his resignation was not linked to his professional activities there can have been no objection to his re-appointment.

Hart's first wife certainly died in suspicious circumstances. Late one night in November 1861, when looking for a 'black draught', she mistakenly took some tincture of aconite.[72] During the night she vomited, but this caused no anxiety as it was attributed to the black draught. Rosetta Hart's error was discovered only on the following morning by which time 'all cause for alarm seemed to have subsided'. What happened next does not show Hart in a very good light. The *Medical Times and Gazette* reported that:

> Dr. Richardson [a general practitioner] saw the lady at eleven in the forenoon, and thought her quite out of danger. It seems that some vomiting had excited Mr. Hart's apprehension, and a question was raised as to the propriety of checking this symptom. Dr. Richardson thought it was not advisable to interfere. He was called again at one o'clock, and found the lady dead. It then appeared that two or three doses of hydrocyanic acid had been given to check the vomiting.[73]

The *Gazette* was then edited by Hart's friend, James Fernandez Clarke. He claimed to be providing a true account of Mrs Hart's death in order to scotch rumours; in fact the *Gazette* account suggests that Hart bungled or did worse.

The inquest was held on 8 November. Because the Middlesex coroner's records for 1861 have not survived, we have no information about how Rosetta Hart might have mistaken tincture of aconite for a black draught or why, and in what concentration, Hart gave her the hydrocyanic acid. The verdict of the court was 'accidentally poisoned by tincture of aconite'.[74] On the basis of the *Gazette*'s report, this was certainly giving Hart all the best of it. If the verdict had been 'poisoned by prussic acid' he would surely have faced criminal proceedings. Squire Sprigge, the biographer of Thomas Wakley and editor of the *Lancet*, later told Edward Muirhead Little that, 'When I came to look into the crime story, which was more or less traditional in this office, I came to the conclusion that it was without foundation.'[75]

[72] A 'black draught' was a common aperient medicine made from senna, bruised ginger, liquorice, Epsom salts, sal volatile, cardamons, and water. The dose for an adult was a wineglassful. Aconite is derived from the roots of monkshood or wolfbane. An analgesic, it was formerly used to prepare liniments in cases of tooth-ache or muscle pain. It is regarded as too toxic to be used today. *Enquire Within upon Everything* (London: Houlston and Sons, 1894), p. 118; *Concise Medical Dictionary* (Oxford: Oxford University Press, 1987).

[73] *Medical Times and Gazette*, 16 Nov. 1861, 509. Hydrocyanic (prussic) acid is 'an intensely poisonous volatile acid that can cause death within a minute if inhaled'. But 'properly diluted' Victorians administered it in cases of dyspepsia. Robert Christison, *A Treatise on Poisons* (Edinburgh: A & C Black, 1829), pp. 555–82; *Hooper's Medical Dictionary* (London: Longman, n.d. 1854?); *Concise Medical Dictionary* (note 72); *Journal*, 23 April 1898, 1098.

[74] The Middlesex coroner was Thomas Wakley, who was then Hart's employer. His name appears on Rosetta Hart's death certificate. This might arouse suspicions of favouritism were it not for the fact that Wakley was not sitting in November 1861 owing to ill-health (he died the following year). I am grateful to Mary Bostetter for this information.

[75] *BMJ* mss. Ernest Hart File. Squire Sprigge to E. M. Little, 10 June 1929.

However, aided by Frank Danby's 1887 novel, *Dr. Phillips: A Maida Vale Idyll*, in which a clever Jewish doctor who is sub-editor of a medical journal kills his wife, Hart became known as 'the doctor who murdered his wife'.[76]

In the absence of an authenticated, signed confession, we shall never know whether Hart was a murderer. The episode will remain one of the several mysteries associated with him. But what is clear is that the death of Rosetta Hart in 1861, that is, well before Hart joined the *BMJ*, can have had nothing to do with his resignation as editor in 1869. It is difficult to understand how the two events were ever linked. The explanation seems to lie, as Sprigge intimated, in the power of office myth, under the influence of which several murky events in Hart's past became mixed. As a deputy editor of the *BMJ* wrote in 1967, when discussing the break in Hart's editorship, 'it is generally believed . . . that Hart had to take time off to defend himself against having committed the gravest crime in the calendar. There was some doubt about what happened to £800 of the Association's income, but that was really a triviality.'[77]

Although there is no clear evidence of what Hart did or where he went in 1869–70, it has been sometimes stated that he fled abroad. A report in the *Medical Press and Circular*, which admittedly is inaccurate in a number of other details, indicates that he went to the United States, 'where he remained for a couple of years'.[78] If he went to America he certainly did not remain there for two years, for he was back in England by May 1870, in which month he attended a BMA meeting.

The *Lancet*'s report of the Leeds debate on the *Journal* provides an important clue to the resignation riddle. In this account Dr Davey's speech on the subject of the £802 was much more fully reported than in the *Journal*, where it was summarized in a mere three lines. Moreover, the *Lancet* report referred to the fate of the money, on which point the *Journal* was silent. The *Lancet* reported Davey as saying:

> He did not see why, if the editor contributed a certain number of papers, for which he was overpaid, it should not be made apparent to the members of the Association. They were all bound together in one common and good cause. Why should there be any secrecy in a matter of that kind? No one would object to pay the editor for his services. He, for one, would rather see him overpaid than underpaid; but let all transactions be clear and above-board.[79]

This is the clearest indication we are ever likely to have that some of the £802 found its way into Hart's pocket. It seems reasonable to conclude that he was

[76] Frank Danby was the *nom de plume* of Julia Frankau. In 1929 Mrs Frankau's son told E. M. Little that 'I have . . . frequently heard my mother say that she drew the principal character in "Dr. Phillips" from Ernest Hart, whom I believe she knew intimately'. *Ibid.*, letters of 11, 17 June 1929.

[77] *Ibid.*, T. D. V. Swinscow to R. A. Barley, 21 Aug. 1967.

[78] *Medical Press and Circular*, 12 Jan. 1898, 40.

[79] *Lancet*, 31 July 1869, 179.

paying himself handsomely, from funds over which he exercised complete control, for the articles he wrote, and that neither the practice nor the sums were being disclosed. If so, Hart's behaviour, while not dishonest, was morally questionable. After Hart returned as editor he, along with his junior editors, continued to receive additional payments as contributors. But these payments were never itemized in the Association's published financial statement and seldom mentioned elsewhere. If the arrangement had been known to the membership the protests would certainly have been long and loud.[80]

In a sense the resignation and murder mysteries are irrelevancies, for Hart's historical importance is as an outstanding editor. There was, however, one scandal—that associated with the German Emperor, Frederick, and his British physician, Morrell Mackenzie—which arose directly out of Hart's editorial work and therefore merits consideration. But first, we should look into what happened at the *Journal* after Hart's resignation, and the circumstances in which he returned to his post.

At the end of July 1869 Council decided to advertise for a new editor in the *BMJ*, the *Lancet*, and the *Medical Times and Gazette*. There were 14 candidates, and at its meeting in August Council selected Jonathan Hutchinson as Hart's successor. It is worth noting that it imposed a limit of £500 a year on the amount available to him for paying contributors.[81] Council also resolved that 'in future all sums paid to any contributor to the *Journal* exceeding five pounds shall be paid by the Treasurer and that all such sums below five pounds shall be paid by the Editor who shall communicate to the Treasurer, in confidence, a list of such contributors with the respective sums paid to them.'[82]

Hutchinson, born in Selby, Yorkshire, in 1828, had been a BMA member since 1858. At the time of his appointment he was senior surgeon to the London Hospital and lecturer in surgery at the medical school as well as surgeon to Moorfields Ophthalmic Hospital and to the Hospital for Skin-Diseases. He was also one of the leading lights in the New Sydenham Society, a body whose main object was the translation of continental medical monographs at reasonable cost. Although questioning whether his growing practice and other appointments would allow him the time to edit the *Journal*, the *Medical Press and Circular* regarded Hutchinson as an excellent

[80] BMA records provide a precise indication of Hart's editorial income. His salary on appointment was £250 p. a. Following several increases it reached £500 p. a. in 1875. After 1888 his income frequently exceeded £1100 p. a., of which £750 was salary. Other editorial staff were also paid for contributions. In 1887 there was discussion about paying editorial staff inclusive salaries rather than payments for contributions, but these came to nothing while Hart was editor. BMA mss. MCSC, III, Journal and Finance Committee, 19 Jan. 1887, 1449; Minutes of Council, V, 15 Jan. 1890, 1455; 15 April 1891, 1700; VI, 19 April 1893, 2095.

[81] BMA mss. CCMB (1868–75), 30 July 1869, 82–3; 24 Aug. 1869, 86–7; 3 Dec. 1869, 95–7.

[82] *Ibid.*

choice as editor of the *BMJ* and used the occasion of his appointment to attack his predecessors:

Under his guidance the Association may hope to see the tone of their Journal greatly raised, and its respectability vastly increased. He is not likely to fill its columns with ungenerous assaults upon individuals, nor with desperate attacks upon classes in the Profession. He will not set class upon class, nor college against college, nor, we hope, submit his own unbiassed judgment to the control of a clique. The Journal may thus become a more ready means for intercommunication between members. These will, perhaps, no longer be obliged to send their papers elsewhere for publication, while money is lavished in getting up sensational reports.[83]

Hutchinson held office for less than a year, so it is superfluous to examine the development of the *Journal* during his editorship. However, it is interesting to note that, at the BMA's annual meeting in 1870, Charles Chadwick, the Association's retiring president, launched an attack, which was greeted with applause from the floor, upon the *Journal*'s 'apathetic attitude . . . in this recent reform struggle'.[84] Chadwick went on to stress the key importance of the impending selection of a new editor (Hutchinson having resigned by this time):

. . . the choice of Editor now to be made during this present meeting, must prove an important turning point in your history. It is fairly in your hands to determine what kind of JOURNAL you will have; and according with that resolve must be the selection of your Editor. Once appointed he must have your complete and undeviating support in carrying out your wishes.

Is there a hint here of why Hutchinson resigned and Hart returned? Could the uninspired new man have been asked to resign so that the dynamic, successful, and re-available Hart could put the *Journal* back on course? Alternatively, perhaps Hutchinson was only too pleased to vacate the editorial hot seat and escape the brickbats which tended to fly its way. Some years later he claimed to have resigned the editorship because he found 'its duties incompatible with my other work'. He went on to say that 'what I enjoyed most in connection with the office was the getting rid of it.'[85] Conversely, his biographer states that he 'thoroughly enjoyed' editing the *BMJ* and that being a 'born journalist' he had no difficulty in writing leaders and working up favourite projects.[86] In fact, Hutchinson decided to resign at least as early as March 1870, giving as his reasons ill-health (though he survived till 1913) and pressure of work.[87]

[83] *Medical Press and Circular*, 1 Sept. 1869, 191–2.

[84] *Ibid.*, 20 Aug. 1870, 201. A Medical Act Amendment Bill had been before Parliament that year.

[85] *Journal*, 19 Aug. 1876, 231.

[86] Herbert Hutchinson, *Jonathan Hutchinson. Life and Letters* (London: Heinemann, 1946), p. 87.

[87] BMA mss. CCMB (1868–75), 5 May 1870, 115–16.

The *Medical Press and Circular*, despite having approved Hutchinson's appointment to the *BMJ*, later claimed that his performance as editor was so poor 'that Mr. Hart was welcomed back with open arms to the post in spite of the strenuous opposition of certain influential persons who neglected no weapon, however disreputable, to prevent his re-accession to power . . . .'[88]

After his departure, Hutchinson's relationships with *Journal* and Association remained amicable; he was a regular contributor to the former and an eminent member of the latter for many years. Indeed, he became president of the BMA's Metropolitan Counties branch.[89] On 2 July 1870 the *Journal* announced that the office of editor was about to fall vacant. Potential applicants were invited to apply within four weeks. On this occasion there were nine candidates, three of whom—Alexander Henry, Prosser James, and Fairlie Clarke—had also applied in 1869. A notable new applicant was the surgeon Lawson Tait, who, perhaps because he was passed over, became one of Hart's most persistent and hostile critics over the next three decades.[90]

At Newcastle, in August, Council unanimously re-elected Hart as editor. Their decision, they explained, was based upon his previous success in the post and the receipt of strong testimonials in his favour from some of the leading lights of the medical profession.[91] Hart was able to resume his distinguished journalistic career, to be interrupted again only by ill-health and death.

As a postscript to this episode, it is instructive to look at the *Journal*'s payments to contributors in the years after Hart's reappointment. The financial statement for 1870, for only about one-third of which was Hart editor, shows that in that year over £935 was paid to contributors, presumably through the channels agreed at Leeds. Although this was well in excess of

88 *Medical Press and Circular*, 12 Jan. 1898, 40–1.

89 After leaving the *Journal* Hutchinson became a Fellow of the Royal Society in 1882 and President of the Royal College of Surgeons in 1889. In 1908 he received a knighthood. He served as president of most of the London medical societies and was a member of two Royal Commissions, on smallpox and fever in London hospitals in 1881 and on vaccination in 1890–96. Hutchinson specialized in ophthalmology, dermatology, neurology, and 'above all syphilis'. In consequence, he became known as the 'greatest general practitioner in Europe'. He received many honours and also became prosperous, owning 300 acres in Surrey. However, his *Dictionary of National Biography* (note 25) entry criticizes his judgement; for example, even after the discovery of the leprosy bacillus, he clung to his theory that the disease was caused by consumption of rotten fish. The scurrilous Frank Harris ridiculed Hutchinson's persistent attachment to this idea. See *My Life and Loves* (London: Corgi, 1964 edn), p. 728.

90 BMA mss. CCMB (1868–75), Copy of letter from Lawson Tait dated 3 Dec. 1873, n.p.; MCSC, V, Journal and Finance Committee, 7 May 1874. Another reason for the antipathy between these two assertive and obstinate men was their difference over vivisection, Tait being passionately opposed to the practice. Hart was also an enthusiast for aseptic surgery, whereas Tait was hostile. One thing they had in common was a love of Japanese art. Personal antipathy did not prevent Tait from submitting to the *Journal*, and Hart accepting for publication, many papers over the same period. See W. J. Stewart McKay, *Lawson Tait. His Life and Work* (London: Baillière, 1922).

91 *Journal*, 13 Aug. 1870, 177.

the figure which had sparked all the controversy a year earlier, it was accepted without demur by the annual meeting at Plymouth in 1871.[92] In 1871 contributors received the very much smaller total of £486, but in the following year payments were higher than ever at £952.[93] On this occasion the matter was raised at the annual meeting when a member explained that he had tried unsuccessfully to discover to whom this 'large sum' had been paid. He resented the Association's 'policy of concealment' and asked the audience whether they 'thought the money was well and usefully spent in the JOURNAL'—an inquiry which elicited cries of 'yes, yes'.[94] These developments throw into new relief the events surrounding Hart's payment to contributors of £802, for they tend to exonerate him. If £952 could be paid to contributors under a system which vetted Hart's payments, it suggests that there may have been little of a truly 'shady' character in his earlier behaviour. We can now turn to the Morrell Mackenzie/Emperor Frederick affair.

The honour of the Association

The German Empire was created by 'blood and iron' in 1871 after Prussia's military defeat of France. Its first emperor was William of Prussia, who became William I of Germany. William's son, Frederick, married a daughter of Queen Victoria, the Princess Royal. An anglophile, widely regarded as a cultured and refined man, the Crown Prince had little in common with his son, who, as Emperor William II, led Germany into the First World War. It has sometimes been suggested that, had Frederick been emperor for years rather than weeks, the course of German history, and therefore of world history, might have been different. As it was, when he acceded to the throne, the cancer of the throat which was to kill him was already far advanced. It was in the controversy over Frederick's medical treatment that Hart—and the *BMJ*—became embroiled. On 19 May 1887 Queen Victoria received a telegram from her daughter informing her that the Crown Prince's doctors, who had been treating a throat infection for some months, were contemplating tracheotomy. However, before operating they wished to consult Morrell Mackenzie, Britain's foremost throat specialist. The Princess Royal begged her mother to send Mackenzie to Germany to save her husband from the operation. Victoria's medical advisers vouched for Mackenzie's competence

[92] *Ibid.*, 12 Aug. 1871, 190–4.

[93] *Ibid.*, 10 Aug. 1872 177; 9 Aug. 1873, 171.

[94] Requests at annual meetings for details of payments to contributors occurred on several other occasions during Hart's editorship. See e. g. *ibid.*, 30 July 1892, 255; 5 Aug. 1893, 321. But from 1886 the published balance sheet ceased to itemize payments to contributors separately. Instead, this sum was lumped in (with salaries, engraving, and reporting) as part of an item called 'editorial expenses'. This meant that it was no longer possible to see what individual staff salaries were. BMA members complained on several occasions about the deficiencies of the financial statement made available to them.

but expressed doubts about his personal qualities, stating that he was grasping and unpopular. By 20 May Mackenzie, who had received his own telegram, was in Berlin.[95]

On 28 May the *Journal* published reassuring news. A growth on Frederick's left vocal cord had been causing concern for some months. Although partially destroyed by electric cautery several months earlier, it had thereafter grown 'so rapidly as apparently to warrant the worst suspicions of the medical men who had charge of the case, as to the malignant nature of the growth'.[96] However, Mackenzie and Professor Virchow 'have dispelled these apprehensions for the time, and the treatment carried out by the former has thus far been so successful as to give grounds for hope of a favourable issue'. Mackenzie's treatment was intra-laryngeal removal of the growth rather than excision of the larynx, as had been favoured by the Crown Prince's German specialists. In reporting these happy tidings the *Journal* warned that benign growths often became malignant, but expressed the sentiment that 'Dr Mackenzie's fellow-countrymen cannot but feel a certain pride in his having so well upheld the credit of English medicine abroad.'[97] Other publications adopted a still more chauvinistic attitude, referring to the triumph of British surgery over German. Already the case had become tainted by international rivalry.

Two correspondents, who doubted the wisdom of Mackenzie's treatment and detected inaccuracies and complacency in the *Journal*'s leading article, took the *Journal* to task. One, Henry Butlin, a BMA Council member, stated presciently that the 'occurrences of the last few days do not afford the least proof that Dr. Mackenzie is right and the German physicians are wrong, and I do hope that our journals, whether lay or medical, will refrain from any expressions of triumph until we are in a position to know that Dr. Mackenzie has really "well upheld the credit of English medicine abroad".'[98]

However, many people must have regarded this as gloomy in the extreme, for the Crown Prince was soon well enough to make an extended visit to Britain in connection with Victoria's Jubilee celebrations. The *Journal* published a series of optimistic bulletins, announcing in July that Frederick's health was so good that he no longer required a resident physician. But before the month was out renewed growth required further cauterization, notwithstanding which the *Journal* remained entirely sanguine.[99] In September Mackenzie received a knighthood 'in recognition of the great service he has rendered the royal families of England and Germany—and, it may be

[95] E. Longford, *Victoria R.I.* (London: Pan, 1966), pp. 625–6; Sir Morrell Mackenzie, *The Fatal Illness of Frederick the Noble* (London: Sampson Low, 1888), p. 3.

[96] *Journal*, 28 May 1887, 1169.

[97] *Ibid.*

[98] *Ibid.*, 4 June 1887, 1240–1.

[99] *Ibid.*, 11 June 1887, 1288; 18 June 1887, 1345, 1348; 25 June 1887, 1397; 2 July 1887, 31; 9 July 1887, 77; 16 July 1887, 139; 6 Aug. 1887, 319; 15 Oct. 1887, 841; 22 Oct. 1887, 899.

added, the whole of Europe—by his skilful treatment of the Crown Prince'.[100]

With the approach of winter the Crown Prince travelled south to San Remo. From there, in November, the *Journal* received a telegram which was 'by no means calculated to allay the most serious apprehensions'. Another, and this time unquestionably malignant, tumour had been discovered. The *Journal* anticipated further criticism of Mackenzie's treatment and a renewed upsurge of international jealousy. Two weeks later, in a leading article which studiously avoided all mention of the Crown Prince's case, the *Journal* reviewed the success of operations for removal of the larynx. It concluded that 'complete excision for carcinoma . . . is highly unsatisfactory. As a rule it appears to mean death, as an exception it signifies a short but harassed lease of life . . . .'[101] This could leave nobody in doubt that the *Journal* gave its full support to Mackenzie. But in case it did, another column explicitly backed the British surgeon and gave him the freedom of its pages to justify his treatment.[102]

In February 1888 tracheotomy was performed; in March the aged emperor died and Frederick returned to Berlin as his successor. In April he conferred the Hohenzollern Order of the Second Class and Star upon Mackenzie. But the Emperor's pleasure was not shared by all of his subjects. Mackenzie received death threats, became embroiled in an acrimonious public squabble with members of the German medical profession, and instituted libel actions against two newspapers which had accused him of professional incompetence.[103]

When Frederick died in June 1888 the *Journal* defended Mackenzie's treatment and expressed the hope that the last had been heard of the 'unseemly disputes' between the medical advisers.[104] In fact, they had barely started:

> . . . the mutual ill will of the doctors flared into a furious argument, conducted in public, in which medical knowledge, international politics, and professional rivalry were inextricably mingled. With horrified distaste the medical profession watched as accusatory pamphlets and counterblasts were exchanged like blows between the contending factions.[105]

At base the issue was simple. If the larynx had been removed when Mackenzie was first called in, as the German specialists had recommended,

[100] *Ibid.*, 10 Sept. 1887, 605.

[101] *Ibid.*, 12 Nov. 1887, 1065; 19 Nov. 1887, 118–19.

[102] *Ibid.*, 1127–8; 17 Dec. 1887, 1357; see 23 June 1888, 1351–2. Mackenzie's book (note 95) on the case sold nearly 100 000 copies in its first fortnight of issue, but Mackenzie was censured by the Royal College of Physicians for criticizing colleagues and breaking confidences. *Journal*, 3 Nov. 1888, 1030; 9 Feb. 1889, 324.

[103] *Ibid.*, 14 April 1888, 812; 28 April 1888, 919; BMA mss. Hastings Library, Morrell Mackenzie file, M. M. to C. L. Taylor, postmarked May 1888; 'One of the German Secret Union to M.M.', postmarked Nov. 1888.

[104] *Journal*, 23 June 1888, 1343–4.

[105] P. Vaughan, *Doctors' Commons*, p. 140 (note 4).

would Frederick's life have been saved? In deciding against excision, had Mackenzie taken an overly optimistic view of the case, adopted inappropriate treatment, and thereby condemned his patient to premature death? The *Journal* consistently rejected any such suggestions, arguing that in the circumstances Mackenzie's judgement and actions had been exemplary.

On 13 October 1888, under the heading 'The Handwriting of the Dying Emperor', Hart reproduced two short notes written by Frederick shortly before his death. These have been termed 'sensational', but such a description is more appropriate to the controversy they engendered than the information they contained. One, a response to a suggested change of medicine, read: 'The same Hovell just tried. Before Bergmann illtreated me'. Hovell, it should be noted was Mackenzie's English assistant; von Bergmann, Professor of Surgery at the University of Berlin had been one of Frederick's most eminent medical attendants. At most, the note indicates that the patient had more faith in his British than his German doctors. But this was hardly a sensational revelation. The mere fact that Mackenzie had been called in at all indicated a degree of dissatisfaction with the treatment hitherto available. The second note merely expressed sympathy with Hovell over the death of his father, and one wonders why Hart bothered to publish it at all.[106]

Publication of these notes gave rise to a storm of protest. The *Lancet* stated that a

> circumstance much to be regretted in this miserable business is the publication—in a quarter, too, where it might be expected more prudent counsels would have prevailed—of a statement alleged to have been written by the dying Emperor, in which he expressed an unfavourable opinion of the merits of the treatment carried out by one of his medical attendants.

It took the view that Frederick's opinion was valueless and that publication of the facsimiles 'can therefore only have the effect of intensifying yet more the feeling of personal rancour imported into a controversy already sufficiently pronounced, and of rendering more dense the cloud of prejudice'.[107]

One hundred and eighty-six members of the BMA, including many of the leading lights of the profession, signed a memorial deprecating the appearance in the *Journal* of the facsimile of the late emperor's 'script'. They regarded publication

> as a violation of professional confidence, and its appearance in the BRITISH MEDICAL JOURNAL as discreditable to the medical profession of this country. They accordingly request the President and Council to take such immediate action as may be required to clear the Association and profession from the discredit now attaching to them in respect of this matter.[108]

[106] The source of these notes was kept secret, but it is probable that they came from Mackenzie via Charles Taylor, who had been Mackenzie's assistant and then was on the *Journal* staff. See R. S. Stevenson, *Goodbye Harley Street*, p. 87 (note 4).

[107] *Lancet*, 20 Oct. 1888, 778–9.

[108] *Journal*, 1 Dec. 1888, 1244.

At a special meeting held at the Strand office a memorandum drawn up by Hart was read. This explained that the 'script' was merely the exact verbal form of an expression of opinion publicly discussed elsewhere. It was also revealed that Hart had furnished the *Journal* Committee with documentary evidence 'which he considered to afford strong reason for believing that the publication of this opinion did not constitute any breach of confidence'. Nevertheless, Hart also expressed regret that it should have appeared in the *Journal*. The meeting ended with Council passing a resolution deprecating the publication of details in violation of professional confidence and also 'their own regret that, under any circumstances, that document was published'.[109]

Here, however, the matter did not end. One hundred and one of the signatories of the original memorial, at a meeting held on 12 December under the presidency of Sir Joseph Lister, passed two resolutions. One regretted that Council had not gone further in deploring the offence and had done nothing to prevent its repetition. The other called for Council to tender Bergmann 'an adequate apology'. At their meeting in January 1889 Council decided to send Bergmann a copy of their November resolution, but declined to go further, believing that they 'have done everything which was necessary to vindicate the honour of the Association and of the profession'.[110]

At least one member resigned from the BMA because the 'Committee controlling the JOURNAL' took insufficient action: 'If practitioners are to become news and gossip-mongers, there is an end of all confidence between the public and the profession, while for us all personally, there must be an end of self-respect.'[111] But here the controversy over the 'script' came to an end or, more accurately, changed character, for over the next few months a great deal of dissatisfaction was expressed about the general character of the *Journal*. This was surely inspired by a lingering sense of outrage felt by those upset by Hart's conduct in the Morrell Mackenzie affair, for many of those involved in the earlier protests, including Lister, were also to the fore in the new dispute.

On 20 February 1889 one of the *Journal*'s rivals, the *Medical Press and Circular*, published a letter, 'signed by several leading members of the profession', which, while praising the *Journal* as a financial and scientific success, argued that 'the best interests and the honour of the Association would be greatly promoted by a change in the character of the JOURNAL.'[112] Its authors disapproved of the *Journal*'s 'anonymous articles and reviews and multifarious advertisements' which, they claimed, 'are not

[109] *Ibid.*

[110] *Ibid*, 29 Dec. 1888; 19 Jan 1889, 152-3; Sir Rickman John Godlee, *Lord Lister* (Oxford: Clarendon Press, 1924), p. 477. Lister's part in criticizing Hart must have been painful to both men for, as we shall see, a decade earlier Hart had championed Lister and his antiseptic system in the face of fierce criticism.

[111] *Journal*, 2 Feb. 1889, 261.

[112] The names of the signatories were given in the *Journal*, 16 March 1889, 620.

suitable for the organ of our Association, for the sayings and doings of which our members individually are responsible'. They wanted the *Journal* to be a 'faithful exponent' of BMA business and to carry reports of scientific work. Beyond this, they wished all articles, reviews, and notes to be signed by their authors, and also pressed for much stricter control of advertisements. They were prepared to accept the financial loss which the new policy might entail because 'our individual self-respect is a matter of higher moment than flourishing finances.'[113]

The BMA Council regretted that the letter writers had neither seen fit to take their complaints to the Association's *Journal* and Finance Committee nor sought to publish them in the *BMJ*. It rejected their criticisms and suggestions for improvement. In a letter to branch presidents, the President of Council and the Association Treasurer urged them against supporting the dissidents.[114] When the matter was considered by the Association's *Journal* and Finance Committee, it refuted the idea that BMA members were collectively responsible for what appeared in the *Journal*. The true position was that such responsibility had always rested with the editor, subject to the control of Council and the *Journal* Committee. On the proposals that articles should be signed and advertisements vetted, the Committee observed that many *Journal* contributors held high office. Few of those who wrote on matters such as military, naval, Poor Law medicine, and public health would be prepared to continue if they lost their anonymity. On advertising, the Committee found that it was vital to the Association's financial health and performed a useful function for readers. They stated that advertisements were already strictly vetted and sometimes rejected. The Committee made the general point that the *Journal*'s rapidly growing circulation indicated widespread satisfaction with it.[115] The report was received and entered on the minutes, though it was not formally approved by Council, an omission that the dissidents seized upon with alacrity.[116]

At a special meeting the Journal and Finance Committee considered a memorandum from Hart, requesting more frequent communication with Council and the establishment of a Committee of Reference which should meet weekly to assist him with matters relating to *Journal* policy which, hitherto, he had had to decide alone. It is not clear what Hart's motive was in making such a request, but it seems likely that it was an attempt to defuse criticism by spreading formal responsibility for some of the contentious matter which appeared in the *Journal*. It is unlikely that Hart desired to transfer any real power into other hands.

The *Journal* Committee resolved that a Reference Committee be appointed which would meet in the *Journal* offices every Thursday morning. The new committee would take charge of the section of the *Journal* which

113 *Ibid.*
114 *Ibid.*
115 *Ibid.*, 4 May 1889, 1025–6.
116 *Ibid.*, 1 June 1889, 1252.

discussed new inventions and remedies—in other words, that section where accusations of patronage were liable to be made. Proofs of all articles would be forwarded for comments to the committee members. Proposed alterations to these and any questions of policy which arose would then be discussed with the editor at the weekly meeting, which occasion would also provide an opportunity for the General Manager to raise questions about questionable advertisements.

When one sees the duties which were to be undertaken by the new committee, it seems unlikely that busy professional men could have carried them out in full.[117] At first Hart's critics seemed to have been mollified by this new development, though they reserved judgement pending scrutiny of its operation. However, scarcely two months had elapsed before Lister and his colleagues were addressing new complaints to Council:

GENTLEMEN,—Many members of the Association have been much disappointed to find that the hopes which they had been led to entertain of an improvement in the conduct of the JOURNAL have not been fulfilled. So strong is this feeling that a large number of men in influential positions in the profession, warmly attached to the Association, but jealous of its honour and despairing of seeing the improvement they desire, have expressed their determination to resign their membership.

The letter concluded with a request that Council 'take such steps as shall make the JOURNAL in all respects worthy of the Association'.[118] Before Hart published this letter, but after he knew of its existence, he wrote a vigorous defence of the *Journal* and his own part in its success.[119] To the dissidents the President of Council replied that 'you may safely leave the honour of the Association where it has been safely preserved for so many years.'[120] Council and the General Meeting endorsed this response at the BMA meeting at Leeds in August, 1889.[121]

Council attempted to heal the breach by offering a meeting to discuss the matter, but in November the dissidents met and resolved to carry out their threat of resignation. As a result, a total of 67 London members left the Association, though Lister was not among them.[122] In the 1890 Report of Council Hart received enthusiastic backing for his conduct of the *Journal*:

The JOURNAL under the able editorship of Mr. Ernest Hart, continues to increase in utility and popularity. Socially, scientifically and politically it is a great success, and your Council feel that they have much cause to congratulate themselves that it has

[117] As early as 1891 there was a proposal to scrap the Reference Committee, but the Journal and Finance Committee rejected it. BMA mss. MCSC, V, Journal and Finance Committee, 20 Oct. 1891, 1875.

[118] *Journal*, 31 Aug. 1889, 493.

[119] *Ibid.*, 10 Aug. 1889, 321–2.

[120] *Ibid.*

[121] *Ibid.*, 17 Aug. 1889, 381.

[122] *Ibid.*, 25 Jan. 1890, 206; 26 July 1890, 226. The original list contained more names, but some, perhaps including Lister, changed their minds.

taken its position as one of the leading medical journals of the day, and is to be found in circulation over the whole scientific world.[123]

Hart had not only survived once again; he had emerged triumphant.

The end

In 1883, at the age of 48 Hart was diagnosed as suffering from diabetes. According to his *BMJ* obituary, 'from the time that it was discovered . . . till his death, fourteen years later, he always suffered more or less from the dyspeptic and nervous troubles with which that disease torments its victims.'[124] He also suffered from depression and, in 1890 and 1895, experienced severe attacks of pneumonia. In 1886, when he was 50, an acquaintance described him as looking 'old and ill'.[125]

Ill-health prompted many of Hart's frequent visits abroad in the 1880s and 1890s, for he found nothing so beneficial as a sea-journey. Germany, France, Egypt, Gibraltar, Tangiers, Corfu, Madeira, the Canary Islands, India, Burma, the United States, Canada, and the West Indies were all visited in these years, and not merely for holidays. In 1893 he attended and addressed the American Medical Association's conference in Milwaukee. During his North African vacation in the following spring he wrote a series of articles on Tangiers as a health resort, while, on his return journey, he stopped off in Gibraltar, to assist in the formation of a BMA branch, and Paris, where he spoke on cholera. The following year saw him lecturing on public health in the Indian subcontinent. Even during his 1897 visit to the West Indies, in the course of which he was seriously ill, he attended a host of offical functions and produced a series of articles for the *Journal* on the value of the islands as a health resort.[126] Hart's ceaseless activity cannot have improved his health. In India, in 1895, dysentery brought him close to death; during his visit to the West Indies he was a virtual invalid.[127] It may be that Hart's deteriorating health contributed to errors of judgement, for example, over publication of the 'script', and added to the irascibility of an already 'difficult' personality.

In the early 1890s Hart performed much of his editorial work at his Wimpole Street home. In 1896 he sold the London house and much of his Japanese art collection, resolving to live and work entirely in Hertfordshire. During the summer of 1897 he performed most of his editorial work recumbent in his Totteridge garden. His clerk travelled out from London

[123] *Ibid.*

[124] *Ibid.*, 15 Jan. 1898, p. 184. Insulin treatment was not available till the 1920s.

[125] Diary of Jeannette Marshall, 6 March 1886. I am grateful to Zuzanna Shonfield for this reference. See her *The Precariously Privileged. A Professional Family in Victorian London* (Oxford: Oxford University Press, 1987).

[126] *Ibid.*, 27 March 1897, 817–18.

[127] *Journal*, 15 Jan. 1898, 184.

daily to assist him, though until September 1897 Hart continued to meet the Reference Committee once a week in London.[128] It should not be assumed that Hart mellowed and entered into semi-retirement some years before his death. He remained a forceful character who continued to court controversy throughout his last years. Legal actions and the threat of such actions had regularly punctuated Hart's editorship, and continued to occur in the 1890s. Until close to the end he remained very much in charge of the *Journal*. Neither did the *Journal*'s vitality fail as the editor's infirmity increased. Hart was mentally alert till the day he died. Some of the best socio-medical exposées—for example, of massage parlours, opiate abuse, the 'new mesmerism', conditions in Irish workhouses and infirmaries, and the 'barrack life of pauper children'—were published in the mid-1890s. At the same time, the *Journal* published brilliant work on the newly-discovered X-ray.

Despite his removal from London, Hart's health continued to decline. In June 1897 herpetic spots on his right leg and foot ulcerated and became gangrenous; the foot was amputated in September. In October Hart requested leave of absence from the *Journal* in order to convalesce in Madeira.[129] However, he never boarded the *Athenian* to make the voyage, repairing instead to Brighton, where he died on 7 January 1898.

During his lifetime Hart had been a consistent advocate of the then comparatively unusual practice of cremation. One of its foremost advocates, the surgeon Sir Henry Thompson, was a close friend. Together, they had been leading figures in the foundation of the Cremation Society in 1874.[130] After a memorial service in Marylebone Parish Church Hart was himself cremated at Woking. His ashes were interred in the Jewish cemetery at Willesden in north London.

Within days of his death the Journal and Finance Committee recommended that Hart's assistant editor, Dawson Williams, be appointed as his successor, and that Charles Taylor be promoted to the position of assistant. Council duly accepted these recommendations. Neither post was advertised. In a report to Council its president, Robert Saundby, paid tribute to Hart's contribution to the *Journal* and the Association, adding that no one could doubt the great extent to which the *Journal* under Hart had been responsible for the BMA's success. But the ambivalent attitude of the Association towards Hart is perhaps illustrated by its response to Mrs Hart's invitation that it participate in the establishment of a memorial to her late husband. During 1897 Hart had been engaged in the acquisition of land, formerly in the possession of Sir Thomas Spencer Wells, for the extension of Hampstead

[128] *Ibid.*, 185; BMA mss. MCSC, VIII, Journal and Finance Committee, 21 Oct. 1896, 3336. He chaired his last meeting of the Parliamentary Bills Committee on 13 July 1897.

[129] *Ibid.*, VIII, 20 Oct. 1897, 3760–1.

[130] Zachary Cope, *The Versatile Victorian. Being the Life of Sir Henry Thompson, Bt. 1820–1904* (London: Harrey and Blythe, 1951), pp. 121–2, 141.

Heath. Alice Hart saw the completion of this project as a fitting memorial to her husband and invited Saundby to address a meeting to discuss it. Saundby declined to attend, adding somewhat insensitively that he was 'not altogether convinced that such a strictly parochial affair as the extension of Hampstead Heath is one that concerns anyone but the Hampstead ratepayers, or at most the citizens of greater London'. In reply, Mrs Hart thanked Saundby for his 'frank expression of opinion'. Council referred the question of a memorial to the Journal and Finance Committee. The BMA's ultimate decision was to establish 'The Ernest Hart Memorial Scholarship for Preventive Medicine', tenable for a period of two years and worth £100 p.a.[131]

[131] BMA mss. MCSC, VIII, Journal and Finance Committee, 20 April 1898, 3801–2; *Journal*, 16 July 1898, 197.

5
Campaigns and controversies

Many social questions have a medical dimension, and one of the features of Ernest Hart's *BMJ* was the amount of attention it paid to social medicine. Between the late 1860s and the end of the century few subjects of socio-medical importance escaped the penetrating gaze of Hart and his contributors. Furthermore, the *Journal* sought not only to inform its readers of developments relating to these subjects but often to influence those developments or to initiate public debate. Four topics in which the *Journal* took a particularly strong interest were the Contagious Diseases Acts, baby farming, compulsory vaccination, and vivisection.

The Contagious Diseases Acts

Historians have recently devoted much attention to the Contagious Diseases (CD) Acts, which regulated prostitution in the so-called 'garrison towns'. These Acts have been seen as an example of class and gender domination, of the double standards of Victorian society, of the growing regulatory power of the State, and of the activities of an interest group, as well as a catalyst of the women's movement.[1] Less notice has been taken of the role of the medical profession in making, extending, and repealing the Acts. Yet medical men played a notable part in these activities, and between 1864 and 1886 the *BMJ* carried many articles and expressed firm opinions on the Acts.

The Contagious Diseases Act, 1864, which was passed as a temporary measure, provided for the medical inspection of prostitutes in 11 towns in southern England and Ireland which contained a large military or naval presence. Its main objective was to control the spread of venereal disease in the armed forces by removing infected prostitutes from circulation. Doctors were responsible for examining 'common prostitutes' brought to them by the police, diagnosing the presence of disease, and treating infected women in the so-called lock hospitals in which they could be interned for up to three months.

The passage of the Act attracted comparatively little attention. With its euphemistic title it was rushed into law virtually unknown to the general public. However, the *Journal*, then edited by Markham, drew attention to the

[1] See in particular, J. Walkowitz, *Prostitution and Victorian Society* (Cambridge: Cambridge University Press, 1980); Paul McHugh, *Prostitution and Victorian Social Reform* (London: Croom Helm, 1980).

'The Day's Doings.' Glasgow Police raid brothel, 1871. Source: Mary Evans Picture Library.

bill soon after it was brought before Parliament. It was highly critical of a measure which allowed the police to arrest any woman on suspicion that she was suffering from venereal disease. A leading article described it as the most 'iniquitous interference with the liberty of the subject' for over 200 years.[2] The *Journal*, however, made little comment on the extension of the Act, in 1866, by the terms of which Windsor was added to the list of garrison towns, and known prostitutes became subject to fortnightly medical examination.

Opponents of the CD Acts condemned State endorsement of vice, interference with civil liberty, and the harsh treatment of women. They also questioned the statistical evidence that the Acts were achieving anything. Supporters, on the other hand, pointed to fewer cases of venereal disease, fewer prostitutes in the regulated areas, improved public order on the streets, and the reform of 'fallen women'. On the basis of these alleged successes, doctors and others began to campaign in 1867 for extension of the Acts to all large towns and sea ports.

This movement began with the Harveian Society, of which Hart was to be president in 1868, and quickly led to the formation of the Association for Promoting the Extension of the Contagious Diseases Act of 1866 to the

[2] *Journal*, 9 July 1864, 42; see 23 July 1864, 94. In 1870, when Hutchinson was editor, a reference to the CD Acts declared that 'we do not fear for the "liberty of the subject" '. *Ibid.*, 9 April, 365.

Civilian Population (CDAA).[3] This body 'depended heavily on the medical press . . . to promote its cause'.[4] The *Journal*'s reports of these developments made it clear where its sympathies lay, for they described the Association's objectives as 'purely sanitary, and as such they cannot fail to be commended by everyone who is at all aware to what extent the best blood and fibre of this country is being destroyed by a most pernicious disease'. On the other hand, the *Journal* saw opponents of the Acts as 'friends of contagion'.[5]

In 1867–8 the *Journal* carried regular reports on the value of the Acts, including a series of articles by the surgeon Berkeley Hill, who was the CDAA's secretary. Hart and Hill were then close friends; in 1870 they were to visit France together and collaborate on a paper arising out of their experiences.[6] In 1868 they undertook a systematic study 'of the extent to which the public women of London are afflicted with contagious disease, and what means of cure are open to them; also, whether it would be practicable to apply to them the regulations that control the common prostitutes of garrison towns'. Hill published an account of their findings in the *Journal.* Hart helped Hill draw up a memorial calling for extension of the Acts, which was sent to the President of the Privy Council and published as a parliamentary paper.[7]

Although, in 1868, a select committee of the House of Lords supported the case for extension, the campaign was dealt a blow by a negative report from the Medical Officer of the Privy Council, John Simon. A select committee of the House of Commons, in 1869, proposed extension to five more garrison towns and various changes in the existing law, including a maximum period of internment of nine months rather than three, the moral and religious instruction of women so interned, permanent application of the Acts, and extension of their jurisdiction to a 10-mile radius of each regulated town. These changes were incorporated in the last of the CD Acts, that of 1869. But the terms of this measure fell well short of the extensionists' demand that the Acts should operate in non-garrison towns.[8] Nevertheless, the passing of the Act represented a high-water mark for supporters of the Acts, because no

[3] The Harveian Society was founded in 1831. Its founders were concerned to advance medical knowledge and the status of medicine. See Sir D'Arcy Power (ed.), *British Medical Societies* (London: Medical Press and Circular, 1939), p. 91.

[4] J. Walkowitz, *Prostitution and Victorian Society*, p. 80 (note 1). Walkowitz singles out the *Lancet*, but gives more references from the *BMJ*. On the extensionist movement see P. McHugh, *Prostitution and Victorian Social Reform*, pp. 44–5 (note 1).

[5] *Journal*, 6 July 1867, 11; 20 July 1867, 47; 12 Aug. 1871, 184; J. Walkowitz, *Prostitution and Victorian Society*, p. 79 (note 1).

[6] This was 'Surgical Visit to the Seat of the [Franco-Prussian] War'. *Journal*, 15 Oct. 1870, 420. In 1888 Hill was among those who criticized Hart for publishing Emperor Frederick's 'script'. See *ibid.*, 1 Dec. 1888, 1244.

[7] *Ibid.*, 16 May 1868, 486; 23 May 1868, 505; *Parliamentary Papers* (1867–8) **LV**: 421; Frank Mort, *Dangerous Sexualities: Medico-Moral Politics in England Since 1830* (London: Routledge and Kegan Paul, 1987), p. 76.

[8] J. Walkowitz, *Prostitution and Victorian Society*, p. 86 (note 1).

further amendments were made; moreover, 1869 saw the mobilization of a movement that led to the suspension and repeal of the Acts.

In early 1870 the repeal movement, of which Josephine Butler and James Stansfield MP were two leading members, began to gather strength at an astonishing pace. Repeal societies and ladies' committees sprang up all over the country while, in March, a weekly journal, *Shield*, was launched. A repeal bill was brought before Parliament as early as April. In the same month Sir Henry Storks put himself forward for election to Parliament in the Newark by-election. As a staunch supporter of the CD Acts, he attracted the full attentions of the opposition movement. On the day of the election he withdrew, and an abolitionist was elected. The *Journal* saw this as 'not a little' ominous and, correctly, predicted that the prospects for extending the Acts had been reduced to zero, for MPs would not court unpopularity by expressing agreement with the objectives of the CD Acts. Consequently, 'to prevent the repeal of the present Act will probably be as much as it is possible to do for the present.'[9] But under Hutchinson's editorship the *Journal* was, in any case, ambivalent about the value of the Acts. It recognized that as long as most soldiers and sailors were prohibited from marrying, fornication and venereal disease were inevitable. It followed that there was a public health problem which required tackling. On the other hand, if illicit sexual intercourse was rendered safer (but not risk free), the incidence of venereal disease could be expected to increase. The danger was that 'there may be no gain as regards the sum total of syphylitic misery. We may find that we have irretrievably lost in morality and gained not at all in health'.[10]

In May 1870, during the debate on the repeal bill, the government announced its willingness to set up a Royal Commission to examine the administration and operation of the Acts. The *Journal*, in a leading article which may have been written by Hart, welcomed this development as a means of allaying public 'fears and doubts' and of terminating the prevailing 'unpleasant and mischievous agitation'.[11] When, in the following year, the Royal Commission reported, it produced no clear recommendations, but, in addition to several minority reports, a main 'report so anodyne that both sides could use it to support its contentions'.[12] Its main recommendations were for abandoning periodic examination and strengthening the powers of the authorities to detain prostitutes in hospitals and of the police to attack prostitution. Paul McHugh states that 'nobody could be satisfied with this indecision', but the *Journal*, presumably because the report proposed no serious interference with the legislation, termed it 'moderate, sensible and

[9] *Journal*, 9 April 1870, 365.

[10] *Ibid.*, 18 June 1870, 633.

[11] *Ibid.*, 28 May 1870, 553. This and other articles in the office set of *Journal*s are initialled 'EH'.

[12] P. McHugh, *Prostitution and Victorian Social Reform*, p. 65 (note 1). See *Parliamentary Papers* (1871) **XIX**: pp. 1–27.

deliberate'. Thereafter, it maintained a steady stream of propaganda in favour of the Acts and against those who pursued a 'fanatical crusade' in favour of a 'free trade in contagion'.[13]

In conducting his campaign in support of the Acts, Hart showed none of the doubts of Markham or the ambivalence of Hutchinson, but only an unquestioning belief in his case. This is well illustrated in an 1875 leading article dealing with the Metropolitan Police report on the working of the CD Acts in 1874. The report, the *Journal* suggested,

> proves indisputably that these Acts, of which the main object is to restrain the spread of disease, are effectual instruments not merely for improving public decency, but for repressing vice and immorality among the reckless and ignorant, by removing temptation, and by helping those who have fallen to regain steady habits and a respectable position.[14]

At the end of the 1870s, after 10 years of activity, supporters of the CD Acts seemed to have withstood the best efforts of the abolitionists, for 'the repeal movement was stagnating'.[15] But in 1879 the government appointed a select committee of inquiry into the working of the Acts. This was re-appointed for subsequent parliamentary sessions, and sat for a total of four years. As important as this appointment was the result of the 1880 General Election. This brought Gladstone back into office as the prime minister of a Liberal government that was sympathetic towards moral reform in general and repeal of the CD Acts in particular. Moreover, many of the government's backbench supporters had been assiduously wooed by the repealers.

When the select committee reported, in August 1882, it recommended neither extension nor repeal of the Acts. The *Journal* expressed disappointment that the committee proposed to retain the existing regulations without recommending their application to every military station: 'practical reformers will altogether fail to understand the logic of maintaining the Acts because of their demonstrated utility, and at the same time consenting to paralyse their efficiency.'[16] But this disappointment was as nothing compared with that of the following April when the parliamentary leader of the abolitionists, James Stansfield, gained a Commons majority of 72 for his motion condemning the compulsory examination of women under the CD Acts. The compulsory principle had been upheld by the select committee; it was, in fact, at the heart of the regulatory system. Without it there could be no system. The *Journal* predicted dire consequences, including the return of juvenile prostitution, rampant soliciting on the streets, and the downfall of many reformed prostitutes in the garrison towns. All this it characterized as

[13] P. McHugh, *Prostitution and Victorian Social Reform*, p. 66 (note 1); *Journal*, 29 July 1871, 129; 18 May 1872, 529–30.

[14] *Ibid.*, 5 June 1875, 748.

[15] P. McHugh, *Prostitution and Victorian Social Reform*, p. 203 (note 1).

[16] *Journal*, 6 Jan. 1883, 26.

'the sacrifice of the innocent to the ignorant sentimentality of the friends of free trade in disease'.[17] The government immediately moved to suspend the Acts, which, although not formally repealed till 1886, were now, for all practical purposes, dead.

The contagious diseases question raised issues of public health and morality. Under Hart the *Journal*, in common with most medical opinion, supported the Acts on sanitary grounds. It was defeated by the full strength of Victorian morality. Josephine Butler disliked men doctors, and it has been observed that the repeal campaign represented 'part of a libertarian reaction against medical expertise'.[18] In claiming a monopoly of wisdom, not only on the CD Acts but also on compulsory vaccination and other subjects, the medical profession helped to stir up opposition. The regulators have also been accused of perpetuating double standards and of discriminating against women. But, stripped of their moral overtones, the CD Acts were not unlike the food adulteration acts. In both cases the principle of *caveat emptor* was replaced by a regulatory code which sought to protect consumers by imposing obligations and restrictions on the suppliers of goods and services, in the one case with widespread approval, in the other with great public disapproval. But though the principles behind these two pieces of legislation may have been similar, for most Victorians prostitution and venereal disease could not be viewed in morally neutral terms. This was the error of those who championed the CD Acts. In the last analysis it was the reason why the legislation was lost.

Baby farming

Through his activities in the Harveian Society Hart was already associated with the campaign against baby farming when he took over as editor of the *BMJ*, for in May 1866 John Brendon Curgenven, then the society's honorary secretary, proposed that it should look into the social aspects of child murder. His fellow-members responded with enthusiasm, and a committee, on which Hart sat, was appointed to investigate the matter.[19]

Baby farming comprised the practice of taking in infants to nurse or rear in exchange for payment. It could entail the systematic neglect, mistreatment,

[17] *Ibid.*, 28 April 1883, 825. The *Lancet* was similarly disturbed. See 17 March 1883, 486; 4 Aug. 1883, 192. See F. Mort, *Dangerous Sexualities: Medico-Moral Politics in England since 1830*, p. 106 (note 7).

[18] P. McHugh, *Prostitution and Victorian Social Reform*, p. 25 (note 1).

[19] *Parliamentary Papers* (1871) **VII**: Select Committee on the Protection of Infant Life, Evidence, p. 627; George K. Behlmer, *Child Abuse and Moral Reform in England 1870–1908* (Stanford: Stanford University Press, 1982), p. 22; Ivy Pinchbeck and Margaret Hewitt, *Children in English Society* (London: Routledge, 1973), p. 616. Curgenven was honorary secretary of the CDAA. Another member of the committee was Charles Drysdale, who later became one of the medical opponents of the CD Acts. P. McHugh, *Prostitution and Victorian Social Reform*, pp. 44–5 (note 1).

and sometimes murder of unwanted children placed with professional foster parents, many of whom were concerned more with financial gain than with providing proper care for their charges. Although baby farming was not synonymous with infanticide, it was often 'an overt means of rapidly disposing of babies, whose presence in the world was inconvenient to their parents'.[20]

Infanticide came to public attention in the 1860s, when newspapers were full of reports of dead babies being dumped in ponds, canals, and privies or secreted under floorboards. Then, in 1865, came the sensational and well-publicized trial of Charlotte Winsor. Winsor, who took in illegitimate children at 3 shillings per week, also 'put them away', that is, killed them, for fees ranging between £3 and £5. She was convicted of murdering an infant who had been found wrapped in newspaper at the side of a Devonshire road.[21]

The Harveian Society's infanticide committee met regularly during the second half of 1866. It gathered a substantial amount of evidence, on the basis of which it compiled 20 recommendations for reform. But, although the society gained an interview with the Home Secretary in January 1867, it secured no commitment to reform from a government preoccupied with the franchise question.[22] Meanwhile, of course, Hart had succeeded to the editorship of the *BMJ*, thereby acquiring a platform from which to argue the case for reform. Up to this point 'the allegations of criminality associated with baby-farming were vague and unsubstantiated. More than anyone else the person responsible for making tangible these hazy suspicions of foul play was Ernest Hart . . . .'[23]

In common with other newspapers and periodicals, the *Journal* had woken up to the problem of infanticide during the 1860s. In 1865 it carried, among other stories, John Simon's remarks about 'some country districts of England where child killing by opium is monstrous'. In the following year it had reported the work of the Harveian Society. But the space given to the subject greatly increased with Hart's appointment. The second issue for which he was responsible included the address of W. Tyler Smith, president of the Harveian Society, on 'Infanticide and Excessive Infant Mortality', which he had delivered to the society's annual meeting. In October Hart published his first baby farming story—an account of an inquest which revealed that the four children of a hairdresser's wife had died 'whilst out at nurse'.[24]

[20] *Journal*, 15 Oct. 1870, 415–16. Ann R. Higginbotham, '"Sin of the Age": Infanticide and Illegitimacy in Victorian London', *Victorian Studies* (1989) **32**: 319–38.

[21] G. K. Behlmer, *Child Abuse and Moral Reform in England 1870–1908*, pp. 20–2 (note 19).

[22] *Parliamentary Papers* **VII**: (1871), S. C. on Infant Life, Evidence, pp. 627–8.

[23] G. K. Behlmer, *Child Abuse and Moral Reform in England 1870–1908*, pp. 25 (note 19).

[24] *Journal*, 5 Aug. 1865, 131; 12 Jan. 1867, 21–5; 19 Oct. 1867, 343.

In December Hart published the first of his many leading articles on baby farming. In this he re-stated the recommendations of the Harveian Society's report and expressed the wish that the Home Secretary would give attention to the question.[25] But Hart was not content to remain merely an observer and commentator. In January 1868 he embarked on a campaign to identify, track down, and expose individual baby farmers. His object was less to bring retribution upon the guilty than to create a wave of public indignation that would compel government interest and action. In this he was triumphantly successful, providing an instructive example of the constructive power of the press.

Hart's first step was to inspect registers of births and deaths in order to pinpoint houses in which a large number of infants had died. But because registration of births, unlike deaths, was not compulsory, he had to try a different tack. With his assistant, Dr Alfred Wiltshire, he inserted advertisements in the press, including the *Clerkenwell News*, a newspaper notorious for its baby farming advertisements, in which he masqueraded as a father-to-be and offered a fee for the adoption of a child. Within a week he had received 333 written replies and several personal applications. Wiltshire then followed up many of these with personal visits to meet 'nurses', inspect premises, and inquire into the precise nature of the services offered. It emerged that while 'there are a large class who take charge of infants with really good intentions' (though good intentions were not necessarily synonymous with good practice), there were many cases of systematic mistreatment. In one house a 'Mrs____' was minding seven infants. She would adopt them for £10 or £15 down or take them on a weekly basis at 4s 6d or 5s. Wiltshire found these children to be neglected, malnourished, and living in conditions of appalling squalor. Further inquiry revealed that during the preceding two years Mrs____ had registered the deaths of seven children, none of whom had survived beyond 12 months.[26]

These and other revelations prompted questions in Parliament, one of which was posed by Lord Shaftesbury on Hart's behalf.[27] The government's view was that, though baby farming might be a disgrace, if crimes were being committed it was for the police rather than government to take action. The Duke of Marlborough, who answered Shaftesbury, observed that there was no need for a government inquiry since the matter had already been 'thoroughly exposed in the able papers in the British Medical Journal'. Nevertheless, he acknowledged that the subject was of great importance and

[25] *Ibid.*, 21 Dec. 1867, 570.

[26] *Ibid.*, 28 March 1868, 301–2. This account was included in the last of a series of articles on baby farming and baby murder. See 25 Jan. 1868, 75; 8 Feb. 1868, 127; 22 Feb. 1868, 175; 29 Feb. 1868, 197; 21 March 1868, 276. Hart gave an account of his inquiry to the Select Committee in 1871. See *Parliamentary Papers* (1871) **VII**, Select Committee on the Protection of Infant Life, pp. 628–30.

[27] 3 *Hansard*, 90 (12 March 1868), col. 1450; 193 (28 July 1868), cols. 1896–7.

that it might be possible to put an end to abuses by licensing and inspecting the people or premises concerned. The government, the Duke indicated, would consider the matter during the summer recess with a view to drawing up a bill.[28]

The *Journal* was well satisfied with the progress it had achieved:

> We publish, with great gratification, this record of the public usefulness of our inquiries into the subject of baby-farming. Not only has the object, which we announced at the outset, of invoking the attention and intervention of the Government to restrict this system of organised murder, been realised; but the statement of the Duke of Marlborough indicates that the Government are likely, in the legislative measure which they propose to base upon our papers, to adopt precisely the suggestions which we made as to the remedies for the evil.[29]

This satisfactory rate of progress was, however, not maintained. As Hart later said, the subject of baby farming 'went to sleep' between autumn 1868 and summer 1870.[30] There were two reasons for this. First, the General Election of November 1868 brought the defeat of Disraeli's Conservative government and the election of the Liberals under Gladstone. Although Gladstone's administration was neither more nor less committed to social reform than its predecessor, it was not bound by the promises given by the Duke of Marlborough. Moreover, it became absorbed by two issues: Ireland and elementary education. Second, Hart's 'missing year' (1869–70) meant that baby farming stopped getting the amount of coverage in the *BMJ* that had prevailed in 1868.

The subject was resurrected in June 1870 with the discovery in Brixton of the decomposed bodies of two infants. Police inquiries connected these finds, and others made in neighbouring streets, to the premises of Margaret Waters and her sister, Sarah Ellis. In their house were found 11 drugged and starving infants, five of whom shortly died.[31] In due course Waters was convicted of murder and hanged. The Waters case gave the *Journal* an opportunity to return to the subject of baby farming. It quickly recognized that the case would do much to advance the chances of legislation.[32] In two articles that probably were written by Ernest Hart, it commented on the Brixton deaths and went on to express regret that its 1868 exposés had not led to government action. Thereafter it maintained the pressure for compulsory registration of

[28] *Ibid.*; *Journal*, 1 Aug. 1868, 121; I. Pinchbeck and M. Hewitt, *Children in English Society*, p. 616 (note 19).

[29] *Journal*, 1 Aug. 1868, 121.

[30] *Parliamentary Papers* (1871) **VII**, Select Committee on the Protection of Infant Life, p. 631.

[31] On the connection between baby farming, infant mortality, and child doping see Virginia Berridge and Griffith Edwards, *Opium and the People. Opiate Use in Nineteenth Century England* (London: Yale University Press, 1987 edn), pp. 97–105.

[32] G. K. Behlmer, *Child Abuse and Moral Reform in England 1870–1908*, pp. 28–9 (note 19); *Journal*, 9 July 1870, 44; 1 Oct. 1870, 362–3; 15 Oct. 1870, 415–16.

births, including of stillbirths, registration of baby minders, and the regulation of adoption.[33]

In October Curgenven, W. T. Charley, Conservative MP for Salford, and others, including Hart, formed the Infant Life Protection Society (ILPS).[34] In the following month Hart was a member of an ILPS deputation which laid before the Home Secretary, Henry Bruce, a draft bill for the prevention of baby farming. Its principal objectives were those for which the *Journal* had been pressing since 1868.[35] In January 1871 Hart and Charley met George Goschen, President of the Poor Law Board, in order to argue the case for the bill, which was introduced in the Commons in February. In April Hart was part of another ILPS deputation to the Poor Law Board, the presidency of which had passed to James Stansfield. Both Bruce and Goschen had expressed support for the proposed reforms, but Stansfield harboured doubts about getting the bill through Parliament. He persuaded the delegation to agree to suspension of the bill and the appointment of a select committee of inquiry.

The *Journal* saw this solution as 'the best which can be desired. It is possible that such an inquiry may lead to alterations in the bastardy laws, and so go to the root of the evil, of which unregulated baby-farming is one of the branches.'[36] In taking this line the *Journal* allied itself less with the bill's promoters, and more with the views of the National Society for Women's Suffrage (NSWS) whose leader, Lydia Becker, criticized the bill precisely because it failed to tackle the root causes of baby farming, namely, inequitable bastardy laws, the social stigma of illegitimacy, and ignorance of child-rearing.[37] However, the NSWS was also concerned that the bill gave men powers to dictate on what it saw as women's business and also that it threatened to extend the power of the State. There is no evidence that the *Journal* shared the first of these worries; as regards the second, Hart's *Journal* was a consistent advocate of measures that eroded the voluntary principle and enlarged the role of the State in medico-social questions.

According to one commentator, the appointment of the select committee benefited the reformers because it 'gave the cause a national forum'.[38] The

[33] *Ibid.*, 18 June 1870, 633; 25 June 1870, 657; 2 July 1870, 15; 9 July 1870, 44; 15 Oct. 1870, 415–6. In three letters to the *Pall Mall Gazette*, Hart reviewed the findings of his earlier inquiry and repeated his suggestions for reform. *Parliamentary Papers* (1871) **VII**, Select Committee on the Protection of Infant Life, p. 631.

[34] *Journal*, 22 Oct. 1870, 443; I. Pinchbeck and M. Hewitt, *Children in English Society*, p. 617 (note 19).

[35] *Journal*, 12 Nov. 1870, 534.

[36] *Ibid.*, 21 Jan. 1871, 76; 11 Feb. 1871, 150; 8 April 1871, 376.

[37] I. Pinchbeck and M. Hewitt, *Children in English Society*, p. 617 (note 19). The position of the emergent women's movement is well discussed by G. K. Behlmer, *Child Abuse and Moral Reform in England 1870–1908*, pp. 33–5 (note 19). The relationship between child neglect and bastardy law is discussed in Lionel Rose, *Massacre of the Innocents: Infanticide in Britain 1800–1939* (London: Routledge and Kegan Paul, 1986). See also U. R. Q. Henriques, 'Bastardy and the New Poor Law', *Past and Present* (1967) **37**: 103–29.

[38] G. K. Behlmer, *Child Abuse and Moral Reform in England 1870–1908*, p. 36 (note 19).

Committee called Hart as its first witness and Alfred Wiltshire as its second. Hart was asked mainly about his 1868 inquiry and his ideas for reform.[39] When the Committee reported in July its main recommendations were for compulsory registration of births, compulsory registration of private houses used as lying-in establishments, and registration of baby minders. The *Journal* made no comment, but the ILPS quickly moved to prepare a bill based on the select committee's proposals.[40] In order to minimize opposition the bill was watered down more than its promoters would have wished. For example, minders who took in single children would not be obliged to register. The *Journal* recognized the absence of 'effective inspection clauses, which are undoubtedly necessary for the efficient working of the Bill'.[41]

As it reached the Statute Book the Act provided that any person, excluding relatives, guardians, and certain others, who took in more than one infant under the age of 12 months for longer than 24 hours had to register with their local authority. Authorities could refuse to register unsuitable premises and could impose a limit on the number of infants taken in by any one individual. Minders were required to keep records of where their charges came from and to whom they were discharged. Infant deaths had to be reported directly to a coroner.[42]

In his first report as chairman of the BMA's Parliamentary Bills Committee, to which position he was appointed in 1872, Hart expressed satisfaction with the new legislation which, he affirmed, was 'mainly founded upon the inquiries instituted by the BRITISH MEDICAL JOURNAL, and upon the subsequent efforts of the editor and Mr. J. Brendon Curgenven'. It would, he believed, be 'most useful' in affording 'medical men the opportunity of interfering successfully to save life, to avert disease, and to arrest crime in a large class of cases in which they have hitherto been helpless and distressed spectators of excessive mortality and scarcely cloaked wrong-doing'.[43] In the event this proved an overly optimistic assessment.

The Infant Life Protection Act, 1872, has been called 'a resounding failure', and the *BMJ* accused of 'premature optimism' in suggesting, in 1876, that the Act had ended the practice of baby farming.[44] Although it is true that the Act failed to deliver what had been hoped of it, only a selective reading of the evidence can support the claim that the *BMJ* was blind to its shortcomings. The *Journal* recognized in March 1872 the lack of appropriate inspection clauses. Occasionally the *Journal* praised the Act, but it often

[39] *Parliamentary Papers* (1871) **VII**: Select Committee on the Protection of Infant Life, pp. 627–41.

[40] *Journal*, 20 Jan. 1872, 76.

[41] *Ibid.*, 9 March 1872, 272.

[42] *Infant Life Protection Act, 1872*, 35 & 36 Vict. c. 38.

[43] *Journal*, 17 Aug. 1872, 191.

[44] G. K. Behlmer, *Child Abuse and Moral Reform in England 1870–1908*, pp. 38–9 (note 19). On the shortcomings of the Act see I. Pinchbeck and M. Hewitt, *Children in English Society*, p. 597 (note 19).

acknowledged its weaknesses, attributing these to the compromises struck during the parliamentary process. The result, as a leading article put it in 1875, was that, though the Act established the principle of state protection of infants, 'the *application* of the principle was of the most limited character.'[45]

In fact, the '1872 Act was constantly sniped at by the *British Medical Journal* which in the late 1870s was regularly reporting inquests on infants from unregistered baby farms.'[46] As time passed the *Journal*'s dissatisfaction increased. By 1879 it was calling for 'stringent amendments' of the Act, including its application to older children and the registration and inspection of houses where even an individual child was taken in to nurse by those who were unrelated to it.[47] In the following year Hart was one of a deputation which met Disraeli's Home Secretary, Cross, and, after the General Election, Sir William Harcourt.[48] But at this stage the government took no action. The *Journal* maintained intermittent though unavailing calls for reform throughout the 1880s and early 1890s. Despite the breaking of further scandals in 1888, which made additional legislation a real possibility, no amendment of the law ensued.[49]

In 1896, the year which saw the trial and execution of Mrs Dyer of Reading, a baby minder who strangled her charges and threw them in the Thames, the *Journal* undertook a second investigation and published a six-part series of reports on 'baby farming and its evils'.[50] This was followed by the passing of the Infant Life Protection Act, 1897, which, though still exempting the 'one-child' minder, raised the age of protection to five years. But the new Act, about which the *Journal* was less than enthusiastic, was the result of 'eight years of sustained reform agitation', in which the NSPCC (founded in 1889) loomed large, rather than of *BMJ* investigations.[51] By the 1890s leadership of the now 'gigantic' child protection movement had passed to other hands. But Hart and the *Journal* continued to play an influential role. For example, in the 1890s the *Journal* took up the question of conditions and educational standards in Poor Law 'barrack schools' and argued successfully for the establishment of a government inquiry.[52]

The *BMJ*'s greatest contribution to the child protection movement was its

[45] *Journal*, 16 Jan. 1875, 84–5.

[46] L. Rose, *Massacre of the Innocents: Infanticide in Britain 1800–1939*, p. 111 (note 37).

[47] *Journal*, 27 Sept. 1879, 511; see 10 May 1879, 715; 20 Sept. 1879, 469; 14 Feb. 1880, 256; 31 July 1880, 175; 12 March 1881, 400.

[48] *Ibid.*, 1 May 1880, 666–7; 31 July, 1880, 175; 21 Aug. 1880, 295.

[49] *Ibid.*, 13 Oct. 1888, 825–6, 852. A government bill was prepared and a select committee sat in 1890. L. Rose, *Massacre of the Innocents: Infanticide in Britain 1800–1939*, p. 159 (note 37).

[50] *Journal*, 22 Aug. 1896, 463; I. Pinchbeck and M. Hewitt, *Children in English Society*, pp. 597, 620 (note 19).

[51] *Journal*, 1 Oct. 1898, 1017; G. K. Behlmer, *Child Abuse and Moral Reform in England 1870–1908*, pp. 156–7 (note 19); L. Rose, *Massacre of the Innocents: Infanticide in Britain 1800–1939*, pp. 160–1 (note 37).

[52] G. K. Behlmer, *Child Abuse and Moral Reform in England 1870–1908*, p. 203 (note 19).

exposure in 1868 of the baby farming scandal. The *Journal* did not single-handedly cause the Infant Life Protection Act to be passed, but it undoubtedly exerted a powerful influence. On one level it can be argued that its revelations achieved comparatively little of a practical nature since the 1872 Act failed to put an end to baby farming abuses. But this is too narrow a view. Although it did not discover baby farming, the *Journal* was instrumental in bringing it to public attention; in so doing it gave impetus to the development of a child protection movement concerned not only with baby farming but with the whole subject of child abuse. This was no mean achievement for a weekly periodical.

Compulsory vaccination

Vaccination was an aspect of medicine in which the State played an important role from an early date. As noted in Chapter 3, by 1853 vaccination had become, in principle, if not in practice, free, non-pauperizing, and compulsory. In the 1860s, legislation introduced the machinery for enforcement, which sought to overrule parental choice and make compulsion a reality. But this led to a backlash of opinion against the destruction of individual rights, with the ultimate result that the compulsory principle perished. The *Journal* was at the very least an interested observer of all these developments, while Ernest Hart was an ardent supporter of compulsory vaccination. As the proposer of an Animal Vaccine Establishment to supply safer and more readily obtainable calf lymph to take the place of 'arm to arm' vaccination, he was also actively concerned with the question.[53] Hart's commitment to compulsory vaccination, along with his advocacy of vivisection, did much to deny him election to Parliament in 1885.[54]

The *Journal* had enthused over the arrival of free vaccination in 1840, describing it as 'the most beneficial legislation' ever secured by the medical profession.[55] But the results were not as impressive as this statement might suggest. The incidence of vaccination varied from place to place and, though deaths from smallpox declined, they still occurred at a rate of around 5000 a year.[56] In the early 1850s the Epidemiological Society of London recom-

[53] *Journal*, 29 Nov. 1879, 843–52; 27 Dec. 1879, 1036–41; 30 July 1887, 246–7; 22 Aug. 1896, 454; 19 June 1897, 1644.

[54] R. M. MacLeod, 'Law, Medicine and Public Opinion: The Resistance to Compulsory Health Legislation 1870–1907', *Public Law* (1967) 196; Dorothy Porter and Roy Porter, 'The Politics of Prevention: Anti-Vaccinationism and Public Health in Nineteenth Century England', *Medical History* (1988) **32**: 231–52; *East London Observer* 28 Nov. 1885. Hart's pamphlet, 'The Truth About Vaccination', 'fully set out . . . the advantages of compulsory vaccination'. *Journal*, 3 July 1880, 1.

[55] R. J. Lambert, 'A Victorian National Health Service: State Vaccination 1855–71', *Historical Journal* (1962) V: 2; *Journal* 3 July 1880, 1; 19 June 1897, 1642–3.

[56] R. J. Lambert, *Sir John Simon 1816–1904 and English Social Administration* (London: Macgibbon and Key, 1963), pp. 252–3.

1873

HIGH LIFE IN THE COUNTRY

Doctor : 'I AM PLEASED TO SAY, MRS. FITZBROWNE, THAT I SHALL BE ABLE TO VACCINATE YOUR BABY FROM A VERY HEALTHY CHILD OF YOUR NEIGHBOUR, MRS. JONES——'

Mrs. Fitzbrowne : 'OH, DEAR, DOCTOR! I COULD NOT PERMIT THAT. WE DO NOT CARE TO BE MIXED UP WITH THE JONESES IN ANY WAY.'

High Life in the Country: from *Mr Punch Among the Doctors*. Source: Bodleian Library, Oxford.

mended compulsory infant vaccination with a central medical administration to register vaccinations and prosecute defaulters. Lord Lyttelton's 1853 Act gave effect to the compulsory principle, but the *Journal*, though recognizing that the existing law left much to be desired, questioned the need to 'enforce by legal compulsion that which it ought to offer as a boon'.[57]

In the event the principle of compulsion had little practical impact for some time owing to the absence of means to enforce it. Although this was provided by an Act of 1861, Lord Chief Justice Cockburn's judgement in *Pilcher* v. *Stafford* that parents could not be convicted a second time for failing to have a child vaccinated meant that continuous avoidance could not be repeatedly and effectively penalized. The result, as the *Journal* later recalled, was that compulsion was 'imperfect' and 'as regards a great part of the kingdom, illusory'.[58]

This was the position when Hart joined the *Journal*. Once editor he immediately nailed his colours to the mast. One of his first leading articles, discussing the onset of London's latest smallpox epidemic, condemned the 1853 Act as a failure and regretted parents' 'criminal neglect' of vaccination.

[57] *Ibid.*; *Journal*, 25 March 1853, 248–9; 15 April 1853, 313.

[58] Pilcher *v*. Stafford. Best and Smith Queen's Bench Reports (1864), 775; *Journal*, 3 July 1880, 3; R. J. Lambert, Sir John Simon, p. 393 (note 56).

It pointed out the need for new law and administration if the 'silent enemy to mankind' were to be overcome.[59] Within months the Vaccination Act, 1867, was law. This introduced no new principles but sought to secure the quality of vaccination and, more controversially, to ensure observance of the law, which was to be achieved largely through the 'astounding' clause 31. By this, defaulters were liable to continuous and cumulative fines or imprisonment. This clause, it has been argued, possessed 'a stringency utterly unprecedented in English health legislation'. In its first reference to the bill the *Journal* made no mention of clause 31, but it did give warm support to the principle of compulsion.[60]

Soon after the passing of the new Act anti-vaccinators in London and the provinces began to organize opposition. The *Journal*, especially during the smallpox epidemics of the early 1870s, was unashamedly hostile to this 'rabid', 'reckless', and 'pestiferous' movement of the 'ignorant' and 'wrong-headed' which was intent on poisoning 'the mind of the public on a subject of such enormous importance'. It criticized Northampton magistrates for showing 'a dangerous and cruel tendency to leniency' in their treatment of non-vaccinators, and stressed that only by 'a rigid enforcement of vaccination' can 'the health of the people ... be protected, and smallpox reduced to its smallest proportions, and ultimately exterminated'.[61] The *Journal*'s position was clearly expressed in a leading article published in 1883:

> The opponents of compulsory vaccination insist strongly on the violation of "freedom of conscience" and of "parental rights" implied in the enforcement of the compulsory clauses of the Act. They forget, however, that the State has a stake in the welfare of the child as well as the parent, and that it has repeatedly affirmed its right to interfere between the parent and the child, if interference be necessary. The State has repeatedly declared that certain things shall be done for the child regardless of the opinion, or of the consent of the parent, when it has been clearly shown that what was to be done was for the benefit of the child. In the case of vaccination, therefore, which protects the child from the danger of a deadly and loathsome disease, the State is quite consistent in having recourse to compulsion, even in face of the protest of the parent.[62]

The article went on to point out that vaccination protected the community as well as the individual, and that the State's duty to the community justified it in overruling individual rights. All this was quite different in tone from the pre-Hart *Journal*.

In many ways, but particularly in its hostility to State intervention, to the principle of compulsion, and to the medical profession, the anti-vaccination

[59] *Journal*, 16 Feb. 1867, 174–5; see 9 March 1867, 268; 18 May 1867, 573–4.

[60] R. J. Lambert, *Sir John Simon 1816–1904 and English Social Administration*, p. 393 (note 56); *Journal*, 11 May 1867, 542–5.

[61] *Ibid.*, 10 Oct. 1868, 394; 2 Jan. 1869, 16; 12 June 1869, 545; 9 Oct. 1869, 397; 4 June 1870, 583–4; 12 May 1877, 586–7.

[62] *Ibid.*, 17 Feb. 1883, 320–1; see 16 April 1887, 841–2.

movement had much in common with the campaign against the Contagious Diseases Acts. There was also a similarity in the nature of the debate between the conflicting parties, for much of it turned on the interpretation of statistics, in the one case of venereal disease, in the other of mortality from smallpox. Did the statistical evidence prove that vaccination lowered the incidence of smallpox? The *Journal*'s answer was unequivocal: 'more lives are saved by vaccination', it asserted in 1886, 'than by any other means which medical men possess for combating disease.'[63] But there was much to be said on both sides. Hart's pamphlet 'The Truth About Vaccination', brought him personally into the debate.[64]

In the 1870s anti-vaccinationists were mainly concerned with establishing the right of conscientious objection and with mitigating the penalties imposed upon defaulters. Many campaigners were out-and-out crackpots, but the argument that multiple penalties could severely and unfairly punish people such as Charles Nye, who, having seen two of his children die soon after vaccination, refused to allow a third to be vaccinated, had some validity.[65] In 1880 the government, persuaded that real injustice was being done to genuine conscientious objectors, proposed to relax the full rigour of the law. Faced with the prospect of a bill to abolish multiple penalties, Hart argued that the 'very large majority of defaulters are persons who are indolent and apathetic on the subject of vaccination', and attacked the government proposals as 'legislation for the benefit of the few at the expense (the very terrible expense) of the many ... [which would] virtually ... condone the permanent violation of a most necessary and health-preserving law'. The BMA's Parliamentary Bills Committee, with Hart at its helm and the *Journal* as its mouthpiece, co-ordinated opposition to the bill. The result was that the government abandoned its plans.[66]

From 1880 some anti-vaccinationists began to set their sights not merely on mitigation of penalties but on total repeal of the Vaccination Acts. In 1885 mass demonstrations in Leicester showed the strong representation of artisans and workers in the movement.[67] The *Journal* carried a blatantly contemptuous article on the events in 'that misguided town'.[68] Before the year was out Hart stood in the General Election as a 'radical' candidate for the predominantly working-class constituency of Mile End. The dominating national issue in the election was Irish Home Rule, but Hart's support of

[63] *Ibid.*, 21 Aug. 1886, 404. See also 17 Feb. 1883, 321; 31 March 1883, 628–9.

[64] *Ibid.*, 27 March 1880, 484; 15 Oct. 1881, 636. See also 4 May 1878, 648–9; 7 Dec. 1878, 845; 13 May 1882, 707–8.

[65] R. M. MacLeod, 'Law, Medicine and Public Opinion: The Resistance to Compulsory Health Legislation 1870–1907', 118, 189 (note 54).

[66] *Ibid.*, 193; *Journal*, 3 July 1880, 1–6; 10 July, 1880, 51, 62; 17 July 1880, 75; 31 July 1880, 171, 178; 21 Aug. 1880, 296–7; 28 Aug. 1880, 351–2.

[67] *Ibid.*, 189, 193, 195–6.

[68] *Journal*, 4 April 1885, 707.

compulsory vaccination and vivisection were key factors in his heavy defeat by a Conservative (2091 votes to 1442) and the demise of his political ambitions. Anti-vaccinators and anti-vivisectionists 'expended a deal of money in opposition to him'. As the *Journal* commented, 'Mile End was continuously flooded with placards and handbills of a somewhat violent character, proceeding from the headquarters of the Antivaccination and the Antivivisection Societies.'[69]

In 1886 James Stansfield, Gladstone's President of the Local Government Board, suggested to a deputation from the London Society for the Abolition of Compulsory Vaccination that it should seek the appointment of a Royal Commission on the Vaccination Acts. The *Journal* responded favourably.[70] But it was only in 1889 that J. A. Picton, the anti-vaccinationist MP for Leicester, successfully requested the Conservative Home Secretary, Henry Matthews, to make such an appointment. The *Journal* again welcomed the prospect of an inquiry and expressed 'the hope that as an inquiry has been decided upon, the whole question will be thoroughly threshed out and definitively settled, so that an agitation which greatly unsettles the mind of the people, and leads them into severe danger, may receive a quietus from the irresistible logic of ascertained facts.'[71] The Commission contained 'some of the nation's foremost medical men', including Jonathan Hutchinson.[72] It sat for seven years, producing an interim report in April 1892 which recommended the cessation of repeated penalties and preferential treatment of those imprisoned under the Vaccination Acts.[73] These recommendations, which pointed the way to a non-compulsory system, disappointed Matthews, and, although the chairman of the Commission, Lord Herschel, wanted them implemented without delay, the Conservative government declined to act. For its part the *Journal* feared that the recommendations would accelerate the trend towards non-compliance with the law.[74]

In 1895 Hart produced a lengthy four-part report for the *Journal* on 'Vaccination as a Branch of Preventive Medicine'. This he concluded with the claim that the evidence in favour of vaccination was 'overwhelming' whereas the argument on the other side was untrustworthy, thin, and

[69] For Hart's views on vivisection see pp. 111–18. R. D. French, *Vivisection and Medical Science in Victorian Society* (Princeton: Princeton University Press, 1975), p. 167; R. M. MacLeod, 'Law, Medicine and Public Opinion: The Resistance to Compulsory Health Legislation 1870–1907', 196 (note 54); *Journal*, 5 Dec. 1885, 1077–8; *East London Observer*, 28 Nov. 1885; Robert Farquharson, *In and Out of Parliament* (London: Williams and Norgate, 1911), p. 117.

[70] *Journal*, 24 April 1886, 791.

[71] *Ibid.*, 13 April 1889, 842–3.

[72] R. M. MacLeod, 'Law, Medicine and Public Opinion: The Resistance to Compulsory Health Legislation 1870–1907', 199 (note 54).

[73] *Parliamentary Papers* (1892) **XLVII**, Royal Commission on Vaccination, Fifth Report, 1; *Journal*, 14 May 1892, 1032.

[74] *Ibid.*, 23 April 1892, 869–70; R. M. MacLeod, 'Law, Medicine and Public Opinion: The Resistance to Compulsory Health Legislation 1870–1907', 201–2 (note 54).

exaggerated. He urged Parliament not only to maintain compulsory vaccination but to introduce compulsory re-vaccination.[75] In the following year one whole issue of the *Journal* (23 May 1896) was devoted to a celebration of the centenary of Edward Jenner's first vaccination. This issue signalled a change in the *Journal*'s view on compulsion. A leading article reviewing the law on vaccination took its usual line in support of compulsion. But it also acknowledged that there should be a right of conscientious objection, urging only that the procedure for registering such objection should entail as much trouble to the objector as attendance at a vaccination station. This grudging change of heart was caused, as was later made clear, by recognition that the compulsory principle created resistance to vaccination, while also making martyrs of those who were repeatedly prosecuted, thereby giving 'to agitators a handle which they would otherwise never have possessed'.[76] But it represented a transformation of attitude on the part of the *Journal* and a recognition that the anti-vaccinators had won a significant victory.

The Royal Commission produced its final report in August 1896. This was largely pro-vaccinationist in character, but, as the *Journal* noted, though 'the essential fact of the report is the vindication of the merits of vaccination, the recommendations are limited by the claims of popular prejudice and political interests'.[77] But it is going too far to suggest that the *Journal* believed that 'the concessions made by the Commissioners . . . destroy[ed] the very basis of the Vaccination Acts'. In fact, it believed that

> The medical and scientific aspects of vaccination have never before been so powerfully contended for and upheld as they are in the report of the Royal Commission on Vaccination; and we can afford to smile when people of the mental calibre of antivaccinists can maintain in the face of such a document, that their victory 'is all along the line'.[78]

The *Journal* did not criticize the Commission for recognizing the legitimacy of conscientious objection, for it knew this to have become inevitable. Its only significant criticism was that, having accepted the importance of re-vaccination, the Commissioners had failed to recommend that this be administered on the same basis as primary vaccination—that is, that it be mandatory unless a statutory declaration of objection be made. In fact, the BMA's Parliamentary Bills Committee resolved in October 1896 that it would lobby for such a clause in any future legislation.[79]

By the time Henry Chaplin, Conservative President of the Local Government Board, introduced a bill to give effect to the Royal Commission's

[75] *Journal*, 6 April 1895, 765–6.

[76] *Ibid.*, 23 May 1896, 1300; see 7 Nov. 1896, 1397–8.

[77] *Ibid.*, 22 Aug. 1896, 453.

[78] R. M. MacLeod, 'Law, Medicine and Public Opinion: The Resistance to Compulsory Health Legislation 1870–1907', 203 (note 54); *Journal*, 12 Sept. 1896, 669; 19 Sept. 1896, 770–2.

[79] *Ibid.*, 31 Oct. 1896, 1332–3; 2 Jan. 1897, 32–3.

recommendations (March 1898), editorship of the *BMJ* had passed to Dawson Williams. The bill contained no mention of re-vaccination, and this, a leading article in the *Journal* suggested, was its 'great defect'. It also made no provision for conscientious objection, but on the other hand it did provide for the abolition of repeated penalties. The *Journal* preferred to reserve judgement on whether this would mean greater take-up of vaccination.[80] However, in the course of the bill's passage through Parliament, and for blatantly electoral reasons, the Conservative government adopted several amendments which went towards satisfying the objectives of anti-vaccinationists and further alienating majority opinion in the medical profession. The Act allowed for the exemption of parents who could satisfy magistrates of their conscientious objection; penalties for objectors who declined or failed to do this were limited to two or one in full amount. As one commentator has stated, 'the Act conceded everything . . . except complete repeal.' For the *Journal* it was a 'defective piece of legislation'.[81] It consoled itself with the hope that a measure introducing re-vaccination was not far away, but in fact worse rather than better was to come, for an Act of 1907 allowed parents to avoid vaccination by making a simple declaration before a magistrate. This 'virtually ended compulsory vaccination'.[82] The cause to which the *Journal* had given unremitting support had died.

Vivisection

Vivisection became a matter of deep controversy during the last quarter of the nineteenth century. Hart and the *BMJ* played prominent roles in this controversy as defenders of vivisection. In fact, the *Journal*'s coverage of the subject far exceeded that of any other periodical. Between about 1875 and 1885 it carried more than twice the amount of material as the *Lancet*.[83] Hart was described by anti-vivisectionist opponents as the medical profession's 'chief wire-puller', while the *Journal*'s attitude, it has been said, was characteristically 'hard line'. The *Lancet*, by way of contrast was 'always somewhat more moderate' than the *BMJ*. Indeed, towards the end of the campaign against the 1876 Cruelty to Animals Bill, which introduced the first controls on vivisection, the *Journal* criticized the *Lancet*, not altogether justly, for

[80] *Ibid.*, 26 March 1898, 838–40.

[81] *Vaccination Act, 1898*, 61 & 62 Vict. c. 49; R. M. MacLeod, 'Law, Medicine and Public Opinion: The Resistance to Compulsory Health Legislation 1870–1907', 205–7 (note 54); *Journal*, 13 Aug. 1898; 5 Nov. 1898.

[82] R. M. MacLeod, 'Law, Medicine and Public Opinion: The Resistance to Compulsory Health Legislation 1870–1907', 209 (note 54).

[83] Nicolaas Rupke, 'Pro-Vivisection in England in the Early 1880s: Arguments and Motives', in N. Rupke (ed.), *Vivisection in Historical Perspective* (London: Croom Helm, 1987), p. 191.

Stupidity and Science: from *Punch*. The original caption reads: Operating Professor. 'By this experiment we have ascertained that we can alleviate the sufferings of our fellow creatures! I may further add—' Policeman (*interrupting*). 'No, you mayn't! We've had enough o' this sort o' thing! You must move on!' Professor. ' "Move on"? We can't *move on* if *you* interfere!' The figure seated by the microscope is Ernest Hart. Source: Bodleian Library, Oxford.

acting 'feebly' and leaving the profession 'altogether in the lurch' in the struggle against the anti-vivisectors.[84]

Concern about cruelty to animals was well established by the time Queen Victoria came to the throne.[85] Acts of 1822 and 1835 had outlawed cruelty to domestic animals, while the Society for the Prevention of Cruelty to Animals (later the RSPCA) was founded in 1824. But, despite sporadic controversy about vivisection, there was before 1870 'no mass coverage, and, therefore, no mass awareness' of this question. The RSPCA, for example, showed little interest. Lack of sustained opposition reflected the comparative rarity of vivisection. This in turn was indicative of the backwardness of British experimental medicine compared with that of continental Europe.[86]

[84] R. D. French, *Vivisection and Medical Science in Victorian Society*, pp. 58, 70, 130 (note 69); *Journal*, 12 Aug. 1876, 222.

[85] See Keith Thomas, *Man and the Natural World* (London: Allen Lane, 1983).

[86] R. D. French, *Vivisection and Medical Science in Victorian Society*, pp. 18–27, 34–7 (note 69). See also Brian Harrison, 'Animals and the State in nineteenth-century England', *English Historical Review* (1973) **88**: 786–820; James Turner, *Reckoning with the Beast* (Baltimore: Johns Hopkins University Press, 1980). Stimulating studies of vivisection are to be found in Coral

During this period of quiescence, when Streeten was editor, the *Journal* published a leading article on vivisection. This presented not a forthright defence of the practice but, rather, a thoughtful appraisal of the arguments for and against it. The article condemned the 'wretched and reckless disregard for the sufferings of animals shown, especially, by some foreign experimentalists', and also questioned the notion that vivisection was justified if carried out on a limited basis, only in the pursuit of knowledge, and if conducted with the minimum of suffering. It concluded that

On the whole . . . we admit that where the end in itself is a lawful one, animal life would seem to be placed at our disposal, it is evident that any unnecessary waste of it is morally and indefensibly wrong, and that when the occasional infliction of a certain amount of suffering for purposes of rendering animals subservient to the use of mankind is necessary, every precaution should be taken to confine this amount within the smallest possible limits, whatever may be the object for which it is had recourse to.[87]

Decades later some anti-vivisectionists held opinions not far removed from these.

The beginnings of the public debate about the rights and wrongs of vivisection can be traced to 1870, at around which time, 'a small group of experimentally inclined British physiologists many of them with continental educations, accepted recently developed institutional positions from which they and their allies were to dominate the science'. At about the same time the Royal College of Surgeons began to require greater knowledge of physiology on the part of would-be practitioners. In consequence, vivisection became more frequently practised.[88]

One trigger for the debate was the publication of Burdon Sanderson's *Handbook for the Physiological Laboratory*, a manual which, in giving directions for carrying out experiments on animals, seemed to suggest that students of physiology needed to undertake (sometimes painful) experiments as part of their routine training.[89] Also important was the controversy over

Lansbury, 'Gynaecology, Pornography, and the Antivivisection Movement', *Victorian Studies* (1985) **28**: 413–38 and the same author's *The Old Brown Dog: Women Workers and Vivisection* (Madison, Wisconsin: University of Wisconsin Press, 1985). See also Harriet Ritvo, *The Animal Estate. The English and other Creatures in the Victorian Age* (Cambridge, Massachusetts: Harvard University Press, 1987).

[87] *Journal*, 10 July 1844, 216–18.

[88] R. D. French, *Vivisection and Medical Science in Victorian Society*, p. 42 (note 69); see Mark N. Ozer, 'The British Vivisection Controversy', *Bulletin of the History of Medicine* (1966) **40**: 162–3.

[89] J. Burdon Sanderson (ed.), *Handbook for the Physiological Laboratory* (London, 1873). See Stewart Richards, 'Vicarious Suffering, Necessary Pain: Physiological Method in Late Nineteenth-century Britain' in N. Rupke (ed.), *Vivisection in Historical Perspective*, pp. 125–48 (note 83). Though Hart was a personal friend of Sanderson, in 1882 the *BMJ* published an article urging that it 'will be a disaster for Oxford' if Sanderson, then Jodrell Professor at University College London, were to be appointed to the newly created Waynflete Chair of Physiology at Oxford. See *Journal*, 11 Nov. 1882, 956; University College London, Burdon Sanderson Papers, Mss/Add 179/4/ 75–8, Hart to Burdon Sanderson, 7 Nov. 1882, 10 Nov. 1882.

the allegedly cruel experiments of Professor Moritz Schiff in Florence. In a leading article published in January 1874 the *Journal* offered a staunch defence of Schiff and of vivisection in general.[90] This, the *Journal*'s first discussion of the subject for many years, clearly established the views it was to hold for years to come. As yet it was merely an observer of distant events, but before the year was out the BMA and its *Journal* were to be in the front line of the controversy as a result of a demonstration performed by a French vivisector at the BMA's annual meeting in Norwich.

In this experiment Eugene Magnan injected one dog with absinthe in order to induce epilepsy, and another with alcohol in order to demonstrate its contrary effects. The first dog died, the other recovered. Some of those present at the demonstration voiced protests and physically disrupted the lecture; the RSPCA subsequently became involved and a prosecution was instituted under existing legislation. In the absence of Magnan, who had returned to Paris, the prosecution failed, though the magistrates considered it a proper one for the Society to bring. The case gained nationwide publicity and constituted a propaganda victory for the RSPCA.[91]

At the time the *Journal* made no editorial comment on these events, but it was clear where its sympathies lay. Although one of the prosecution witnesses at the trial was Sir William Fergusson, the BMA's President for 1875, the *Journal* attacked both the bringing of the prosecution and 'the quality of mind of gentlemen who can go into court as accusers of their brethren on a matter as to which, according to their own statements, they are profoundly ignorant ... '. After the trial was over it published a leading article entitled: 'WHAT HAS VIVISECTION DONE FOR HUMANITY?' In this it listed 22 advances in physiology, 10 in medicine and surgery, and six in therapeutics and relief of pain which could not have been achieved without animal experimentation. Subsequent articles extended these lists.[92] At the end of January another leading article suggested that there could be no valid objection to experiments carried out on anaesthetized animals and

> It is only when the experiments involve suffering that a difference of opinion may be entertained as to their justifiableness. We think they ought not be performed, unless it can be distinctly shown that instruction cannot otherwise be communicated in matters of fundamental importance. We think that, if the objects for which experiments on animals are undertaken are fairly considered, there is no more reason for

[90] *Journal*, 3 Jan. 1874, 18; R. D. French, *Vivisection and Medical Science in Victorian Society*, p. 50 (note 69). See Patrizia Guarnieri, 'Moritz Schiff (1823–1896): Experimental Physiology and Noble Sentiment in Florence' in N. Rupke (ed.), *Vivisection in Historical Perspective*, pp. 105–24 (note 83).

[91] The defendants were the four Norwich doctors who had arranged Magnan's demonstration. The BMA paid the defence costs. See R. D. French, *Vivisection and Medical Science in Victorian Society*, pp. 55–8 (note 69). The *Journal* carried a report of the court case. See 12 Dec. 1874, pp. 751–4; 26 Dec. 1874, 828; 10 June 1882, 874; 19 June 1897, 1575–6.

[92] *Ibid.*, 9 Jan. 1875, 56. See 2 Jan. 1875, 25; 16 Jan. 1875, 90.

accusing the operators of cruelty, than there is for accusing of inhumanity a surgeon who inflicts pain for a benevolent motive.[93]

This was to be the *Journal*'s standard line over many years.

During 1875 two bills to regulate vivisection were brought before Parliament. In contrast to the more moderate views of the *Lancet* and the *Medical Times and Gazette*, the *Journal* was strongly opposed to both. But in May, Richard Cross, Disraeli's Home Secretary, announced the government's intention to appoint a Royal Commission of Inquiry.[94] The *Journal* reacted favourably to this news: 'The institution of an inquiry will be satisfactory to all; at least, we shall now have the real facts impartially investigated, and candidly stated.'[95]

The Royal Commission was given a wide brief: 'to inquire into the practice of subjecting live animals to experiments for scientific purposes, and to consider and report what measures, if any, it may be desirable to take in respect of any such practice'.[96] The Commission's task was one 'of finding a way to regulate vivisection that would prevent abuse and calm public disquiet while permitting maximum progress in scientific research'. The *Journal* argued that the Commissioners faced the responsibility of deciding whether physiology, which had already contributed so much to medicine, was to be allowed to flourish in Britain, or be 'confined to continental countries where laboratories are built, professorships endowed, and the expenses of experiments defrayed by the governments'.[97]

When the Commission reported in January 1876, it admitted the impossibility of outlawing vivisection, and, indeed, the necessity for it, but, recognizing that the practice could give rise to abuses, the Commissioners proposed controls. Their main proposal was for the licensing of vivisectors. These licences would carry conditions requiring that avoidable suffering should not be inflicted. They would be revocable on proof of abuse, subject to a right of appeal. Following well-established precedent, the regulations would be administered and enforced by a government inspectorate.[98]

The Commission's report was so cautiously worded that both supporters and opponents of vivisection 'could read into . . . [it] . . . what they wished'.[99] Certainly the *Journal*, in common with most of the rest of the medical press, reacted favourably. It noted that the inquiry had failed to uncover any case of cruelty perpetrated in the course of animal experiments. It felt that the

[93] *Ibid.*, 30 Jan. 1875, 149, 159. See 5 June 1875, 749.

[94] R. D. French, *Vivisection and Medical Science in Victorian Society*, pp. 61–79 (note 69).

[95] *Journal*, 29 May 1875, 716; Richard B. Fisher, *Joseph Lister 1827–1912* (London: Macdonald and Jane's, 1977), p. 219.

[96] *Parliamentary Papers* (1876) **XLI**: 277.

[97] R. D. French, *Vivisection and Medical Science in Victorian Society*, pp. 91 (note 69); *Journal* 3 July 1875, 26

[98] *Parliamentary Papers* (1876) **XLI**: 277.

[99] R. D. French, *Vivisection and Medical Science in Victorian Society*, pp. 110 (note 69).

proposed regulations would prove valuable in defusing public disquiet while imposing no great barrier to scientific progress.[100]

In May 1876 Lord Carnarvon introduced the government's 'Bill for the Prevention of Cruelty to Animals'. He claimed that it was based on the findings of the Royal Commission, but it differed in several crucial respects. It required that potentially painful experiments on living animals should be carried out only by licensed persons on registered and inspected premises. Thus far it was largely uncontroversial, though the bill's very title, carrying, as it did, the implication that vivisection and cruelty were synonymous, was a provocation to practitioners and advocates of vivisection. But much more controversial were the clauses that permitted only experiments which offered the prospect of advancing knowledge, which would be useful in saving or prolonging human life, or in alleviating human suffering. Furthermore, experiments on cats and dogs were expressly forbidden.[101] The *Journal* had consistently maintained that it was not always possible to forecast the results of experiments or their ultimate value to humanity. Neither had it ever accepted the argument that cats and dogs were inappropriate subjects for scientific experiments. Indeed, it believed that experiments on these animals could be of fundamental importance.[102]

When the BMA's Parliamentary Bills Committee, under Hart's chairmanship, discussed the bill with the teachers of physiology, they produced a string of important objections. Other medical bodies, including the GMC and Royal Colleges, also took exception to the measure, but it was Hart who shouldered much of the responsibility for organizing opposition against the 'insulting and mischievous' bill. In this respect his role has been termed 'crucial': 'if it had not been for the decided movement of Mr. Ernest Hart it [the medical profession] would have been absolutely silent on the matter, and as a consequence we should have had the Act passed in its original form . . . .' Hart employed the *Journal* to foster and co-ordinate opposition. For example, the 3 June leader, 'Experiments on Animals', was reprinted and made available on request; similarly, the *Journal* carried the BMA's petition against the bill, emphasizing that it was available to non-members, including the public, and encouraged readers to obtain signatures. Over 2000 members of the Association signed this petition. The *Journal* urged BMA members to protest against the bill to their MPs, while Hart himself headed BMA deputations in interviews with Lord Carnarvon and Richard Cross.[103]

As a result of these representations Lord Carnarvon introduced conces-

[100] *Journal*, 19 Feb. 1876, 227–9.

[101] R. D. French, *Vivisection and Medical Science in Victorian Society*, pp. 115 (note 69).

[102] *Journal*, 10 June 1876, 739.

[103] *Ibid.*, 27 May 1876, 677; 3 June 1876, 690, 692–7, 701–2, 707–8; 10 June 1876, 739; 24 June 1876, 794–8; 1 July 1876, 24; 8 July 1876, 49; 15 July 1876, 80; 10 June 1882, 885; R. D. French, *Vivisection and Medical Science in Victorian Society*, pp. 125–6, 130–2 (note 69); H. Lawson, 'The Vivisection Clamour', *Popular Science Review* (1876) **XV**: 398.

sions in the hope of making the bill acceptable to medical opinion. But although the *Journal* acknowledged that these improved the bill, it remained dissatisfied, believing that the bill would 'still hamper and annoy men who have the highest credentials to public confidence'. It concluded that 'the best thing that could happen to the Bill would be, that it should be thrown out altogether.'[104] Hart resolved to fight for further concessions. On 11 July he led a huge deputation of BMA members to protest to the Home Secretary against the bill. This meeting and other lobbying convinced the government that its revised bill remained unacceptable to the profession. Cross and Carnarvon decided that compromise might be possible if they could consult the scientists without Hart being present. After discussions held on 22 July the vivisection bill was further amended to the effect that experiments did not have to be always confined to laboratories; that special certificates to experiment on cats, dogs, horses, mules, and asses would be required only if anaesthesia were not used; that prosecutions would require Home Office sanction; and that the bill was confined to warm-blooded animals.[105]

The *Journal* still considered the bill to be illogical, partial, and unnecessary, but pronounced itself 'by no means ill-pleased with the bill as it stands, considering the extreme ignorance, the hysterical calumny, and the worse than theological odium with which the controversy was initiated'.[106] As amended, it could at least be declared 'harmless to science'. With another amendment—to the effect that the Act would apply to vertebrates, rather than warm-blooded animals, with which the *Journal* was by no means pleased—the bill received the Royal Assent.

In some ways the *Journal* recognized the 1876 Act as a positive reform and not merely a needless inconvenience. Hitherto a physiologist had run the risk of prosecution for cruelty, as had happened at Norwich in 1874. For licensed persons this risk was removed by the new measure. Because of this there was some justice in the claims of anti-vivisectionists that the 1876 Act was one for the protection of physiologists. At the same time, the *Journal* believed that the Act would advance the cause of kindness to animals in general, for it was impossible that the principle of protection would be confined to cases where pain was inflicted for scientific purposes. In this way the profession could be said to be setting an example for the community at large, where real cruelty to animals was to be found, while suffering no substantial inconvenience itself. For this satisfactory outcome, Hart claimed, much credit was due to the BMA, its Parliamentary Bills Committee, and, by implication, himself.[107]

The Act can be assessed in several ways. The fact that it was passed at all meant that the perceived slur on physiologists remained. Since some scien-

[104] *Journal*, 24 June 1876, 786.
[105] R. D. French, *Vivisection and Medical Science in Victorian Society*, pp. 137–9 (note 69).
[106] *Journal*, 12 Aug, 1876, 221–2.
[107] *Ibid.*, 19 Aug. 1876, 245.

tists, including eminent individuals such as Lister and Lauder Brunton, had their applications for licences rejected, it can be argued that progress in research was retarded.[108] On these grounds the 1876 Act may be interpreted as a victory for anti-vivisectionists and a defeat for the likes of Ernest Hart. On the other hand experimental medicine was not stopped in its tracks in 1876 but 'enjoyed a spectacular growth' after 1882. This is reflected in the statistics of animal experiments, the number of which rose from 311 in 1880 to 95 731 in 1910. Moreover, 'from the late 'eighties on, the medical and scientific interest seems to have been generally satisfied with the adminstration of the Act.'[109] In contrast, following the dismissal of the prosecution brought against David Ferrier, in 1881, anti-vivisectionists experienced 'a final and total loss of faith in the Act'.[110] After 1876 the anti-vivisectionist movement became abolitionist rather than regulatory in character. It introduced a string of unsuccessful bills to suppress animal experimentation and became increasingly frustrated with its failure to make progress.

It has been suggested that Hart, 'an advocate of mass agitation rather than diplomacy by the few', successfully 'aroused the rank and file of the [medical] profession, developing a power base from which a few leaders could negotiate in camera with the politicians'.[111] That he was able to operate in this way and to such effect was testimony to the influence of the *BMJ*. There are good grounds for viewing the outcome of the *Journal*'s campaign to uphold animal experiments as one of its most notable successes.

An interventionist journal?

In its attitude towards the CD Acts, baby farming, compulsory vaccination, and other socio-medical topics, Hart's *Journal* was repeatedly in favour of government intervention. Freedom of choice to avoid vaccination, or to engage in a free trade in prostitution and infants produced disease, misery, degradation, cruelty, and premature death. The *Journal* saw State regulation as the best way of controlling social evils arising from the unfettered operation of individualism and the marketplace. But in none of these cases was the *Journal* notably successful in securing a realization of its vision.

Far from the CD Acts being extended throughout the country, they

[108] *Ibid.*, 27 Aug. 1881, 365–6; See Andrew H. Ryan, 'History of the British Act of 1876: An Act to Amend the Law Relating to Cruelty to Animals', *Journal of Medical Education* (1963) **38**: 182–94; Mark N. Ozer, 'The British Vivisection Controversy', *Bulletin of the History of Medicine* (1966) **40**: 158–67.

[109] R. D. French, *Vivisection and Medical Science in Victorian Society*, pp. 214–5, 392–3 (note 69); *Journal*, 11 June 1892, 1264; 22 Aug. 1896, 464–5.

[110] Judith Hampson, 'Legislation: A Practical Solution to the Vivisection Dilemma?', in N. Rupke (ed.), *Vivisection in Historical Perspective*, p. 315 (note 83); R. D. French, *Vivisection and Medical Science in Victorian Society*, p. 202 (note 69).

[111] *Ibid.*, pp. 210, 408–9.

foundered on the reef of feminist and moral outrage. No one could accuse the *Journal* of not occupying the high moral ground in its defence of infants and children, but its campaign against baby farming did not meet with immediate and resounding success. The goal of universal vaccination proved unattainable owing to the strength of the opposition it engendered. The basic reason for the *Journal*'s limited success in these areas is that its interventionism ran counter to prevailing *laissez-faire* ideology. The strength of this ideology was a formidable barrier to even the strongest arguments for State regulation.

Many historians now dismiss the traditional notion of mid-Victorian England as a haven of *laissez-faire*. They emphasize the distinction between ideas and actions and claim that in reality State intervention was the order of the day even when *laissez-faire* was routinely considered to be king. But the power of the State to command and control was more circumscribed than is now often thought. Moreover, the State was often less keen to extend its role than is sometimes assumed. Even where legislation was passed, it often reached the Statute Book in a weaker form than reformers wanted. Moreover, in many instances the law was not always easily enforced. Certainly, the history of the CD Acts, the Infant Life Protection Act, 1872, and compulsory vaccination undermines the notion of an interventionist tide. In each of these cases thoroughly interventionist objectives had been either considerably diluted by the time they became law, or proved less than fully attainable in practice.

The *Journal*'s views on vivisection were staunchly anti-regulationist and apparently, therefore, at odds with its policy towards the other questions considered in this chapter. In fact, there were parallels. Its hostility towards anti-vivisectionists stemmed partly from the belief that misplaced humanity threatened to cripple the advance of medical science and thus add to the sum of human misery. In this sense its outlook was consistent, for it professed to support venereal disease control, baby farming regulations, and compulsory vaccination on the grounds of public interest. The *Journal* was also constant in its belief that the public should be willing to trust doctors to take decisions in the best interests of society. Thus, a recurring theme in the *Journal* during the campaign against regulation of animal experimentation was that the planned legislation insulted the profession, not only by implying that it was heartless and careless of suffering but also by suggesting that it could not be trusted to behave responsibly.

In its desire to uphold the honour and status of medical men, Hart's *Journal* was no different from that of his predecessors. One of the things which marked it out was its readiness to tackle socio-medical issues of vital importance to the well-being of the population at large. Although this had occasionally been done by earlier editors, there was a change of emphasis under Hart. He had a passionate interest in social medicine and did not shrink from systematically employing the *BMJ* to foster and project his vision of society. This made his *Journal* constantly controversial and provocative, but it also did much to transform it from a 'parish pump magazine' into a mature, stimulating, and widely respected 'mirror of medicine'.

6
Science and internationalism

Classic papers

The Victorian and Edwardian *BMJ*, though well known for its socio-medical campaigns and its efforts to advance the profession, was perhaps most important for its coverage of scientific and clinical medicine. Over this period it monitored all important developments in medical science, published many ground-breaking papers, championed the work of Lister and others, and made a notable contribution to the early history of British radiology. Such work can be assessed both qualitatively and quantitatively. Hence it is possible to evaluate the *Journal*'s record in publishing classic papers and also its coverage of innovations in anaesthesia, antisepsis, and radiology.

Since there is a publication, Garrison and Morton's *Medical Bibliography*, which purports to list all classic books and papers in medical science, there is a convenient way of judging journals in terms of the number of ground-breaking articles they published at any given time.[1] On this basis a journal achieving a high number of 'Garrison and Morton' entries might be thought to be performing better than one that achieved few or none. This, of course, is flawed reasoning, for the importance of a paper on, say, paediatrics cannot be realistically appraised in relation to one on, for example, genito-urinary disease. Moreover, if each Garrison and Morton entry is deemed to be of equal merit, the effect may be to undervalue certain papers while overvaluing others. Lister's most important article, for example, will rate no higher than a paper that adds far less to the sum of human knowledge and, by consensus, is of much lesser consequence. Furthermore, a journal may make a valuable contribution to knowledge and practice in ways other than by publishing original papers—for example, by translating or summarizing work published elsewhere. Thus, 'when Wertheim in 1905 wrote his great paper on extended abdominal hysterectomy for cancer [Dawson] Williams undertook to have the MS. translated and published in full in the *Journal*, and from that time the operation became widespread in Great Britain.'[2] Such a contribution to clinical practice will not be registered in Garrison and Morton. It is still nevertheless worth examining the number of Garrison and Morton entries

[1] Leslie T. Morton, *A Medical Bibliography (Garrison and Morton). An Annotated Check List of Texts Illustrating the History of Medicine* (4th edn Aldershot: Gower, 1983).

[2] *Journal*, 10 March 1928, 421.

achieved by the *Journal.* To make the exercise more worthwhile, we shall also look at the *Lancet*'s record. Entries in Garrison and Morton are banded into five-year periods, beginning with 1840, the *Journal*'s first year of publication. The data are presented in more visual form in Figures 1 and 2.

Although launched in 1840, the *Journal* carried no papers destined to secure a Garrison and Morton entry until the period 1855–9 when it published two, both appearing in 1858. One was by Henry Silvester (1828–1908) on artificial respiration: 'A new method of resuscitating still-born children, and of restoring persons apparently drowned or dead'.[3] The other, which is, in fact, the earliest *BMJ* listing in Garrison and Morton, was a letter written by none other than David Livingstone (1813–73), the Scottish missionary and explorer. This was written on 22 March while Livingstone was aboard SS *Pearl* off the coast of Senegal, West Africa.[4] It described the use of arsenic in treating 'nagara' (sleeping sickness) in horses: 'Arsenic as a remedy for the tsetse fly'. Probably the first man to make use of a treatment suggested by James Braid (1795–1860), the father of modern hypnotism,[5] Livingstone is renowned for achieving many 'firsts'; it is intriguing that he was also the first to publish a classic paper in the *British Medical Journal.*[6]

Six years passed before William Tilbury Fox (1836–79) published in the *Journal* his findings 'On impetigo contagiosa or porrigo' (impetigo of Tilbury Fox) in which this skin disease was first described.[7] In the same year Henry Carden (?–1872) described his technique for 'Amputation by single flap' which entailed cutting through the femur just above the knee joint.[8] Until the 1870s, however, the *Journal*'s record in carrying 'key' papers was unimpressive. After 35 years in existence its total was a mere nine, though one of these was Joseph Lister's (1827–1912) 'Method of Antiseptic Treatment Applicable to Wounded Soldiers in the Present War' (i. e. the Franco-Prussian, 1870–1), and another, Joseph Clover's (1825–82) 'Description of a new double current inhaler for administering ether'.[9] Over the same period the *Lancet* totalled 23. But things began to change in the 1870s as the Ernest Hart 'revolution' took effect. In 1875–9 alone the *Journal* carried nine classic papers. These included contributions by William Gowers (1845–1915) on the state of the arteries in Bright's disease,[10] John Wolfe (1824–1904) on skin

[3] *Ibid.*, 17 July 1858, 576–9.

[4] *Ibid.*, 1 May 1858, 360–1.

[5] L. T. Morton, *A Medical Bibliography (Garrison and Morton)*, p. 704 (note 1).

[6] Another man who was to achieve fame outside the world of medicine, Conan Doyle, had his first medical publication published in the *Journal.* See 20 Sept. 1879, 483; 17 April 1948, 740–1.

[7] *Ibid.*, 16 Jan. 1864, 78–9; 30 April 1864, 467–9; 7 May 1864, 495–6; 21 May 1864, 553–5; 4 June 1864, 607–9. In 1873 Tilbury Fox published in the *Journal* the first description of dyshidrosis (a form of skin eruption) 27 Sept. 1873, 365–6.

[8] *Ibid.*, 16 April 1864, 416–21.

[9] *Ibid.*, 3 Sept. 1870, 243–4; 15 March 1873, 282–3.

[10] *Ibid.*, 9 Dec. 1876, 743–5.

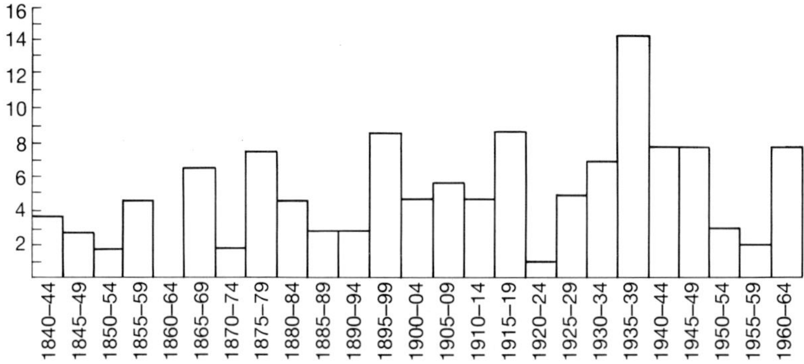

Figure 1: *Lancet* Citations in Garrison and Morton, 1840–1964

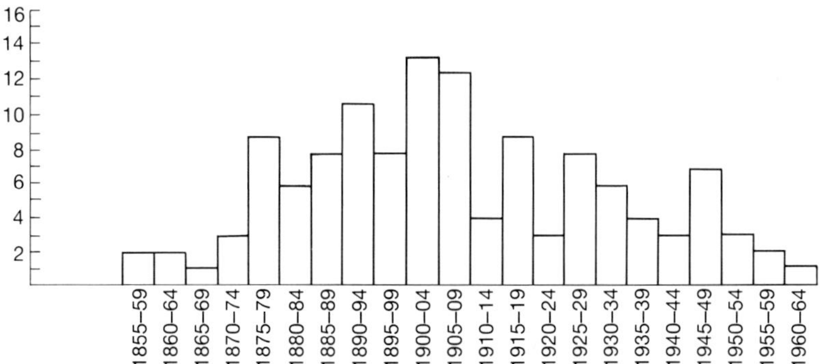

Figure 2: *BMJ* Citations in Garrison and Morton, 1840–1964

grafts,[11] Clover (again) on ether inhalation,[12] Robert Lawson Tait (1845–99) on gynaecology,[13] and Thomas Spencer Wells (1818–97) on surgical forceps.[14]

Thereafter Hart maintained a splendid record in publishing high-quality scientific and clinical material. During the 1880s and 1890s some of the leading figures of the day reported their findings in the *Journal.* These included Lawson Tait (notwithstanding his loathing of Hart),[15] Felix Semon (1849–1921),[16] William Osler (1849–1919),[17] Alexander Rennie (1859–1940),

[11] *Ibid.*, 18 Sept. 1875, 360–1.

[12] *Ibid.*, 15 July 1876, 74–5; 20 Jan. 1877, 69–70.

[13] *Ibid.*, 31 May 1879, 813–14.

[14] *Ibid.*, 21 June 1879, 926–8; 5 July 1879, 3–4. The second part of this paper concluded with the words 'to be continued', but it never was.

[15] *Ibid.*, 14 May 1881, 766–7; 28 June 1884, 1250–1; 22 March 1890, 651–61.

[16] *Ibid.*, 1 Dec. 1883, 1072.

[17] *Ibid.*, 7 March 1885, 467–70; 14 March, 522–6; 21 March, 577–9.

Victor Horsley (1857–1916),[18] Patrick Manson (1844–1922), and Ronald Ross (1857–1932). Rennie's paper on the plague was 'the first seriously to support the theory of transmission of the plague bacillus by rats and to present evidence in support of the theory'.[19] Manson and Ross published much of their work on malaria in the *Journal*.[20] Manson's June 1898 paper, entitled 'Surgeon-Major Ronald Ross's Recent Investigations on the Mosquito–Malaria Theory', secured for Ross his place in medical history as the discoverer of the link between the insect and the disease. 'You have done a great work,' wrote Manson to Ross, 'and your deed will not be forgotten. You will see from the last *British Medical Journal* that I have secured your priority in discovery, and have nipped what may have been an attempt at stealing'.[21] Ross was awarded the Nobel Prize for 1902.

Allowing for Hart's year-long absence from the editorial chair and also for time lags between receipt and appearance of articles, we can treat Hart's editorial tenure in this context as 1870–99 inclusive. During that period the *Journal* carried 46 classic papers; over the same period the *Lancet* published 30. This meant that their overall totals between 1840–99 were the same, that is, a score of 51 each. It seems reasonable to conclude that by the end of the Hart era the *Journal* had replaced its great rival as Britain's leading scientific medical journal. But was this status maintained?

The *Journal*'s position was held, indeed, strengthened, during Dawson Williams' editorship, though it could be argued that Williams was Hart's beneficiary. Certainly, his most fertile period occurred during his early years in office. In the early 1900s he published a string of important papers, many on communicable and tropical diseases, by major figures in medicine. These included further contributions from Gowers, Horsley, and Manson, from William Boog Leishmann (1865–1926), and from Almroth Wright (1861–1947), the originator of modern vaccine treatment, on typhoid inoculation.[22]

Manson's 1900 paper gave experimental proof of the link between mosquitoes and malaria. He allowed his son to be bitten by infected insects brought from Rome. The young man developed malaria, which was then

[18] *Ibid.*, 28 Nov. 1891, 1139–43.

[19] *Ibid.*, 15 Sept. 1894, 615–16; L. T. Morton, *Medical Bibliography (Garrison and Morton)*, p. 683 (note 1).

[20] See *Journal*, 8 Dec. 1894, 1306–8; 30 Jan. 1897, 251–5; 18 Dec. 1897, 1786–88; 26 Feb. 1898, 550–1; 18 June 1898, 1575–7.

[21] Philip H. Manson-Bahr, *The Life and Work of Sir Patrick Manson* (London: Cassell, 1927), p. 170. Friendly relations between Ross and Manson ended in 1912–13, when the pugnacious and litigious Ross threatened his former mentor with a libel action. The story is related in Eli Chernin, 'Sir Ronald Ross vs. Sir Patrick Manson: A Matter of Libel' *Journal of the History of Medicine and Allied Sciences* (1988) **43**: 262–74. See also the same author's 'Sir Ronald Ross, Malaria, and the Rewards of Research', *Medical History* (1988) **32**: 119–41.

[22] *Journal*, 22 Jan. 1900, 122–9. This paper, by Leishman and Wright, reported the results of antityphoid inoculation. For Leishman's other major papers see 21 Sept 1901, 757–8; 30 May 1903, 1252–4; 21 Nov. 1903, 1376–7; 6 Feb. 1904, 303. On Wright see Z. Cope, *Almroth Wright: Founder of Modern Vaccine Therapy* (London: Nelson, 1966), especially Chapters 3 and 4.

cured by quinine.[23] Wright had a long struggle to gain acceptance of his methods of inoculation. The *Journal* became the forum of debate on his theories and practices. Gowers described myopathy, a form of muscular dystrophy,[24] while Horsley wrote on the function of the motor area of the brain.[25]

If we treat Williams's tenure of office as being 1900–29, we find that a further 51 classic papers appeared in the *Journal* in this period, 27 of them in the decade 1900–1909. Over the same 30 years the *Lancet*'s score was 31. By the end of the Williams era the *Journal* had published 10 or more classic papers in three five-year periods, the last of which was 1905–9. The *Lancet* had never achieved this feat and did so only once afterwards (1935–9). By 1929 the *Journal*'s aggregate of Garrison and Morton entries stood at 102, compared with the *Lancet*'s 82. Thereafter the position began to change. In the 35 years, 1930–64, the *Journal* carried another 26 ground-breaking papers whereas the *Lancet* carried 44 with as many as 15 in 1935–9. As a consequence it regained its pre-eminence as the leading medical scientific weekly. Its total score over the whole period 1840–1964 stands at 133, against the *BMJ*'s 127.

What conclusions can be drawn from these statistics? Figure 1 shows that in terms of publishing major scientific and clinical papers the *Journal* was at its most productive during the last quarter of the nineteenth century and the first of the twentieth. This period, encompassing the editorial careers of Hart and Williams, coincided with a period of great vitality in other respects, for example, in terms of campaigning socio-medical journalism, so there are good grounds for regarding it as the *Journal*'s golden era. Before the mid-1870s and since 1930 the *BMJ*'s record in scientific publishing was and has been eclipsed by that of its major rival. For the earlier period this may be explained by the *Lancet*'s being established earlier and the influence of its dynamic founder. Under Thomas Wakley's leadership it secured an eminence which the *Journal* found hard to challenge. It is a measure of Hart's greatness that the late Victorian *Journal* did mount a successful challenge and attain the pre-eminent position in British medical journalism. Its relative decline as a scientific force since about 1930 must be attributed, at least in part, to the failure of Gerald Horner, Dawson Williams's successor, to maintain the high standards of his two immediate predecessors during his editorship between 1928 and 1946.

Anaesthesia

From the start the *Journal*'s editors claimed to be interested in 'scientific and

[23] *Journal*, 29 Sept. 1900, 949–51.
[24] *Ibid.*, 12 July 1902, 89–92.
[25] *Ibid.*, 17 July 1909, 125–32.

practical subjects of inquiry'.[26] They published clinical lectures and case notes with the object of keeping their readers, most of whom were general practitioners in the provinces, abreast of new developments. The discovery and introduction of inhalational anaesthesia coincided with the *Journal*'s early years.

The effects of the introduction of safe and effective anaesthesia have been immense, for before its discovery surgical treatment was severely circumscribed by the pain and shock which surgery inflicted. Operations had to be completed rapidly if patients were to recover, so not only was much of the body beyond the reach of surgical intervention but many potentially viable operations, for example, repair of damaged limbs, could not be attempted; amputation was the order of the day. However, far-reaching as the implications of the discoveries of the 1840s were, it has been suggested that they were seen as having no great importance until the following decade.[27] Do the pages of the *Journal* confirm this suggestion?

Its first reference to the use of ether in surgery was in January 1847 when it gave details of several operations. The article quoted at length from a letter written by Dr John Ware, a professor of medicine in Boston, Massachusetts. In his letter, written in November 1846, Ware wrote of 'a mode of rendering patients insensible to the pain of surgical operations by the inhalation of the vapour of the strongest sulphuric aether'. The *Journal* also drew attention to Robert Liston's operations performed at University College Hospital in December 1846. His amputation of a thigh and removal of a nail are usually recognized as being the first performed in Britain on anaesthetized patients. Liston's satisfaction with ether elicited his famous remark that 'This Yankee dodge beats mesmerism hollow'. The *Journal* documented other cases in which British surgeons quickly followed Liston's example in using anaesthetic.[28] It also described the inhalers used by Liston and others. The *Journal*'s assessment of these developments was that

> The announcement of a new means of performing surgical operations without pain has excited much general interest, and been already so extensively diffused throughout the country, that it is now merely necessary to bring forward, from time to time, such evidence of the efficiency of the new mode, as shall enable us to estimate its advantages, and to appreciate aright those circumstances under which it may hereafter be available, or otherwise, for affecting the end in view.[29]

In March 1847 Streeten published a leading article on anaesthesia. Noting that the practice 'has taken so fast a hold of almost every professional man in

[26] *Ibid.*, 3 Oct. 1840, 2.

[27] C. and G. Lawrence, *No Laughing Matter. Historical Aspects of Anaesthesia.* Catalogue of an exhibition held at the Wellcome Institute for the History of Medicine, 8 June to 25 September 1987. (London: Wellcome Institute for the History of Medicine/Science Museum, 1987), p. 12.

[28] *Journal*, 27 Jan. 1847, 54–5.

[29] *Ibid.*, 13 Jan. 1847, 27–8.

this country', he felt impelled to advise against over-enthusiasm. He seems to have felt that the discovery of a means of safely alleviating pain during surgical operations was too good to be true. Indeed, the same number of the *Journal* carried the first account of a death of an anaesthetized patient.[30] The *Journal*'s caution was in marked contrast to the excitement of the profession, both in Britain and on the continent. A letter from Paris, written in February 1847, noted that 'The mind of the profession here, is entirely occupied upon the aether question, to the temporary exclusion of all others.'[31] George Humphry, surgeon to Addenbrooke's Hospital, Cambridge wrote in the *Journal* in 1848, of the more recently discovered chloroform, as a 'wondrous boon'. Although urging discretion in the 'employment of such very powerful agents', he was already convinced that 'by no previous discovery, except perhaps that inestimable one of vaccination, has so much pain been saved at so little cost.'[32] Hence, anaesthesia seems to have been recognized by the profession in the 1840s as an innovation of the utmost importance.

Towards the end of 1847 the *Journal* published James Simpson's paper reporting the 'Discovery of a New Anaesthetic Agent More Efficient than Sulphuric Aether'.[33] The new agent was chloroform. Simpson, who was Professor of Midwifery at Edinburgh University and Physician Accoucheur to Her Majesty in Scotland, claimed to have been using chloroform in surgery, midwifery, and dentistry 'for some time previously'. In fact, the accidental discovery had occurred on 4 November, its first use in dental, obstetric, and surgical cases taking place in the course of the next week. Simpson's paper in the *Journal* is dated 15 November, the very day for which he subsequently claimed that 'the anaesthetic effects of chloroform were discovered', that is, finally established in surgery.[34]

Simpson believed that chloroform had several advantages over ether. First, a smaller quantity was needed to achieve the same effect, so it was cheaper and easier to transport. Second, its action was quicker, more complete and longer lasting. Third, no special inhaler was needed, merely a handkerchief or piece of sponge. Fourth, it was pleasanter for the patient to inhale and also for those in attendance at the operation. Simpson's paper was of major importance. It appeared in the *PMSJ* at a time when some members of the Association were questioning the *Journal*'s scientific value.

A major stimulus towards the acceptance of anaesthesia came in April 1853 when Queen Victoria gave birth to her eighth child. Under the direction of her physician, Sir James Clark, John Snow, who has been called 'the first

[30] *Ibid.*, 10 March 1847, 129.

[31] *Ibid.*, 139.

[32] *Ibid.*, 9 Aug. 1848, 427.

[33] *Ibid.*, 1 Dec. 1847, 656–8. The paper was published in the *Lancet* first. See 20 Nov. 1847, 549.

[34] See A. J. Youngson, *The Scientific Revolution in Victorian Medicine* (London: Croom Helm, 1979), Chapter 2.

professional anaesthetist', gave a small amount of chloroform—enough to soothe, rather than produce insensibility—during the final stages of labour.[35] The Queen was delighted 'beyond measure' with the 'blessed chloroform', and Sir James informed Simpson that it had speeded Her Majesty's recovery.

The use of chloroform in the royal birth was a tremendous boost in favour of its acceptance; after all in a good many cases, as the *Journal* had documented, anaesthesia had resulted in death.[36] The *Journal*, then edited by Cormack, was quick to recognize that the royal experience would have important implications:

> The responsible position, and the acknowledged skill of the physicians who sanctioned the inhalation of chloroform, the Royal Majesty of the patient, and the excellence of her recovery, are circumstances which will probably remove much of the lingering professional and popular prejudice against the use of anaesthesia in midwifery . . . .[37]

In contrast, the *Lancet* expressed astonishment that HM physicians could have sanctioned the use of chloroform, preferring to believe that it had all been a pretence.[38]

Cormack certainly believed that he had 'scooped' his rival by publishing the story not only first but accurately.[39] He consolidated his triumph a month later with an article by Snow 'On the Administration of Chloroform During Parturition'.[40] In July he published another paper by Simpson on 'The Propriety and Morality of Using Anaesthetics in Instrumental and Natural Parturition'.[41] In this Simpson answered those critics who opposed anaesthesia in labour on the grounds that it interfered with a natural function involving natural pain. Victoria's biographer states that 'It might well be claimed that Queen Victoria's greatest gift to her people was a refusal to accept pain in childbirth as woman's divinely appointed destiny.'[42] When this statement was made in the early 1960s it was uncontroversial. More recently some feminist historians have taken a different view, arguing that anaesthesia has deprived women of 'their rightful experience of, and control over, a supremely feminine function'.[43] The *Journal*'s editorial line was clear:

> From a careful perusal of most of that which has been written on the subject, as well

[35] C. Singer and E. A. Underwood, *A Short History of Medicine* (Oxford: Oxford University Press, 1962), p. 346. Pelling suggests that Snow's work on anaesthesia 'may have been of higher intellectual quality than his work on cholera'. Margaret Pelling, *Cholera, Fever and English Medicine, 1825–1865* (Oxford: Oxford University Press, 1978), p. 204.

[36] *Journal*, 1 April 1853, 281.

[37] *Ibid.*, 15 April 1853, 318; see 11 Aug. 1877, 175.

[38] *Lancet*, 14 May 1853, 453; see *Journal*, 27 May 1853, 450. See A. J. Youngson, *The Scientific Revolution in Victorian Medicine*, pp. 122–4 (note 34).

[39] *Journal*, 3 June 1853, 478.

[40] *Ibid.*, 10 June 1853, 500–2.

[41] *Ibid.*, 8 July 1853, 582–9.

[42] E. Longford, *Victoria R.I.* (London: Pan, 1966), p. 292.

[43] C. Lawrence and G. Lawrence, *No Laughing Matter*, p. 41 (note 27).

as from some personal experience of the practice, we may ... state, as our own humble opinion that the cautious inhalation of the vapour of chloroform during labour is entirely free from danger, and calculated to afford merciful relief from pain, in one of the most agonizing trials of humanity.[44]

The *Lancet*, however, remained unpersuaded and for some years continued to ignore the connection between anaesthetics and obstetrics.[45]

If Queen Victoria's experience gave encouragement to the use of anaesthesia in childbirth, the Crimean War soon provided an opportunity to test its value in warfare. Here too Cormack showed enthusiasm. Naval and military surgeons were liberally supplied with chloroform but advised not to use it in operations on gunshot wounds or other severe injuries. In a leading article Cormack expressed astonishment at this recommendation, for in civil and foreign military practice it had been found to work well in such cases. Except in major battles, such as that of the Alma, where manpower shortages made anaesthesia less feasible because its application required a second attendant, Cormack believed it to be invaluable.[46] In December the *Journal* published an article on 'Amputation at the Shoulder-Joint Under the Influence of Chloroform, in a Case of Gun-Shot Wound'. Its author confirmed Cormack's observation 'that the state of constitutional alarm or shock which succeeds any bad injury need not of necessity preclude the exhibition of chloroform'.[47]

In fact, the *Journal* has published more seminal articles on anaesthesia than on any other subject. In the 1870s Clover published his two papers on ether inhalers.[48] In the 1880s Sir William Macewan (1848–1924) published his 'Clinical Observations on the Introduction of Tracheal Tubes by the Mouth, instead of Performing Tracheotomy or Laryngotomy', which described giving chloroform through a metal tracheal tube introduced by the mouth (endotracheal anaesthesia).[49] In the 1920s Yandell Henderson's (1873–1944) 'Lecture on Respiration in Anaesthesia',[50] Elmer McKesson's (1881–1935) 'Administration of Gas-Ether',[51] and Sir Denis Browne's (1892–1967) 'Anaesthesia for Tonsillectomy and Removal of Adenoids'[52] were all published in the *Journal*.

Lister and antisepsis

If anaesthaesia was one of the two most important advances affecting surgery

[44] *Journal*, 27 May 1853, 450.
[45] A. J. Youngson, *The Scientific Revolution in Victorian Medicine*, pp. 123–4 (note 34).
[46] *Journal*, 17 Nov. 1854, 1029–30.
[47] *Ibid.*, 22 Dec. 1854, 1143.
[48] *Ibid.*,15 March 1873, 282–3; 15 July 1876, 74–5.
[49] *Ibid.*, 24 July 1880, 122–4 and 31 July 1880, 163–5.
[50] *Ibid.*, 19 Dec. 1925, 1170–5.
[51] *Ibid.*, 11 Dec. 1926, 1113–17.
[52] *Ibid.*, 6 Oct. 1928, 632.

in the nineteenth century, Lister's antiseptic system was the other. Until it came into common use, those who survived the surgeon's knife, or, for that matter, childbirth, faced the awful threat of post-operative sepsis, in the form of pyaemia, septicaemia, erysipelas, puerperal fever (in childbirth), and hospital gangrene.[53] In 1867 Joseph Lister, then Professor of Surgery at Glasgow University, published his first paper on antisepsis in the *Lancet*.

Lister's work owed a heavy debt to the researches of Louis Pasteur. It was Pasteur who had discovered that the air carried micro-organisms or germs which produced putrefaction; he demonstrated that this putrefaction could be avoided if the micro-organisms were filtered out of air reaching putrescible matter. Lister's achievement was in deducing that micro-organisms were the cause of post-operative sepsis, in recognizing that Pasteur's discovery could be of relevance in surgery, and in evolving practical methods for preventing the entry of germs into surgical wounds. What was necessary, he wrote in the *Lancet*, was to cover a wound with a dressing—he initially used carbolic acid—powerful enough to kill the germs which caused suppuration without damaging living tissue.[54] Of course, this oversimplifies Lister's principle, which consisted, notwithstanding the misapprehensions of some contemporaries, of more than sloshing carbolic acid on to wounds.

Though Lister was still refining his theories and practices at the end of the century, the essentials of his antiseptic principle were established in the period 1867–1871. Today it may seem little more than a truism, but the fact is that his was a major breakthrough which 'did more than anything before or since to reduce the risks of surgery'.[55] Despite, or perhaps because of, the importance of Lister's discovery, the British medical establishment was reluctant to accept it. Indeed, although Lister's findings were first published in the *Lancet*, that journal was for some time 'no supporter of Lister'. In 1871 it criticized his address on the antiseptic principle, delivered to the annual meeting of the BMA, observing in a leading article that 'Disbelievers in the marvellous efficacy of carbolic acid could not fail to notice that with every public appearance Professor Lister's solutions become weaker and weaker, while his faith appears to grow more and more'.[56]

In August 1867 Lister read a paper on 'The Antiseptic Principle in the Practice of Surgery' to the BMA's surgical section at the annual meeting in Dublin. This paper was published in the *Journal* (and simultaneously in the *Lancet*), with no editorial comment, in September. It was one of his

[53] Before Lister's innovations the method of dealing with hospital gangrene was to burn away the mortified flesh with caustics. G. T. Wrench, *Lord Lister: His Life and Work* (London: Fisher Unwin, 1913), p. 32.

[54] A. J. Youngson, *The Scientific Revolution in Victorian Medicine*, pp. 144–5 (note 34).

[55] *Ibid.*, p. 157.

[56] Quoted in P. Vaughan, *Doctors' Commons. A Short History of the British Medical Association* (London: Heinemann, 1959), p. 107; see *Lancet*, 23 Oct. 1875, 597; A. J. Youngson, *The Scientific Revolution in Victorian Medicine*, pp. 193 (note 34).

fundamental statements.[57] In the following years the *Journal* published many of Lister's papers on his system. It was still doing so as late as 1908, when Lister was 81.[58] But the *Journal* was perhaps less notable as publisher of Lister's work, than as a vigorous champion of it. As one of Lister's biographers has it, Hart's 'advocacy of Lister ... [was] ... so potent for good'.[59]

In January 1868 Hart published a paper by James Syme on antisepsis. Syme, for many years Lister's friend and mentor, as well as his father-in-law, had held the chair of clinical surgery at Edinburgh University since 1833. In the 1850s he was reckoned to be 'the most distinguished surgeon in Britain and perhaps in Europe'.[60] He was also 'the first of the old school of surgeons to recognize Lister's greatness'.[61] Syme had tried the antiseptic system and was persuaded of its value. His *BMJ* paper sought 'to illustrate and recommend the antiseptic principles of practice introduced by Mr. Lister, which, although of the greatest value, there is reason to fear are not yet generally understood or adopted'. It concluded with a vigorous defence of Lister:

> From such cases as those which have just been related, it is evident that there has taken place in surgical practice an improvement which promises to produce a great diminution of human suffering and danger. Some attempts have been made, anonymously and otherwise, to filch away from Mr. Lister the credit justly due to him for devising and establishing the antiseptic system, by representing the use of carbolic acid previously for other purposes as an anticipation of his treatment. But, although the agent was not new, the principles of its employment, the modes of its application, and the results of its effects, being so entirely original, I venture to hope that the members of my profession will no longer tacitly sanction such disingenuous and ungenerous conduct.[62]

[57] *Journal*, 21 Sept. 1867, 246–8; A. J. Youngson, *The Scientific Revolution in Victorian Medicine*, pp. 159–60 (note 34); Sir Rickman John Godlee, *Lord Lister* (Oxford: Clarendon Press, 1924 edn), p. 192

[58] In 1868 and 1869 the *Journal* published Lister's address to the Medico-Chirurgical Society of Glasgow on the 'Antiseptic System of Treatment in Surgery' and his inaugural lecture as Professor of Clinical Surgery at Edinburgh University, in which he tackled further the subjects of the germ theory and antiseptic system. In 1871 it published his Address in Surgery delivered to the 39th Annual Meeting of the BMA in Plymouth. Four years later the *Journal* carried Lister's 'Address on the Effect of the Antiseptic Treatment Upon the General Salubrity of Surgical Hospitals' given to the BMA's Edinburgh meeting. Over the years the *Journal* published many more of Lister's papers and addresses. See 18 July 1868, 53–6; 1 Aug. 1868, 101–2; 31 Oct. 1868, 461–3; 14 Nov. 1868, 515–17; 3 April 1869, 301–4; 4 Dec. 1869, 601–4; 3 Sept. 1870, 243–4; 14 Jan. 1871, 30–2; 26 Aug. 1871, 225–33; 27 June 1908, 1557; R. B. Fisher, *Joseph Lister 1827–1912* (London: Macdonald and Jane's, 1977), p. 273.

[59] G. T. Wrench, *Lord Lister*, p. 290 (note 53). See also R. B. Fisher, *Joseph Lister 1827–1912*, pp. 228–9 (note 58).

[60] A. J. Youngson, *The Scientific Revolution in Victorian Medicine*, p. 138 (note 34); see also pp. 30–2; G. T. Wrench, *Lord Lister*, pp. 37–62 (note 53).

[61] *Ibid.*, p. 156.

[62] *Journal*, 4 Jan. 1868, 1–2; G. T. Wrench, *Lord Lister*, p. 156 (note 53).

As Syme's remarks make clear, the opposition to Lister and his so-called 'carbolic acid mania' was gathering. This was at least partly due to the fact that, if Lister's theory and system were correct, then distinguished 'pre-Lister' surgeons stood to lose all claim to seniority and eminence and to be reduced, in effect, to mere novices.[63]

Among Lister's critics there were those who denied the germ theory and refused to accept that the air was contaminated with malignant organisms which could set up mortification in surgical wounds. If Lister were right, they wondered, why was not a simple abrasion, burn, or scald 'a death-warrant, without hope of reprieve'?[64] It was not, of course, necessary to accept the germ theory in order to value the antiseptic system. Its usefulness was established if it could be shown that it appreciably reduced post-operative infection and increased the incidence of recovery. But there was by no means universal agreement that it did. James Simpson and Lawson Tait were two of many illustrious anti-Listerites. Simpson argued that Lister's system was neither original nor effective. Tait refused to use anything but unboiled tap water; as late as 1898 he continued to deny Lister's contribution to surgery and medicine.[65]

At the BMA's annual meeting in Leeds in 1869 Thomas Nunneley, who delivered the Address in Surgery argued against the antiseptic system, claiming that its results were no better than those obtained when it was not used:

> During the last three years, since 'the antiseptic treatment' has been in vogue, I have not allowed one of my patients to be treated with carbolic acid; while my colleagues have very extensively employed it and . . . fairly tried it. The result is, that my cases without it are as good as theirs with it.

As a result, Nunneley stated, many of his colleagues who had adopted it were abandoning it as untrustworthy. Lister wrote to the *Journal* pointing out that Nunneley had misunderstood his published views, and there followed a lengthy correspondence about the merits of Lister's innovations.[66] In September the *Journal*, then edited by Hutchinson, published its first leading article on the controversy: 'Carbolic and the Treatment of Wounds'. This was a cautious assessment which paid tribute to Lister's achievements and urged that discussion of the subject should avoid the 'personal element'. But the main conclusion was that judgement of 'Lister's method' should be suspended pending 'the result of accumulated experience'.[67]

[63] A. J. Youngson, *The Scientific Revolution in Victorian Medicine*, p. 191 (note 34).

[64] *Journal*, 7 Aug. 1869, 152.

[65] A. J. Youngson, *The Scientific Revolution in Victorian Medicine*, pp. 162–72 (note 34); *Journal*, 15 May 1886, 921–3; F. B. Smith, *The People's Health, 1830–1910* (London: Croom Helm, 1979), 274–5; R. B. Fisher, *Joseph Lister 1827–1912*, pp. 308–9 (note 58); R. J. Godlee, *Lord Lister*, Chapter xiv (note 57).

[66] *Journal*, 7 Aug. 1869, 152–6; 21 Aug. 1869, 227; 28 Aug. 1869, 256–7; R. B. Fisher, *Joseph Lister 1827–1912*, p. 168 (note 58); R. J. Godlee, *Lord Lister*, pp. 311–13 (note 57).

[67] *Journal*, 4 Sept. 1869, 269–70.

During 1870 the *Journal*'s own correspondent wrote articles on the antiseptic system in the Edinburgh and Glasgow Royal Infirmaries, while a leading article, probably written by Hart, discussed its use in Berlin.[68] All of these and other communications in the early 1870s gave positive assessments. But in 1873 a more critical note was struck. At the BMA's annual meeting in London in that year, John Wood, of King's College, London, questioned the originality and effectiveness of Lister's system.[69] A few weeks later the *Journal* devoted a leading article to Wood's address. In this it was noted that the 'theoretical groundwork of Professor Lister's method has been rudely assailed, and has been but feebly defended. To re-establish it in the belief of the general professional public, experimental proof is required, which as yet has not been furnished by its author or any of his disciples.' The article went on to inquire whether there was evidence in Edinburgh that complications of wounds were less frequent in the antiseptic than the non-antiseptic wards.[70]

This editorial was less an attack on antisepticism than a criticism of Lister's failure to promote it and answer his critics.[71] Wood's attack and the *Journal*'s leader drew a sharp retort from Lister, who implied that Wood's failures originated in defective practice.[72] Notwithstanding this whiff of criticism, it is undoubtedly true that, as one of Lister's biographers puts it, the *BMJ* was 'Lister's chief supporter'.[73] This was well illustrated in 1877 when Lister first rejected, then accepted the post of Professor of Surgery at King's College Hospital, London.

Wood's criticism of Lister was symptomatic of the views of the metropolitan medical establishment. For, while the antiseptic system was becoming widely accepted and practised in Scotland, the English provinces, and Europe, in London and the pages of the *Lancet* there was continued resistance, not to say hostility and ridicule.[74] It was against this background that, in 1877, Lister was offered the position at King's formerly occupied by Sir William Fergusson. Fergusson's natural successor by reason of seniority would, in fact, have been John Wood, but the *BMJ* enthusiastically supported those 'influential persons at the College' who wanted to offer the post to Lister.[75] Partly because of the terms of the original offer, Lister

[68] *Journal*, 19 March 1870, 285–6; 9 April 1870, 361; 28 May 1870, 557.

[69] *Ibid.*, 9 Aug. 1873, 146–52.

[70] *Ibid.*, 30 Aug. 1873, 264–5.

[71] Lister is often termed cool, aloof, reserved, grave, and unapproachable. According to A. J. Youngson, *The Scientific Revolution in Victorian Medicine*, p. 159 (note 34), he 'was neither an eager nor a skilful controversialist'.

[72] *Journal*, 13 Sept. 1873, 339.

[73] G. T. Wrench, *Lord Lister*, p. 269 (note 53). See R. B. Fisher, *Joseph Lister 1827–1912*, p. 228 (note 58).

[74] *Journal*, 26 May 1877, 657; *Lancet*, 20 Nov. 1875, 743; G. T. Wrench, *Lord Lister*, pp. 264–7 (note 53); A. J. Youngson, *The Scientific Revolution in Victorian Medicine*, pp. 189–90 (note 34); R. J. Godlee, *Lord Lister*, pp. 320–31, Chapter XXI (note 57).

[75] *Journal*, 17 Feb. 1877, 212–13; R. B. Fisher, *Joseph Lister* 1827–1912, pp. 224–5 (note 58).

initially rejected the opportunity to return to his native city. The *Journal* commented:

> King's College thus suffers an irreparable loss; and the loss is hardly less to the surgical school of London generally, since it could not but have been of the highest interest and value to the metropolitan school of surgery to have had the antiseptic system of surgery carried out in its midst by the distinguished surgeon with whose name that system is identified throughout the world, and under whose auspices its greatest triumphs have been achieved.[76]

But Lister appreciated the importance of converting leaders of the profession in London. When he was given the opportunity to teach clinical medicine, to manage his own separate wards, and to appoint his own Edinburgh-trained house surgeons, dressers, and nurses, he changed his mind.[77] The *Journal* greeted his arrival in the capital with great satisfaction; the *Lancet* preserved a discreet silence. During Lister's early years at King's the *Journal* was 'his only staunch ally'. For his part, Lister was grateful for the support that Hart had given through the pages of the *Journal*.[78]

Lister soon made converts of many of those, including Wood, who had formerly opposed him. The year 1879 was a 'decisive one in the history of Listerism'. Lister was acclaimed at the Sixth International Congress of Medical Science in Amsterdam, and his methods were warmly endorsed by leading metropolitan surgeons at a meeting of the south London district of the BMA's Metropolitan Counties branch.[79] Towards the end of the year the *Journal* reviewed the great man's triumph and its own part in bringing it about:

> We heartily congratulate ourselves and the profession that Mr. Lister's coming to London has been so speedily followed by a signal triumph of that great principle in surgery which had been accepted everywhere else almost before it was even listened to in London. It was with the conviction that this necessary triumph would follow, that we strongly urged the authorities at King's College to put aside small traditions and petty jealousies, and to invite the great London surgeon ... to assume the mantle ... of Fergusson .... Mr. Lister has been but two years in London, and already he may say that he 'came, saw, and conquered'; for the principle of antisepticism has now so strongly asserted itself in London hospitals, that it is bound to make its way and to establish itself here as firmly as elsewhere throughout the world.[80]

Lister's success was accelerated by a paper that his registrar, Watson Cheyne, published in the *BMJ*. This provided a statistical analysis of Lister's operations since 1871, and thereby supplied an omission, for Lister had

[76] *Journal*, 31 March 1877, 401.

[77] Between 1869 and 1877 Lister had occupied the chair of clinical surgery at Edinburgh.

[78] *Journal*, 6 Oct. 1877, 489; G. T. Wrench, *Lord Lister*, p. 273 (note 53); R. B. Fisher, *Joseph Lister 1827–1912*, pp. 229, 301 (note 58).

[79] *Journal*, 20 Sept. 1879, 453–9; 6 Dec. 1879, 906–13; G. T. Wrench, *Lord Lister*, pp. 278–91 (note 53); R. B. Fisher, *Joseph Lister 1827–1912*, p. 252 (note 58).

[80] *Journal*, 13 Dec. 1879, 943; see also 20 Sept. 1879, 468.

frequently been criticized for failing to publish, and even of suppressing, statistics of his cases. As recently as August 1879 the *Journal* itself had observed 'that there is something, we will not say suspicious, but at any rate strange, in the persistent avoidance of the challenge so often thrown out to Mr Lister and his followers to show, by actual comparison, whether, and if so, how far, their results are really superior to those of surgeons who do not admit their theory.'[81] Of Cheyne's account the *Journal* said: 'The result shown is so marvellous a triumph over accidents known to be inseparable from a series of such operations till Lister robbed them of their danger, that they require no comment'.[82] They may have required no comment from the *Journal*, but they elicited comments a-plenty from James Spence, who, as Professor of Surgery at Edinburgh University, had been a senior colleague of Lister's.

Motivated, it has been said, by envy, Spence launched 'the last and bitterest attack against Lister' in the pages of the *BMJ*.[83] In two papers entitled 'Surgical Statistics', Spence sought to show how his simpler methods of dressing were superior to those pioneered by Lister.[84] His argument was comfortably refuted by both Lister and Cheyne, while the *Journal*, in a later editorial, concluded that 'the result of the discussion has only been to bring out in more striking contrast the imperfections of "simple" methods of dressing in the hands of a most distinguished surgeon, when compared with the brilliant results of treatment conducted on strict Listerian principles.'[85] In a later letter Spence dismissed this leading article as 'distorted' and complained that Hart had suppressed parts of his original text. Hart replied that he had cut only such 'objectionable . . . acrimonious personal remarks' that were 'scarcely worthy of so eminent a surgeon'. On this note he decreed that the controversy should cease.[86]

Although Lawson Tait continued to hold out against the antiseptic principle, the controversy over it effectively ceased in 1879.[87] Eighteen years later, in its Queen's Jubilee number, the *Journal* summed up antisepsis as 'the most powerful agency in the development of surgery' which 'has made operative proceedings possible which only twenty-five years ago would have

[81] *Ibid.*, 9 Aug. 1879, 232. See A. J. Youngson, *The Scientific Revolution in Victorian Medicine*, p. 192 (note 34); *Lancet*, 16 Oct. 1875, 565.

[82] *Journal*, 29 Nov. 1879, 859–64, 869; G. T. Wrench, *Lord Lister*, p. 284 (note 53).

[83] *Ibid.*

[84] *Journal*, 24 Jan. 1880, 119–21; 20 March 1880, 434–8.

[85] *Ibid.*, 14 Feb. 1880, 237–41; 10 April 1880, 559.

[86] *Ibid.*, 29 May 1880, 831–2; G. T. Wrench, *Lord Lister*, p. 286 (note 53); R. B. Fisher, *Joseph Lister 1827–1912*, pp. 258–9 (note 58).

[87] On Tait's views see W. J. S. McKay, *Lawson Tait. His Life and Work* (London: Baillière, 1922), pp. 364–96. His position is demonstrated in his article, 'The Antiseptic Theory Tested by the Statistics of One Hundred Cases of Successful Ovariotomy', *Journal*, 14 Feb. 1880, 243–4. See also his 'Address on the Present Aspect of Antiseptic Surgery', *Journal*, 27 Sept. 1890, 728–32; R. B. Fisher, *Joseph Lister 1827–1912*, pp. 308–9 (note 58).

been justly condemned as criminal; has freed surgical wards from pyaemia and allied scourges . . . and has reduced the mortality of lying-in hospitals, which, without such precautions, have generally been hotbeds of septic disease.'[88] If this was a valid judgement, as it surely was, the *BMJ* might also have looked back with satisfaction at the support it had given to Lister when he was under attack from many quarters. Because Lister was a poor propagandist and unskilful disseminator of his results, it was important that those convinced by his methods should support him. In this respect he was well served by the *Journal*, which thereby performed an important function in hastening acceptance of antisepsis.

The *Journal* and the Roentgen ray

In November 1895 Professor Wilhelm Conrad Roentgen, building on the work of Crookes, Hittorf, Lenard, Ruhmkorff, and others, made his famous discovery of a ray—he called it the X-ray—capable of penetrating wood, paper, cloth, and other materials and silhouetting bones within living flesh. News of his discovery, which was made known to the world early in the following year, rapidly reached the United Kingdom, where it excited the attention of the London and provincial press.[89] On 11 January the *Lancet*, in a jocular, sub-Dickensian editorial, became the first English-language medical journal to cover the news. Only in the following week did it concede that the discovery could have implications for medical and surgical practice.[90]

The *Journal*'s first reference to the Roentgen Ray, as it was normally termed at this time, came on 18 January when it published four paragraphs from Arthur Schuster, Professor of Physics at Owen's College, Manchester, on 'The New Kind of Radiation'.[91] Roentgen had sent copies of his paper to two British physicists, Schuster and Lord Kelvin. Schuster, as his daughter, Nora, related in an article published in the *Journal* nearly 70 years later, 'was so immediately fascinated by it that he kept his pretty young wife, the cabby, and the horse waiting outside in the chill winter evening (on the way from the railway station) while he read the pamphlet twice over in his laboratory.'[92] Professor Schuster's communication gave the gist of Roentgen's paper and affirmed that 'a most important discovery . . . [with] . . . many possible medical applications . . . has been made.'[93]

[88] *Journal*, 19 June 1897, 1522.

[89] The best history of radiology is E. H. Burrows, *Pioneers and Early Years. A History of British Radiology* (St Anne, Alderney: Colophon, 1986). See also R. F. Mould, *A History of X-Rays and Radium with a Chapter on Radiation Units: 1895–1937* (Sutton: IPC, 1980).

[90] E. H. Burrows, *Pioneers and Early Years*, p. 18 (note 89).

[91] *Journal*, 18 Jan. 1896, 172–3. The *Journal* discussed the question of a name for the X-ray in an indecisive leading article. The term Roentgen Ray was dropped, because of its Germanic origins, in the First World War. *Journal*, 14 March 1896, 677–8.

[92] *Ibid.*, 3 Nov. 1962, 1164.

[93] *Ibid.*, 18 Jan. 1896, 172–3.

Thereafter material dealing with the new X-rays became a regular feature in the *Journal.* Once Roentgen had made his methods public it was possible for anyone with sufficient knowledge of physics and access to the appropriate equipment to replicate his results, and on 25 January the *Journal* included an X-ray photograph of his own hand taken by the electrical engineer, A. A. Campbell Swinton. This is thought to have been the first X-ray picture to be taken in Britain.[94] It was now clear that X-rays worked and that they had medical and surgical applications. On 1 February a leading article in the *Journal* stated:

It is some time since a scientific discovery of real importance has excited so much interest and popular attention as Roentgen's recent work on certain hitherto unknown rays of light has done. Nor is the reason of the popular interest difficult to find, for the application of the discovery to the photography of hidden structures is a feat sensational enough and likely to stimulate even the uneducated imagination.[95]

On 8 February the *Journal* 'secured a scoop' with the announcement that it had commissioned Sydney Rowland to produce a series of reports 'on the application of the new photography to medicine and surgery'.[96]

Sydney Domville Rowland was only 24 years of age when he became the *Journal*'s special commissioner on X-rays. He had been educated at Berkhamsted Grammar School and Downing College, Cambridge, where he took a first-class honours degree in natural sciences. At Cambridge he had been president of the Natural History Society; he had also been university demonstrator in zoology and physiology. In 1895 he was awarded a scholarship to pursue his medical studies at St Bartholomew's Hospital. But according to the writer of his *Journal* obituary, 'I don't think the clinical side of medicine ever appealed to him, and much of his time was spent in studying the development of *x* rays, which had just been discovered, and their application to medicine. He was also obliged to devote much of his energy to gaining subsistence.'[97] In fact, Rowland was Ernest Hart's nephew, and Hart had borne the financial responsibility of his education:

I have the very highest opinion of Mr. Rowland's capacity and character in every relation of life. He is a connection of mine by marriage, and I was so much impressed with his character and capacity that I undertook to bear the whole cost of his education. I have been training and intend him for staff work on the *Journal*, for which I consider him eminently fit. I think it is of great advantage to the *Journal* to have members of staff on whose personal devotion the Editor can count; and I have long felt the want on the *Journal* of a member of the staff who shall have special scientific capacities, knowledge and connections.[98]

[94] *Ibid.*, 3 Nov. 1962, 1165; Gerald Larkin, *Occupational Monopoly and Modern Medicine* (London: Tavistock, 1983), p. 61.

[95] *Journal*, 25 Jan. 1896, 238; 1 Feb. 1896, 289–90.

[96] *Ibid.*, 8 Feb. 1896, 361.

[97] *Ibid.*, 17 March 1917, 375.

[98] BMA mss. MCSC, VIII, Journal and Finance Committee, 14 April 1897, 3673.

In 1896 Rowland was due to take his final medical examinations, but Hart persuaded him to postpone these in order that he might work for the *Journal* on X-rays.

Hart provided his new reporter with much *Journal* space and in less than 18 months Rowland produced a total of 17 articles on 'the new photography', 13 of which were published in the first half of 1896. In April or May 1896 Rowland began his own journal, *Archives of Clinical Skiagraphy*, though his association with it lasted only two years.[99] He was a great enthusiast for his subject, and reading his reports still gives a real sense of witnessing the week-by-week progress of early British radiography as new inventions, techniques, and photographs are brought to readers' attention. Rowland travelled the country giving demonstrations with his own apparatus, which he was constantly refining, making contact with leading radiographers whose work he reported, and producing for the *Journal* copy, often accompanied by high-quality reproductions, which took it to the forefront of the new science.[100] For example, his article of 22 February 1896 dealt with work in progress in Sheffield, where Christopher Addison had succeeded in taking X-ray photographs of the blood vessels in a human hand and kidney. These, 'probably the first human angiograms ever performed', were reproduced as glossy prints in the *Journal*.[101] In March Rowland himself took, on a 14-minute exposure, a remarkable picture of the skeleton and deep visceral region of the head and trunk of a 3-month-old baby. This was reproduced as a double page spread in the *Journal* for whom it was 'hailed as a scoop'. Interest in the photographs was so enormous that Rowland gave his negatives to the London Stereoscopic Company, asking them to handle requests for copies.[102]

In effect Rowland turned the *BMJ* temporarily into 'a journal of radiology in miniature'. In so doing 'he played a crucial part as a medical publicist of the new method at an early stage when its protagonists in London were still seeking clinical credibility'.[103] Because the *Journal* was such a widely read and highly respected periodical, it provided the ideal forum for such publicity.

[99] This continued as *Archives of Skiagraphy* and *Archives of the Rontgen Ray* till 1915. See W. R. Le Fanu, *British Periodicals of Medicine* (Oxford: Wellcome Unit for the History of Medicine, 1984), 645, 656, 670; E. H. Burrows, *Pioneers and Early Years*, pp. 144–9 (note 89).

[100] Rowland provided demonstrations at the BMA's annual meeting in Carlisle. See *Journal* 1 Aug. 1896, 284. On his own experiments and refinements see 7 March 1896, 620. Rowland possessed 'a sound knowledge of engineering principles' and was a competent mechanic. His *Journal* obituary records that he was 'never happier than when devising technical means for attacking some problem or making the apparatus to be used in the investigation'. 17 March 1917, 375.

[101] *Ibid.*, 22 Feb. 1896, 495–6; E. H. Burrows, *Pioneers and Early Years*, p. 21 (note 89). This was the same Addison who went on to serve as Lloyd George's Minister of Health and Labour's post-1945 leader of the House of Lords.

[102] *Journal*, 28 March 1896, between 798–9, see 807–8; E. H. Burrows, *Pioneers and Early Years*, p. 19 (note 89).

[103] *Ibid.*

Accordingly, Rowland is now recognized as one of the pioneers of early British radiography, while the *Journal* is credited for nurturing the new science.[104] In contrast, the *Lancet* gave it much less space. Such coverage as it provided failed to match the exciting visual impact of its rival's, for it was either unable or unwilling to reproduce high-quality glossy photographs.

Notwithstanding the recognition accorded to Rowland's achievements by posterity, his work for the *Journal* earned him scant credit with the mandarins in the BMA. In order to perform his work as commissioner Rowland had purchased the equipment necessary to take X-ray pictures. The cost of this apparatus was over £98—a not inconsiderable sum when it is recalled that at the same time Hart was trying to have his nephew appointed to the *Journal* staff at a salary of £100 p.a. When Rowland submitted his accounts the Journal and Finance Committee resolved 'That Mr. Sydney Rowland be informed that he has no authority to order apparatus in the name of the British Medical Association, or pledge its credit in any way'.[105] Subsequently, Messrs Newton & Co of Fleet Street, who marketed the first focus tube (which enabled sharper pictures than those achieved by Roentgen to be produced), sent the Association a bill for £28 4s in respect of 'goods ordered by Mr. Sydney Rowland in the name of the Association'. As a result, Rowland was summoned to appear before the committee to explain himself.[106] The committee's proceedings have not survived, though we do know that Rowland's expenditure was accepted. That the acceptance was grudging is indicated by the committee's decision, at the same meeting, 'that Mr. Rowland be requested to furnish the General-Secretary with a list of the instruments belonging to the Association in his possession'.[107]

During 1896 Hart had appointed Rowland, as he had long intended, to a permanent position on the *Journal*. But, as we have seen, Rowland was not at this stage a qualified practitioner, having abandoned his medical studies in order to undertake his X-ray assignment. As a result, the Journal and Finance Committee referred his appointment back to the Reference Committee for reconsideration, resolving that Rowland's salary should be no more than £50 p.a. Hart, though by this time a very sick man, was furious with this decision. He wrote a memorandum pointing out his nephew's high scientific attainments and asserting his right as editor to appoint whomsoever he pleased to the *Journal* staff. With the Reference Committee urging compromise, the Journal and Finance Committee decided to postpone further consideration of the matter, agreeing instead to appoint a committee 'to

[104] *Ibid.*, pp. 18–20; see also R. F. Mould, *A History of X-Rays and Radium with a Chapter on Radiation Units: 1895–1937*, p. 1 (note 89).

[105] BMA mss. MCSC, VIII, Journal and Finance Committee, 20 Jan. 1897, 3609.

[106] *Ibid.*, 14 April 1897, 3672.

[107] *Ibid.*, 14 July 1897, 3724; see 20 Oct. 1897, 3761.

consider the course most desirable to take with the object of facilitating the resignation of Mr. Hart'.[108]

Rowland gained his qualification in 1897 but his days with the *Journal* were numbered, for his tenure of office depended upon his sick uncle's survival. When Hart died in the following January, Rowland could not long survive. In fact he received notice to quit in October 1898. His subsequent career makes interesting reading. After leaving the *Journal* he never returned to the subject of radiography. At the end of 1898 he took up an appointment as a bacteriologist with the Lister (at that time Jenner) Institute, where he remained for the rest of his career. He did important work in connection with plague in India. With the outbreak of the First World War he joined the Royal Army Medical Corps as a lieutenant (he was subsequently promoted to major). While investigating meningococcus carriers, he contracted the cerebro-spinal fever from which he died in 1917.[109]

Rowland's anonymous obituary in the *BMJ* states that he was not 'entirely successful' in either his X-ray or editorial work. It goes on to suggest that he would never have made a successful medical journalist for he was 'singularly devoid of any literary faculty'. We do not know the extent to which Rowland's copy for the *BMJ* was sub-edited, but the available evidence indicates these judgements to be harsh; both the *Journal* and the early development of radiography were well served by Rowland's work.

There is a remarkable postscript to the *Journal*'s coverage of the early history of radiography. In September 1916, under the heading, 'The Delineation of Internal Organs by an Electrical Method', the *Journal* carried a two-page account of a new system for depicting the inside of the living body without resort to surgery. The process, which put the *Journal*'s correspondent in mind of both X-ray photography and wireless telegraphy,

> appears to succeed just where *x*-ray photography fails, or, rather, it takes up the task of producing pictures of structures hidden far below the surface of the body just at the point where *x*-ray photography ceases to perform it effectively. In other words, the new work attempts the delineation not of dense structures such as bone, but of living soft organs, such as the liver, the kidneys, and the intestines.[110]

The alleged technique had been devised by one James Shearer, a Scottish-born, American-educated surgeon who was serving as a sergeant with the RAMC in France. By means of simple apparatus and electricity generated by the human body, a needle etched the outline of internal organs on to waxed paper revolving on a cylinder. This outline could then be converted into a photograph. When the authorities ascertained that Shearer possessed special electrical knowledge which might be put to use to further the war effort, he

[108] *Ibid*, 20 Jan. 1897, 3607–8; 14 April, 1897, 3672–74.
[109] *Journal*, 17 March 1917, 375–6; *Lancet*, 7 April 1917, 552.
[110] *Journal*, 30 Sept. 1916, 459–60.

was provided with opportunities to develop a 'discovery' that had given rise 'to a host of rumours, surmises, and conflicting views'.[111]

The author(s) of this and another *Journal* article dealing with Shearer's invention admitted that the results it produced were 'puzzling', even 'quite incomprehensible, if not incredible'. But he had no doubt as to their genuineness: 'It is certain . . . that they can be and are obtained.'[112] However, Shearer's account of how his technique worked was sheer gobbledegook:

> the process interposes between two alternating electric fields of equal strength—and at the precise point where they meet—a third electric field, whose facultative potential force is thus released and can be converted into dynamic power. It is this released circuit which operates the recording needle, and the pattern tapped out on the revolving cylinder varies with the shape of the organ furnishing that circuit.[113]

The *BMJ*'s account of Shearer's invention attracted considerable attention. Shearer was given additional facilities to pursue his research, including the assistance of a 'physicist of high repute'. In October the *Journal* made known its intention of printing a full account of his latest results in the near future.[114]

The account never appeared. In March 1917 the *Journal* published a short retraction: 'we have reason to believe that the inventor has failed to satisfy the physicists consulted as to the truth of his claims.'[115] According to the author of a recent history of radiography, Shearer was tried by court martial and sentenced to death by firing squad. His sentence was commuted to one of penal servitude, but he died in prison a year later.[116]

The International Medical Congresses, 1867–1913

The nineteenth century saw a proliferation of conferences and congresses, many of which were devoted to medical and surgical matters. As the century progressed more and more of these meetings became international.[117] Most were on a small scale and dealt with the various specializations of medical science, but in 1867 there began in Paris a series of regular, large-scale

[111] *Ibid.*

[112] The absence of *Journal* contributor lists makes it impossible to identify the correspondent, but it is possible that it was Dawson Williams. He visited France in September 1916 and would certainly have been interested in a revolutionary medical development such as Shearer's purported to be. One of the articles discussing the 'delineator' was written by 'a civilian at the front'.

[113] *Journal*, 30 Sept. 1916, 460.

[114] *Ibid.*, 21 Oct. 1916, 565.

[115] *Ibid.*, 24 March 1917, 401.

[116] See R. F. Mould, *A History of X-Rays and Radium with a Chapter on Radiation Units: 1895–1937*, p. 42 (note 89); Stephen Lock, 'Misconduct in Medical Research: Does it Exist in Britain?', *Journal*, 10 Dec. 1988, 1531–5.

[117] See Winifred Gregory (ed.), *International Congresses and Conferences, 1840–1937. A Union List of Their Publications Available in Libraries of the United States and Canada* (New York: Wilson, 1938). In researching this section I have benefited greatly from information and advice provided by Godelieve van Heteren, whose PhD thesis, 'British–German Connections in Medicine, 1858–1914, the Problem of Influence' (London University) is in preparation.

congresses, unrestricted by subject matter and intended for the profession at large, which continued until brought to an end by the First World War. These were the International Medical Congresses (IMC). The first IMC attracted over 1200 participants, and, although subsequent gatherings were on a more modest scale, the London Congress of 1881 was a giant affair with 3182 in attendance, of whom over 1000 came from overseas. Even this was dwarfed by the massive dimensions of some of the later IMCs, the largest for which figures have survived being Moscow (1897), where more than 7500 were present.

At first, and to some extent throughout, the British were lukewarm in their response to the IMC movement. Unlike some European governments, the United Kingdom sent no official representative to Paris. Indeed, only 72 Britons, amongst whom were few of any distinction, registered for the Congress. Of these, many were undoubtedly lured more by the glamour of a spell in the French capital than by the attractions of scientific discourse.[118] However, at the outset Ernest Hart and the *BMJ* expressed considerable enthusiasm for the IMC principle. The *Journal* gave publicity to the forthcoming Paris programme and regretted the lack of interest in it shown in Great Britain.[119] Hart attended the Congress (along with a former *BMJ* editor, Andrew Wynter) as the BMA's representative, and in all probability wrote the substantial reports on its proceedings that appeared in the *Journal* during August and September. Hart also made a speech at the Congress banquet at which he 'expressed a hope that an opportunity would be given, by a meeting of the Congress in London, for the medical men in England to demonstrate their confraternity with the profession abroad'.[120]

When it was all over, the *Journal* acknowledged that Paris had established the 'principle of a congress', but it was not uncritical of the way that principle had been put into effect. It particularly regretted the rigid management of proceedings, which prevented any meaningful discussion taking place, the airing of petty national jealousies, and the failure to make the occasion more of a social event.[121]

The next four IMCs were held in Florence (1869), Vienna (1873), Brussels (1875), and Geneva (1877). All were more or less ignored by the British; only Florence attracted more than seven British participants. The *Journal*, then edited by Jonathan Hutchinson, had a correspondent at Florence, but he was unimpressed by what he saw: '. . . if the first international Congress of Paris was a failure, this second is a decided *fiasco*.'[122] Vienna passed virtually unnoticed,[123] while the prospect of Brussels failed to send the *Journal*'s

[118] *Journal*, 21 Sept. 1867, 254–5.
[119] *Ibid.*, 20 July 1867, 48; 3 August 1867, 91.
[120] *Ibid.*, 31 Aug. 1867, 187, 189–92; see also 24 Aug. 1867, 167–8; 7 Sept. 1867, 212–13.
[121] *Ibid.*, 21 Sept. 1867, 254–5.
[122] *Ibid.*, 16 Oct. 1869, 427.
[123] *Ibid.*, 20 Sept. 1873, 355–6.

reporter into paroxysms of expectation: 'The past experience of these "international" congresses appears to have been sufficiently satisfactory to prolong their existence till this the fourth session . . . .'[124] Two years later, the *Journal* gave the Geneva Congress even less space than it had devoted to proceedings at Vienna four years earlier.

The *Journal*'s attitude changed abruptly with the Amsterdam Congress of 1879. Although this also attracted few British participants (20 out of a total registration of 600), it was extensively and enthusiastically reported by the *Journal* (some 20 000 words spread over more than 13 pages of one issue).[125] The Congress was graced by the presence of Lister and Lawson Tait, both of whom read papers, as well as Hart, who played an important part in the proceedings. He presented a paper ('Sur la Propagation de Fièvres Typhoides par Lait de Vache Infectée et sur la Prevention'), was elected an honorary president, and proposed a toast at the farewell banquet.[126]

Robert Brudenell Carter later suggested to William MacCormac, organizer of the 1881 London IMC, that Hart had proposed London as the next venue:

I DULY RECEIVED YOUR CIRCULAR TOUCHING THE INTERNATIONAL MEDICAL CONGRESS. IS IT NOT THE THING AT WHICH, LAST YEAR, AT SOME FOREIGN CAPITAL, DR. DRYSDALE AND MR. ERNEST ABRAHAM HART WERE SO GOOD AS TO TAKE UPON THEMSELVES TO REPRESENT THE ENGLISH PROFESSION, AND TO INVITE THE ASSEMBLED DELEGATES TO COME TO LONDON? IF SO, HAVE WE ANY SECURITY THAT THE DR. DRYSDALES AND THE ERNEST ABRAHAM HARTS OF OTHER COUNTRIES, IF SUCH THERE BE, WILL NOT POSE AMONGST US AS RESPECTABLE MEMBERS OF THE MEDICAL PROFESSION? I CONFESS I RATHER SHRINK FROM THE POSSIBILITY, AND WHILE I ADMIT HART'S CLEVERNESS IN INDUCING HONOURABLE MEN TO ALLOW THEIR NAMES TO BE DRAGGED THROUGH THE DIRT AT HIS TAIL, I HAVE NO AMBITION TO MAKE ONE OF THE PROCESSION.[127] [caps. in original]

Although Hart had proposed a London meeting in 1867, the suggestion which led to the choice of London for 1881 actually originated with Dr Warlomont of Brussels. He floated the idea during one of the Amsterdam sessions. Professor Donders of Utrecht, President of the Amsterdam Organizing Committee, then asked those present if anyone wished to oppose the proposal. As his question elicited only applause he declared London to be

124 *Ibid.*, 18 Sept. 1875, 374.

125 *Ibid.*, 20 Sept. 1879, 453–66.

126 See *Congrès Periodique des Sciences Médicales 6me. Session. Amsterdam Sept. 1879. Compte-Rendu Publié avec le Concours des Secrétaires des Sections par M. Guye et MM. de Perrot, Stokvis et Zeeman* (Amsterdam, 1880), II, pp. 94–119.

127 Royal College of Surgeons. MacCormac Papers. R. Brudenell Carter to Sir William MacCormac, 31 May 1880. Charles Drysdale read a paper on the regulation of prostitution to the general assembly of the Amsterdam Congress.

chosen.[128] Hart then rose to invite IMC members participating in the Congress also to attend the BMA's annual meeting in Ryde if the two events were sufficiently close together. Brudenell Carter was, therefore, misinformed.[129]

The London International Medical Congress of 1881 lasted for one week in early August. With an attendance list that included such medical 'superstars' as Koch, Lister, Pasteur, and Virchow, it constituted one of the most distinguished gatherings of medical men of that or any other era.[130] The Executive Committee of the Congress included an ex-*Journal* editor, Jonathan Hutchinson, who also held several other official posts, while Hart served on the Reception Committee and also as a council member of the section on State Medicine.[131]

In its reporting of the Congress the *Journal* gave no hint of the reservations expressed about previous IMCs. The words 'brilliant, 'splendid', 'powerful', 'overwhelming', and 'genius' are scattered throughout its accounts and leaders:

> The London session of the International Medical Congress has been inaugurated with even more than all the amplitude, brilliancy and completeness which could have been anticipated. In William MacCormac a new Carnot has been found, and success has been organised on a scale suitable to the metropolis of Great Britain and to the famous city of four millions. Medicine has never been more fully represented, or more publicly honoured, than in the great assemblage of Wednesday, the third of August, when the Royal Princes of the great Teutonic and English empires, standing side by side on a platform graced and dignified by the most representative and illustrious of physicians and surgeons of the world, declared the Congress of 1881 open for its work. By the side of Paget and Jenner stood Langenbeck, Pasteur, Virchow, Charcot, Donders, Austin Flint, and Pantaleone.[132]

So convinced was Hart of the importance of the occasion that he planned to publish a daily edition of the *BMJ* in order to do justice to the papers presented and proceedings conducted in the 15 separate Congress sections. But the organizers made such thorough arrangements for reporting 'as to relieve the medical journals of any very urgent duty in this respect . . . the arrangements are so complete, as largely to supercede the ordinary functions of the weekly journals.' Nevertheless, most of the 6 August and much of the following week's issue of the *Journal* were devoted to the reprinted addresses

[128] *Compte-Rendu*, I, p. 155 (note 126); *Journal*, 20 Sept. 1879, 454.

[129] Brudenell Carter's scathing comments about Hart were not out of character for he possessed a combative character and vitriolic tongue, see *Lancet*, 6 Oct. 1923, 726; *Plarr's Lives of the Fellows of the Royal College of Surgeons of England*, vol. 1 (Bristol: Wright, 1930), pp. 201–2. As a journalist with the *Lancet* he would have known Hart well. He had been an applicant for the editorship of the *BMJ* in 1869, when Hutchinson was appointed.

[130] Alex Sakula, 'Baroness Burdett-Coutts' Garden Party: The International Medical Congress, London, 1881' *Medical History* (1982) **26**: 183–90.

[131] *Journal*, 17 July 1880, 104; 22 Jan. 1881, 138.

[132] *Ibid.*, 6 Aug. 1881, 230–1; 13 Aug. 1881, 290-2.

and reports of Congress affairs. As late as October the *Journal* was still allocating substantial space to Congress proceedings.

The London IMC has been described as 'arguably the greatest and most historic medical congress ever held'.[133] But it is not easy to evaluate its practical achievements. It may have 'proved to be a landmark in the general acceptance of the role of the new science of bacteriology in medicine, surgery, and public health'.[134] It is doubtful, however, whether the progress of the new science would have been seriously impeded if the Congress had never taken place. In the last analysis the real importance of the London IMC lay in the less tangible achievements of inspiring scientific endeavour and promoting international harmony among medical men.

The eighth IMC was held in Copenhagen in 1884. It profited greatly from the interest aroused by the London Congress. Although the numbers attending were scarcely more than half those present in London three years earlier, this is explained by the smaller number of participants from the host nation. The number of foreign participants was greater than ever before, and the Congress again attracted men of great eminence, including Pasteur and Virchow. The *Journal*, which devoted much space to Congress affairs, was warmly congratulatory in its assessment and enthusiastic about the prospect of reconvening in Washington, DC, in 1887.[135]

In the event, Washington, possibly because of the travelling entailed, attracted relatively few British participants, though overall attendance exceeded 5000, including many Europeans. The *Journal* accorded the Congress little attention and expressed dissatisfaction with various aspects of it, particularly the narrowness of the programme and the absence of several leading medical men. The final verdict was that 'an opportunity has been missed, and though many of the discussions and papers will no doubt be remembered and valued, we fear that the abiding impression . . . will be one of disappointment.'[136] Disenchantment was, however, 'nipped in the bud' by the Berlin Congress of 1890.

Berlin attracted almost 6000 participants, of whom 358 came from Great Britain and Ireland. The German government saw it as an outstanding propaganda opportunity and spared no expense to make the occasion a triumphant success. The *Journal*, mindful of the standing of German science, arranged for 15 reporters to cover the proceedings.[137] It judged that

> whether for its remarkable assemblage of the most eminent representatives of cosmopolitan medical science or for its endless round of scientific and social activity,

[133] A. Sakula, 'Baroness Burdett-Coutts' Garden Party: The International Medical Congress, London, 1881', 183 (note 130).

[134] *Ibid.*, p. 184.

[135] *Journal*, 23 Aug. 1884, 373.

[136] *Ibid.*, 17 Sept. 1887, 632.

[137] *Ibid.*, 16 Aug. 1890, 415.

the Berlin Congress must be pronounced to have far exceeded any which has preceded it; and it will certainly be difficult in the future for any capital to surpass the feat which Berlin has accomplished.[138]

The 1890 IMC was perhaps the high point of the series. Certainly the *Journal* did not feel that the Rome Congress of 1894 equalled that of Berlin. Indeed, it found the scientific work presented there to be disappointing. A leading article warned against the dangers of IMCs becoming 'international picnics'.[139] In 1897 the *Journal* was too preoccupied with the BMA's first overseas annual meeting to pay much attention to events at the Moscow Congress. Although it had a special correspondent in Russia who summarized proceedings and gave some account of the social side of the event, this was the first IMC which failed to gain attention in a leading article.

The Paris Congress of 1900 did inspire editorial comment, albeit somewhat jaundiced in tone:

fairly successful as the meeting in Paris was in some ways, it will hardly be contended that, apart from the festivities for which Paris offers such exceptional facilities, anything was done there that could not have been equally well done without the pride, pomp and circumstance of an International Congress.[140]

Nevertheless, the *Journal* was far from advocating their termination, and it continued to report future IMCs, at Madrid (1903), Lisbon (1906), Budapest (1909), and London (1913) with greater or lesser enthusiasm. Lisbon was reported as extensively as any, though the *Journal*'s correspondent had reason to complain of organizational defects and of the participants' preference for activities other than the furtherance of medical science: 'the inclination for work does not appear to be increasing.'[141]

This sort of criticism became a commonplace of the *Journal*'s reporting of the IMCs. But editorials persisted in regarding them as valuable, if flawed, occasions: 'to our mind there can be no question that science would lose greatly by the discontinuance of these periodical assemblies.'[142] In truth, however, by 1913, if not long before, the IMCs had outlived their usefulness. Progress in medical science made it impossible to produce a manageable programme which could appeal to the profession as a whole. Smaller, specialist congresses multiplied to meet the demand. The *Journal* index for 1913 shows the extent of such gatherings, devoted to everything from anatomy to zoology. To cover the full panoply of medicine it became necessary for IMC organizers to establish more sub-sections, with more speakers, and yielding ever longer transactions. Thus, whereas one volume of proceedings had sufficed to record the first Paris Congress, the transactions

138 *Ibid.*, 394.
139 *Ibid.*, 14 April 1894, 814.
140 *Ibid.*, 18 Aug. 1900, 437–8.
141 *Ibid.*, 5 May 1906, 1051.
142 *Ibid.*, 2 Aug. 1913, 266.

of the second filled as many as 17 volumes. Those who had predicted that the Congresses would be 'crushed by their own immensity' proved correct.[143] Nevertheless, in their heyday the IMCs, for all their faults, performed a valuable function, particularly in terms of fostering international understanding and inspiring medical research. The British were seldom to the forefront of the IMC movement, but Ernest Hart was one of its champions and through the *BMJ* he played an important part in stimulating and maintaining interest in the United Kingdom.

[143] *Ibid.*, 2 May 1903, 1053.

7
Professional and non-professional

Cycles and cars

When Hart became editor of the *Journal* the nation was firmly in the railway age. When he died it was on the brink of the age of the motor car. But in the 1880s, especially for practitioners living in country districts, the transport question of greatest moment was whether to stick with their horses or buy a bicycle, tricycle, or even the ill-fated quadricycle.

From the 1870s technical improvements such as pneumatic tyres and chain-driven rear wheels transformed the nature of cycling by making it feasible for people other than the young and athletic. Consequently it gained great popularity as a recreation for middle-class men, while doctors and clergymen found the bicycle 'of great practical assistance, especially in rural work'.[1] In the 1880s the practicalities, pleasures, and perils of cycling were regularly discussed in the *BMJ*'s correspondence columns.[2] The subject was first raised in 1878 when George Stilwell, a doctor living in Epsom, complained about the dangers posed to pedestrians and equestrians by reckless cyclists. The physician H. J. Kendrick Vives, who was president of Littlehampton Cycling Club, replied by extolling the bicycle as a form of transport for doctors with country practices. It was, he claimed, suitable for all but the hilliest terrain, could be ridden with dignity and ease even by the elderly if they had been brought up to it, and it did away with the expenses of a stable. In short:

> No more convenient machine than this could have been invented for medical purposes. The bicycle occupies scarcely any room, is always available and gives no trouble on reaching the patient's house. An urgent summons arrives; you mount the machine, and have reached your destination in the time that it would usually take to 'find the man, and get the horse ready'. Thus I have officiated at many midwifery cases where otherwise my services would have arrived too late; and have thus expeditiously reached the scene of accidents, often to the satisfaction of my patients.[3]

[1] David Rubinstein, 'Cycling in the 1890s', *Victorian Studies* (1977) **21**: 47–71. Benjamin Ward Richardson, who later founded the Society of Cyclists and became President of the Tricycle Union, refers to an exhibition of bicycles at the 1877 Sanitary Congress in Leamington. But his account suggests that they were very much a novelty for medical men at this time. See *Vita Medica. Chapters of Medical Life and Work* (London: Longman, 1897), pp. 241–2.

[2] See e.g. *Journal*, 27 May 1882, 805; 20 Oct. 1888, 915; 27 Oct. 1888, 973; 3 Nov. 1888, 1032; 10 Nov. 1888, 1087.

[3] *Ibid.*, 16 Nov. 1878, 757; 30 Nov. 1878, 824.

GENTLE EXERCISE.

Mrs. Jones. "COME ON, OLD SLOWCOACH! LET'S RACE UP THIS NEXT HILL, OR WE'LL BE LATE FOR TEA!"

[*Jones is beginning to doubt the wisdom of having sold his Pony and Trap, and taken to Bicycles. He lives seven miles from a Town where Mrs. J. takes him shopping four times a week with the greatest regularity.*

Gentle Exercise: from *Punch*. Source: Mary Evans Picture Library.

Vives's letter elicited several queries and recounted experiences. How long, inquired 'A Would Be Cyclist' did it take to become a proficient cyclist; which was the best model; was it true that the vibration of cycling caused spinal injury? Another correspondent told of a chapter of accidents, expense, and inconvenience with horses and grooms which must have been the common lot of many practitioners. Such problems had been removed by a 'Salvo' quadricycle which, for a purchase price of £19, had supplied 'an antidote to one of the greatest banes of practice'—that is, maintaining stables.[4]

The 'Salvo' was manufactured by Starley Brothers of Coventry, one of the

[4] *Ibid.*, 14 Dec. 1878, 503. See 25 Jan. 1879, 133; 1 March 1879, 338.

The Passing of the Horse: from *Mr Punch's Motoring Book*. Source: Bodleian Library, Oxford.

companies involved in perfecting the 'safety bicycle, whose chain-driven rear wheel gradually became identical in size to the front wheel'.[5] Mention of their machines in the *Journal* brought them numerous inquiries from country practitioners. Some of these must have led to purchases, for the pages of the *Journal* indicate that many GPs were 'doing their rounds' on a 'Salvo'.[6]

After a while discussion began to centre less exclusively upon the use of cycles for practitioners. In 1881 'Nestor' suggested that, with the advent of

[5] D. Rubinstein, 'Cycling in the 1890s', 48 (note 1). See Geoffrey Williamson, *Wheels Within Wheels: The Story of the Starleys of Coventry* (London: Bles, 1966).

[6] *Journal*, 25 Jan. 1879, 133; 25 Oct. 1879, 681; 6 May 1882, 685; 10 June 1882, 894.

improved machines, tricycle exercise could 'form a powerful adjunct in the management of a class of female complaints'. Another correspondent agreed that doctors might consider recommending tricycling 'as a most useful and enjoyable method of affording exercise to both sexes'.[7] This was a far cry from earlier queries as to whether cycling could cause hernias, varicose veins, haemorrhoids, urethral stricture, 'and various forms of cardiac and nervous disease'.[8] In 1889, prompted by publication of Oscar Jennings's pamphlet, '*La Santé par le Tricycle*', the *Journal* carried a leading article on cycling and health. In this it placed cycling behind only rowing and horse riding as a form of exercise. While regretting the 'silly craze' of racing and record-breaking, it considered that 'Cycling as a therapeutic agent has a considerable future.' It warned, however, that it should not be taken up too early in life lest round, stooping shoulders be the result: 'a convenient rule is to avoid recommending it till a lad has passed the age when the chief growth in height takes place.' It also recommended that cyclists should be dressed 'from head to foot' in woollen clothing and should 'as far as possible abstain from alcoholic beverages while on a journey'.[9]

In 1896, in the middle of the cycling 'boom', the *Journal* published a 10-part report on 'Cycling in Health and Disease', specially written for it by E. B. Turner, FRCS, vice-president of the National Cyclists' Union.[10] Turner urged the benefits of cycling, even for mothers, the aged and, in certain cases, the sick, provided that over-exertion was avoided. His advice, which was praised by the cycling editor of the *Sunday Times*, led to another rash of correspondence on the subject.[11]

The *BMJ*'s coverage of cycling reflected society's enthusiasm. In the 1880s and 1890s bicycles and tricycles had a profound social impact from which medicine and the medical profession were not exempt. The *Journal* played an important role in helping to spread the cycling habit among practitioners, in promoting the products of certain manufacturers, and in allaying fears that it could injure health. By the mid-1890s it was beginning to pay attention to a form of transport that was to have a far greater social impact than the bicycle—the motor car.

Britain might be said to have entered the age of the automobile in December 1894 when Henry Hewetson imported the first car, a Benz, from Germany.[12] Within two years the *Journal* published its first query, from a

[7] *Ibid.*, 2 April, 1881, 539; 9 April 1881, 582.

[8] *Ibid.*, 4 Sept. 1880, 414; 16 July 1881, 109; 23 July 1881, 144; 2 Feb. 1889, 252–3; 16 Aug. 1890, 399; 6 Sept. 1890, 610; 20 Sept. 1890, 713; 4 Oct. 1890, 824; 18 Oct. 1890, 937; 1 Nov. 1890, 1049; 8 Nov. 1890, 1104.

[9] *Ibid.*, 2 Feb. 1889, 252–3.

[10] D. Rubinstein, 'Cycling in the 1890s', 51 (note 1).

[11] *Journal*, 9 May 1896, 1158; 16 May 1896, 1211–12; 30 May 1896, 1336–7; 6 June 1896, 1399; 4 July 1896, 38; 11 July 1896, 98–9; 25 July 1896, 203; 8 Aug. 1896, 367; 22 Aug. 1896, 469–70.

[12] Harold Perkin, *The Age of the Automobile* (London: Quartet Books, 1976), p. 7.

general practitioner in Rhyl, Dr Hughes Jones, as to the suitability of the new form of transport for medical men.[13] The question was referred to the secretary of the Society of Arts, who advised the *Journal*'s correspondent to await developments before making any purchase. Indeed, at this time legislation restricted the speed of the so-called road locomotives to 2 mph in towns and 4 mph in the country, limits which rendered motorized transport impractical. It was only in November 1896 that these restrictions were relaxed, thereby removing one of the barriers to the development of a domestic motor industry.[14]

In fact, Hughes Jones's letter was not quite the first occasion on which the *BMJ* had considered the motor car. This had occurred nearly a year earlier in an article entitled 'Mechanical Road Carriages: Horseflesh v. Steam'. Even at this early date the *Journal* believed that, 'provided a good mechanical horse can be found', there was 'no contest'.

Of the advantages of mechanical over animal traction there can be no question. The mechanical horse unlike his living rival, only eats when he is at work. He does not want his meals served with regularity when he is at home in his stable. His food costs a great deal less. He is never sick or sorry, never tired. He will go on all day, and if need be all night. He does not require a stable. He does not grow ill or die. He will not run away. He does not deposit ordure on the roads.

On the negative side, the motor car might break down or 'even blow up', would wear out, 'though very slowly', and required 'a certain amount of skilled attendance'. However, the *Journal* was forced to conclude that until the terms of the Highways and Locomotives Act were modified, 'we shall probably have to content ourselves with looking on at the progress made in other countries.'[15]

This was the first of very many articles and letters tackling the question of 'motor cars for medical men'. As with bicycles, many of the letters sought or offered advice on the value of a car in medical practice. This enthusiastic appraisal was published in 1897:

Mine is a four-seated victoria with hood and a 4½ h.p. motor. it will carry four, and go up gradients as steep as one in eight. I have run sixty miles a day for three days in one week, and have often made twenty or thirty calls in the day with it. The cost of running varies from ½d. to 1d. per mile according to size and gradients.[16]

'GEEGEES' believed it was 'a great advantage to be able to go ten miles an hour for an indefinite time and without the fear of knocking up your horses or having them catch cold while waiting'.[17] A correspondent in 1899 was even

[13] *Journal*, 31 Oct. 1896, 1363.
[14] William Plowden, *The Motor Car and Politics 1896–1970* (London: Bodley Head, 1971), pp. 21–2.
[15] *Journal*, 7 Dec. 1895, 1434–5.
[16] *Ibid.*, 3 April 1897, 895.
[17] *Journal*, 11 Dec. 1897, 1770.

more positive, predicting that professional and business travel would soon be 'almost entirely by the motor car'.[18] But not everyone was so easily persuaded. 'E. H. R.', for example, wrote that 'It is surprising what a number of trifles throw your car out of use just when you want it.' Moreover, 'if something goes wrong and you are alone and have to put things right yourself, you will need a good wash before you will be presentable in the sick room.'[19] In 1903 'A Sadder and a Wiser Man' described his experiences since purchasing a car for £350, as 'one continued bother, worry, and annoyance in every way from the very first'.[20] Most correspondents, however, regarded the motor car, particularly in terms of its speed and economy, as a marked improvement over the horse and carriage.[21]

For its part the *Journal* took some convincing that reliable and practical machines were available.[22] It was not until 1904, after reliability trials on small cars at Hereford, that it was ready to endorse the automobile as a sound investment for doctors:

> . . . it is clear that very much more can now be expected than was the case a year or two ago. In short, great progress has been made, and though, from the number of more or less marked failures, it is obvious that many, if not the majority, of cheap cars still stand in the need of improvement, it is equally obvious that the man of modest aspirations can 'horse' himself satisfactorily for £200 or less, provided he use sufficient discrimination.[23]

Thereafter the *Journal* regularly carried motoring items.[24] Though stopping short of recommending particular models, it clearly felt it should advise readers on the problems and opportunities provided by automobile ownership. Doctors constituted a sizeable potential market for motor cars; in consequence, models such as the Gregoire and the de Dion Bouton were advertised in its pages as 'the medical man's favourite car' and 'the reliable car for professional men'.[25]

Motoring magazines, including *Autocar*, also aspired to offer specialist advice to doctors on purchases, but the *Journal* believed that these had too great a stake in the success of the automobile to be able to offer truly objective advice. It therefore urged its readers to study its articles rather than be swayed by 'paeans of praise' emanating from elsewhere.[26] Certainly, there was no shortage of information from the *BMJ*. As the popularity of

[18] *Ibid.*, 1 July 1899, 57.

[19] *Ibid.*, 22 July, 1899, 253–4; 18 May 1901, 1220.

[20] *Ibid.*, 3 Jan. 1903, 44; 30 Jan. 1904, 288.

[21] *Ibid.*, 10 March 1906, 586; 16 June 1906, 1407.

[22] *Ibid.*, 27 Nov. 1897, 1603; 16 Sept. 1899, 732–3; see 14 Sept. 1901, 755.

[23] *Ibid.*, 1 Oct. 1904, 857.

[24] *Ibid.*, 23 March 1907, 695–7; 30 March 1907, 757–8; 6 April 1907, 821–12; 13 April 1907, 883–6; 20 April 1907, 943–4; 27 April 1907, 1001–4; 4 May 1907, 1069–72; 11 May 1907, 1133–5; 18 May 1907, 1190–1.

[25] See e.g. *Ibid.*, 22 Dec. 1906 (advertising section) p. 45.

[26] *Ibid.*, 25 June 1904, 1505–6. See 14 April 1906, 884.

motoring increased (the number of cars on the road grew from 8465 in March 1904 to over 53 000 in 1910 and 132 000 in 1914), so the *Journal*'s coverage became ever more comprehensive.[27] It encompassed not only the positive side of motoring, but also less pleasant aspects such as accidents, insurance, drunken driving, prosecutions, pollution, and taxation.

In 1911 H(ugo) Massac Buist began his long association with the *Journal* as its motoring correspondent. Buist was then only 33, but he already had achieved much as a motoring, boating, and aviation pioneer. In 1904 he made the world's first motor mountaineering tour; in the following year he established, with Charles Rolls, the London–Monte Carlo record. He then took part in the first cross-Channel motor boat trial before taking up ballooning and flying. He wrote 'thousands' of articles for many journals on aviation, motoring, and manufacturing problems.[28]

Buist was a prolific contributor to the *BMJ*. His first articles dealt with the 10th 'International Motor Carriage Show', which was promoted by the Society of Motor Manufacturers and Traders at Olympia in 1911.[29] The main object, indeed, Buist's main object over the many years that he wrote for the *Journal*, was to provide authoritative advice to doctors considering buying a car. In 1912 Buist covered not only the motor exhibition but also the 'cycle car' and motor cycle show at Kensington 'for the medical man of slender means'.[30] From 1914 he began to write on more general motoring questions, hitherto largely the preserve of the *Journal*'s correspondence columns. Thus, in the first half of the year he contributed pieces on fuel for medical men's motor cars, some phases of the light car problem, the multiplication of accessories, lessons of the light car trials, and lessons of the tourist trophy race.[31] By this time Buist was providing virtually all of the *Journal*'s motoring 'copy'.

The outbreak of war did not restrict his contributions, for not only did he continue to produce his usual column, he also started a series on motor ambulances and wrote on such questions as the requisitioning of motors and the fuel problem. In the second half of 1914 Buist published 10 articles, running to some 23 000 words. The contraction in British production of non-military vehicles and the impossibility of obtaining imported models during the war led to a dramatic shrinkage of the 'motor cars for medical men' series from early 1915, though Buist still wrote on military ambulances and

[27] Figures from W. Plowden, *The Motor Car and Politics 1896–1970*, Appendix B (note 14).

[28] *Who Was Who, 1961–1970*. See *The Times*, 18 April 1966. I have been unable to discover a relationship between H. M. Buist and R. C. Buist who was chairman of the *Journal* Committee before the First World War.

[29] *Journal*, 11 Nov. 1911, 1302–4; 18 Nov. 1911, 1364–6. Although the *Journal* began to cover the Olympia Motor Show in 1907, articles were unsigned until 1911.

[30] *Ibid*., 9 Nov. 1912, 1315–18; 16 Nov. 1912, 1399–1402; 23 Nov. 1912, 1479–80; 30 Nov. 1912, 1555–6.

[31] *Ibid*., 3 Jan. 1914, 40–2; 21 March 1914, 663–6; 25 April 1914, 924–5; 23 May 1914, 1135–7; 20 June 1914, 1361–3.

discussed the implications of fuel shortages, lighting regulations, and the problem of obtaining spare parts.[32]

After the war Buist reported on the Paris and Olympia motor shows. He found that, while quality was higher than in 1914, the price of cars had outstripped the average increase in medical incomes. Nevertheless, he was able to list a range of cars priced between £195 and £800 which might attract medical visitors to Olympia. Buist's articles often stressed the overseas competition faced by British manufacturers such as Rover, Wolsley, Morris, and Standard, and made a point that was to be made time and again by the domestic industry over the decades, 'that we are sending money overseas for a number of commodities which we could produce at home. If we do not order from home sources tens of thousands of skilled workers fail to secure work and, therefore, go on the dole; hence there is a double bill to pay, one direct and the other indirect.'[33] As early as 1919 Buist was speculating on the circumstances that might lead to Japanese domination of the world motor industry.[34]

Buist's last signed articles for the *Journal* appeared in 1925. Thereafter the motoring column was produced by 'our motoring correspondent'. Whether Buist remained responsible for any of them is unknown, though later in the 1920s, and throughout the 1930s, articles were initialled C. J. W. Buist and his successors were largely concerned with stressing the positive side of motoring and the opportunities it provided for medical men. Throughout the interwar period a regular feature every November was the report from the Motor Show at Olympia (Earls Court from 1937) with details of what was new in motor car production. But motoring has always had negative aspects such as noise, pollution, accidents, and congestion. In the 1920s and 1930s such topics supplied a larger proportion of the *Journal*'s motoring copy. In 1925 a *Journal* leader, prompted by the rising tide of road casualties, considered the advisability of requiring drivers to take tests of physical fitness to drive. The BMA went on to play a part in drawing up regulations, under the Road Traffic Act, 1930, governing the physical and mental fitness of prospective drivers.[35] But the vast numbers of accidents led the *Journal* to devote increasing space to eyesight, epilepsy and driving, drunken driving, street lighting, and so on.

By the 1930s motoring had lost much of its novelty: there were, after all,

[32] *Ibid.*, 29 May 1915, 932–3; 2 Jan. 1915, 42–5; 16 Jan. 1915, 132–3; 7 Aug. 1915, 222–4; 15 Jan. 1916, 96–7; 12 Feb. 1916, 243–4; 11 March 1916, 379–80; 15 April 1916, 557–8; 1 July 1916, 17–18; 12 Aug. 1916, 224–62; 2 Dec. 1916, 762–5; 16 Dec. 1916, 846; 13 Jan. 1917, 57; 20 Jan. 1917, 85–6; 27 Jan. 1917, 123–4; 17 Feb 1917, 228–9; 30 June 1917, 877–8; 20 Oct. 1917, 521–4.

[33] *Ibid.*, 3 Feb. 1923, 207–8; 13 Oct. 1923, 667–8; 3 Nov. 1923, 819–24.

[34] *Ibid.*, 23 Nov. 1918, 576–7; 28 Dec. 1918, 720–1; 10 May 1919, 580–1; 8 Nov. 1919, 601–4.

[35] *Ibid.*, 24 Jan. 1925, 174–5; 22 Nov. 1930, 882–4. Systematic figures for road traffic accidents were not kept until 1926 when there were 4886 road deaths. This figure rose to a peak of 7300 in 1934, a figure not surpassed till the 1960s. It is perhaps no coincidence that the 1930 Act had abolished the speed limit. W. Plowden, *The Motor Car and Politics 1896–1970*, p. 127 (note 14).

more than three million vehicles in use by 1939. The *Journal*'s coverage dwindled accordingly, though its motoring correspondent continued to provide news of the latest models. The *Journal* also continued to perform a service to readers by supplying information on tax liabilities and concessions as they affected motoring medical men. But, as with other financial matters, these were more the province of the BMA in its dealings with government than of the *Journal*. There were also organizations other than the BMA, and periodicals other than the *BMJ*, to which doctors, along with their fellow citizens, could turn for motoring information.

Health and fitness

The *Journal* tended to see cycling as either a useful form of transport or a means of gentle exercise; it had little sympathy with cycling as a sport. This typified its attitude, up to the 1890s, to sports and games in general, for until then it tended to represent them as risky and senseless pastimes. Neither was its distaste confined to those activities, such as swimming or rowing the English Channel, which an 1885 editorial castigated as 'foolhardy feats'.[36] Danger lurked on every street corner: 'Top-spinning, for instance, appears at first sight to be a tolerably innocent amusement, but, when it is practised on the pavement of a busy thoroughfare, the lash of the whip, which is used to impart the necessary movement of rotation, is apt to find its way into the faces of the passers-by, or into their eyes.'[37]

There was even greater concern about 'tip-cat', a game with a long tradition, which London children resurrected in the summer of 1886. Tip-cat was played with two sticks, one of which was pointed at both ends. The pointed stick was made to jump by tapping one end and then, while airborne, violently projected 'with the utmost indifference to the direction it is about to take', by means of a blow with the other stick. A *Journal* editorial called upon the metropolitan police to take action to curb this and similar dangerous pastimes.[38]

But the *Journal*'s special distaste was reserved for football, whether played under Rugby or Association rules.[39] Football, in its many divergent forms, was a long-established sport. The Association game was codified in 1863, while the Rugby Football Union dates from 1871. Professional soccer with its large crowds, gate money, and commercialization began to take off in manufacturing towns in the 1880s, a decade which saw 'an astonishing

[36] *Ibid.*, 15 Aug. 1885, 308.

[37] *Ibid.*, 8 May 1886, 897–8.

[38] *Ibid.*, 15 May 1886, 949. Tip-cat had flourished on previous occasions, including 1853.

[39] In 1884–5 the *Journal* enthusiastically greeted the prospect of Harvard University banning football. See 23 Feb. 1884, 380; 10 Jan. 1885, 86.

BARBARIANS AT PLAY.

John Bull. "PLAY FOOTBALL, BY ALL MEANS, MY BOY—BUT DON'T LET IT BE THIS BRUTAL SORT OF THING!"

Barbarians at Play: from *Punch*. Source: *Punch*.

increase in sport' in general.[40] In the same decade the press began to pay serious attention to organized sport, particularly football.[41]

The *Journal* was not blind to the national upsurge of interest in football. It carried occasional reports of Hospitals' Cup rugby matches—in 1882, for example, a correspondent reported of the drawn fixture between St Bartholomew's and St George's that 'a more exciting game could hardly be imagined'—but, like the *Lancet*, it concentrated upon the accidents, injuries,

[40] David Rubinstein, 'Sport and the Sociologist, 1890–1914', *British Journal of Sports History* (1984) **1**: 16. On the origins and development of Victorian sport see Bruce Haley, *The Healthy Body and Victorian Culture* (Cambridge, Mass., and London: Harvard University Press, 1978) and J. A. Mangan, *Athleticism in the Victorian and Edwardian Public School* (Cambridge: Cambridge University Press, 1981).

[41] J. Walvin, *The People's Game* (London: Harvard University Press, 1975), p. 63. On sports journalism see B. Haley, *The Healthy Body and Victorian Culture*, pp. 138–40 (note 40) and Tony Mason, 'Sporting News, 1860–1914' in M. Harris and A. Lee (eds), *The Press in English Society from the Seventeenth to Nineteenth Centuries* (London: Associated University Presses, 1986), pp. 168–86.

and violence of the football field.[42] It regularly called for rule changes to render matches safer, for police intervention to control brutal play, and even for total prohibition of the game. In this respect, the *Journal* represented part of the 'backlash' against the Victorian mania for athleticism.[43] An 1884 report encapsulates the *Journal*'s position:

> The result, on one day recently, of four football fights—it is a gross misuse of language to call them 'games'—was that two young men lost their lives, and two sustained fractures of the leg .... It is a great pity that what might be a manly and health-giving game should have been allowed to degenerate into a kind of organised faction fight ... the death of a young man who perishes in the attempt to emulate the tactics of a goat or a bull may not perhaps be any great loss to the community, but what we complain of is that such conduct should be held up before the eyes of a number of young men and lads as an example to be followed.[44]

On another occasion the *Journal* noted, with no hint of mirth, that 'it is very unpleasant to read of young men being kicked to death, even though it is all done in a friendly way.'[45] Nor was its concern limited to thuggery and fractures, for the *Journal* opined that 'the severe strain put by football for an hour, or an hour and a half, once a week, on the constitution of young men and lads who for the rest of the week follow sedentary occupations cannot but be injurious; not only broken bones and heads, but diseases of the heart and nervous system are thus brought about.'

By 1886 the *Journal* was terming football an 'obsolete' sport and noting that its popularity among 'the better class' of medical student was declining. In the near future, it anticipated, the place of football would be taken 'by more intelligent and manly ways of spending Saturday afternoons'.[47] Several correspondents, it should be noted, took exception to the *Journal*'s rabid anti-athleticism.

The *Journal* mentioned cricket much less than football, though in 1884 it did draw attention to 'certain dangerous abuses which have crept into the noble game'. But two years later an editorial urged the Football Association to follow the example of the MCC by compiling and enforcing good rules.[48] Of course, the greatest of all cricketers, W. G. Grace, was a medical man and in June 1895 a *Journal* correspondent pointed out that, while honours and compliments were being bestowed upon Grace 'on all hands', there was 'alas! not a sign of recognition from the members of his own profession'.[49] He

[42] *Journal*, 4 Feb. 1882, 171; see 20 March 1886, 541.
[43] See B. Haley, *The Healthy Body and Victorian Culture*, pp. 222–6 (note 40).
[44] *Journal*, 22 March 1884, 572. See 11 Dec. 1880, 933; 4 Dec. 1886, 1115.
[45] *Ibid.*, 4 Dec. 1886, 1115.
[46] *Ibid.*, 6 Dec. 1884, 1149–50. See 18 Nov. 1876, 660.
[47] *Ibid.*, 30 Oct. 1886, 831. See Peter Bailey, *Leisure and Class in Victorian England* (London: Routledge and Kegan Paul, 1987), who notes that the middle classes tended to reject professional football and regard it as morally suspect. See pp. 143–4.
[48] *Journal*, 22 March 1884, 572; 4 Dec. 1886, 1115.
[49] *Ibid.*, 8 June 1895, 1307.

called upon the Association to mark Grace's achievement with, perhaps, a banquet, at its next annual meeting. That same month the *Daily Telegraph* launched a 'shilling testimonial' in recognition of Grace's achievements. The *Journal* greeted this with enthusiasm, observing that 'every medical man must feel a certain ... personal pride in the reflection that Dr. Grace is a working member of our profession, and has shown that medical studies and practice are not incompatible with the highest development of athletic skill and pluck.' It invited readers to contribute to the Grace Testimonial through its offices. Among the first subscribers were Hart (£5), Dawson Williams (£1), *BMJ* compositors (14s), and the *BMJ* clerks (10s). Their enthusiasm fired by these examples, *Journal* subscribers contributed almost £50 to the testimonial.[50]

The late-nineteenth century witnessed not only an upsurge of interest in sport and games but also considerable concern about the physical fitness of the nation's children. An 1889 editorial in the *Journal* expressed the hope that 'physical training in schools will be largely extended'.[51] Two years later a leading article on public schools emphasized that 'physical training is, equally with mental training, an integral factor of all true education.' It recommended that every schoolchild, boy or girl, should undertake military drill and be taught to swim. It commended cricket as a summer game and, more surprisingly in view of its strictures of recent years, football:

> where boys are properly graded, as they always should be, in respect of age, weight and size, football can be strongly recommended for all except those few whom the medical officer will certify as unfit for this more violent form of exertion. If the game is a rougher one for all concerned, its average of accidents is not greater than—and certainly, amongst boys, is not so serious as—that of the injuries which occur during the pastimes that obtain during the warmer months, while its encouragement of the virtues of pluck, forbearance and good temper, its excellent value of wind and muscle, its need of rapid judgement and ready resource, are qualities which deservedly recommend it as a method both of physical training and of moral education.[52]

What was unsuitable for the student and young man was, apparently, ideal for the public schoolboy, but a more plausible explanation for the *Journal*'s apparent inconsistency is that between the mid-1880s and the early-1890s it was belatedly converted to the cult of athleticism. Indeed, the same article went on to recommend running, fencing, boxing, and, indeed, all sports other than throwing the hammer and putting the weight.[53] By the end of the century sport formed a regular part of BMA annual meetings. Although participants did not play football, the 1896 meeting at Carlisle featured an

[50] *Ibid.*, 22 June 1895, 1406. See e.g. 6 July 1895, 43; 24 Aug. 1895, 499.
[51] *Ibid.*, 25 May 1889, 1183.
[52] *Ibid.*, 17 Jan. 1891, 136.
[53] *Ibid.* See 7 Feb. 1891, 295–6.

England versus Scotland golf match, with the Scots gaining a comfortable victory, and a cricket match in which rain stopped play.[54]

By this time the *Journal* was taking the view, increasingly popular in the medical profession and elsewhere, that good health depended not merely on medicine and surgery, but also on a healthy lifestyle, including a sensible diet and temperate habits. The most celebrated writings on food in the nineteenth-century medical press were the *Lancet*'s disclosures about food adulteration in the 1850s. Over a three-year period Arthur Hassall published the results of some 2400 food analyses. These reports led directly to changed methods of food manufacture, parliamentary investigation, and legislation to control adulteration.[55] Although the *BMJ* also touched upon the question from time to time, and was a supporter of anti-adulteration laws, it was, in its treatment of the subject in the 1850s, only hanging on to the *Lancet*'s coat tails.[56] During Hart's editorship the *Journal* took a stronger interest in food and drink. In 1869 it carried analytical reports and comments on beer, still the staple drink of the British working man.[57] Although concerned about the continuation of adulteration, for the Adulteration of Foods Act, 1860, was ineffective, it also turned its attention to the question of healthy and economical eating.[58]

Insufficient milk, meat, and vegetables, inadequate cooking facilities and equipment, expensive fuel, the absence of a plentiful water supply, and an abundance of ignorant and overworked housewives were responsible for the diet of the Victorian urban poor being 'truly appalling'.[59] Several authors sought to remedy the situation by writing recipe books of cheap economical dishes. One of these was Sir Henry Thompson, a close friend of Hart, who published his book *Food and Feeding* in 1880. The *Journal* commended Thompson's work and urged doctors to encourage healthier, more economical, and more exciting eating.[60] Hart, who regarded himself as something of a dietitian, wrote a series of leading articles entitled 'The Doctor in the Kitchen' in which he spoke of extravagant consumption of meat, ignorant neglect of vegetables, and unskilful waste in cooking.[61] These articles advocated greater use of beans, lentils, green vegetables, fish, rice, cheese,

[54] *Ibid*, 15 Aug. 1896, 393–4.

[55] John Burnett, *Plenty and Want. A Social History of Diet in England from 1815 to the Present Day* (London: Scolar Press, 1979 edn), pp. 240–67.

[56] See e.g. *Journal*, 11 Feb. 1853, 116; 1 March 1856, 173; 23 Aug. 1856, 725; 28 April 1860, 323.

[57] *Ibid.*, 23 Jan. 1869, 83–4; 6 March 1869, 218; 28 Aug. 1869, 245.

[58] On the 1860 Act see J. Burnett, *Plenty and Want*, pp. 257–8 (note 55).

[59] *Ibid.*, pp. 185–6. See Margaret Hewitt, *Wives and Mothers in Victorian Industry* (London: Rockliff, 1958).

[60] *Journal*, 7 June 1879, 859. See Z. Cope, *The Versatile Victorian. Being the Life of Sir Henry Thompson, Bt. 1820–1904* (London: Harrey and Blythe, 1951), p. 91. By 1910 Thompson's book had gone through 12 editions.

[61] Hart had lectured on dietetics in the 1850s. See *Jewish Chronicle*, 21 March 1856, 20 June 1856.

and macaroni—something of a departure for the *BMJ*, which in the past had tended to poke fun at vegetarians. But Hart's greatest scorn was reserved for the poverty of English cooking in which—in marked contrast to France, where humble ingredients yielded excellent results—roast, boiled, or grilled meat was usually accompanied by 'a limited repertory of vegetables' served plain-boiled, watery, and tasteless.[62] Hart's articles passed on advice on how nutritious, palatable meals might be economically produced from simple, inexpensive ingredients. In the following year his lecture for the National Health Society on the same subject was reported by *The Times*.[63] But, at least as far as the urban poor were concerned, Hart seems to have been one of those who accused housewives of mismanagement and waste while ignoring the hardships under which they laboured.[64]

If Hart held firm opinions about food, he was equally opinionated on the subject of drink. For much of the nineteenth century alcohol was heavily prescribed as a medicine. Before Hart's editorship the *Journal* sometimes expressed faith in its medicinal value, dismissing teetotallers as cranks. But at other times it was more doubtful: 'Are we healthy people who daily swallow these things poisoning ourselves, and are teetotallers only wise?' Moreover, it blanched at the news that, in 1864, 4619 patients in the London Hospital had consumed 1558 gallons of wine, 359 gallons of brandy, and 77 gallons of gin.[65] Under Hart the *Journal* became more sympathetic towards the temperance movement, observing that as a cause of death and disease alcohol 'tower[ed] as a giant over its puny rival [syphilis]'.[66] In 1871 Hart helped compile the 'Medical Declaration Respecting Alcohol', the text of which argued that 'inconsiderate prescription of large quantities of alcoholic drinks by medical men' had encouraged drunkenness.[67] It called for more responsible prescribing. The *Journal* supported the movement to establish 'inebriate retreats' for the incarceration and treatment of habitual drunkards and, reflecting Hart's involvement with the coffee tavern movement, favoured positive measures to wean drinkers to alternative pleasures.[68]

[62] *Journal*, 20 Sept. 1879, 466–7; 27 Sept. 1879, 505–6; 4 Oct. 1879, 546–7; 11 Oct. 1879, 584–5; 25 Oct. 1879, 671–3.

[63] *Ibid.*, 5 June 1880, 861.

[64] J. Burnett, *Plenty and Want*, p. 186 (note 55).

[65] *Journal*, 9 March 1861, 259; 23 March 1861, 309; 6 April 1861, 366; 5 Oct. 1861, 360–2; 2 Nov. 1861, 468–9; 9 Nov. 1861, 507–8; 23 Nov. 1861, 557–9; 14 June 1862, 629–30; 9 Sept. 1865, 262–3; 9 Dec. 1865, 614.

[66] *Ibid.*, 4 June 1870, 580–2; 23 March 1872, 315.

[67] *Ibid.*, 30 Sept. 1871, 389; 23 Dec. 1871, 737; 11 Oct. 1879, 585.

[68] *Ibid.*, 8 Feb. 1879, 215; 16 Aug. 1879, 249; 26 Aug. 1882, 373. See E. Hepple, *Coffee Taverns, Coffee Houses and Coffee Palaces: Their Rise, Progress and Prospects* (London, n.d.); James Freeman Clarke, 'Coffee House and Coffee Palaces in England' (Boston, 1882). On habitual drunkenness see Roy M. MacLeod, 'The Edge of Hope: Social Policy and Chronic Alcoholism, 1870–1900' *Journal of the History of Medicine* (1967) **xxii**: 215–45; Jenny Mellor *et al.*, ' "Prayers and Piecework": Inebriate Reformatories in England at the End of the Nineteenth Century' *Drogalkohol* (1986) **3**: 192–206.

Although the *Journal* was critical of the nation's diet and love of drink, its attitude towards tobacco, to which Hart himself was hopelessly addicted, was complacent. In 1857 it devoted considerable space to ridiculing those who drew attention to the health risks, including carcinomas, of smoking. There was, it averred, 'no tittle of evidence ... [that] ... tobacco is really prejudicial to the human constitution'. Moreover, 'when one surgeon boldly asserts that tobacco causes cancer ... we think it right to appeal to the calm judgment of unbiased men.'[69]

In 1888 the *Journal* dismissed newspaper reports that smoking could cause malignant throat disease as mere products of the 'silly season'.[70] Although willing to concede that boys should not smoke cigarettes, the *Journal* continued to express the view that moderate smoking 'cheered and lightened the working hours', and to represent those who connected it with diseases such as cancer as fools or bigots.[71] These views persisted well into the twentieth century.

Sex

It is a commonplace that sex was the great unmentionable in polite Victorian society. As a result there is a dearth of material on sexual behaviour and attitudes.[72] Prime sources for the Victorian period are works of pornography, of which there is no shortage, and medical books and journals. Although neither can be deemed to provide a comprehensive or typical insight into Victorian sexuality, it is instructive to look at the *BMJ*'s references to sex. In their approach to sexual matters medical practitioners have been called 'accomplices of ... learned ignorance' and purveyors of anxiety. Does the *Journal*'s coverage confirm the description?[73]

Spermatorrhoea, or the involuntary discharge of seminal fluid, has been called 'a fiction of Victorian quackery'.[74] In 1843 it was discussed in two

[69] *Journal*, 14 Feb. 1857, 133–5; 28 Feb. 1857, 174–5, 179–80; 12 March 1870, 267.

[70] *Ibid.*, 25 Aug. 1888, 444.

[71] *Ibid.*, 9 Feb. 1889, 316; 15 Nov. 1890, 1161;/ 4 April 189, 770–1; 4 July 1891, 19; 26 March, 1892, 675; 2 April 1892, 750; 2 Feb. 1895, 270–1; 18 Jan. 1896, 165. Juvenile smoking was condemned by the Inter-Departmental Committee on Physical Deterioration and proscribed under the terms of the Children's Act, 1908.

[72] On the reticence of autobiographers to discuss sexual matters see John Burnett (ed.), *Destiny Obscure. Autobiographies of Childhood, Education and Family from the 1820s to the 1920s* (London: Allen Lane, 1982), pp. 43–7.

[73] Peter Gay, *Education of the Senses* (Oxford: Oxford University Press, 1984), p. 294. See Eric Trudgill, *Madonnas and Magdalens. The Origins and Development of Victorian Sexual Attitudes* (New York: Heinemann, 1976), p. 50.

[74] M. Jeanne Peterson, *The Medical Profession in Mid-Victorian London* (Los Angeles and London: University of California Press, 1978), pp. 244–5; Paul Atkinson, 'Fitness, Feminism and Schooling' in Sara Delamont and Lorna Duffin, *The Nineteenth Century Woman. Her Cultural and Physical World* (London: Croom Helm, 1978), pp. 101–2; E. Trudgill, *Madonnas and Magdalens*, pp. 53–4 (note 73).

lengthy articles by a future editor of the *Journal*, W. H. Ranking, who claimed to have identified several strains of the disorder. His treatment of the subject established a tone that was to endure for decades. Ranking associated a formidable list of symptoms with the condition. The patient's 'mind becomes enfeebled and incapable of protracted attention, the memory fallacious and uncertain, and the patient feels that he is no longer fitted for his usual avocations. His disposition undergoes an equal change; he becomes morose and suspicious, fond of solitude, lachrymose upon trivial occasions . . .'. There was much more in this vein, including uneven temper, hypochondriasis, eccentricity, giddiness, tinnitus, emaciation, dejection, inability to look people in the eye—'as if conscious that the expression of his countenance would reveal his wretched condition'—loss of appetite, colic, and flatulence. Indeed, there seem to be few symptoms that could not justify a diagnosis of spermatorrhoea.

Appropriate treatment depended on the particular form of the 'disease'. If it was occasioned by 'general debility', tonics, cold showers, and 'the occasional employment of the organs' in sexual intercourse ('upon the principle that a weakly frame generally is strengthened by the moderate employment of the exercise specially adapted to each of its parts') were recommended. But if the complaint was brought on by 'undue exertion of the sexual organs'—Ranking neglected to explain at which point moderate employment became undue exertion—more extreme measures were called for including—in addition to the ubiquitous cold showers—sexual abstinence, temperance, soft mattresses, sleeping face up, and avoidance of highly seasoned foods. However, Ranking placed greatest reliance upon cauterization or injecting the urethra with nitrate of silver.[75]

Of course, 'undue exertion of the sexual organs' was a long-winded euphemism for that *bête noire* of the Victorians (though not only of the Victorians), masturbation—'the crime of masturbation' as one *Journal* contributor put it.[76] The medical profession associated it with a string of physical and mental disorders. Henry Maudsley was but one distinguished British doctor who associated the 'vicious habit' of 'self abuse' with insanity. He published an 'important' article on the question in the *Journal of Mental Science* in 1868.[77] His paper was presented at a meeting of the Harveian

[75] *Journal*, 14 Oct 1843, 26–9, 31; 4 Nov. 1843, 93–5. Other authorities favoured injections of opium and acetate of lead, which was said to be less painful and incapacitating, but which can hardly have been more therapeutic. The principal authority on spermatorrhoea was J. L. Milton whose *On Spermatorrhoea* went through 12 editions between 1854 and 1857. See E. Trudgill, *Madonnas and Magdalens*, p. 53 (note 73); Jean L'Esperance, 'Doctors and Women in Nineteenth Century Society: Sexuality and Role' in John Woodward and David Richards (eds.), *Health Care and Popular Medicine in Nineteenth Century England* (London: Croom Helm, 1977), pp. 107–12.

[76] *Journal*, 29 July 1853, 673.

[77] This was 'Illustrations of a Variety of Insanity' XIV (July 1868). See P. Gay, *Education of the Senses*, p. 298 (note 73).

Society on 5 March. Hart, who was then the Society's president, occupied the chair and contributed to the discussion, which was reproduced in the *BMJ*. Whereas all the other speakers were convinced of the connection between masturbation and insanity, Hart took a more balanced view, arguing that 'masturbation might, as was well known, be carried on for years, and to a great extent, without any injury whatever.' Although couched in the courteous tones of academic debate, Hart's response to Maudsley's paper represented a stinging refutation:

by grouping together the various mental and emotional symptoms found associated with one case and another, with the view of characterising a particular form of disease, a description merely was obtained, which was to be found equally applicable to many persons against whom not a suspicion of the practice of self-abuse could be raised.[78]

By the end of the century the *Journal* seemed to endorse the opinion of Sir James Paget that, although masturbation was a nasty practice, it was no more harmful than sexual intercourse practised with similar frequency.[79]

In fact, under Hart the *Journal* paid little attention to the subject of masturbation. When raised it was in the correspondence columns, which tended to be a refuge for all manner of eccentricity. In 1874 'An Old Member' (presumably no pun was intended) requested advice on curbing excessive masturbation on the part of a 7-year-old boy whose behaviour was causing him to become weak and thin. The following week four replies were published. These recommended blistering the penis with a hot iron or other means, or circumcision. Some weeks later a correspondent from Maidstone suggested that a child's nurse might often be the villain of the piece:

I had a very shocking and distressing case a year or so ago, when a bright intelligent little boy, about six years old, was taken into the bed of his nurse-girl every night, placed between her legs, and kept there more or less all night. After a while it came to the knowledge of his mother, and of course the nurse was instantly dismissed. But imagine her horror on finding that he afterwards got into the bed of a little sister about a year younger than himself, and did the same thing as with the nurse; and still later, when they were separated and carefully watched at night, he would seek an opportunity in the day time and throw her down on the floor for the same purpose.[80]

[78] *Journal*, 18 April 1868, 387–8.

[79] *Ibid.*, 30 Nov. 1895, 1399. See H. Marsh (ed.), *Sir James Paget Clinical Lectures and Essays* (London, 1875); E. H. Hare, 'Masturbatory Insanity: the History of an Idea', *Journal of Mental Science* (1962) **108**: 1–25; R. H. MacDonald, 'The Frightful Consequences of Onanism: Notes on the History of a Delusion', *Journal of the History of Ideas* (1967) **XXVIII**: 423–31; Alex Comfort, *The Anxiety Makers (London: Panther, 1967), Chapter 3; R. P. Neuman, 'Masturbation, Madness and the Modern Concepts of Childhood and Adolescence', Journal of Social History* (1975) **8**. 1–2, J. L'Esperance, 'Doctors and Women in Nineteenth Century Society', pp. 107–12 (note 75).

[80] *Journal*, 5 Dec. 1874, 727; 12 Dec. 1874, 759; 2 Jan. 1875, 33. Similar discussions recurred almost verbatim in later years. See Nov. 30 1889, 1259; 7 Dec. 1889, 1315; 19 Jan. 1895, 179; 26 Jan. 1895, 235.

In this case boarding school proved the solution, but the writer suggested that nurses needed careful watching.

For a minority of women and girls there was the more drastic solution of clitoridectomy, or surgical removal of the clitoris. In fact, this was presented by its main English exponent, Isaac Baker Brown, as a cure for a pattern of female afflictions arising from 'peripheral excitement of the branches of the pudic nerve', i.e. masturbation. In 1866 Brown published a short work, *On the Curability of Certain Forms of Insanity, Epilepsy, Catalepsy, and Hysteria, in Females.* The *Church Times* saw Brown's treatment as being 'incontestably' successful in curing epilepsy and urged clergymen to draw the attention of medical men to it.[81] However, the book was unfavourably reviewed in the *Journal*, where the reviewer recognized Brown's methods for what they were—a knife-happy assault on masturbation.[82] If, as Brown admitted, patients who had gone through clitoridectomy still needed 'careful watching and moral training', was there not, the reviewer inquired, a serious question mark against the value of the operation?

The review's appearance prompted considerable correspondence on the subject of clitoridectomy. Thomas Littleton, observing that 'what is sauce for the goose is sauce for the gander', inquired mischievously whether Brown would 'resort to an analagous deprivation in cases of the same disease similarly induced in the male'.[83] The answer was no, for Brown viewed clitoridectomy as akin to circumcision rather than penile amputation.

In November 1866 Charles West, in a trenchant critique of Brown, stated that he had not 'in the whole of my practice seen convulsions, epilepsy or idiocy *induced* by masturbation in any child of either sex. . . . Neither have I seen any instance in which hysteria, epilepsy, or insanity in women after puberty was *due* to masturbation as its efficient cause.' When the Obstetrical Society of London discussed the issue in December, Brown received virtually no support.[84] The *Journal* too was inclined to disagree with Brown, though it considered that his treatment warranted a proper trial. Its main concern, however, was with 'the public discussion before mixed audiences, of sexual abuses. It is a dirty subject, and one with which only a strong sense of duty can induce professional men to meddle; and then it needs to be handled with an absolute purity of speech, thought, and expression, and, as far as possible in strictly technical language.'[85]

Early in 1867 there were suggestions that some of Brown's patients had been 'terrorised' into consenting to clitoridectomy while others had undergone it without their knowledge.[86] As a result his fellowship of the Obstetrical

[81] *Ibid.*, 28 April 1866, 456.
[82] *Ibid.*, 438–40.
[83] *Ibid.*, 19 May 1866, 537; 16 June 1866, 654.
[84] *Ibid.*, 24 Nov. 1866, 585.
[85] *Ibid.*, 15 Dec. 1866, 664–5, 672–8.
[86] *Ibid.*, 19 Jan. 1867, 61.

Society was terminated.[87] With the disgrace of its chief advocate and practitioner, clitoridectomy rapidly became a thing of the past.[88]

What all this signified, of course, was the prevalence of profound sexual ignorance, not only on the part of many doctors but in society at large. This ignorance was nurtured by the social purity movement which campaigned against prostitution, 'smut', pornography, and vice in general. The movement was particularly active in the 1880s when it agitated for a Criminal Law Amendment Act to raise the age of consent and suppress brothels. It was given a huge boost by W. T. Stead's exposé of child prostitution and the white slave trade in the *Pall Mall Gazette* in 1885.[89] The *Journal* used the occasion of Stead's 'Maiden Tribute of Modern Babylon' articles to launch an appeal for sex education. A leading article observed that complete ignorance regarding the sexual organs and the sexual functions was 'sedulously fostered' in the country's schools and by society at large. In consequence some men and many 'cultivated and refined women' grew up and married 'in complete sexual ignorance'. The *Journal* believed that this state of affairs led to marital unhappiness and an unhealthy fascination on the part of the young with a subject which, because of the conspiracy of silence, was considered lewd and obscene. Its solution was for schools to tackle the subjects of elementary anatomy and physiology including, at the appropriate time, of the sexual organs.[90]

This proposal went down like the proverbial lead balloon. An Irish headmaster believed that few teachers would be capable of teaching the

[87] *Ibid.*, 6 April 1867, 387–8, 395–410. Brown subsequently resigned his fellowship of the Medical Society of London.

[88] See J. B. Fleming, 'Clitoridectomy—the Disastrous Downfall of Isaac Baker Brown, FRCS, 1867', *Journal of Obstetrics and Gynaecology of the British Empire* (1960) **67**: 1017–34; Susan Kingsley Kent, *Sex and Suffrage in Britain, 1860–1914* (Princeton: Princeton University Press, 1987), pp. 47, 61, 116–19; Jeffrey Weeks, *Sex, Politics and Society. The Regulation of Sexuality Since 1800* (London: Longman, 1981), p. 43; Lorna Duffin, 'The Conspicuous Consumptive: Woman as Invalid', in S. Delamont and L. Duffin, *The Nineteenth Century Woman*, pp. 42–3 (note 74). The fate of Baker Brown and 'his' operation might seem to give the lie to Duffin's implication that there was a more or less unified conspiracy of male doctors intent on assaulting their female patients. However, Kent suggests that Brown's punishment was for the bad publicity he brought the profession, not because his operation was deemed to be mistaken and inappropriate. But she fails to cite the newspapers in which this bad publicity was given, and takes no account of the *BMJ*'s treatment of the case. In sum, this interpretation appears to be based on a selective reading of the evidence.

[89] See E. J. Bristow, *Vice and Vigilance. Purity Movements in Britain Since 1900* (Dublin: Gill and Macmillan, 1977), pp. 106–14; F. Mort, *Dangerous Sexualities: Medico-Moral Politics in England since 1830* (London: Routledge and Kegan Paul, 1987), pp. 103–5; E. Trudgill, *Madonnas and Magdalens*, pp. 49–52, 197–9 (note 73).

[90] *Journal*, 15 Aug. 1885, 303; 19 Sept. 1885, 561; E. Trudgill, *Madonnas and Magdalens*, pp. 59–62, (note 73). Smith makes the point that it is 'hard to document ... inferences about disastrous innocence on wedding nights'. F. Barry Smith, 'Sexuality in Britain, 1800–1900' in Martha Vicinus (ed.), *A Widening Sphere. Changing Roles of Victorian Women* (London: Methuen, 1977), p. 195. The *Lancet*'s response to Stead's revelations was to rue public discussion of sexual matters and to stress the importance of religion and purity. See 22 Aug. 1885, 350–1.

subject. As for unmarried female teachers, 'there are surely many of them ... who would far rather at once resign their offices than instruct the young in such extremely delicate matters.' Another correspondent, who signed himself 'A Doctor and a Father', sympathized with the *Journal*'s objectives but suggested that they could be best realized if a committee of medical and clerical authorities collaborated in producing a book explaining 'the laws of generation ... with appropriate scriptural references'. This would be given to all children on their 12th or 13th birthday for them to read 'at leisure and in private'. Other writers inveighed against this proposal and, indeed, against any effort to exchange what one termed 'the old sweet symplicity [sic] and innocence of our English homes, for the doubtful blessing of such early physiological knowledge'. In these inauspicious circumstances, the *Journal* quietly dropped the topic.[91]

The task of exploring sexuality and disseminating findings was largely left to isolated individuals ploughing a lone furrow. In the early twentieth century the *Journal* carried reviews of several works on sexual psychology and pathology, notably Krafft-Ebing's *Psychopathia Sexualis* (1899) and Havelock Ellis's *Studies in the Psychology of Sex* (1897–1900). The reviewer of the former found it 'nauseous', while Ellis's work was described as 'disgusting' and 'scientifically valueless':

> It seems as if he [Ellis] argued that since most of the facts bearing upon his subject are dirty and disgusting, therefore any and every dirty and disgusting fact is a proper one to be recorded in his book, and the consequence is that he frequently presents the appearance of bedaubing himself with filth without serving any useful purpose.[92]

Ellis's publisher, George Bedborough, was prosecuted for obscene libel and corrupting public morals, with the result, as Ellis's *BMJ* obituary put it, that Britain was put 'out of the running ... in the study of sex for a good many years'.[93] In reporting the Bedborough case the *Journal* took a more tolerant line than its reviewer. Although it saw Ellis's subject matter as 'extremely disagreeable', it could not fault the author's treatment.[94] When Ellis died in 1939 the *Journal* described him as 'a singularly high-minded soul, filled with a vivid sense of the beauty of the world and of the potential beauty of human life in it'. A fortnight later a correspondent drew attention to the great change in attitude which had occurred in the *Journal*'s columns in a comparatively short time.[95]

For a publication which highlighted the scandals of infanticide and baby farming and was anxious to dispel sexual ignorance, it is curious that the

[91] *Journal*, 19 Sept. 1885, 579; 30 Jan. 1886, 236; 13 Feb. 1886, 331. See A. Comfort, *The Anxiety Makers*, p. 15 (note 79).

[92] *Journal*, 8 Feb. 1902, 339–41; 22 July 1939, 203–4.

[93] *Ibid.*, 22 July 1939, 203–4.

[94] *Ibid.*, 5 Nov. 1898, 1466.

[95] *Ibid.*, 22 July 1939, 203–4; 5 Aug. 1939, 320.

Victorian *Journal* almost totally ignored the related question of contraception. In so far as it was discussed, it was in terms of disapproval. The medical profession as a whole oscillated between studied indifference and overt hostility to contraception. One historian of birth control gives four reasons for these attitudes. First, the profession's reluctance to accept the importance of preventive medicine in any field; second, its inherent distaste for the subject; third, its confusion of contraception with abortion; and fourth, its belief that contraception damaged health.[96]

In a leading article entitled 'Social Dialectics' the *Journal* angrily rejected a suggestion made at a meeting of the Dialectical Society that the question of 'how could married persons limit the number of their offspring without injuring their health' was mainly a medical one. 'We believe,' said the editorial, 'that our profession will repudiate with indignation and disgust such functions as these gentlemen wish to assign to it.' The *Journal*'s repudiation was strong enough for the society to contemplate libel action.[97] If birth control was not a medical question, one might suppose that it was a topic for lay consideration. However, the *Journal* ignored popular works on contraception such as George Drysdale's *Elements of Social Science* (1854), Charles Knowlton's *Fruits of Philosophy* (re-published in 1876), and Annie Besant's *Law of Population* (1878), as well as the Bradlaugh–Besant trial of 1876.[98] Moreover, its position in the case of *H. A. Allbutt* versus *General Medical Council* showed that it simply did not want such matters to be made accessible to the general public.

Henry Allbutt, organizer of the Leeds neo-Malthusian movement and a cousin of the more famous Clifford Allbutt, was the first 'English doctor [to] put his name to a birth control tract'.[99] This was *The Wife's Handbook* (1886), a work which described contraceptives such as the condom, sponge, and diaphragm. In 1887 the Leeds Vigilance Association drew the attention of the General Medical Council to the pamphlet. A GMC committee

[96] Angus McLaren, *Birth Control in Nineteenth Century England* (London: Croom Helm, 1978), p. 118; see Peter Fryer, *The Birth Controllers* (London: Secker and Warburg, 1965); John Peel, 'Contraception and the Medical Profession', *Population Studies* (1964–5) **xviii**: 133–45.

[97] *Journal*, 1 Aug. 1868, 113; 8 Aug. 1868, 141; 20 March 1869, 212. These views were also held by the *Lancet* and the *Medical Times and Gazette*. See A. McLaren, *Birth Control in Nineteenth Century England*, pp. 129–30 (note 96); A. Comfort, *The Anxiety Makers*, pp. 157–8 (note 79); J. L'Esperance, 'Doctors and Women in Nineteenth Century Society', p. 107 (note 75); J. Peel, 'Contraception and the Medical Profession', 134–5 (note 96); P. Fryer, *The Birth Controllers*, pp. 124, 130 (note 96); Richard Allen Soloway, *Birth Control and the Population Question in England, 1877–1930* (Chapel Hill, North Carolina: University of North Carolina Press, 1982), p. 112; J. A. Banks, *Prosperity and Parenthood, A Study of Family Planning Among the Victorian Middle Classes* (London: Routledge and Kegan Paul, 1954), p. 146.

[98] Charles Bradlaugh and Annie Besant were prosecuted for re-publishing Knowlton's pamphlet. See J. A. Banks and Olive Banks, 'The Bradlaugh–Besant Trial and the English Newspapers', Population Studies (1954–5) **VIII**: 22–34.

[99] A. McLaren, *Birth Control in Nineteenth Century England*, pp. 112, 132 (note 96). See A. Comfort, *The Anxiety Makers*, pp. 165–6 (note 79).

appointed to inquire into the facts of the case found that 'the pamphlet was extensively sold [its price was only 6d], and that, besides containing much that was offensive to taste and professionally objectionable, it taught how sexual intercourse might be indulged in without fear of pregnancy supervening ... '.[100] Although the Committee acknowledged that Allbutt 'did not distinctly recommend that kind of indulgence unless avoidance of pregnancy was advised by the doctor', the GMC still decided that he had committed the offence 'of having published and publicly caused to be sold a work ... at so low a price as to bring the work within the reach of the youth of both sexes, to the detriment of public morals'. In so doing, it judged, Allbutt was guilty of 'infamous' professional conduct; the Council ordered his name to be erased from the *Medical Register*.[101]

Over the next 18 months Allbutt attempted to get this verdict overturned in the courts. But in July 1889 the Court of Appeal concluded that it had no authority to review GMC decisions. In a leading article on the decision the *Journal* showed little sympathy for Allbutt. It believed 'that injury is done to the medical profession by one of its members publishing in a cheap and popular form information which, however legitimate in its proper place, may be used for the worst purposes'.[102] But in fact, as is shown by its attitude to the Allbutt case, its Social Dialectics editorial, and its customary silence, the nineteenth-century *BMJ* saw contraception as an inappropriate topic for medical men, no matter how treated.[103]

It took a world war to temper the profession's antagonism. The extent of venereal disease among British troops fighting in the First World War persuaded the government, on medical advice, to issue condoms.[104] The primary objective, of course, was not to control fertility but to keep fighting men fit and in the field. But one historian suggests that the distribution 'marked more clearly than any other single event the end of "Victorian England" '.[105] *BMJ* attitudes were changing too, for in 1918 it felt able to 'commend' Marie Stopes' *Married Love*, a book which, three decades earlier, would have been anathema.[106] But artificial contraception remained a matter of controversy for years to come.

The consequences of the Victorian silence on contraception were

[100] *Journal*, 26 Nov. 1887, 1162.

[101] *Ibid.*, 3 Dec. 1887, 1222; J. Peel, 'Contraception and the Medical Profession', 135–6 (note 96). The *Handbook* went into a 45th edition in 1913.

[102] *Journal*, 13 July 1889, 88. See 28 May 1887, 1177.

[103] On the Allbutt case see J. A. Banks, *Victorian Values. Secularism and the Size of Families* (London: Routledge and Kegan Paul, 1981), pp. 110–12; J. A. Banks, *Prosperity and Parenthood*, pp. 156–7 (note 97); E. O. Bristow, *Vice and Vigilance*, p. 126 (note 89); P. Fryer, *The Birth Controllers*, pp. 170–1 (note 96); R. A. Soloway, *Birth Control and the Population Question in England, 1877–1930*, p. 116 (note 97).

[104] A. McLaren, *Birth Control in Nineteenth Century England*, p. 136 (note 96).

[105] *Ibid.*, p. 136.

[106] *Journal*., 4 May 1918, 410.

unwanted conceptions followed by attempts to procure abortion.[107] In 1895 the *Journal* complained about the 'flood' of newspaper advertisements offering 'female pills' guaranteed to remove 'obstructions' or get rid of the 'consequences' of marriage.[108] Indeed, in a period of two years the notorious Chrimes brothers, who placed such advertisements, received over 10 000 requests for their useless abortifacients.[109] The *Journal* regarded the 'immoral advertisements' as 'a direct incentive not only to undesirable practices among the married, but to all sorts of immorality among the young, by holding out a relief if difficulties arise'. As such, it was for the police 'to put a stop to what is a public incitement to crime'.[110] Because abortion was illegal the Victorian profession failed to discuss it as a medical, social, or moral issue in the pages of either the *BMJ* or the *Lancet*. Abortion was regarded as disgraceful, but so too, apparently, was the information that might have curtailed recourse to it.

Doctors in petticoats

Victorian beliefs about women's sexuality, psychology, and physiology profoundly affected attitudes towards women in the workplace and women as citizens. Nowhere was this more the case than in the question of whether it was appropriate for women to train as doctors. Notions of propriety made many people, not only male doctors, baulk at the idea of women studying medicine, particularly if they were to do so alongside men. Others expressed more concern that women would add to the competition for patients and fees, thereby impairing the livelihoods of male practitioners. To say that this issue split the medical profession in two is only partially true, for most medical men long remained implacably opposed to the prospect of women doctors. Certainly until the 1870s the *BMJ* showed every sign of illiberalism and misogynism.

The presence of women in the labour market was no new phenomenon in the nineteenth century. Women had long constituted a sizeable proportion of the gainfully employed. Though protective legislation (for which many women were less than grateful) and restrictive practices by male workers limited their employment opportunities, the number of women workers increased by almost two millions (from 2.8m to 4.75m) between 1851 and 1901. In certain industries, such as pottery manufacture, domestic service, or parts of the textile trade, they predominated. But most working women were in low paid, manual jobs; social convention ensured that employment

[107] A. McLaren, *Birth Control in Nineteenth Century England*, p. 238 (note 96).

[108] *Journal*, 14 Dec. 1895, 1509.

[109] When the Chrimes brothers tried to blackmail as well as cheat their customers, their cruel swindle was exposed. Accounts of this case are given by A. McLaren, *Birth Control in Nineteenth Century England*, pp. 232–40 (note 96) and the same author's 'Abortion in England, 1890–1914', *Victorian Studies* (1976–7) **20**: 381–7. See *Journal*, 22 Oct. 1898, 1270; 14 Jan. 1899, 110–11.

[110] *Ibid.*, 14 Dec. 1895, 1509; J. A. Banks, *Prosperity and Parenthood*, pp. 157–9 (note 97).

OUR PRETTY DOCTOR

Dr. Arabella: 'WELL, MY GOOD FRIENDS, WHAT CAN I DO FOR YOU?'
Bill: 'WELL, MISS, IT'S ALL ALONG O' ME AND MY MATES BEIN' OUT O' WORK, YER SEE, AND WANTIN' TO TURN AN HONEST PENNY HANYWAYS WE CAN; SO, 'AVIN' 'EARD TELL AS *YOU* WAS A RISIN' YOUNG MEDICAL PRACTITIONER, WE THOUGHT AS P'R'APS YOU WOULDN'T MIND *JUST* A-RECOMMENDIN' OF *HUS* AS NURSES!'

Our Pretty Doctor: from *Mr Punch Among the Doctors*. Source: Bodleian Library, Oxford.

opportunities for middle-class women were severely limited. The 1911 census showed that women were in a tiny minority in the professions.[111]

For centuries the 'wise woman' had held an important, albeit lowly, place in medical practice. Until the eighteenth century some women occupied a relatively high status in the medical hierarchy. But a combination of circumstances meant that by the nineteenth century 'good-class medical practice had closed to women, apparently for ever'.[112] Medical reform institutionalized the male monopoly. During the 1860s a few women tried to challenge this position and enter the medical profession. A pioneer figure was Elizabeth Garrett, the first woman (in 1865) to obtain a legal qualification to practise medicine in Great Britain. Another, the first woman to have her name placed on the *Medical Register* (in 1859) was the English-born American Elizabeth Blackwell. She had graduated in medicine from the University of Geneva, New York State, in 1849. When, 10 years later, she

[111] See Jane Lewis, *Women in England, 1870–1950* (Brighton: Wheatsheaf, 1984), p. 195; Lee Holcombe, *Victorian Ladies at Work* (Newton Abbot: David and Charles, 1973); Angela V. John (ed.), *Unequal Opportunities Women's Employment in England, 1880–1918* (Oxford: Basil Blackwell, 1986), p. 17.

[112] Jo Manton, *Elizabeth Garrett Anderson* (London: Methuen, 1965), p. 60.

visited England the *Journal* marked the occasion in a leading article heavy with sarcasm:

> . . . is not the idea of a female practitioner . . . lamentably ridiculous . . . ? Call to mind all things that are done in the ordinary course of hospital duties, or even of general practice in town or country; and imagine, good reader, if you can, a British lady performing them . . . Is it compatible with the attributes of woman, that she should arm herself with a medical education and medical diplomas, and put herself forward to practise medicine? Certainly not.[113]

The *Journal* accepted that women had a place in the sick room, but felt that their role should be in offering sympathy, tenderness, and devotion. It was for men to exercise judgement, make decisions, and take prompt action. 'When woman undertakes . . . the duty of man, then she goes beyond her province, and loses all title to our respect.' However, as far as British women were concerned, the *Journal* had few worries: 'there is no fear that the British matron and the British damsel will be tempted, by any cry of woman's dignity or of false delicacy, to do aught that shall diminish the esteem and affection with which they have ever been regarded.'[114]

This seemed an accurate assessment until Elizabeth Garrett made her determined bid for a medical career. After abortive attempts to pursue her medical studies at the Middlesex Hospital and to matriculate at London University she unsuccessfully sought admittance to St Andrews University in 1862. Her rebuff there prompted the *Journal* to return to 'the female doctor question'. It had not changed its views:

> It is, indeed, high time that this unnatural and preposterous attempt on the part of one or two highly strongly minded women to establish a race of feminine doctors should be exploded. How is it possible, in accordance with any of the notions of propriety and of sentiment which we feel towards the female sex in this country, for any man of proper feeling to sit by the side of a lady at a dissecting-table or in an anatomical lecture-room?[115]

If there was a demand for 'doctors of the female gender', or 'doctors in petticoats' as the *Journal* later put it, then those who wanted them should establish segregated training schools. But at this time, and for several years to come, the *Journal* made it clear that it had little sympathy with the idea of women practitioners.[116] Jonathan Hutchinson, like his predecessors in the editorial chair, was an out and out opponent, though he did recognize that Garrett's achievement in gaining an MD in Paris in 1870 was testimony to her 'indomitable perseverance and pluck'.[117]

[113] *Journal*, 9 April 1859, 292–3.

[114] *Ibid.*

[115] *Ibid.*, 22 Nov. 1862, 537–8. The *Lancet* took a similar view, see 6 July 1861, 16; 3 Aug. 1861, 117–18.

[116] See *Journal*, 23 April 1864, 452; 14 May 1864, 534; 9 March 1867, 269; 16 March 1867, 293; 2 April 1870, 338–9; 7 May 1870, 474–5; 9 July 1870, 41–2.

[117] *Ibid.*, 18 June 1870, 636; 19 Aug. 1876, 232–5.

Under Hart's editorship, however, *Journal* attitudes began to mellow. Hart was a personal friend of Garrett Anderson (as she was from 1871), and published some of her papers in the *BMJ*.[118] After his death she noted that when on the *Lancet*'s staff he had made unfriendly comments about her early struggles. Subsequently, however, possibly because his second wife had studied medicine herself, he gave his 'hearty support to the movement for introducing women into the medical profession . . . [and] . . . did all he could consistently with his position as Editor of the *Journal*, to befriend the movement'.[119]

Hart did not believe in the joint tuition of male and female students. Neither did he feel that women doctors could ever be very numerous or the equal of men, for the 'physical weakness and sexual disadvantages of women for arduous and public pursuits' rendered most of them inherently unsuitable for medical work. Consequently: 'If the profession of medicine were thrown open to women as freely as it is to men—as we have always thought it ought to be—it may reasonably be doubted whether more than a few would ever adopt it, and whether a very small proportion of that few would succeed in it.'[120] But, as even this passage indicates, he was far more liberal than many contemporary male doctors. Thus, a leading article in 1871 stated that 'we desire, and we believe the profession at large desires, to see oppressive barriers removed from before ladies who wish to qualify for medical practice in obstetrics and diseases of women.' '[W]e do not approve', said a later note, 'of the exclusion of women from examination from medical or any other degrees, when they have gone through the required curricula of study, and are able to satisfy the same intellectual tests as men.'[121] Such opinions were far removed from those expressed by Hutchinson and Hart's other predecessors. They were also far in advance of those held by many medical men and institutions, including the BMA, in later years.[122] In 1878, the year in which the Association voted to deny women membership, the *Lancet* could still maintain that the medical education of women violated 'the laws of decency'.[123]

In 1869 Sophia Jex-Blake and six other women had begun to receive, amid considerable controversy, separate tuition in the medical faculty of Edinburgh University. In 1873 the Court of Session decided, on appeal, that the

[118] See e.g. 14 Dec. 1872, 669; Diary of Jeannette Marshall, 15 Nov. 1883. I am grateful to Zuzanna Shonfield for a transcript of references to Hart in the diary.

[119] *Journal*, 15 Jan. 1898, 182.

[120] *Ibid.*, 20 Sept. 1873, 357.

[121] *Ibid.*, 23 Sept. 1871, 356; 14 Oct. 1871, 455; J. Manton, *Elizabeth Garrett Anderson*, p. 284 (note 112).

[122] See e.g. the case against women practitioners made by Septimus Sibley, Hutchinson's successor as president of the BMA's Metropolitan Counties branch. *Journal*, 1 Sept. 1877, 283.

[123] *Lancet*, 5 Jan. 1878, 18; see J. L'Esperance, 'Doctors and Women in Nineteenth Century Society', p. 118 (note 75). The *Journal* was constrained from criticizing BMA decisions by the convention that it did not oppose Association policy. See 15 Jan. 1898, 182.

university's constitution provided only for the education of males, and that women were, therefore, not entitled to attend classes and graduate. This was a severe setback and one which the *Journal* considered unfair. Hart did what he could to offer practical support. When, in 1874, Jex-Blake founded the London School of Medicine (later incorporated in the Royal Free Hospital), he served as a governor and, with his wife, who had studied medicine in Paris, 'gave a handsome scholarship to the school'. In 1875 he alerted Garrett Anderson, newly elected to the BMA, that the Association's annual meeting was likely to mount an attempt to exclude women.[124]

By the late 1870s, with women entering the medical profession in a steady trickle, the *Journal* ceased to pay much attention to the 'lady doctor' question. Of course, women still had a long way to go before gaining full acceptance as the equals of men as medical practitioners. Even when qualified, the barriers they faced were formidable, not least because they were ineligible for the military and naval, Poor Law, and other public appointments which often provided men with valuable early experience. By 1881 only 21 women were on the *Medical Register*. But in comparison with the other professions—the Church, the armed forces, and the law remained completely closed to women throughout the nineteenth century—much had been achieved. By 1895, 264 women were registered as doctors.[125]

Advertising

The *Journal* was financed in three ways: by subvention from BMA funds, by sales, and by advertising. Advertising revenue became an increasingly important source of income for the *Journal* and, indeed, the Association. As a passage in the *Journal* in 1867 noted, 'the income derivable from advertisements is . . . a consideration in the management of this as of other journals. Without such an income, a first class journal, such as alone is worthy of the Association, could not be furnished for the moderate annual subscription.'[126] In fact, by the end of the nineteenth century *Journal* advertising and sales were sometimes providing a larger proportion of BMA income than subscriptions. On the other hand, *Journal* production costs—in excess of £26 500 in 1899—accounted for a far larger slice of BMA expenditure than any other item. In that year advertisers paid over £19 300 for space in the *Journal*. Without this substantial revenue either Association subscriptions would

[124] *Ibid.*; 10 Oct. 1874, 469; J. Manton, *Elizabeth Garrett Anderson*, pp. 254–6 (note 112). The BMA's 1878 decision to exclude women did not debar Garrett Anderson as it was not retrospective.

[125] Duncan Crow, *The Victorian Woman* (London: Allen and Unwin, 1971), p. 322.

[126] *Journal*, 9 Nov. 1867, 440.

have been far higher (and what might this have done to membership figures?) or the *BMJ* would have been a very different publication.[127]

In 1861 the charges to advertisers were:

	£	s	d
Five lines and under	0	2	6
Each additional line	0	0	6
A whole column	2	5	0
A whole page	5	0	0

These figures were reduced for serial insertions. In 1898 the scale was:

	£	s	d
Eight lines and under	0	4	0
Each additional line	0	0	6
A whole column	1	17	6
A whole page	5	5	0

In view of the *Journal*'s larger dimensions and vastly greater circulation, the increased charges over this period were modest. In fact, some advertisements would have been less costly at the end of the century than 40 years earlier. It may be that the small rise in the cost of space in the *Journal* reflected the competitive market for advertising in the late nineteenth century.[128] What is beyond dispute is that the *Journal*'s increased revenue from advertising derived less from selling space at higher prices than from the inclusion of ever more advertising copy. In fact, an 1889 issue contained over 62 pages of advertising (against 56 of editorial matter). In 1891 the ratio was 74 : 52 and, in 1899, 80 : 64.

What was advertised in the *Journal*? In 1840, when advertisements usually covered about three columns, they were mainly for medical books, surgical aids, and medical schools. They were bald, unillustrated descriptions of products that were clearly expected to sell themselves once brought to readers' attention. On 7 November 1840 a bookseller, a tailor, and an insurance company advertised their services. The tailor, in what was the closest approach to the 'hard sell', offered 'superfine' dress coats at £2 7s 6d and 'the very best that can be made' at £2 15s.[129]

[127] On the importance of advertising to the growth and survival of nineteenth century newspapers in general, see Terry Nevett, 'Advertising and Editorial Integrity in the Nineteenth Century' in M. Harris and A. Lee, *The Press in English Society from the Seventeenth to Nineteenth Centuries*, pp. 149–67 (note 41).

[128] See *ibid.*, p. 153. The *Journal* was not in competition with the general press for all its advertising, but by the 1880s many producers of non-medical goods, such as bicycles, whisky, cigars, and bread, were advertising in the *Journal*.

[129] *Journal*, 7 Nov. 1840, 112.

By the 1850s there had been little change in the type of advertising. Medical books continued to predominate, though by now a few professional posts were also appearing. For example, in 1854 the Southern and Toxteth Hospital in Liverpool advertised for a junior house surgeon. Candidates were required to possess a diploma from one of the Royal Colleges of Surgeons and the licence of the London Society of Apothecaries. A salary of 50 guineas a year plus board and lodging in the hospital was offered.[130]

By the 1860s the *Journal* was carrying a far more extensive range of advertising. This may be explained by the abolition of excise duty in the 1850s and the mid-Victorian 'consumer boom'. The first patent baby food was marketed by Liebig in 1867. In August the *Journal* included an inauspicious news report that in French trials four infants to whom it was given had died.[131] Although the *Journal* contained advertisements for Liebig's Extract of Meat ('highly strengthening for children and invalids'), I have been unable to discover advertisments for its baby food. However, rival companies, Savory and Moore and Anglo-Swiss Condensed Milk, both advertised their infant food in the *BMJ*. Savory and Moore's advertisement for its 'food for infants and invalids', which came in tins priced between 1s and 10s, included a quotation from the *Lancet* that it was '"a real improvement" on the ordinary kind of Liebig's food'. Anglo-Swiss's 'Pure Swiss Milk (Preserved)' cited a recommendation from Baron von Liebig and a *BMJ* report. Moreover 'Its UNIFORMITY and PURITY render it specially adapted for INFANT'S FOOD and for HOSPITAL PURPOSES. All things considered, it will be found as CHEAP for FAMILY USE as ordinary Milk. It may be used as an equivalent to cream.'[132] Examination of the *Journal*'s report shows that, though it recognized the 'great dietetic value' of the condensed milk, it did not comment on its value as infant food.[133]

The *Journal*'s practice of evaluating baby foods and other products in its editorial columns, such assessments sometimes being used by manufacturers in their advertising, raises the question of whether the *Journal* engaged in 'puffing'. A 'puff' may be defined as an advertisement masquerading as editorial matter. Put another way, it is a news item extolling the virtue of a product, for which payment is made. Newspaper 'puffs' were usually charged at a higher rate than mere advertisements, presumably because they carried greater authority and hence might be expected to be more powerful persuaders. Quacks and vendors of patent medicines were among those who relied on puffing.[134] Although we have no direct evidence that the *Journal* engaged in the practice, circumstantial evidence suggests that during Hart's

[130] *Ibid.*, 20 Jan. 1854, 76.
[131] *Ibid.*, 3 Aug. 1867, 91.
[132] *Ibid.*, 21 Dec. 1867, n.p.
[133] *Ibid.*, 2 Nov. 1867, 384.
[134] See T. Nevett, 'Advertising and Editorial Integrity in the Nineteenth Century', pp. 154–64 (note 127).

editorship it may have done so, for it carried regular reports on new commercial products. Moreover, we know that Apollinaris, the bottled water company in which Hart reputedly had a stake and which regularly advertised in the *Journal* using a *BMJ* quotation, did seek to induce the press to 'puff' its product.[135]

A popular advertising technique was to incorporate the endorsement of a medical practitioner or publication into the copy promoting a product. Dahl's dyspepsia cakes were advertised with five such endorsements, while Pears relied heavily on Mr James Startin's recommendation to sell their soap:

> the eminent surgeon writes: 'I always use it myself and recommend to my patients PEARS' SOAP in preference to any other as being more free from excess of alkali and other impurities prejudicial to the skin.'

Medical endorsement of commercial products was to become a controversial ethical issue. As we shall see (Chapter 8), in the early twentieth century the BMA's Ethics Committee, encouraged by the membership, began to look closely at products advertised in the *Journal*.

Food and drink advertisements were prominent in the *Journal* from the 1860s. Most of these products were claimed to have health-enhancing or preserving properties (for example, mineral waters, pepsin globules, saccharated wheat phosphates, cod liver oil, and beef essence). This also applied to some alcoholic beverages, with one enterprising distiller in the 1880s advertising his 'diabetes' whisky. With the awakening of public concern about food and drink adulteration, many advertisers stressed the purity of their wares, sometimes publishing complex reports of chemical analyses. As Burnett states:

> By the late fifties 'Pure and Unadulterated' had become the stock advertising slogan of dealers anxious to cash in on the newly awakened fears of the public—all too frequently it was the same spirit of commercialism which had prompted adulteration in the first instance which now made it more profitable to offer, usually at a somewhat higher price, a commodity which was 'guaranteed pure' and bore the certificate of a doctor or analyst.[136]

For the rest, medical publications, life insurance, pharmaceutical preparations, and surgical aids and instruments made regular appearances in the 1860s, as did invalid carriages, water beds, and (a hardy perennial) 'Walters' India-Rubber Urinals' as 'worn by all Travellers and in all climates'.

Since the *Journal*'s early days teaching institutions had used its pages to seek students; by the 1860s, other establishments such as lunatic asylums for the middle classes and retreats for those of 'INTEMPERATE HABITS, or otherwise requiring Moral Restraint' were also using it in their search for

[135] *Ibid.*, pp. 163–4.
[136] J. Burnett, *Plenty and Want*, p. 251 (note 55).

clients.[137] Perhaps most fascinating are the advertisements offering practices or partnerships for sale. These were often inserted by J. Baxter Langley, whose Professional Agency and Medical Transfer Office in Lincoln's Inn Fields dated from 1848:

Partnership.—The incumbent of a practice in the suburb of a large manufacturing town, realising about £1000 a year, and capable of great increase, is willing to receive a partner on favourable terms. The incomer must be doubly qualified and have at least £500 at command.

In a large country town, a well established Practice for transfer. Receipts £430 a year, capable of great increase in the hands of a young and active man. Appointments yield £100 a year. The whole connexion is believed to be perfectly transferable. The expenses are very moderate and house rent small.[138]

The late Victorian and Edwardian period saw a great blossoming of the art of advertising. The *Journal*'s advertising pages for the 1880s and 1890s make fascinating reading, not only for the sometimes exotic products which found their way there but also for the skill with which they were presented. In contrast, the advertisments of today or of the 1840s seem pale and uninteresting. Take, for example, the advertisements carried in two issues of the *Journal*, one from December 1889, the other from December 1899.

On 7 December 1889 books, booksellers, and medical journals, such as the *Practitioner*, were, as ever, well to the fore. In addition, there were many advertisements for 'chemical and medical preparations'. By the late nineteenth century some pharmaceutical companies had huge advertising budgets—Beecham is said to have spent £120 000 in 1891.[139] Some products, such as cocoa, malt extract, cod liver oil, infant, and invalid foods, sit somewhat uncomfortably under the 'chemical and medical preparations' designation. Still more improbable are 'Savars Cubeb Cigarettes' which, it was claimed, 'always relieve and frequently cure Asthma, Throat Cough, Bronchitis, Influenza'. A London chemist recommended his 'ozone cigarettes', priced 2s 6d per box, for the 'immediate relief and subsequent cure' of the same afflictions. He thoughtfully provided directions for use: 'A cigarette may be lighted at either end, and a large volume of smoke should be drawn from the mouth, then a full inspiration taken to convey it into the air tubes, when instant relief will be afforded.' More conventional tobacco products, regularly advertised in the *Journal* at this time, were still in evidence as late as the 1950s. Advertisements for alcoholic drinks, including brandy, sherry, and Guinness, continued into the 1960s. Equally, if not more, alarming than tobacco and alcohol, though certainly typical of the time, were

Houdé's Pastils of Hydrochlorate of Cocaine, [which] through the insensibility they

[137] *Journal*, 28 Sept. 1867, n.p.

[138] *Ibid.*

[139] T. Nevett, 'Advertising and Editorial Integrity in the Nineteenth Century', p. 151 (note 127).

1. *Journal* editors. Top left: John Walsh (1849–53). Top right: William Harcourt Ranking (1849–52). Bottom left: Andrew Wynter (1855–60). Bottom right: William Orlando Markham (1860–66). Source: *British Medical Journal*.

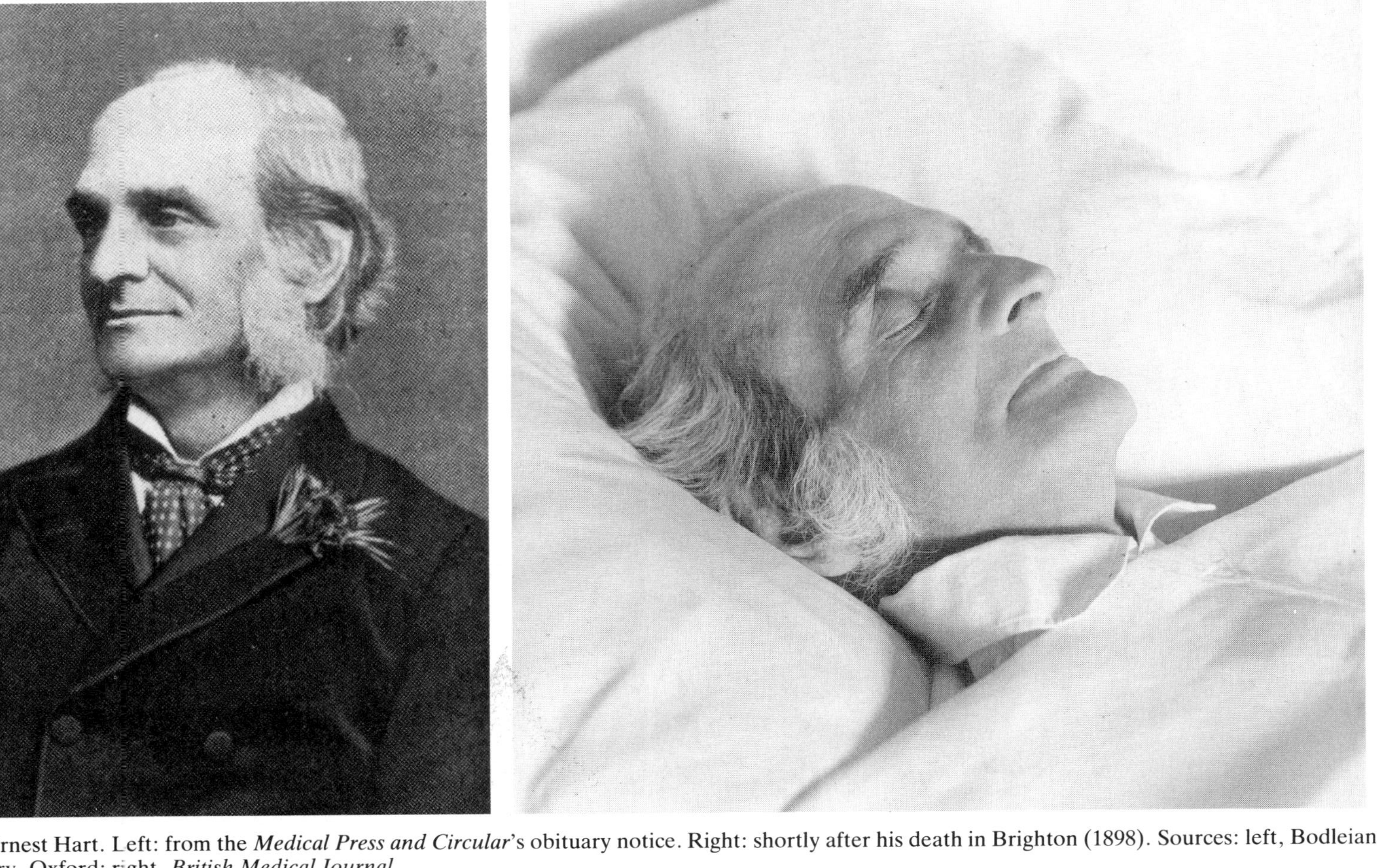

2. Ernest Hart. Left: from the *Medical Press and Circular*'s obituary notice. Right: shortly after his death in Brighton (1898). Sources: left, Bodleian Library, Oxford; right, *British Medical Journal*.

3. *Journal* editors: Top left: Jonathan Hutchinson (1869–70). Top right: Dawson Williams (1898–1928). Bottom left: Norman Gerald Horner (1928–46). Bottom right: Hugh Clegg (1947–65). Source: *British Medical Journal.*

4. Top: Infected public water supplies could rapidly spread enteric diseases. Bottom: Crimean war casualties who were presented to Queen Victoria at Chatham (1855). Sources: top, Wellcome Institute Library. London; bottom, Trustees of the Imperial War Museum, London.

5. Top: Vaccination in the 1870s. Bottom: Fodder for the baby farmers? Street urchins in the 1890s. Sources: top, Wellcome Institute Library, London; bottom, The Children's Society.

6. Top left: Morrell Mackenzie. Top right: Joseph Lister. Bottom: Elizabeth Garrett Anderson. Sources: top left, British Medical Association; top right, Wellcome Institute Library, London; bottom, Royal Free Hospital Medical School.

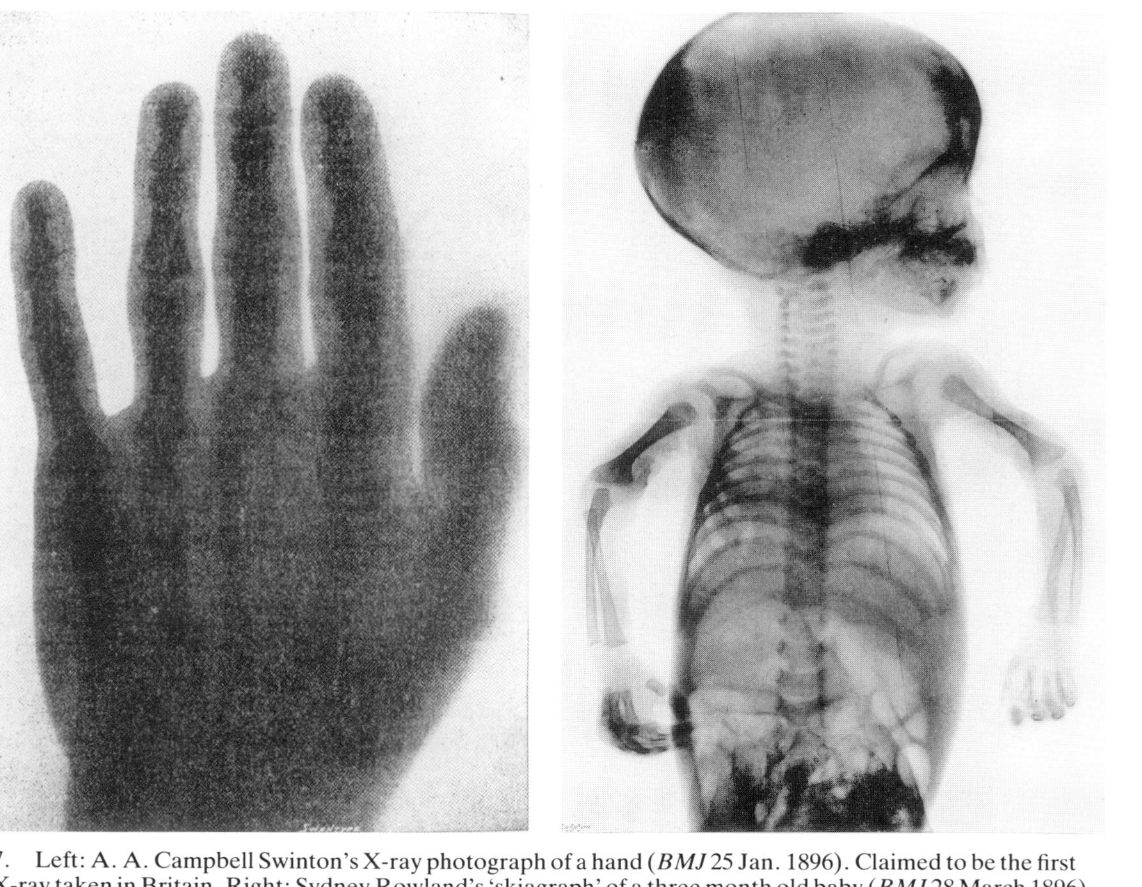

7. Left: A. A. Campbell Swinton's X-ray photograph of a hand (*BMJ* 25 Jan. 1896). Claimed to be the first X-ray taken in Britain. Right: Sydney Rowland's 'skiagraph' of a three month old baby (*BMJ* 28 March 1896). Source: Wellcome Institute Library, London.

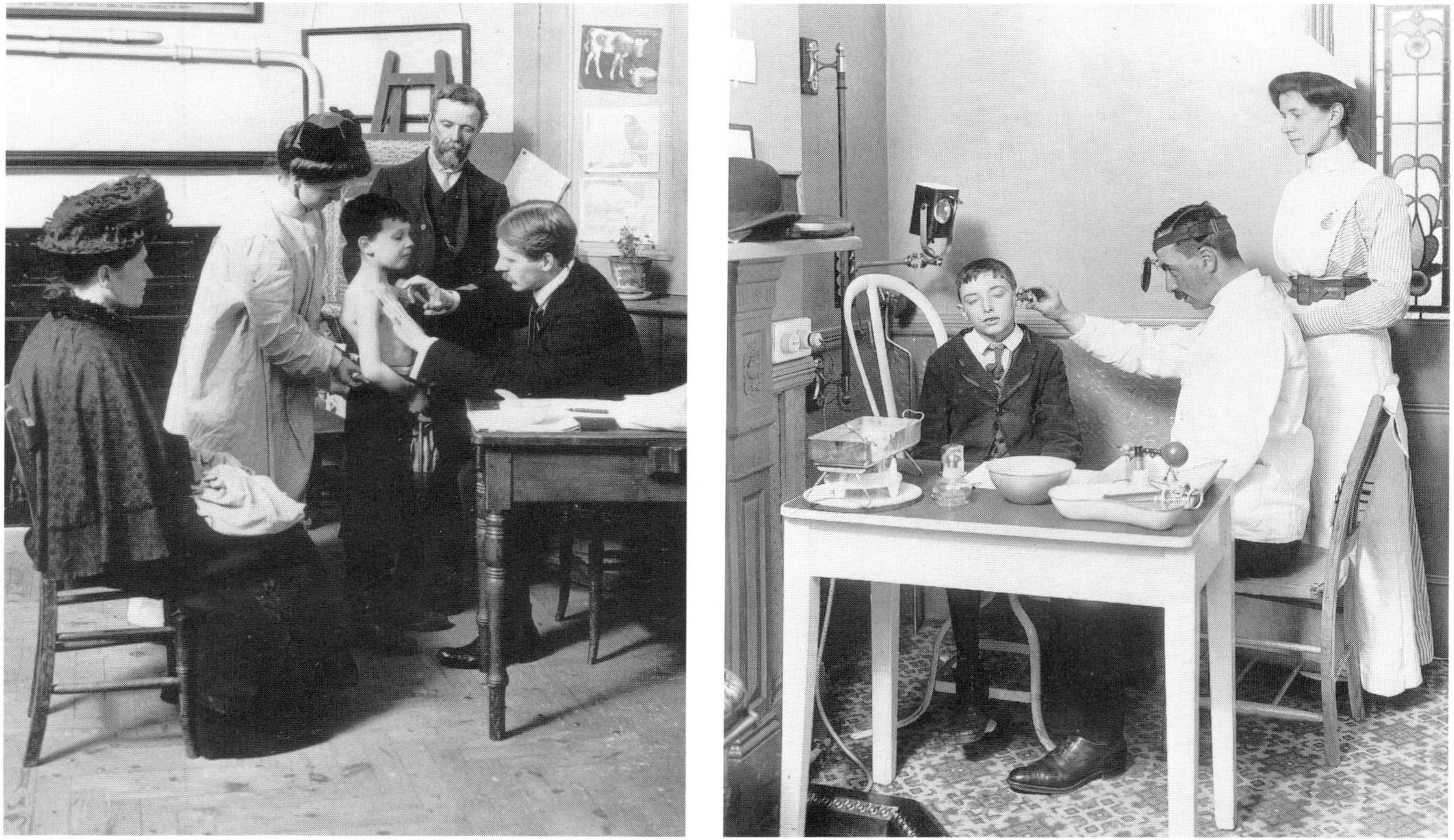

8. Left: Medical Inspection in a London County Council School (1912). Right: Wandsworth Medical Treatment Centre (1913). Source: Greater London Photographic Library.

9. First World War medicine. Top: 'Blighty Junction'. Transporting the wounded on a hand propelled double deck trolley. Bottom: Advance dressing station on the Western Front. Source: Wellcome Institute Library, London.

10. Top left: Pietro Annigoni's portrait of Lord Moran (1951). Top right: Austin Bradford Hill in 1954. Bottom: Stanley Morison. Sources: top left, Royal College of Physicians; top right, Wellcome Institute Library, London; bottom, Times Newspapers Ltd.

11. Left: David Lloyd George. Right: Marie Stopes. Source: Mary Evans Picture Library.

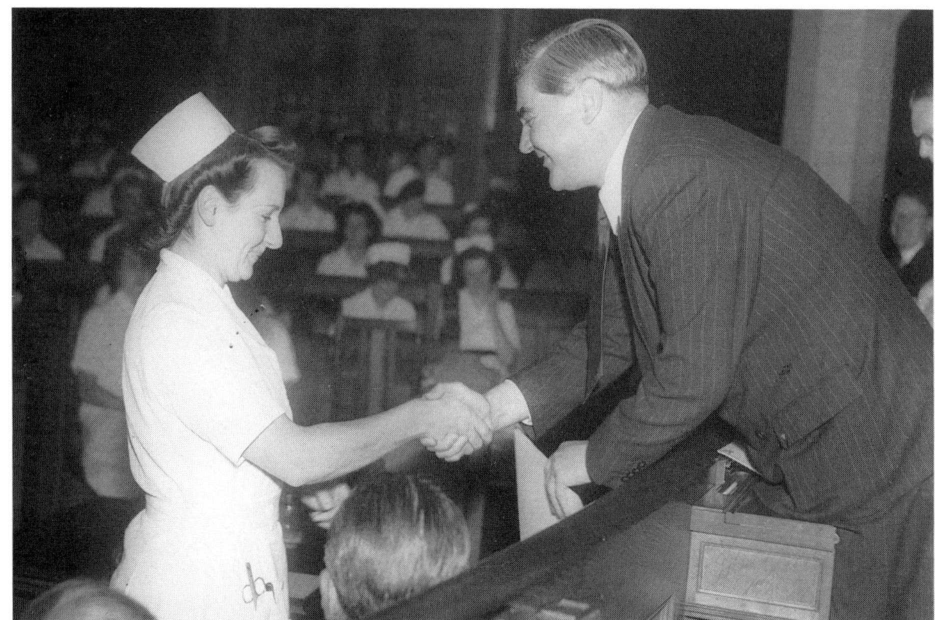

12. Top: Aneurin Bevan presents nurses' awards. Bottom: Second World War. East End underground shelter. Sources: top, The Hulton Picture Company; bottom, Trustees of the Imperial War Museum, London.

produce ... procure the greatest relief and soothe the pain in Sore Throat, Hoarseness, Loss of Voice, Laryngitis, Inflammatory Conditions of the Fauces, Palate and Pharynx, Fits of Coughing, Whooping Cough and Asthmatic Complaints.

With a recommended dose of six to eight pastils per day, they were, not surprisingly, said to help remove prickling and titillation in the throat, to strengthen the vocal cords, to be 'useful' in diseases of the oesophagus and the stomach, 'sea-sickness, gastritis, gastralgia, vomiting etc'. No wonder that the same issue of the *Journal* in which this appeared also included an advertisement for a Private Home for Ladies in Leicestershire where the 'morphia habit and the abuse of drugs' could be treated. In December 1899 the pharmaceutical company Bayer was advertising heroin as a treatment for various pulmonary ailments.[140]

The third largest group of advertisements in 1889 was those for homes, asylums, health resorts, and hotels. These featured, perhaps surprisingly, hydropathic establishments as well as inebriate retreats and mental asylums. Their inclusion illustrates the *Journal*'s practice at this time of accepting advertisements regardless of BMA policy. Income was the priority. Drawings of homes and asylums were sometimes reproduced in advertisements. They were generally described as being spacious, well-appointed, warm, and comfortable. One wonders whether the reality always matched the publicity. Advertisements in this category were often quite specific about the social class of their clientèle; for example, the Leicestershire home for lady inebriates stressed that it accepted clients only from the 'Upper and Higher Middle-Classes'. Clearly class distinction was to be upheld as much among drunks and drug addicts as in the rest of the population. These establishments seldom publicized their fees, but in 1889 £52 was enough to secure a year's board at James Murray's Royal Asylum in Perth.

Health resorts were often discussed in the *Journal*'s editorial columns from the 1880s. In 1889 a short-lived *Journal of British and Foreign Health Resorts* was launched. The *BMJ*'s advertising columns reflected such developments. In 1899 as many as four Egyptian hotels offered themselves as winter health resorts. One, the Tewfik Palace, near Cairo, offered golf, shooting, riding and driving, and boating on the Nile, as well as the services of a medical director and physician and a lady superintendent who took responsibility for nursing and massage. Its prices were not disclosed, but a 65-day cruise of the West Indies with the Royal Mail Steam Packet Co. could be had for £65. Beside all this the lure of Aberystwyth paled somewhat, notwithstanding its 'perfect drainage', an endorsement by Sir James Clark, and its claim to be 'The Biarritz of Wales'.

To put the prices for hotels and asylums into a context of medical salaries,

[140] See Virginia Berridge and Griffith Edwards, *Opium and the People. Opiate Use in Nineteenth-Century England* (New Haven and London: Yale University Press, 1987 edn) pp. xix–xx.

it is necessary only to turn to the *Journal*'s situations vacant pages. Certainly those who were attracted by positions such as that of junior house surgeon at the Royal London Ophthalmic Hospital in City Road, or a similar post at Hull Royal Infirmary, where the annual salaries were £50 and £40, plus board and lodging, respectively, were unlikely to be among the Royal Mail's passengers. Indeed, West Indian voyages would have been beyond the pocket of most general practitioners, who, it seems from the practices offered for sale in the 1899 *BMJ*, were doing very well to achieve an income in excess of £700.

8
Wars and welfare

A great and wise editor

When he became editor in 1898, Dawson Williams had already had a long association with the *Journal*, for he had become a contributor in 1881, its Hospital Reporter in 1884, a principal sub-editor in 1886, and assistant editor in 1895. In the course of Hart's final illness, and during his several long absences from London, Williams had been acting editor. He was editor in his own right for almost 30 years. On his retirement, in 1928, only two months before his death, he had completed 47 years with the *Journal*. No other member of the editorial staff has ever had such a long period of service. It is unlikely that any will ever surpass it. Williams was the first editor to occupy the editorial chair on a full-time basis and the first to attain it through internal promotion.[1]

Williams differed from his predecessor in several respects. He was 'well above six feet in height' and a commanding presence, whereas Hart was small and frail looking. Their personalities also contrasted. Whereas Hart was mercurial, raffish, devious, combative, and controversial, Williams was dignified, respectable, straightforward, modest, and tactful. But in some respects they were similar. Both lived and breathed for their work; moreover, both were powerful characters who ran the *BMJ* as an out and out autocracy. Scott Stevenson, who worked under Williams as a sub-editor in the early 1920s, remembered him as someone with 'an air of authority and wisdom' who 'did not suffer fools gladly'. He had 'more influence than any other individual of his time on the policy of the BMA . . . I . . . never lost the feeling in his presence that I was a schoolboy up in front of the headmaster.'[2]

Dawson Williams inherited a thriving publication, but Hart would have

[1] Williams was appointed editor by the BMA's Council on the recommendation of the Journal and Finance Committee. The position was not advertised and no other candidates were considered. On the two occasions on which Hart had been appointed he had had to compete against other applicants. Williams received his knighthood in 1921–'too late to do any good' as he once remarked. In the same year he was awarded the BMA's gold medal of merit. He became a CBE in 1919 and received honorary degrees from Glasgow, Durham, and Sheffield. BMA mss. MCSC, IX, JFC, 19 Jan. 1898, 3975. See P. Vaughan, *Doctors' Commons. A Short History of the British Medical Association* (London: Heinemann, 1959), pp. 144–8; *Who Was Who, 1916–1928*; E. M. Little, *History of the BMA* (London: British Medical Association, n.d., 1932?), pp. 231–2; *Journal*, 10 March 1928, 414–25; *The Times*, 2 Jan., 28 Feb. 1928.

[2] R. Scott Stevenson, *Goodbye Harley Street* (London: Christopher Johnson, 1954), p. 83.

been a difficult 'act' for anyone to follow. It is to Williams's credit that he was not overawed by the task. Although his *Journal* was 'safer' and less controversial than Hart's, reflecting his more cautious personality and limited interest in medical politics, its scientific reputation was maintained if not enhanced. Williams regarded the BMA's main task as being to nurture medical science. Its main hope of doing this was through the *BMJ*, which its editor regarded as 'post-graduation training brought to the practitioner's door'. Williams therefore believed the *Journal* to be the most important element of the Association.

Williams's editorship was not, however, an unqualified success. Although the *Journal* flourished during his first two decades in charge, after the First World War it entered a period of relative decline. Of course, this is a subjective judgement. On almost any quantitative criterion, it continued to thrive. Circulation and advertising revenue increased, while the number of high-calibre original articles remained high. But possibly these achievements were the product of past success. During the 1920s the *Journal* became staid and unimaginative. Why this was so is debatable, but it is likely that Williams overstayed his time in office. At the end of the war he was 64 years old, with *BMJ* connections stretching over a period of 37 years. During the 1920s he was often in poor health—in 1920, for example, he was thought to have heart disease and given two weeks to live.[3] Anxious about how he would spend his retirement, he stayed in post until almost 74. It was too long.

Dawson Williams, the eldest of the seven children of the rector of Burnby, was born at Ulleskelf in the East Riding of Yorkshire on 17 July 1854. He was educated at Pocklington Grammar School and University College Hospital, London, having been unable, like Hart, though for different reasons (presumably financial), to proceed from school to Cambridge. He was an outstanding student, and graduated MB (Hons.), BCh (1879), MD (1881), and MA (1897). He was elected MRCS in 1878, MRCP in 1885, and FRCP in 1895. On qualifying he served briefly as house-physician and ophthalmic and obstetric assistant at University College Hospital before moving to the Victoria Hospital for Children and, later, the Brompton Hospital for Consumption. Meanwhile, he was building up his practice as a consulting physician in Harley Street. Having gained an introduction to Hart, he took up medical journalism in order to augment his income. In 1884, after having contemplated joining the Indian Medical Service, he moved to the East London Hospital for Children at Shadwell as assistant physician (physician from 1894). On the insistence of the BMA, Williams resigned his position at the East London in 1902 when he became a full-time editor. He did, however, continue as a consulting physician. His main professional interest was in paediatrics, and his only book, *Medical Diseases*

[3] R. Scott Stevenson, *In a Harley Street Mirror* (London: Christopher Johnson, 1951), p. 5.

of Infancy and Childhood (1898), dealt with this field. Williams married in 1882; his wife died in 1917.[4]

During Williams's first 20 years as editor his assistant was Charles Louis Taylor (1850–1920). Born at Peterhead, Aberdeenshire, Taylor spent much of his childhood and youth in Europe. He became Sir Morrell Mackenzie's secretary in 1880. His first *Journal* appointment was as 'technical reader' in 1886. On the basis of salary—he received £50 a year more than Williams—it seems that Taylor initially occupied the more senior position. In fact, Taylor was not medically qualified. Although he trained at University College Hospital, where he was Williams's contemporary, he never sat the qualifying examinations. He had previously trained in Spain for the Roman Catholic priesthood before deciding, after several years, that he lacked vocation. Scott Stevenson explained this repeated failure to qualify in terms of 'some sort of neurosis'. Taylor was, however, a talented journalist. His 'wide learning, ready pen, and high standard of work were of the greatest value to the *Journal*.' William Osler, Regius Professor of Medicine at Oxford, once wrote to him: 'we really ought to give you an M.D. degree somewhere, with all your knowledge and considering all you have done.' Taylor resigned from the *Journal* in 1917, as a result of ill-health. He died in 1920.[5]

In 1898 the only other member of the permanent editorial staff was Sydney Rowland. When, at the end of the year, Rowland's services were dispensed with, the task of editing one of the world's largest (around 4000 pages a year) and most reputable medical journals fell upon just two men. A new sub-editor, Guy Stephen, was appointed in 1900. Born in 1858 Stephen had spent many years with the Foreign Office medical service. He later served in France with the British Expeditionary Force, during which time he also acted as the *BMJ*'s correspondent on the western front. Stephen did not rejoin the editorial staff at the end of the war. He died in 1932.[6]

Until the 1920s the *Journal*'s editorial staff never numbered more than three. In the latter part of the First World War Dawson Williams edited the *Journal* alone. During the early 1900s the staff were all ailing men. For a time Williams suffered an 'acute neurosis', which prevented him from performing his duties; Taylor, who was a diabetic, had had a leg amputated; Stephen was 'as deaf as a post'. In July 1910 Williams sustained a fractured leg and other injuries in a road accident. For a while his condition was 'critical'. During his convalescence Taylor stood in as editor.[7]

[4] *Ibid.*, p. 6; *Journal*, 10 March 1928, 414–25; *The Times*, 28 Feb. 1928; *Who Was Who, 1916–1928*; *Munk's Roll* (London: Royal College of Physicians, 1985), **iv**, p. 383–4

[5] R. S. Stevenson, *In a Harley Street Mirror*, p. 6 (note 3); R. S. Stevenson, *Goodbye Harley Street*, pp. 84–5 (note 2); E. M. Little, *History of the BMA*, pp. 227–8 (note 1); BMA mss. Osler File, W. Osler to C. Taylor, 21 Sept. 1912; *Journal*, 3 Jan. 1920, 33–4; 17 Jan. 1920, 101–2; 10 March 1928, 414.

[6] *Who Was Who, 1929–1940.*

[7] BMA mss. MCSC, IX, Journal and Finance Committee, 20 April 1898, 4039–40; 17 July 1898, 4836–7; 12 Oct. 1898, 4120–1; *Journal*, 10 March 1928, 415; R. S. Stevenson, *Goodbye Harley Street*, p. 84 (note 2). *The Times*, 11 July 1910.

Initially Williams's editorial salary was £650 a year, though as early as 1899 it was increased to £750 a year, the sum that Hart had received. When he retired it was £2000 a year. Until the First World War all editorial staff were paid extra for *Journal* contributions. In 1898 Williams received almost £286 in contributor's fees; in 1900 Taylor's fees exceeded £378. In 1907 a Special Finance Enquiry Committee investigated the propriety of paying staff extra for their contributions. Some members thought that the practice was inappropriate, but the committee decided that it should continue.[8] During the war Williams gave up his claim to these additional payments. When Gerald Horner was appointed as Taylor's successor he was placed on an all inclusive salary scale, starting at £750 a year rising to £1000 a year. The long-standing practice of paying editorial staff for their articles thereby came to an end.[9]

Running the *Journal*, 1898–1918

Williams did not rush into making dramatic changes to the *Journal*; instead, he adhered to Hart's proven formula. Circulation increased steadily. By the end of 1913 it had reached about 30 000 a week. (see Table 8.1). In 1899 annual production costs exceeded £26 500 whereas income, mainly from advertising (£19 328), totalled around £22 100. In other words, expenditure exceeded income by some £4400. This deficit was met from BMA funds, the bulk of which came from membership subscriptions. During the Edwardian period the gap between income and expenditure gradually widened. By 1913 production expenses had risen to almost £40 000 a year, while total income was not quite £29 000 (see Table 8.2).[10]

At this time the *Journal*'s financial viability seldom, if ever, troubled the BMA's membership; it tolerated losses of the above order without demur, but at the BMA's Annual Representative Meeting of 1905 a certain amount of criticism was levelled at the *Journal*.[11] This focused on its content and appearance, though principally the latter. The *Journal* was accused of being inferior to the *Lancet* and 'not so effective a recruiting agent as it ought to be'. Its design, little changed since Hart's 1867 reforms notwithstanding

[8] BMA mss. MCSC, IX, Special Finance Enquiry Committee, 28 May 1907, 520.

[9] BMA mss. Minutes of Committees, Conferences and Sub-Committees, Journal Committee, 4 Oct. 1916, 805; *BMJ* Supplement, 11 Aug. 1917, 39.

[10] Given that most copies of the *Journal* were distributed to BMA members as a benefit of membership, that no part of BMA subscription income was earmarked for *Journal* expenses, and that a substantial proportion of the *Journal*'s costs was met from advertising revenue, it is doubtful whether it is fair to speak of its losses or deficits. This question is discussed in detail in Chapter 11.

[11] In 1903 the Association's Annual or Anniversary Meetings became Annual Representative Meetings.

Table 8.1 *BMJ* Circulation 1899–1913

Date	Weekly circulation
Dec. 1899	over 21 000
Dec. 1902	over 21 500
Dec. 1906	23 800
Dec. 1909	24 100
Dec. 1910	25 500
Dec. 1911	28 250
Dec. 1912	30 000
Dec. 1913	30 000

Note: These statistics are taken from the *Journal*'s advertising pages. This information ceased to be given during the war. Special issues might achieve substantially higher circulations e. g. 27 000 for 8 Dec. 1906.

Table 8.2 Summary of *Journal* finances 1899–1913 (£)

Year	Income	Expenditure	BMA Subvention
1899	22 100	26 500	4400
1903	23 500	27 000	3500
1906	25 000	29 200	4200
1910	28 600	35 200	6600
1913	28 900	40 000	11 000

dramatic improvements elsewhere in the the periodical press, was said to be dull and uninviting.[12]

Williams and the *Journal*'s manager, Guy Elliston, examined these criticisms and concluded that changes were needed. In August and September when, in the past, the *Journal* had carried specialist papers read at the annual meeting, the *Journal* would henceforward carry more 'clinical matter of interest to the general practitioner in the United Kingdom'. As for appearance, they recommended that type face, page layout, and page size should be modified, and a cover added. The Journal and Finance Committee accepted these suggestions, favouring a grey tinted cover and an increase in advertising rates to cover the extra cost. These decisions were implemented at the beginning of 1906.[13]

[12] BMA mss. MCSC, XII, Journal and Finance Committee, 11 Oct. 1905, 956–8.
[13] *Ibid.* Council decided also that the front cover should carry the portrait of Sir Charles Hastings. See MCSC, XIV, Minutes of Council, 18 April 1906, 51–2.

The changes seem to have met with the approval of subscribers, and the *Journal* received little more criticism until 1917. In that year, owing to a worrying drop in BMA membership, a Propaganda Sub-Committee, charged with finding ways of increasing recruitment, uncovered a number of complaints about the *Journal*. Most of these questioned its value to general practitioners. Comments from BMA branches included unfavourable comparisons with the *Lancet*, complaints of over- specialization and of too few articles from GPs, plus a proposal that the *Journal* might be made more entertaining if the editor went 'through a course of "live" American journalism'.[14] The chairman of the ethical committee, Dr Biggs, cited a friend who complained that in comparison with the 'eminently practical and useful' *Practitioner* the *BMJ* was 'merely waste paper'. Biggs commented:

> This is a commonly held view among G.P.'s—they recognise the *B.M.J.* as a first class journal and therefore of no use to them. ... This may and does show a narrow outlook, but to busy men with little time for reading it is very natural. As a matter of fact the *Journal* is unpopular among G.P.'s and they only take it because it comes as a part return of their subscription.[15]

Biggs suggested supplying the *Journal* only to those members who wanted it, while all others could subscribe to the Association at a lower rate. In response, Dawson Williams produced a cogent defence of the *Journal*. He emphasized its strengths, the problems of wartime production, and, tellingly, its growing sale to non-members. When Council debated the matter, it agreed that 'the present form of the *Journal* on the whole is suitable and does meet the present needs of the Association.'

Williams's *Journal*, though less political than Hart's, was certainly no stranger to controversy. Victor Horsley, incensed by something Williams had published, once burst into his office and accused him of lying.[16] In the years preceding the First World War, libel actions and threats of such action were frequent occurrences. Law suits could prove expensive. For example, Dr Robert Bell's action cost the BMA over £5000 in damages and costs.[17] It is indicative of the scale of this problem that the Journal Committee set up a

[14] BMA mss. MCCSC, Journal Committee, 4 April 1917, 430–1.

[15] *Ibid.*, 426.

[16] BMA mss. Signed Committee Minutes, 1910–1913, Journal Committee, 29 March 1912, 5–18.

[17] *Ibid.*, 11 Oct. 1912, 3. The article to which Bell took exception was by E. F. Bashford, General Superintendent of Research and Director of the Laboratory of the Imperial Cancer Research Fund. It was entitled 'Cancer, Credulity and Quackery' and appeared in the *Journal*, 27 May 1911, 1221–30, the whole of which issue was devoted to the question of quackery. There is more information on this case in Robert Bell, *Reminiscences of an Old Physician* (London: John Murray, 1924), pp. 271–4 where a report from the *Daily Mirror*, 15 June 1912 is reproduced. In 1923 Bell appeared before the GMC accused of prescribing for a patient's inoperable cancer over a nine-month period without ever seeing her. He escaped erasure from the *Medical Register*. See *BMJ* Supplement, 9 June 1923, 238.

Libel Actions Sub-Committee to handle the matter. Furthermore, Council aided the Newspaper Society in its efforts to reform libel law.[18]

Although affected by the industrial action of print workers during the strike-ridden year of 1911, the *Journal* continued to appear, at a cost of some lost pages and additional expense. At this point the printing and distribution of the *Journal* (though not its composition) were transferred to Odhams.[19] A far graver threat to continuous production was provided by the outbreak of war in 1914. Even before war broke out, the *Journal* lost its 1915 supply of 'band' paper (in which it was despatched) when the German ship carrying it, having arrived in the Port of London in August 1914, departed for Hamburg without unloading its cargo when the captain became uneasy about the international situation.[20]

For reasons of economy, editorial content was reduced by about one-third as early as August 1914. The Epitome of Current Medical Literature was dropped, though reinstated in January 1915 with material from German journals obtained through the USA. It continued for two more years before again being dropped because of staff shortage.[21] Perhaps not surprisingly, in view of the way in which the *Journal* had grown in size over the years, many readers welcomed its smaller dimensions. As Albert Lucas, the chairman of the Journal Committee put it:

> [I] have heard many favourable comments on the reduction in its bulk. The time is not yet ripe to review this fresh position, but I am not at all sure that one of the most instructive lessons we shall have learned will be a sense of proportion, with the conviction that for some years we have tended to overload the *Journal*, and that it is possible to reduce it materially and effect a substantial saving without interfering with its general interest or the efficiency and progress of the Association.[22]

If reduced size was far from being an unmitigated disaster, total war made uninterrupted publication increasingly difficult. Higher postal rates (from November 1915) for newspapers weighing over 6 oz threatened to increase distribution costs by about £1800 a year. In order to avoid such a burden, further cuts in editorial matter and even delivery by hand were considered.

[18] BMA mss. Signed Committee Minutes, 1913–1921, Libel Actions Sub-Committee, 18 Feb. 1914, 1–2. Existing libel law was laid down in Acts of 1843, 1845, and 1888. A 1903 bill, which was unsuccessful, had sought to prohibit actions against the press except with the prior consent of a law officer of the Crown. The 1911 bill sought to define areas which newspapers could freely report, e.g. public meetings, court proceedings, public documents, etc. and in various other ways to alter the balance of the existing law. See *Parliamentary Papers* (1911) **II**, Public Bills, p. 935.

[19] BMA mss. Signed Committee Minutes, 1913–1921, Journal Committee, 8 March 1911, 3–4.

[20] BMA mss. MCCSC, Journal Committee, 6 Jan. 1915, 190.

[21] *Ibid.* The Epitome resumed in September 1919. See BMA mss. JC 2 Oct. 1924, 217–18. The Epitome's future was much discussed during the 1930s. It was finally scrapped in June 1938 and replaced by a 'Key to Current Literature' which sought to guide readers to articles rather than provide summaries. See *BMJ* Supplement, 22 April 1939, 188.

[22] BMA mss. MCCSC, Journal Committee, 6 Jan. 1915, 191. See Editor's Report in *ibid.*, 31 March 1915, 618.

However, the Journal Committee decided to make use of lighter paper, even though this was not 'all that would be desired'. Even this inferior product, which was still more expensive than the *Journal*'s pre-war paper, became difficult to obtain, particularly after imports of paper-making material were halved. In February 1916 the Journal Committee was forced to make further page reductions. In 1917, following the introduction of conscription in the previous year, Odhams imposed their own limits on the volume of material they were prepared to handle.[23]

During the war, production costs rocketed while revenue slumped. The regular war bonuses granted to print workers meant that by the end of 1918 Odhams' printing charges were 81 per cent higher than before the war.[24] The 1914 prohibition on advertising originating from enemy aliens, coupled with a sudden shrinkage in placements from domestic sources, meant an immediate loss of some 20 pages of advertising a week, worth over £10 000 a year.[25] In such conditions it was difficult to raise rates, especially as the *Lancet*'s charges were already lower than the *Journal*'s. But in 1918 these were raised from £10 to £12 per page.[26] If, as occasionally happened, the *Journal* obtained additional advertising and the promise of extra revenue, the financial benefit could be lessened by its having to pay the higher postal rate for exceeding the 6 oz weight limit.[27]

The year 1917 was one of deepening crisis. The Ministry of Munitions' Paper Commission introduced rationing and, although both Lucas and the BMA's president, Clifford Allbutt, petitioned for the *Journal* to receive a priority allocation, 'having regard to its work of national importance', they were unsuccessful.[28] As a result, Lucas reported to his committee that 'the outlook for an adequate supply of paper to continue even the reduced size *Journal* is obscure.' Yet another page cut was implemented. In March 1917 the price of the *Journal* to non- members was raised from 6d to 8d. This was partly to meet rising costs, partly to discourage sales and thereby conserve precious paper reserves. It worked in the first respect, but not the second; in 1917 revenue from sales increased by £1000. From April 1918 the weekly price was set at 1s in the expectation that paper would be saved or additional revenue of over £2000 a year obtained.[29] In December 1917 the Journal Committee discussed the idea of not publishing every third issue. This was rejected, but by July 1918 the *Journal* was down to 22 pages of editorial

[23] *Ibid.*, 5 April 1916, 328–9; 3 Jan. 1917, 99; 4 April 1917, 420–2.

[24] *Ibid.*, 19 Dec. 1917, 1429; Finance Committee, 16 Jan. 1918, 138; 17 April 1918, 455; 16 Oct. 1918, 955.

[25] *Ibid.*, Journal Committee, 5 Jan. 1916, 117–18.

[26] *Ibid.*, Finance Committee, 17 April 1918, 456-7. This was a response to the *Lancet*'s new rates of £8 per page. *The Journal* had last increased its rates in 1914.

[27] *Ibid.*, Journal Committee, 5 Jan. 1916, 123; 15 April 1916, 332. This, of course, became less likely as the *Journal* shrank.

[28] *Ibid.*, 4 April 1917, 420–2.

[29] *Ibid.*, 419–20; Finance Committee, 18 April, 1917, 484; Finance Committee, 17 April 1918, 457.

content as compared with up to 60 during July 1914, itself by no means a record.[30]

During the First World War, in comparison with the Second, the civilian population was little exposed to enemy offensives. However, in 1917 Lucas had warned that production and distribution might be interrupted by air raids. On 29 January 1918 Odhams' printing works were hit by an enemy bomb. The ensuing fire destroyed 75 tons of paper and, although this was covered by insurance, 'the monetary compensation under existing conditions cannot make good the loss of material.' A government priority certificate allowed replacement of two-thirds of the loss and, remarkably, the *Journal* was despatched two days later only a few hours behind schedule. With this exception, the slimmed-down *Journal* continued to be published on time, albeit without a cover (from March 1918) for the remainder of the war.

Secret remedies

Dawson Williams was not such an ardent campaigning journalist as Hart. Neither did he give prominence to social medicine. Women's suffrage and the forcible feeding of suffragettes—topics on which Hart would surely have found much to say—were virtually ignored.[31] However, one campaign which Williams ran with sustained energy was against the so-called secret remedies or proprietary medicines.

Patent medicines had been specifically excluded from the terms of the Pharmacy Act, 1868, and the Sale of Food and Drugs Act, 1875, which among other things regulated the sale of poisons and drugs in late nineteenth-century England. Whether proprietary mixtures were patent medicines was a point decided by the courts only in the 1890s. Until then these preparations, the contents of which were usually a closely guarded secret but which might include poisons within the meaning of the 1868 Act, could be sold to the public without restriction other than that of paying government stamp duty. In the later nineteenth century, with ordinary opium preparations more difficult to obtain, their sales boomed.[32] Individual producers such as James Morison and Thomas Holloway made fortunes.[33]

[30] *Ibid.*, Journal Committee, 19 Dec. 1917, 1431; Finance Committee, 16 Jan. 1918, 139; 17 April 1918, 457; Council Minutes, 23 Jan. 1918, 3.

[31] Brian Harrison, 'Women's Health and the Women's Movement', in Charles Webster (ed.), *Biology, Medicine and Society, 1840–1940* (Cambridge: Cambridge University Press, 1981), p. 48.

[32] The stamp duty on proprietary medicines dated from the 18th century. In 1892 it yielded some £240 000 in government revenue. Many producers hinted that payment of the tax implied State endorsement of their preparations. The *Journal* complained that the stamp 'is generally regarded as a guarantee of the genuineness of the contents of the package'. V. Berridge and G. Edwards, *Opium and the People. Opiate Use in Nineteenth-Century England* (New Haven and London: Yale University Press, 1987), p. 123, Chapters 10, 11; *Journal*, 19 July 1884, 125–7; 12 Jan. 1895, 95; 10 Dec. 1904, 1599; *Parliamentary Papers* (1914) **IX**, Select Committee on Patent Medicines, xxii–xxiii.

[33] E. S. Turner, *The Shocking History of Advertising* (London: Michael Joseph, 1952), pp. 40–6, 61–8.

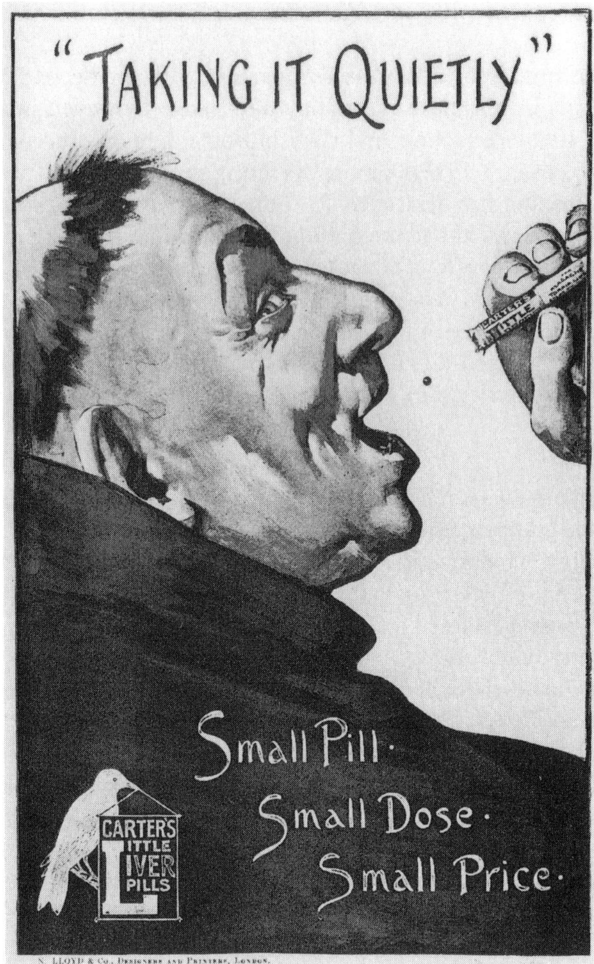

Taking it Quietly. Source: Bodleian Library, Oxford.

In the 1880s the medical profession began to campaign against the proprietary medicine trade which, it was said, supported as many as 1000 owners and 19 000 employees. Deaths caused by proprietary medicines were publicized, and in 1884 the *Journal* welcomed a bill which sought to confine the sale of any product containing a scheduled poison, such as opium, to registered pharmacists.[34] Although this bill failed, the question was one in which the *Journal* continued to take a strong interest. In 1890 a leading article proposed a ban on 'any proprietary medical preparation unless the composition is printed on the cover'.[35]

[34] *Journal*, 29 March 1884, 627.

[35] *Ibid.*, 13 Sept. 1890, 639; 7 Nov. 1891, 1009; 10 Sept. 1892, 602–3; See V. Berridge and G. Edwards, *Opium and the People*, pp. 129–30 (note 32).

It was sometimes suggested that doctors and pharmacists wanted to outlaw or regulate secret remedies in order to protect their monopoly as treaters of the sick and dispensers of medicines. Such imputations were, of course, vigorously denied by the *Journal*.[36] It argued that controls were needed for two reasons. First, to stop the deaths caused by poisonous mixtures, and, second, to prevent addiction to the narcotic substances that were the mainstay of so many 'elixirs', 'syrups', potions, and 'balms'.[37] In other words, it claimed to be motivated simply by concern for the public good. Whether such protestations were entirely ingenuous is a matter of conjecture. Perhaps the professionals were not completely disinterested in adopting the positions they did; on the other hand, professional interests were not bound to conflict with the public good and it can be argued that both the public and the medical profession were victims of the commercial nostrum-mongers.

In 1891 the BMA's Parliamentary Bills Committee, chaired by Hart, pressed for prosecutions to be brought against certain manufacturers and sellers of proprietary medicines containing poisons.[38] Chemical analyses of their products were forwarded to the Treasury solicitor, and in the following year J. T. Davenport, a London chemist, was prosecuted for selling chlorodyne, a preparation which contained opium and chloroform, without indicating its contents on the label. His defence was that, chlorodyne being a patent medicine, the Pharmacy Act relieved him of this obligation. But the court held that as chlorodyne had never been granted letters patent it could not be considered a patent medicine and was, therefore, subject to the terms of the 1868 Act. In so doing it upheld the *BMJ*'s view of the matter:

> The assumption that secret remedies come within the scope of the exemptions provided for patent medicines is utterly unfounded and unjustifiable. They cannot be included under that designation, because they are wanting in that important characteristic which essentially distinguishes patented articles, namely, that of having their composition made public by an official specification of the nature and proportions of their ingredients, and of the modes of preparing them. ... Consequently, secret remedies containing articles which are poisons within the meaning of the Pharmacy Act cannot justly claim to be exempt from the provisions of that Act relating to the sale, dispensing and compounding of poisons.[39]

Davenport was fined £5 plus costs, but more importantly the verdict meant that in future chlorodyne could be sold only by pharmacists and had to be labelled a poison. Since it followed that all other so-called patent medicines were also merely proprietary remedies, they too were placed in the same position. As the *Journal* put it, 'It may therefore be anticipated that the secret sale of poisons in the form of so-called 'patent medicines' will now be

[36] *Ibid.*, Chapter 10; *Journal* 29 March 1884, 627.
[37] *Ibid.*, 26 Dec. 1891, 1359–60.
[38] *Ibid.*, 5 Nov. 1892, 1018–19; see 18 Feb. 1893, 367.
[39] *Ibid.*, 26 Dec. 1891, 1360.

More in That than Meets the Eye. Source: Bodleian Library, Oxford.

subjected to the control we have long contended that it requires.' Encouraged by Hart, the Pharmaceutical Society took action against traders who ignored the implications of *Regina* versus *Davenport*.[40]

Hart and the *Journal* had won an important victory, but not a final one, for when all was said and done, even if the new legal position was perfectly observed, the same proprietary medicines could still be sold, albeit labelled as poisons and from the shelves of pharmacists rather than grocers. Furthermore, the position of proprietary medicines which did not contain poisons (within the meaning of the 1868 Act) was completely unchanged. All that had happened was that a loophole in a far from draconian statute had been closed. A leading article in the *Journal* at the end of 1892 showed a realistic appreciation of what had been achieved:

[40] V. Berridge and G. Edwards, *Opium and the People*, pp. 130–1 (note 32); *Journal*, e.g. 7 Nov. 1891, 1009; 7 May 1892, 978–9, 995–6; 1 Oct. 1892, 745–6, 756; 3 Dec. 1892, 1252; 18 Feb. 1893, 367; 23 Sept. 1893, 699–700; 11 Nov. 1893, 1066–7; 21 April 1894, 870.

Some means should surely and speedily be adopted by the Legislature to protect the credulous portion of the public from squandering their money and perhaps injuring their health for the sole profit of unscrupulous quacks, for the law, as it at present stands, is we fear, wholly insufficient to grapple with this evil.[41]

The *Journal* favoured the adoption in Britain of the German policies of publicizing the contents and true costs of proprietary substances, providing government guarantees of purity, and restricting press advertising.[42] Hart personally sought to persuade newspaper editors to cease 'prostituting their advertisement columns ... to the service of a dangerous and often wicked class of imposters'.[43] This crusade was noticed by *The Times* and taken up by some newspapers, notably, the *Pall Mall Gazette*. In May 1894 Hart persuaded the Parliamentary Bills Committee to have a bill drafted requiring the contents of proprietary medicines to be stated. However, rather than pursuing this limited objective, Hart turned his attention to the whole area of quack practice. During 1894 he was anxious to involve BMA members in a collective investigation of quackery which would generate findings capable of forcing an apathetic legislature to act.[44] But Hart's health was failing fast and his efforts came to nothing.

Dawson Williams took up the question in 1903. He contended that some proprietary remedies were dangerous, many were useless, and most a fraud on a gullible public.[45] He proposed that advertisements should be taxed and the contents of preparations publicized. He made a start on the second objective by summarizing Robert Hutchison's lecture on patent medicines, and reproducing Hutchison's appendix in which were listed the principal ingredients of dozens of preparations, including Beecham's Pills, Eno's Fruit Salts, Mrs Allen's Hair Restorer, and Carter's Little Liver Pills.[46] This was to become the *Journal*'s standard tactic in its war against the manufacturers of proprietary medicine, the objects of which were to alert the public 'to articles which are too often impudent and fraudulent deceptions' and to persuade the government to abolish the stamp duty which conferred a spurious respectability on quack nostrums.[47]

The war began in December 1904 under the heading, 'The Composition of Secret Remedies', and dealt first with some 'cures' for epilepsy. Unlike Hutchison, who had listed only the principal ingredients of various remedies, the *Journal* provided details of quantities and production costs. The report

[41] *Ibid.*, 24 Dec. 1892, 1399.

[42] *Ibid.*, see 21 Jan. 1893, 133; 29 April 1893, 889–90, 911–12; 15 July 1893, 135; 22 July 1893, 191–2; 29 July 1893, 257–8; 28 Oct. 1893, 957–8; 7 April 1894, 760.

[43] *Ibid.*, 27 Jan. 1894, 208.

[44] *Ibid.*, 5 May 1894, 974; 14 July 1894, 95; 21 July 1894, 153; 1 Dec. 1894, 1271.

[45] It was estimated that in the financial year 1907–8 the public spent around £2 423 000 on proprietory medicines. *Secret Remedies* (London: British Medical Association, 1909), p. 184.

[46] See *Journal*, 29 Aug. 1903, 478–9; 26 Sept. 1903, 747; 26 Dec. 1903, 1654. Years later Eno's Fruit Salt was advertised on the *Journal*'s front cover. See e.g. 28 July 1928.

[47] *Journal*, 10 Dec. 1904, 1599–1600.

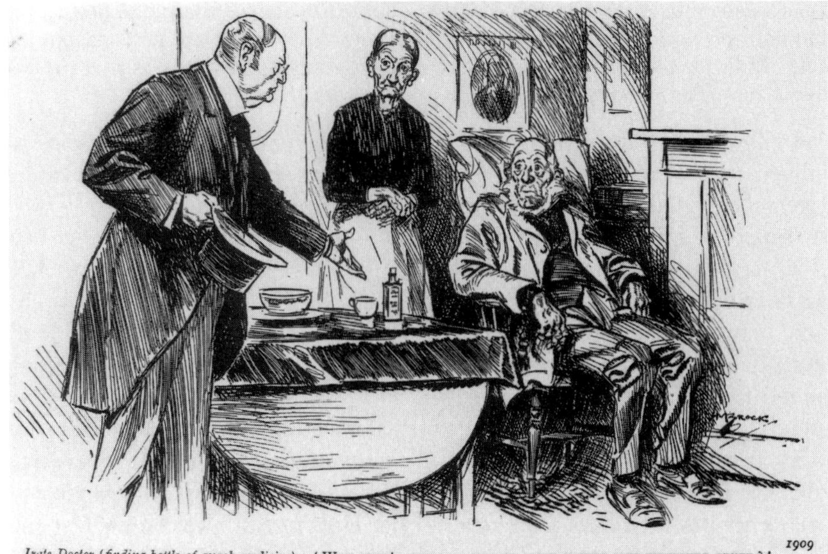

1909

Irate Doctor (finding bottle of quack medicine) : 'Why didn't you tell me you were taking this wretched stuff ?'
Patient : 'Well, it was my missis, sir. She says, "I'll dose you with this, and doctor he'll try his stuff, and we'll see which'll cure you first".'

Why didn't you tell me you were taking this wretched stuff?: from *Mr Punch Among the Doctors*. Source: Bodleian Library, Oxford.

on epilepsy revealed that 'cures' retailing at, in one case, 3s per 3 oz bottle, consisted of ingredients worth no more than 1d. The results of the analyses undertaken by an 'expert chemist and pharmacist' on behalf of the *Journal* were summarized in a leading article:

> With one exception they are weak preparations of well-known drugs supplied at considerably more than the usual cost, and administered without that careful adjustment of dose to the needs of the particular patient, which is, after all, the most essential part in the treatment of epilepsy by bromide salts. The exception contains an old-fashioned herb once praised by the superstitious, but abandoned time and again even by them.[48]

At first sight it is curious that after this initial assault more than 18 months passed before the *Journal* published the second article in its series, this time on headache powders.[49] In fact, the delay was not planned but caused by two factors: the first was the long illness of the pharmaceutical chemist undertaking analyses for the *Journal*; the second was doubt, prompted by a letter from the editor of the *Journal of the American Medical Association* (*JAMA*) as to whether the *BMJ*'s own advertising columns were themselves free of quack

[48] *Ibid.*, 10 Dec. 1904, 1585–6, 1599–1600.

[49] *Ibid.*, 7 July 1906, 27.

nostrums. As a result the BMA set up, on Williams's suggestion, a Proprietary Drugs Committee.[50]

A third article in the *Journal*'s series, on kidney medicines, appeared in December 1906.[51] The tempo increased in 1907 with a further report on kidney pills, followed by analyses of cures for obesity, Burgess's Lion Ointment (a cure-all), blood purifiers, 'female remedies', and numerous reprints from the *Deutsche Medicinische Wochenschrift* of Dr F. Zernik's investigations into German secret remedies.[52] At the end of the year Williams pointed out to the Journal and Finance Committee that 'the results of the analyst had not been challenged in any single instance, although they exposed the flimsiness of the claims made by the proprietors of secret remedies, and the exorbitant prices charged by them for drugs usually of the cheapest and most ordinary description.'[53] In 1908 the series continued with exposures of 'remedies' for baldness, eczema, eye defects, deafness, piles, consumption, teething pain, gout, rheumatism, neuralgia, rupture, catarrh, colds, coughs, obesity (again), and diabetes.[54]

At the end of 1908 Williams decided to call a temporary halt.[55] However, by this time the Journal and Finance Committee had agreed that the articles should be collected and published in book form under the title *Secret Remedies. What they Cost and What they Contain*.[56] They agreed on an initial print run of 2000, a retail price of 1s, and a maximum expenditure of £25 on advertising.[57] The book, published in July 1909, was a huge success which yielded the BMA a handsome profit. Its first two impressions sold out in less than a month, notwithstanding the refusal of newspapers—including the *Daily Express*, the *Graphic*, the *News of the World*, the *Daily Chronicle*, and the *Star*—which were making good money from proprietary medicine

[50] BMA mss. MCSC, XIV, Journal and Finance Committee, 10 Jan. 1906, 214–18. This issue is explored in the next section of this chapter.

[51] *Ibid.*, 216; *Journal*, 8 Dec. 1906, 1645–7.

[52] *Ibid.*, 26 Jan. 1907, 213–14; 6 July 1907, 24–5; 17 Aug. 1907, 393; 31 Aug. 1907, 530–2; 7 Dec. 1907, 1653–8. The German reports began on 3 Nov. 1906 and continued throughout 1907 and 1908.

[53] BMA mss MCSC, XVI, JFC, 22 Jan. 1908, 297. The proprietor of a 'cure' for consumption, C. H. Stevens, later brought a libel action which was decided in the Association's favour. See ibid., XIX, 14 June 1911, 5; Minutes of Committees, Conferences and Sub-Committees, Journal Committee, 6 Jan. 1915, 200; *Journal*, 25 July 1914, 211; 15 May 1915, 871–3; *The Times* 22, 23 July, 23, 30 Oct, 1 Nov. 1912; 17, 24 July 1914. Stevens's activities are discussed in F. B. Smith, *The Retreat of Tuberculosis, 1850–1950* (London: Croom Helm, 1988), pp. 155–62; see the same author's 'Gullible's Travails: Tuberculosis and Quackery, 1890–1930', *Journal of Contemporary History* (1985) **20**: 733–56.

[54] *Journal*, 7 Dec. 1907, 1672–73; 22 Aug. 1908, 518; 21 Nov. 1908, 1578–9; 5 Dec. 1908, 706; 26 Dec. 1908, 1884–5.

[55] BMA mss. MCSC, XVII, Minutes of Council, 27 Jan. 1909, 70–1.

[56] Some analyses, including those dealing with 'female complaints', were omitted from the book. The book contained a chapter (XII) on cancer remedies; these had not been covered in the *Journal*.

[57] BMA mss. MCSC, XVI, Minutes of Council, 28 Oct. 1908, 164–5; Journal and Finance Committee, 21 Oct. 1908, 1092–4. The cost of producing 2000 copies was £110.

advertisements, to accept advertising for the book.[58] Neither did the book obtain many reviews in the general press. Even so, by June 1910 *Secret Remedies* had sold 62 000 copies.[59] In 1912 the Association published a second collection of *Journal* analyses under the title *More Secret Remedies.*[60]

It has been suggested that the *Journal*'s attack on proprietary medicines was 'deadly and skilful'. But what exactly did it achieve? One thing it did not do was to drive them off the market, for these products continued to be widely advertised and, presumably, purchased and used.[61] However, through its books, which sold well in outlets such as station bookstalls it did alert the public to the foolhardiness of spending considerable sums of money on worthless nostrums. It also encouraged the government to point out that stamped medicines were not officially approved medicines. Until 1911 the stamp bore the words: 'This stamp implies no Government guarantee' in what the *Journal* felt was 'rather inconspicuous print'. In that year a new stamp was issued bearing the words 'No Government Guarantee' in larger lettering. The *Journal* commented, 'so far as it goes ... the stamp is an improvement.'[62]

Government was also moved to look more deeply into the whole subject of patent remedies and public policy. In April 1912 a select committee of inquiry was appointed. It would be going too far to suggest that the appointment of this committee was a triumph for the *Journal* alone. Since 1906 the BMA, under instructions from the Annual Representative Meeting, had been actively seeking legislation.[63] Moreover, H. G. Wells's novel *Tono-Bungay* (1909) was a powerful attack on the nostrum-mongers. In parliamentary questions dealing with proprietary medicines in the period 1904–1912, no MP ever mentioned the *BMJ.*[64] But there can be little doubt that the *Journal* was instrumental in giving the matter publicity and in keeping it in the forefront of attention.

The select committee, which was re-appointed for the next two parliamen-

[58] *Parliamentary Papers* (1914) **IX**: Select Committee on Patent Medicines, pp. x–xi. In 1914 it was estimated that advertising for proprietary remedies was worth about £2m per year to the press. See letter of Henry Sewill, *Journal*, 19 Sept. 1914, 522–3. E.S. Turner suggests that the massive growth in newspaper titles after 1855 was based on the fortune spent by quack advertisers. *The Shocking History of Advertising*, p. 78 (note 33).

[59] *Journal*, 16 Oct. 1909, 1174; 6 Nov. 1909, 1368; BMA mss MCSC, XVII, Journal and Finance Committee, 20 Oct. 1909, Appendix C, 1115–7; XVIII, 19 Jan. 1910, 416–17; 22 June 1910, 1301; Minutes of Council, 29 June 1910, 179.

[60] I have been unable to ascertain the sales achieved by this volume, but they were far lower than for the earlier volume. By the end of 1922 it had achieved sales worth some £1400.

[61] E. S. Turner, *The Shocking History of Advertising*, p. 161 (note 33).

[62] *Journal*, 19 Aug. 1911, 392. The *Journal* had criticized Lloyd George for failing to impose a heavier tax on proprietary medicines in his so-called 'People's Budget'. 8 May 1909, 1134–5.

[63] *Ibid.*, 9 Dec. 1911, 1563.

[64] 4 *Hansard* 139 (2 Aug. 1904), 518; 153 (12 March 1906), 921; 160 (12 July 1906), 1059–60; 176 (26 June 1907), 1389; 5 *Hansard* 21 (15 Feb. 1911), 1200; 27 (26 June 1911), 363–4; 27 (5 July 1911), 1302; 30 (6 Nov. 1911), 1269–70; 30 (9 Nov. 1911), 1822; 35 (4 March 1912), 28–9; 35 (19 March 1912), 1712; 36 (1 April 1912), 1012.

tary sessions, completed its inquiry on 4 August 1914, the very day on which Great Britain declared war on the Central Powers. It found that while some proprietary medicines were 'genuine' and 'unobjectionable', there were 'many secret remedies making grossly exaggerated claims of efficacy; causing injury by leading sick persons to delay in securing medical treatment; containing in disguise large proportions of alcohol; sold for improper purposes; professing to cure diseases incurable by medication; or essentially and deliberately fraudulent.'[65] It found that there was almost no legal control over the trade in secret remedies, and recommended that it be brought under regulation. Manufacturers, proprietors, and importers should be registered, certificated, and inspected, while the chemical formulae, ingredients, and proportions of their medicines should be disclosed to the authorities. Their advertising practices should be strictly controlled. Finally, the advertisement and sale of remedies purporting to cure certain diseases and disorders, including cancer, consumption, diabetes, epilepsy, and sexual problems, should be prohibited.[66]

Although the *Journal* was at first somewhat ambivalent about the Committee's report, perhaps because parts of the published minutes of evidence showed it and the Association in an unflattering light (see next section), a leading article published at the end of September demonstrated greater enthusiasm:

> The British Medical Association may congratulate itself on a striking success. But for its persistent efforts pursued through many years, it is exceedingly unlikely that the Select Committee would have been appointed. The statements made with regard to the quack medicine trade by the Association and in the BRITISH MEDICAL JOURNAL have been fully borne out, and a most important part of the inquiry and report of the Committee followed the line indicated by the articles on secret remedies published in the BRITISH MEDICAL JOURNAL, and subsequently collected into the two volumes, *Secret Remedies* and *More Secret Remedies*, published by the Association, many issues of which were quickly exhausted.[67]

In the world crisis that was at hand, the question of proprietary medicines quickly slipped from view, though one major change was made in 1917 when the Venereal Diseases Act prohibited the advertising of 'cures' for syphilis and gonorrhoea. More than 20 years were to pass before the rest of the quack medicine trade was brought under some degree of legal control.[68]

[65] *Parliamentary Papers* (1914) **IX**: Select Committee on Patent Medicines, pp. xxvi.

[66] *Ibid.*, xxvi–xxviii.

[67] *Journal*, 26 Sept. 1914, 548–9. See 12 Sept. 1914, 479–80; 1 Jan. 1916, 22; 12 Feb. 1916, 245–6; *BMJ* Supplement, 31 July 1915, 59.

[68] The Cancer Act, 1939, banned the advertising of cancer cures. The Pharmacy and Medicines Act, 1941, did the same in respect of Bright's disease, cataract, diabetes, epilepsy, fits, glaucoma, locomotor ataxy, paralysis, and tuberculosis. Further controls came after the war. *Journal*, 28 March 1936, 646–7; 15 July 1939, 120; E. S. Turner, *The Shocking History of Advertising*, pp. 227–8 (note 33).

Advertising ethics

As mentioned above, the *Journal*'s analysis of secret remedies was temporarily halted in 1905–6 after receipt of a letter from the editor of *JAMA*, George Simmons, which suggested that the *BMJ* was itself carrying advertising for nostrums. Simmons, who explained that the American Medical Association was campaigning against secret remedies, cited six preparations, four of which had been refused permission to advertise in *JAMA*, that were being advertised in the *BMJ*. His main objection to these products was that they were advertised in the lay press, though he was also concerned that their composition was not disclosed in the advertisements and hence that they might be prescribed by doctors, ignorant of their contents, simply on the claims of their manufacturers. Simmons concluded: 'We shall be glad to have your co-operation, and to co-operate with you in the fight against this nostrum evil. As I said above, it is not a serious one with you yet, but I am positive it will be in time, if it is not checked.'[69]

Responsibility for *BMJ* advertising rested with Guy Elliston, the BMA's general secretary, who also acted as the *Journal*'s business manager. He claimed that his practice had been to deny admission to preparations, 'at least those intended for internal administration, the ingredients of which are not stated in the advertisement'. He also maintained that he rejected 'certain articles largely advertised in the lay press', such as Kutnow's Powder (which was advertised in the *Lancet*), and liaised with the editor over doubtful cases. But in reality the *Journal* did carry advertising for preparations which provided no clue to ingredients and for products which were also advertised in the lay press.

The BMA's Journal and Finance Committee set up a sub-committee to review the matter. This concluded that the manager could safely be left to regulate the admission of advertising provided that he was informed of the ingredients of all preparations advertised. However, Williams insisted that an advisory committee be set up to help him to decide on what proprietary preparations should be noticed in the editorial columns and to advise the *Journal* manager.[70] The Proprietary Drugs Committee, as it was known, drew up a set of rules governing the notice of proprietary preparations in editorial pages. These required full disclosure of ingredients as a precondition for review.[71] But advertising copy continued to be accepted on the manager's discretion. Consequently, the *BMJ* continued with a far more tolerant attitude to proprietary medicines than *JAMA*, which allowed to be advertised only those remedies tested and approved by chemists working in AMA laboratories.[72]

[69] BMA mss. MCSC, XIV, Journal and Finance Committee, 10 Jan. 1906, 214.
[70] *Ibid.*, 214–18.
[71] *Ibid.*, Proprietary Drugs Committee, 9 Feb. 1906, 253–4.
[72] *Ibid.*, Signed Committee Minutes, 1910–13, Journal Committee, 10 Jan. 1913, 5, 8–9.

In 1909 the BMA's Birmingham branch suggested the establishment of a sub-committee to review the *Journal*'s advertising and prevent the inclusion of advertisements containing misleading or exaggerated statements or those for preparations and appliances that were advertised in the lay press. The Journal and Finance Committee rejected the suggestion on the grounds that decisions about advertising had to be prompt, and therefore executive. In any case, 'advertisements such as are referred to in the Resolution of the Birmingham Central Division are not sought, and if tendered are refused.'[73]

Although the *Journal* rejected many advertisements, most of these were for medical appointments deemed to be offered on unsatisfactory conditions or at inadequate salaries.[74] Numerous products of dubious value continued to appear. In 1910 the National British Women's Temperance Association called for the *Journal* to stop taking advertising for so-called medicated wines such as Wincarnis, which the NBWTA described as 'one of the great class of quack secret remedies which are ruining the Medical Profession and the public'. In this instance, urged on by the Annual Representative Meeting, the *Journal* excluded advertising from Wincarnis and also for Hall's wine, a product which contained cocaine.[75] The Association again reviewed its policy on food and drug advertising and decided that those advertisements containing false statements, and those advertised elsewhere in 'a misleading or otherwise objectionable manner', should be rejected.[76] Elliston, who examined how the new policy would affect *Journal* revenue, found that advertisements for alcoholic drinks, including diabetic whisky, and food preparations would remain acceptable. Certain items, including Bragg's Charcoal Biscuits, Kond's Euonymised Cocoa, and Sanatogen, would have to be excluded if they were advertised, as Sanatogen was, in the lay press.[77]

Although most of the advertisements refused by the *Journal* continued to be for medical appointments, the costliest rejections were of foods and drugs, for example, Junora Wine and Sandow Cocoa, the refusal of which, in 1911, meant lost revenue of £332 16s.[78] But even though the *Journal* was monitoring its advertising of food and drug preparations, its policy was not above reproach. In short, as a periodical intent on exposing the proprietary medicine trade and the newspapers profiting from it, the *Journal* was in a vulnerable position.

[73] BMA mss. MCSC, XVII, Journal and Finance Committee, 26 Nov. 1909, 1240–1, 1253.

[74] See e.g. ibid., XVIII, 19 Jan. 1910, 418–19.

[75] *Ibid.*, 22 June 1910, 1300; 19 Oct. 1910, 1677; 21 Dec. 1910, 1855; Minutes of Council, 26 Oct. 1910, 1539–41. In 1914 Coleman's, who made Wincarnis, spent around £50 000 p.a. in advertising it. The company claimed to possess 6000 endorsements from medical men. See *Parliamentary Papers* (1914) **IX**: Select Committee on Patent Medicines, pp. xiii–xiv.

[76] BMA mss. MCSC, XVIII, Journal and Finance Committee, 21 Dec. 1910, 1855.

[77] *Ibid.*, Signed Committee Minutes, 1910–13, Medico-Political and Journal Sub-Committee, 21 Dec. 1910, Appendix.

[78] *Ibid.*, Journal Committee, 5 Jan. 1912, 9.

In 1912, *JAMA* criticized the *Journal*'s (and the *Lancet*'s) advertising practices in its editorial columns. The BMA, it said,

> has . . . neglected to clean its own skirts . . . No attempt has been made . . . to purge the British medical profession of the innumerable fraudulent proprietary remedies with which it is afflicted . . . nostrums . . . hold high revel in the advertising pages of high-class medical journals in Great Britain. . . . Wherein is it any worse for the public to buy medicinal preparations about which it knows nothing, than it is for medical men to prescribe medicinal preparations about which it knows nothing?[79]

JAMA predicted that those with a financial interest in proprietary medicines would be able to resist demands for regulation by pointing to the practices of the medical profession. It forecast that the recently appointed select committee on patent medicines would therefore achieve little.[80]

Sure enough, when Alfred Cox, the BMA's newly appointed medical secretary, appeared as a witness before the select committee on patent medicines, he was subjected to what he later called 'a very searching examination' about the *Journal*'s own advertising by several of its members, two of whom, Sir Henry Dalziel and Harry Lawson, were newspaper proprietors.[81] In the memorandum it submitted to the committee, the BMA had called attention to 'the extent to which financial considerations apparently outweigh all considerations of honourable responsibility on the part of many of the newspapers in this country'. But during Cox's examination 'Attempts were made . . . to show that the Association's position was such that it could not afford to throw stones at other journals. It was pointed out that a large number of the advertisements in the JOURNAL were proprietary remedies.' When confronted with specific examples, Cox defended the Association on the grounds that medical men were capable of judging proprietors' claims in a way that the public was not. But he later acknowledged that he had a 'very awkward' time before the committee and that 'it was evident to me that some of these advertisements were so worded as to make the critical attitude of the Association to other Journals rather difficult to maintain'.[82]

[79] *JAMA*, 3 Feb. 1912, 349.

[80] *Ibid.*

[81] BMA mss. Signed Committee Minutes, 1910–13, Journal Committee, 10 Jan. 1913, 2; *Parliamentary Papers* (1914) **IX:** Select Committee on Patent Medicines, Evidence, pp. 127–30; Dalziel had been Liberal MP for Kirkcaldy since 1892. He was 'connected with several Scottish and London papers' including *Reynolds' Weekly*. Lawson was Liberal–Unionist MP for Tower Hamlets (Mile End). He had been managing proprietor of the *Daily Telegraph* since 1903. Cox had become medical secretary to the BMA only in December 1911. See *Dictionary of National Biography 1931–1940* (London: Oxford University Press, 1949); B. B. Gilbert, *The Evolution of National Insurance in Great Britain: the Origins of the Welfare State* (London: Michael Joseph, 1966), pp. 404–7; P. Vaughan, *Doctors' Commons. A Short History of the British Medical Association*, pp. 204–6 (note 2).

[82] BMA mss. Signed Committee Minutes, Journal Committee, 10 Jan. 1913, 2–4.

Another witness, Ernest Parry, a consulting and analytical chemist, was critical of the *BMJ*'s advertising of diabetic whisky, arguing that, since there was no sugar in whisky, it was not possible to reduce it. He considered that the *Journal*, as a critic of proprietary 'cures' for diabetes, should not have accepted the advertisement, and agreed that the *Journal* was guilty of 'humbug'.[83] As for Cox, he was obliged to confess that things were advertised in the *Journal* of which he personally disapproved.[84]

After his grilling by the select committee, Cox reported his misgivings about advertising to the Journal and Finance Committee, and the whole issue was carefully discussed. Elliston pointed out that refusal to accept advertising for the remedies criticized by the select committee would cost the Association around £1400 a year. He believed there were practical difficulties in controlling unscrupulous proprietors and rejected *JAMA*'s solution as too expensive.[85] All that was agreed was to maintain existing guidelines on the acceptance of advertisements, to insist upon manufacturers supplying product samples, and to decline future advertising for Sanatogen.[86] But advertisements for other questionable preparations, including Angiers Emulsion, which the AMA regarded as a proprietary medicine and was also one of the products to which Cox's attention had been drawn by the select committee, continued to appear in the *Journal*.

In 1915 criticism surfaced within the BMA. The Association's Science Committee felt that the *Journal* Committee had not done enough to exclude unsatisfactory advertising of food and drug preparations. It wanted one of its own sub-committees to deal with the matter. But Council, mindful of the need to reduce BMA business during the war, decided that 'consideration of the whole question be deferred until a more opportune occasion'.[87]

Only in 1920 was the matter placed on a more satisfactory basis, indeed, something akin to what the AMA had adopted and advocated 15 years earlier. In that year the Association adopted the power to suspend or cancel, at a week's notice, contracts for a series of advertisements. It also initiated policies of submitting food and drug samples for chemical analysis, and of refusing advertisements that used the name of a medical practitioner. Finally, the *Journal* began to carry a notice in its index to advertisers to the effect that the Association took no responsibility for the accuracy of advertisers'

[83] *Parliamentary Papers* (1914) **IX**: Select Committee on Patent Medicines, Evidence, p. 600.

[84] *Ibid.*, p. 149.

[85] BMA mss. Signed Committee Minutes, Journal Committee, 10 Jan. 1913, 6.

[86] Sanatogen advertising was later re-admitted but individual advertisements were still being rejected in the 1950s. *Ibid.*, MCCSC, Journal Committee, 4 June 1919, 4; *BMJ* mss. *BMJ* Board of Directors' Report, 31 Dec. 1942; JCM (1953–4), JNL. 19, Journal Committee, 25 Feb. 1954, Minutes.

[87] *Ibid.*, MCCSC, Journal Committee, 31 March, 1915, 615–16; 11 June 1915, 879; 5 Jan. 1916, 119; Science Committee, 10 April 1915, 699–700; 10 July 1915, 947–8; Standing Therapeutic Sub-Committee, 9 July 1915, 940–2.

claims.[88] In 1922 a Food and Drug (Advertisements) Sub-committee was set up to offer advice on doubtful cases.[89]

Even so, the *Journal* continued to carry advertising for quack remedies. In 1924 the chairman of the Canadian Medical Association's Pharmacy Committee criticized the *Journal* for accepting such advertisements. Their appearance in the *BMJ*, he argued, undermined the CMA's efforts to discourage the prescribing of certain products:

> In Canada we have been endeavouring to do what we can to educate the physicians, to the uselessness of such preparations as these, and have made an endeavour to have them excluded from our journal. The answer that we receive almost invariably is that they pay well and that they are appearing in the *British Medical Journal*.[90]

In 1937 a BMA committee found that the *Journal* was carrying advertising for remedies which 'had outlived their usefulness or were making claims which could not be substantiated'.[91] As late as the 1950s some BMA members continued to express concern that advertising for such products as Lucozade and Larson's Swedish Milk Diet was continuing to appear in the *Journal*.

Medicine and welfare

Between 1906 and 1914 the Liberal government introduced a range of welfare reforms including provision of free school meals (1906), school medical inspection (1907), old age pensions (1908), and national insurance against unemployment and sickness (1911) which, with their implications for wealth and income redistribution, some historians have seen as initiating the welfare state. Historians now tend to regard these reforms as a response to internal and external challenges. Britain's international, imperial, and economic power was under threat, most notably by Germany. If this was to be repulsed, it was vital that 'national efficiency' be improved by nurturing a fitter, more capable, and more contented population. At the same time British society, or, rather, its capitalist economy, was threatened from within by socialism; at least some of the Liberal reforms represented an attempt to counter this challenge.

The idea of old age pensions had been much discussed since they were introduced by Germany in 1889.[92] In 1891 the social investigator Charles

[88] *Ibid.*, Journal Committee, 4 Feb. 1920, 5–13; 9 June 1920, 4; Council Minutes, 18 Feb. 1920, 8-10. Since 1911 the BMA had 'deprecated' advertising which used the names of medical practitioners.

[89] *Ibid.*, Journal Committee, 25 May 1922, 871; 5 Oct. 1922, 143.

[90] *Ibid.*, Journal Committee, 5 March 1925, 751–3.

[91] *Ibid.*, *BMJ* mss. JCM (1965–6), JNL. 13, Supplementary Agenda, 10 Nov. 1965.

[92] Though the idea pre-dated the German legislation. See B. B. Gilbert, *The Evolution of National Insurance in Great Britain: the Origins of the Welfare State*, pp. 161–4 (note 81); D. Fraser, *The Evolution of the British Welfare State* (London: Macmillan, 1984), p. 150. On German influences see the writings of E. P. Hennock, especially *British Social Reform and German Precedents* (Oxford: Clarendon Press, 1987).

Booth (the 'father of Old Age Pensions'), read a paper favouring their introduction to the Royal Statistical Society.[93] In this he estimated that around 38 per cent of the population aged over 65, numbering more than ½m individuals, were paupers. In no other age bracket was the proportion of paupers anything like as high. He concluded that a state pension of 5s a week should be granted to everyone of 65 or over.[94]

A *Journal* leader on Booth's address calculated the cost of implementing and administering his proposals. It concluded that there was no justification for indiscriminate payments which would add greatly to taxation, create 'disagreeable ... governmental supervision and control', and establish a precedent for bounties to the necessitous: 'A more intelligent and less degrading treatment of deserving and aged poor persons could surely be effected on a reasonable and less ambitious plan, and one that should give more incentive to individual thrift and independent provision for the needs of old age.'[95]

During the 1890s the pension question was investigated by a Royal Commission and a Departmental Committee. Numerous offical and non-official schemes, for both contributory and non-contributory pensions, were compiled. In 1898 New Zealand passed an old-age pensions act. By this time the *Journal* had enthusiastically espoused the pension principle, motivated, it seems, by the assumption that any legislation was likely also to establish sanatoria for the aged and would, therefore, provide abundant employment for doctors.[96] As it turned out, partly because of the intervening Boer War, the introduction of pensions was still a decade away. Furthermore, the Act as passed was more limited than the *Journal* had envisaged in the 1890s. It provided non-contributory benefits of up to 5s a week (depending on their other income) for those over 70 who passed stringent character tests. In consequence, the *Journal* seems to have largely lost interest in the reform. Its main observation on the bill as it passed through Parliament was that, limited measure though it undoubtedly was, it promised to keep many old people out of workhouse sick wards. This, it anticipated, would be of dubious benefit since the aged 'can hardly receive in their own homes the same care and attention which a Poor-law infirmary affords', it would also throw a large additional burden upon underpaid and overworked Poor Law medical officers.[97]

The origins of school medical inspection were very different from those of old age pensions. The 'real stimulus' both for free school meals and for medical inspection was the Boer War, or, more precisely, what army recruitment seemed to reveal about the physical condition of the British population, for a large number of volunteers were rejected as medically unfit.

[93] Sir Robert Ensor, *England, 1870 1914* (Oxford: Oxford University Press, 1936), p. 237.
[94] *Journal of the Royal Statistical Society* (1891) **54**: 600–43.
[95] *Journal*, 6 Feb. 1892, 291–2.
[96] *Ibid.*, 13 March 1897, 674; 2 April 1898, 902; 3 Sept. 1898, 641; 26 Nov. 1898, 1641.
[97] *Ibid.*, 11 July 1908, 100; see 6 June 1908, 1383.

THE BAIT.

Mr. Lloyd George. "Surely he ought to take this one!"

[October 30, 1912.]

The panel doctor's remuneration under the National Insurance Act was raised to 8s. 6d. per patient.

The Bait: from *Lloyd George by Mr Punch*. Source: Bodleian Library, Oxford.

This led to the appointment of the Inter-Departmental Committee on Physical Deterioration. When the *Journal* discussed this problem in 1903 it spoke of 'weakly men' and feeble girls bringing 'into the world sickly children, who grow up more weak and incompetent than their parents'. This suggests that the *Journal* espoused the notion of a progressive race degeneration. In fact, like the BMA, it was anti-eugenist, opposing any notion of compulsory or voluntary sterilization of the 'unfit'. True to its heritage as a champion of social and environmental reform, it favoured infant and educational welfare in the form of proper feeding and exercise, and through maternal welfare which offered training for motherhood.[98] In November

[98] *Ibid.*, 18 July 1903, 154–6; 25 July 1903, 207–8; 12 March 1904, 625–6; 2 Aug. 1913, 223–4, 225–7; 23 Aug. 1913, 508–9; F. Mort, *Dangerous Sexualities: Medico-Moral Politics in England since 1830* (London: Routledge and Kegan Paul, 1987), pp. 171–2.

Arthur Newsholme, who later became Chief Medical Officer of the Local Government Board, wrote the *Journal*'s leading article which proposed school medical inspection some eight months before it was recommended by the Physical Deterioration Committee.[99]

The *Journal* treated this question of physical deterioration, which became something of a national obsession, very seriously, publishing, between November 1903 and January 1904, a series of articles by Mrs Watt Smyth on 'Physical Degeneration'. These were later issued in book form.[100] At the end of the series a leading article maintained that the existence of 'unfitness is beyond all doubt'. It advocated, among other things, the proper feeding of children and periodical medical examination in schools 'with a view of checking such diseases as spinal curvature, narrow chests, and diseases of the ears, eyes, nose, and throat before they become chronic, and with a view to collecting the weakly ones of each school in order that they may have special classes and suitable physical exercises.'[101]

In July 1904 the Inter-Departmental Committee on Physical Deterioration issued its report. While denying the existence of general progressive deterioration, it accepted that physical unfitness prevailed in the lowest strata of society. It recommended many of the measures suggested by the *Journal* and, consequently, received warm praise in two leading articles:

> The Committee is to be congratulated upon the intelligent and conscientious manner in which it has tackled the social problems placed before it. It has ferreted out the gravest of the causes likely to cause deterioration and it has not been afraid to point out remedies. The report is excellently drawn out . . .'.[102]

From 1904 the feeding and medical inspection of schoolchildren became a much debated subject. The *Journal* 'hoped that we may be able to establish a very thorough, simple, and co-ordinated method of medical inspection throughout the country'. Although it devoted much less attention to the provision of meals, one of the articulated reasons that the *Journal* supported inspection was to facilitate identification of those children in need of feeding.[103]

[99] *Journal*, 14 Nov. 1903, 1288. See B. B. Gilbert, *The Evolution of National Insurance in Great Britain: the Origins of the Welfare State*, p. 93 (note 81).

[100] *Journal*, 21 Nov. 1903, 1338–41; 28 Nov. 1903, 1430–31; 5 Dec. 1903, 1471–4; 12 Dec. 1903, 1555–7; 26 Dec. 1903, 1652–3; 2 Jan. 1904, 45–7; 9 Jan. 1904, 86–8; 16 Jan. 1904, 1402; 23 Jan. 1904, 197–9; 30 Jan. 1904, 272–3. See 6 Aug. 1904, 297. Dawson Williams addressed the BMA's 1905 Annual Representative Meeting on 'Physical Deterioration: Its Causes and Extent', 14 Oct. 1905, 929–31.

[101] *Ibid.*, 6 Feb. 1904, 319–20.

[102] *Ibid.*, 30 July 1904, 248; 6 Aug. 1904, 296–7. *Lancet*, 6 Aug. 1904, 390–2. Gilbert notes that 'doctors generally supported measures designed to extend knowledge of hygiene and domestic science among the poor through training in State schools'. *The Evolution of National Insurance in Great Britain: the Origins of the Welfare State*, p. 92 (note 81).

[103] *Journal*, 29 April 1905, 949; see 17 Feb. 1906, 400–2; 14 April 1906, 878–9; 21 July 1906, 156–7; 8 Dec. 1906, 1660; 12 Jan. 1907, 97–8; 9 March 1907, 582–3.

The Education (Provision of Meals) Act became law in December 1906. It empowered local authorities to provide meals for needy children. Since it proved impossible to recover the cost from parents who, nevertheless, were not pauperized by public provision for their children, it represented a small step towards acceptance by the State of responsibility for the disadvantaged. By the same token, school medical inspection, introduced under the terms of the Education (Administrative Provisions) Act, 1907, was likely to be followed, as it soon was, by school medical treatment. As such it was a step towards a State medical service. Arthur Newsholme, in some respects a critic of the BMA, later gave it much of the credit for the introduction of school medical inspection.[104] In reality much of the credit belonged to the *Journal* for its effective advocacy of the reform.

While questions of old age pensions, free school meals, and school medical inspection were being debated, the Royal Commission on the Poor Laws was sitting (1905–9). A large part of its deliberations was devoted to the question of medical relief. When it finally reported it produced not one, but two voluminous reports. Fourteen commissioners favoured reforming, but retaining, the Poor Law. A minority, comprising the Commission's four socialist members, favoured its abolition, and replacement of the Poor Law Medical Service with 'a unified [State] Medical Service based on Public Health principles' and staffed by salaried medical officers. This would be available to anyone who wished to make use of it, though not necessarily free of charge, without any need to prove destitution.[105]

The minority report was very much at odds with the evidence given to the Commission by the BMA. It may have provided a blueprint for the National Health Service, but the *Journal* rejected it out of hand as 'a discursive document with even its summary of conclusions reading more like an article in a monthly magazine than the serious recommendations of a Royal Commission for fresh legislation ... its proposals with regard to medical relief appear to us to be nebulous and insufficiently considered.'[106] For all its impact on ideas, the minority report, no more than that of the majority, exerted no immediate influence upon legislation. In the last years of peace before the First World War the health debate centred not on Poor Law medical services, but on national insurance.

The architect of national insurance was David Lloyd George, who was Chancellor of the Exchequer in Asquith's 1908–1916 Liberal administration.

[104] Sir Arthur Newsholme, *Fifty Years in Public Health* (London: George Allen and Unwin, 1935), p. 392; B. B. Gilbert, *The Evolution of National Insurance in Great Britain: the Origins of the Welfare State*, p. 93 (note 81).

[105] *Parliamentary Papers* **XXXVII** (1909), Royal Commission on the Poor Laws, Reports.

[106] *Journal*, 20 Feb. 1909, 487–8; Charles Webster, *The Health Services since the War*. Vol. 1, *Problems of Health Care. The National Health Service before 1957* (London, 1988), pp. 17-8; Donald Read, *Edwardian England* (London: Harrap, 1972); D. Fraser, *The Evolution of the British Welfare State*, pp. 158–61 (note 92).

Lloyd George's main concern was with the problem of poverty rather than health care. But poverty was often the result of inability to work, whether as the consequence of sickness, age, or accident, and the main feature of national insurance as implemented was income replacement for the insured worker through sick pay at a rate of 10s a week for 26 weeks and 5s thereafter.[107] The Act also provided for the medical treatment of insured people (though not their dependants), with the object of enabling them to return to work as soon as possible. Treatment was provided by practitioners who were paid a capitation fee based on the number of 'panel patients' they had. Unlike old age pensions, these benefits, which also included a maternity grant of 30s, were to be provided on the contributory principle by means of a weekly stamp for which the employee paid 4d, the employer 3d, and the State 2d. The ramshackle arrangements for the health care of the working classes were barely touched by the National Insurance Act. For example, no move was made to support or develop the hospital system, though provision was made for patients with tuberculosis to be treated in sanatoria.

When Lloyd George introduced his national insurance bill in the Commons in May 1911, he received a 'uniformly favourable' reception from the party leaders. On the other hand, medical reaction was 'immediate and violent'; BMA branches passed condemnatory resolutions.[108] It has been claimed that such a reaction was not shared by the *BMJ*, which 'welcomed the Bill in a mildly laudatory leader'.[109] This is true so far as it goes, but the *Journal*'s approval was more in respect of principles than detail. The *Journal* actually expressed grave doubts about the bill's likely impact on medical incomes. Indeed, its reservations were real enough for it to suggest that the national insurance bill seemed 'seriously to threaten the interests of the medical profession'. The *Lancet*'s reception of the bill was at least as welcoming as the *BMJ*'s.[110]

The BMA's struggle to achieve a better deal for its members began on 1 June when Lloyd George attended its Special Representative Meeting to, as he disarmingly put it, 'talk the matter over' with the profession.[111] The Chancellor's performance, with its shrewd blend of amiability, encouragement, and resolve, was consummate. He conceded little yet won enthusiastic applause from an audience which, hitherto, had regarded him as a sworn enemy and was later to treat him with undisguised scorn. After his departure,

[107] See B. B. Gilbert, *The Evolution of National Insurance in Great Britain: the Origins of the Welfare State*, especially pp. 314–15 (note 81).

[108] *Ibid.*, p. 365. P. Vaughan, *Doctors' Commons. A Short History of the British Medical Association*, pp. 196–7 (note 1); *BMJ* Supplement, 20 May 1911, 244–6; 27 May 1911, 298–302.

[109] B. B. Gilbert, *The Evolution of National Insurance in Great Britain: the Origins of the Welfare State*, p. 365 (note 81).

[110] *Journal* 13 May 1911, 1134–6; 20 May 1911, 1202; *Lancet*, 13 May 1911, 1289–90; 20 May 1911, 1362–3; 27 May 1911, 1435–6.

[111] *BMJ* Supplement, 3 June 1911, 352–60.

the representatives agreed on a six-point policy for an acceptable scheme, which subsequently became known as the 'Six Cardinal Points'. These were:

1. An upper income limit of £2 per week for insured persons.
2. A free choice of doctor for patients, subject to the doctor's agreement.
3. Benefits to be administered by local health committees rather than friendly societies.
4. The method of payment to be determined by a majority of local doctors.
5. Adequate remuneration.
6. Adequate medical representation in the scheme's administration.[112]

The struggle to achieve the Cardinal Points is the stuff of a history of the BMA rather than of the *BMJ*. Nine representative and innumerable divisional meetings were held; 27 000 signatures pledging non-cooperation with any Act which did not accord with BMA policy were obtained; 33 000 resignations from existing appointments with friendly societies were collected and a huge fighting fund accumulated. By the time the bill received the Royal Assent, in December, four of the six points had been conceded; only one and five, both financial, remained. But the BMA was still dissatisfied, and the *Journal*, which had supported the Association throughout the struggle, urged its readers to back the policy of insistence upon the entire six points, without agreement on which there should be no treatment of insured persons.[113] Clearly, it had travelled a long way in the months since May when it had predicted that 'the medical profession will be in full accord ... with the general intentions of the Bill.' At that time, it had said, 'The Bill is a call to a great social duty, and we are confident that the medical profession will not be slow to respond, and to lend every assistance that lies in its power to accomplish the desire of the nation ...'.[114]

Since insurance contributions would not begin till July 1912 (the administrative machinery had to be put in place), while benefits would be payable only from January 1913 (once a fund of contributions had been built up), the doctors had a year in which to press their case for more money. Despite the Act's presence on the Statute Book the profession remained confident that it could get the six points 'without evasion or reservation', its reasoning being that, while the nation could manage without Lloyd George, the sick could not manage without doctors. It believed that all it had to do was hold firm and wait until the Chancellor begged them to accept concessions. As the *Journal* put it in January 1912, 'the profession should stand aside and let the Frankenstein of the Exchequer make what arrangements he can to galvanize into some likeness of life the legislative monster he has created.'[115]

[112] *Ibid.*, 10 June 1911, 410.
[113] *Journal*, 23 Dec. 1911, 1666–7.
[114] *Ibid.*, 13 May 1911, 1136.
[115] *Ibid.*, 6 Jan. 1912, 38; 13 Jan. 1912, 90–1; P. Vaughan, *Doctors' Commons. A Short History of the British Medical Association*, p. 208 (note 1); B. B. Gilbert, *The Evolution of National Insurance in Great Britain: the Origins of the Welfare State*, pp. 407–8 (note 81).

We cannot be sure whether public opinion was on the side of the profession in the struggle, but what seems certain is that it was alienated when the Plender Committee reported in July 1912. This actuarial investigation of medical incomes showed that the typical practitioner would fare rather better under the national insurance scheme than he had in the past.[116] Lloyd George, scenting the propaganda value of the report, released it to the press before discussing it with the BMA. The *Journal* condemned the report as rushed and inaccurate, while the Association repeated its demand for an income limit and a capitation fee of 8s 6d, exclusive of extras. Unable to win agreement, the BMA broke off negotiations.[117]

Lloyd George's response was to resort to the carrot and the stick. On the one hand, he threatened to withdraw medical representation in the administration of the scheme and recruit as salaried employees any doctors willing to ignore the call to solidarity. On the other, he secured Cabinet agreement to an increase in the capitation fee to up to 9s inclusive.[118] The *Journal* suggested that the profession should accept the new deal:

> The alteration of the terms of remuneration now proposed has brought about a new situation, differing materially from that which existed when the Representative Meeting resolved to break off negotiations with the Government. ... The new proposal falls short of what the profession has demanded in many important respects. But the justice of many of the claims put forward by the Association on behalf of the profession is recognized in principle ...'.[119]

However, on 19 December a Special Representative Meeting overwhelmingly turned down the new proposals, despite the fact that in some areas, particularly the poorer ones, a majority of practitioners had joined the panel.

BMA headquarters staff were dismayed, and the SRM decision has been described as being 'more than an act of unwisdom; it was an act of folly'.[120] Although the decision differed from that which it had previously espoused, the *Journal* backed the democratic verdict, saying that 'the Government must understand that the only way in which the Act can be worked is through a frank recognition of the reasonable demands of the Association.'

If the *Journal* truly believed this it was greatly mistaken, for the government, aware of the split in the profession, had merely to wait for the trickle of doctors joining panels to turn into a torrent. By 10 January 1913 15 000 had joined. A week later a Special Representative Meeting formally relieved BMA members of their pledge not to accept service.

Contrasting views have been expressed as to the BMA's success in the national insurance struggle. Writers connected with the Association have

[116] *Ibid.*, pp. 408–9.

[117] *Journal*, 20 July 1912, 133–4; *BMJ* Supplement, 20 July 1912, 98, 120–1; 27 July 1912, 146.

[118] B. B. Gilbert, *The Evolution of National Insurance in Great Britain: the Origins of the Welfare State*, pp. 410–2 (note 81).

[119] *Journal*, 26 Oct. 1912, 1154–5.

[120] B. B. Gilbert, *The Evolution of National Insurance in Great Britain: the Origins of the Welfare State*, p. 413 (note 81).

tended to emphasize its achievement in effecting real improvements in practitioners' terms of service. On the other hand, it has also been suggested that the 'British Medical Association was defeated and crushed'.[121] There is some truth in both assessments, for, though the BMA did win important concessions, its 'all or nothing' approach to negotiations guaranteed its final defeat. Urged on by consultants and specialists, the Association pursued a policy that was not necessarily in the best interests of most of its members. This was a major factor in the decline in BMA membership between 1913 and 1919. As for the *Journal*, although its pages were full of national insurance in the years 1911–1913, it played an unimportant role in determining the question, for in the twentieth century, unlike in the nineteenth, medical politics were the province of the Association. National insurance was the BMA's first major struggle with government; it signified that the days of the *Journal*'s engagement in political activism had ended.

The First World War

The *Journal*'s four issues for July 1914 provide no hint that Great Britain and much of the rest of Europe were on the brink of one of the greatest armed struggles of all time. As late as 1 August the *Journal* was dominated by reports of proceedings and addresses from the BMA's annual meeting, which that year was held in Aberdeen, including an account of the drawn cricket match between BMA and city teams. It all reinforces the notion of a nation blissfully unaware of the impending catastrophe. There was but one short reference to the European crisis:

> The outbreak of a war in the Balkan area, which is creating such confusion in the Chancelleries of Europe and such a disturbance on the markets of the world, is not leaving untouched even the Annual Meeting of the Association. In anticipation of what has actually occurred, more than one Continental authority who was expected to take part in the work of the Sections thought it wise to abandon the project . . .'.[122]

When the next issue of the *Journal* appeared, the country was at war with the Central Powers.

The total of military and naval deaths in the First World War, including those from disease, has been estimated as between 10 and 13 million. British Empire forces sustained around one million dead and over two million wounded; of these about 0.75 million of the dead and 1.7 million of the wounded came from Great Britain and Ireland. Between August 1914 and August 1920 over 2.6 million sick and wounded were brought from abroad to

[121] E. M. Little, *History of the BMA*, pp. 328–30 (note 1); P. Vaughan, *Doctors' Commons. A Short History of the British Medical Association*, p. 209 (note 2); B. B. Gilbert, *The Evolution of National Insurance in Great Britain: the Origins of the Welfare State*, p. 416 (note 81). Vaughan's assessment is more balanced than Little's.

[122] *Journal*, 1 Aug. 1914, 260.

the United Kingdom. At the armistice the medical services attached to the armed forces numbered 144 514 officers and other ranks.[123] These figures provide some idea of the size of the challenge faced by medical personnel in the armed forces. But not only was the scale of the war different from anything experienced before, it was also a new form of warfare, fought with heavy, pointed bullets, high explosives, and chemicals. On the western front it was a static war conducted at close range on heavily manured soil, which made tetanus and anaerobic disease the almost inevitable accompaniment of any wound. Many of the wounded were also traumatized from lying for long periods between trenches.

In 1914 the most recent experience of military medicine of many serving army surgeons had been gained in South Africa during the Boer War. But as Surgeon-General Sir Anthony Bowlby wrote in the *Journal*, 'it was very soon evident that we had to unlearn most of our South African experiences.' Injuries such as comminuted fractures of the femur by bullet wound, which, in South Africa

> never gave the slightest trouble . . . in the present war would almost certainly have resulted in the death of the patients from gangrene, or at least in prolonged suppuration and probable loss of the limb, and many surgeons who are familiar only with South African conditions seem unable to appreciate the completely altered picture of the present war.[124]

Experience soon led to rapid changes in surgical practice. Owing to the risk of infection wounds were left open rather than being rapidly closed. Similarly, a conservative approach to chest, scalp, and abdominal wounds, with the emphasis on resting the patient before operating, gave way to a policy of early surgery. Anti-tetanus serum was found to be effective, while radiology and blood transfusion proved invaluable aids to surgery. Plastic surgery, drug development, skin grafting, and the treatment of burns were all given a fillip by the war.[125]

On the outbreak of hostilities the BMA was quick to point out that 'its machinery [was available] to assist the Government in any appeal it may desire to make to the medical profession.' The government's first priority, as far as the profession was concerned, was to obtain sufficient manpower for the armed forces without depriving civilians of access to medical care. The

[123] Sir W. G. Macpherson (editor-in-chief), *History of the Great War Based on Official Documents. Medical Services. General History* (4 vols. London: Committee of Imperial Defence, 1921), Vol. I, p. xiii; C. R. M. F. Cruttwell, *A History of the Great War 1914–1918* (Oxford: Clarendon Press, 1934), Appendix I.

[124] *Journal*, 25 Dec. 1915, 913, 934–5.

[125] Blood transfusion, though in use before 1914 'was not practised by the majority of surgeons of Great Britain until the war provided them with unparalleled opportunities for its employment'. *History of the Great War*. Sir A. A. Bowlby, Sir Cuthbert Wallace, and Sir Crispin English (eds.), *Surgery of the War* (2 vols. London: Committee of Imperial Defence, 1922); Geoffrey Keynes, *Blood Transfusion* (London: John Wright, 1922); see Lyn Macdonald, *The Roses of No Man's Land* (London: Michael Joseph, 1980), pp. 12, 95–6, 148–50.

association helped co-ordinate arrangements at home while allowing the authorities free access to the *BMJ* for appeals for recruits; as early as 8 August the *Journal* published a two-page 'call' for temporary surgeons and surgeon probationers for the armed services. Thereafter the *Journal*, at official instigation or on its own account, 'directed its efforts to securing an adequate supply of medical officers for the fighting forces'. As Clifford Allbutt, the BMA's president, informed the minister of munitions in 1917, the Association, 'without the assistance of its official organ the *British Medical Journal*, could not have had the same measure of success in securing for the fighting forces and the civil population an adequate medical attendance'. After the war Sir Anthony Bowlby wrote: 'Whoever might have been responsible for the mobilization of the fighting forces of the Crown, there can be no doubt that the mobilization of the medical profession was the work of Dawson Williams.'[126]

As well as assisting the recruitment drive, the *Journal* was used for propaganda. In December 1916 Dawson Williams was informed by an official of the Government Propaganda Committee that

> agents in neutral and friendly countries had intimated . . . that the medical profession, and men of science and education in these countries had 'a very poor opinion' of British medicine and surgery, and the proposal was that a special publication should be prepared to help in removing this erroneous impression.[127]

The editor and Journal Committee felt that such a publication could benefit the *Journal* and Association as well as the national interest and it was agreed that the government should finance a collection of clinical papers, abstracted from the *Journal*, which would deal with military and naval medicine and surgery. The volume was published, with colour plates, in both French (37 000 copies) and English (28 000).[128]

The *Journal* claimed to be 'exceptionally well-informed as to the medical aspects of the present great war' owing to the presence of BMA members 'in every British camp and in every military hospital, whether great or small, both at home and abroad'.[129] Before long its pages were full of the war and war-related material. It largely adhered to medical topics, in the discussion of which it was remarkably dispassionate, usually avoiding critical comment on broader issues or making moral judgements. After the war it was admitted that the organization of army medical services, at least in the early stages, left

[126] *Journal*, 8 Aug. 1914, 308; 13 March 1915, 488; 10 April 1915, 645; 30 March 1918, 375; 20 May 1922, 802; 10 March 1928, 424; BMA mss. MCCSC, Journal Committee, 4 April 1917, 420–1; E. M. Little, *History of the BMA*, p. 241 (note 1). For the BMA's role in organizing civilian health see J. M. Winter, *The Great War and the British People* (Basingstoke: Macmillan, 1986), Chapter 5.

[127] BMA mss. MCCSC, Journal Committee, 4 April 1917, 423.

[128] *Ibid.*, 3 Oct. 1917, 1087; *British Medicine in the War, 1914–1917. Collected out of the British Medical Journal, 1914–1917* (London: British Medical Association, 1917), pp. x, 138.

[129] *Journal*, 7 Nov. 1914, 800.

much to be desired, with textbook methods for the evacuation of casualties breaking down. In France and Belgium this led to 'a rapid and thorough re-organization which stood the test of the war'. Elsewhere improvement was slower and produced 'serious conditions in the field and dissatisfaction in the United Kingdom'. However, the *BMJ* carried no criticism. Similarly, it was only after the war that it revealed that some British soldiers traded in 'tubercle sputum and venereal discharge', so desperate were they to be invalided home.[130]

While it is not surprising that the national interest compelled the *Journal* to abstain from pointing up British deficiencies, rather more puzzling is its objective reporting of the German war effort. While other publications were accusing Germany of committing all manner of atrocities, the *Journal* weighed the evidence before concluding that 'Charges of atrocities made by either side should be received with the critical scepticism we have learned to apply to claims of great victories and statements as to the fighting qualities of our enemies.'[131]

Even the introduction of chemical warfare—chlorine gas was first used by the German army in April 1915—went uncondemned. When mentioned, it was purely in terms of the challenge it presented to medical technology.[132]

The *Journal*'s objectivity was in marked contrast to the views expressed by some of its correspondents. For example, when C. F. Marshall contributed to the long-running discussion about allied manufacture of salvarsan products, he argued that

> Whether English salvarsan is more or less toxic than the German product is immaterial, considering that this drug is not essential in the treatment of syphilis. The labour and ingenuity expended on its manufacture would be better applied in the production of high explosives or poisonous gases, or any other means to rid us of German 'culture,' which has for so long hypnotized and contaminated the civilized world.[133]

[130] *Ibid.*, 11 Nov. 1922, 951; *History of the Great War*. T. J. Mitchell and G. M. Smith, *Medical Services Casualties and Medical Statistics* (London: Committee of Imperial Defence, 1931), pp. 2, 35.

[131] *Journal*, 2 Jan. 1915, 33.

[132] *Ibid.*, 1 May 1915, 774; 8 May 1915, 821; 15 May 1915, 861; 29 May 1915, 940, 944; 5 June 1915, 984–5; 12 June 1915, 1016; David Hamilton, 'Surgery and World War I', Wellcome Symposium on the History of Medicine. Modern Medicine and War, 26 Feb. 1988. L. Macdonald, *The Roses of No Man's Land*, pp. 84–6 (note 125). The use of gas as a weapon was widely condemned at the time though Liddell Hart comments: 'The chlorine gas originally used was undeniably cruel, but no worse than the effect of shell or bayonet, and when it was succeeded by improved forms of gas both experience and statistics proved it the least inhumane of modern weapons ... it was novel and therefore labelled an atrocity by a world which condones abuses but detests innovations'. B. H. Liddell Hart, *History of the First World War* (London: Cassell, 1970 edn), pp. 195–6.

[133] *Journal*, 10 July 1915, 75–6. Salvarsan was an anti-syphilitic drug developed in Frankfurt in 1909. When war broke out its manufacture was exclusive to Hoechst Germany. Since around 20 per cent of British armed forces contracted syphilis, access to an effective drug treatment was vital.

In October 1914 the *Journal* did take to task the President of the AMA, who deplored the loss to the world of those German scientists who had forsaken their laboratories for the battlefields. 'The greatest scientific discoveries of the world,' he said, 'have been made in German laboratories.' A leading article in the *Journal* responded angrily: 'It was not in German laboratories that vaccination, anaesthesia, or antisepsis was discovered. Bacteriology we owe to Pasteur, radium to Madame Curie. The list might be indefinitely extended.' At the time this was as close as the *Journal* came to political comment, though as the war progressed it tended to drop its scientific objectivity and became more willing to characterize Germany and the Germans as savage and barbaric: 'The Germans share with the lower races of mankind a certain cunning . . . .'[134]

Even when dismissive of German medical science and critical of those German scientists who renounced their British academic honours and signed a declaration expressing hatred of Great Britain, the *Journal* was hungry for scientific news from Germany and seriously concerned about the inaccessibility of German universities and publications.[135] From early 1915 its editorial pages began to pay close attention to papers published in the German medical periodicals which reached London via the USA. Of particular interest were those dealing with German experiences of war surgery.

Although the *Journal* did not ignore other theatres of war, it concentrated on France and Belgium. On 17 October 1914 it began publishing articles from its special correspondent on the western front. These were written by Guy Stephen, who, notwithstanding his deafness, had 'a good knowledge of French'.[136] Because of the *Journal*'s reduced size, Williams felt that Stephen could be temporarily spared from his London duties. He produced a stream of brilliant reports which did much to keep *Journal* readers in touch with events in northern France, not least the appalling conditions and dangers of the trenches.

> I do not often see English papers, but when I do it sometimes seems to me that even now the British public does not realise that what is going on in France and Belgium at the present time is a war and not a game played according to definite rules, with every move foreseen. They seem to forget sometimes that at least a million men on each side are trying to kill one another with singularly efficient weapons; that in the course of the struggle the survivors are constantly moving from place to place; and that meantime they have to be fed, kept supplied with ammunition, and the wounded and dead removed out of the way as quickly as possible.

From the general he turned to the particular:

[134] See e.g. 5 Aug. 1916, 184–5; 25 Nov. 1916, 733; 6 Oct. 1917, 457, 459.

[135] *Ibid.*, 31 Oct. 1914, 762; 28 Nov. 1914, 926–7; D. Hamilton, 'Surgery and World War I' (note 132).

[136] BMA mss. MCCSC, Journal Committee, 6 Jan. 1915, 190; R. S. Stevenson, *Goodbye Harley Street*, p. 84 (note 2).

In the wounds seen in France . . . ordinary pus organisms seem to be, initially at any rate, prevented from gaining any foothold by the extraordinary quantity of anaerobic organisms, such as the tetanus bacillus . . . The reason of this bacteriological peculiarity of the wounds is . . . the nature of the country in which the men are fighting. The soil of France, as also that of Belgium, is cultivated to a degree unknown in Great Britain. It has been thoroughly and steadily manured for an untold number of years, and consequently teems with tetanus. In trenches dug out of this soil the men stand for hours and get their clothing and hands caked with mud. It is not surprising, therefore, that when hit by a missile the latter carries in with it millions of anaerobes. This is one of the circumstance which it would seem is not appreciated at home, the result being that the grave infections from which so large a proportion of the wounded suffer are quite wrongly written down as the result of lack of early treatment.[137]

Soon after arriving in France Stephen received a commission as honorary major in the RAMC; he was subsequently promoted to the rank of lieutenant-colonel. When Dawson Williams visited the western front in 1916 he discovered at first hand what a good job Stephen was doing in reporting the war in the west.[138]

The First World War provided an unprecedented challenge to medicine and surgery. In the *Journal*'s opinion, the challenge was triumphantly met. It was highly complimentary both about the organization and the accomplishments of the medical services in the armed forces. It expressed unstinting admiration for 'the adaptability, ingenuity, and perseverance of the British surgeon in face of difficulties undreamt of in any previous campaign'. Indeed, it believed that 'British medicine can look back with pride on the part it has taken in the war and the share it has had in the winning of it. By an appeal to results it is justified before the nations'.[139] For their part, the military authorities expressed satisfaction with the *Journal*'s coverage of medical and surgical questions arising out of the war. Thus, Major T. R. Elliot, medical representative of the Medical Research Committee in France, who later organized the offical medical history of the war, told Williams: 'My opinion about the *B.M.J.* is simply this, that it is the only paper that one can use for the general dissemination of knowledge on medical work during the War . . . The *B.M.J.* has taken the chief place as the diary of men's thoughts from month to month.'[140]

137 *Journal*, 7 Nov. 1914, 804.
138 BMA mss. MCCSC, Journal Committee, 6 Jan. 1915, 190; 4 Oct. 1916, 807.
139 *Journal*, 2 June 1917, 737–8; 16 Nov. 1918, 550.
140 BMA mss. MCCSC, Journal Committee, 4 April 1917, 428; *Journal*, 6 Jan. 1917, 22.

9
Between the wars

Circulation, finance, and staff

Information on *Journal* circulation exists for most years of the 1920s and 1930s. In a period pre-dating independent audits, the main source for such figures is the *Journal* itself—where circulation was sometimes publicized alongside the advertising index—or the annual report of the BMA's Council. Neither the Journal Committee nor the rest of the BMA seem to have placed much emphasis on circulation. Both Dawson Williams and Gerald Horner provided a quarterly report to the Journal Committee, but, while they regularly commented on the *Journal*'s dimensions or the number of contributions and letters received, neither ever mentioned circulation. The annual report of the BMA's Council, which always included a section on the *Journal*, referred to the topic infrequently. The conclusion is that circulation was thought to be unimportant except as an occasional reminder to advertisers. This is perhaps because most of the print-run (around 85 per cent in 1918, and over 92 per cent in 1939) went directly to BMA members as a benefit of membership. Because the *Journal* was not a commercial speculation, did not have to trade at a profit, and had, in some senses, a captive audience, it was under little pressure to chase sales. It was secure in its position as Britain's largest circulation medical journal merely because it was 'the organ of the Association'. All this was a far cry from the Hart years, however, when circulation had been loudly and repeatedly trumpeted in the editorial columns.

In 1918 the *Journal*'s average weekly circulation was 23 546, of which some 3500 copies were sold to non-members. These figures were substantially below pre-war levels, for in December 1913 circulation had been 30 000, some 5500 of which comprised sales. Not since the early 1900s had there been a circulation figure as low as that of 1918. The post-1913 decline was largely a function of falling BMA membership. In 1912 this had reached a peak of 26 568; over the next six years it dropped steadily and by 1918 was down to 19 982. While this decline may be partially attributed to the exigencies of war, a more important factor was disillusion with BMA policy in the national insurance crisis.[1]

After the war, membership recovered; it increased annually until the early

[1] The BMA explained the post-1912 decline in membership in terms of the impact of war and the resignation of those who had joined the Association solely on account of the national insurance upheaval. See *BMJ* Supplement, 3 June 1922, ii. During the Second World War BMA membership and *Journal* circulation rose substantially.

1930s when it stabilized before falling back slightly. The *Journal*'s circulation fluctuated correspondingly. In the late 1930s, when membership picked up again, the *Journal*'s circulation did likewise. By 1939 it had risen to 42 750, a growth of about 82 per cent over the 1918 figure (see Table 9.1). This was an impressive achievement in a period of just over two decades. Yet it was caused entirely by expansion of the Association; sales to non-members actually fell by several hundred between 1918 and 1939 (though revenue from sales was larger owing to the *Journal*'s higher price).

Table 9.1 *Journal* circulation and BMA membership, selected years, 1918–1939

Year	Circulation	Membership
1918	23 546	19 982
1919	24 520	21 355
1920	26 195	22 594
1921	27 247	23 621
1922	27 600	24 282
1923	29 036	26 112
1924	31 339	28 431
1925	33 530	30 524
1926	35 920	32 350
1927	36 688	33 625
1928	37 850	34 558
1929	39 000	35 183
1934	37 750	35 029
1935	37 500	35 383
1937	40 000	37 204
1939	42 750	39 449

Note: As ever, circulation and membership figures could fluctuate in the course of a year. Although it is not always clear, circulation figures generally apply to the average number of copies printed. This could exceed the number distributed to members or sold to subscribers.

These statistics are open to differing interpretations. On the one hand, they may be seen as showing that circulation growth was wholly the product of BMA success and that it owed little or nothing to the *Journal*'s quality. On the other hand, there is no way of knowing how far the *Journal* was responsible for attracting new members into the Association. Given that the *Journal* was an important benefit of BMA membership, it is possible that it had much to do with the Association's inter-war growth. There has long been a myth that under Horner's editorship many BMA members tossed the *Journal* unopened into their wastepaper baskets. But there is no evidence of whether this was a widespread practice. In 1946 a *Journal* correspondent wrote: 'There must be thousands of members of the BMA who joined because it was the cheapest means of obtaining the *Journal.*' Two weeks later came the response that many doctors did not join the Association because part of the subscription went towards a journal they did not want. Douglas Swinscow, who became a deputy editor of the *Journal*, notes in his autobiography that he 'joined the BMA so that I could obtain the *BMJ*'.[2]

In producing the *Journal* the major costs were, in descending order of magnitude, printing, that is, compositors' wages and machining, paper, and postage for despatch. In 1928 these items accounted for around £52 000 (72 per cent) of *Journal* expenditure. Despatch postage alone accounted for almost £14 000, a figure substantially higher than that spent on running the editorial department (£10 600). As for income, most of the money needed to run the inter-war *Journal* continued to come from advertising. In 1913 advertisements had yielded revenue of £24 200. Income from this source fell in the course of the war; in 1918 it amounted to only £17 700. Thereafter it increased considerably (see Table 9.2), though tending to rise or fall according to the state of the national economy. While advertising revenue met most *Journal* expenditure, it was never enough to cover the full running costs. The books had to be balanced by other means, chiefly through sales and by subvention from BMA funds. Table 9.3 gives figures of total annual income and expenditure in the inter-war period along with details of the Association's subsidy.

Table 9.2 *Journal* advertising and sales revenue, 1913–1938 (at five yearly intervals, to nearest £100)

Year	Advertising Revenue	Sales Revenue
1913	24 200	2900
1918	17 700	5900
1923	38 800	7300
1928	51 800	6500
1933	50 500	5600
1938	62 800	6300

Note: In 1913 the price of the *Journal* for non-members was 6d. It was raised to 8d in March 1917, to 1s in April 1918, and to 1s 3d in January 1921. There was no further increase until January 1942. *BMJ* mss. Horner File. Memo. from F. G. Bryan dated 26 Jan. 1968.

Clearly the *Journal*'s financial viability depended on transfers from the BMA's subscription income. Occasionally some members took this to mean

[2] *BMJ* Supplement, 9 July 1949, 34; *Journal*, 7 Dec. 1946, 873; 21 Dec. 1946, 961; *Munk's Roll*, vii (London: Royal College of Physicians, 1985), pp. 103–6; T. D. V. Swinscow, *Reap a Destiny* (Cambridge: Cambridge University Press, 1989), p. 131.

Table 9.3 *Journal* income and expenditure 1913–1938 (at five yearly intervals to nearest £100)

Year	Income	Expenditure	Balance from Subs
1913	28 900	40 000	11 000
1918	24 600	32 200	7 600
1923	47 600	56 800	9 200
1928	60 400	72 500	12 100
1933	58 700	67 600	8 900
1938	70 100	89 300	19 200

that the *Journal* was a 'lame duck', incapable of supporting itself through its own endeavours. For example, at the 1920 ARM Dr Douglas of Fife asked why the *Journal* 'was not a paying concern . . . The Association should not have to pay anything for the JOURNAL at all.'[3] But such a question was hardly justified. The annual deficit was caused entirely by the fact that most copies were not sold but supplied post-free to BMA members. Hence, the size of the subvention may be seen as representing that portion of the BMA subscription allocated to the production of a weekly periodical. On this basis, members were, in 1928, receiving their weekly *Journal* at a cost of between 6s and 7s a year, in other words, for less than 2d a week. It can hardly be argued that this was poor value. As the BMA's Treasurer said in his reply to Douglas:

> if the Association did not have Representative Meetings and did not have to keep an establishment at 429, Strand, and did no medico-political work, and Dr. Douglas simply had to pay two guineas for his JOURNAL delivered to him, the balance sheet would show a profit of £31,000 a year. The JOURNAL was the best paying concern attached to the Association.[4]

Of course, this ducked the question of whether 22 500 people would have subscribed to a journal which did not come automatically as part of a membership package. On the other hand, after the 1860s there was never any serious attempt by members to curtail the *Journal* or separate it from the Association.

The editorship of the *Journal* changed only once in the inter-war years, when Gerald Horner, Williams's assistant editor since 1917, took the editorial chair at the age of 46.[5] Horner faced the challenging task of succeeding a man universally admired but who, perhaps owing to ill-health, had allowed the *Journal* to drift during his final years. Since the end of the

[3] *BMJ* Supplement, 3 July 1920, 3.
[4] *Ibid.*
[5] Horner was customarily known either by his second name, Gerald, or as N. G.

war it had become staid in terms of both appearance and content. Its looks had changed little since Victorian days. There were the same closely printed columns—albeit, since 1903, on a larger page—with scarcely more or better illustrations than Hart had used.[6] Content, too, bore a marked resemblance to that of a decade or even two decades earlier. Comparison of 1907 volumes with those for 1927 reveals contents and layout of remarkable similarity. One notable difference is that the earlier year included the 'secret remedies' reports, which sustained the Ernest Hart tradition of socio-medical journalism. In the inter-war years this tradition more or less perished. With it went the *Journal*'s 'human face'.

Perhaps the most important social phenomena of the inter-war years were economic depression and mass unemployment. Ernest Hart would have found much of medical interest in these evils; his successors found little about which to protest or even comment. In 1931 unemployment reached its peak for the inter-war period, but the *BMJ* index includes no entry for unemployment. The year was also one of deep financial and political crisis, leading to severe cuts in national expenditure on health and social services and the collapse of the second Labour government. All of this passed virtually unnoticed by the *Journal*.

Williams, having been in poor health for some time, retired in January 1928 at the age of 73. It is clear that he went reluctantly. The BMA Council had to use all its powers of persuasion, including the offer of three months' salary in lieu of notice, plus a special 'grant' of £1000 as compensation for loss of office, in order to induce him to leave on the 30th anniversary of his appointment as editor.[7] When his retirement was announced *The Times* devoted a leading article to an assessment of his career.[8] While this was a wordy piece of journalism, long on generalities and short on detail, it was a notable tribute to a man who had done much to develop the *Journal*'s scientific and clinical coverage. Yet for all his achievements, there can be little doubt that Williams remained in office for too long; having 'lived for the *Journal* for the greater part of half a century . . . [he] . . . shrank from the prospect of idleness' and, like Hart, clung limpet-like to the editorial chair.[9] The staffing of the editorial department had been allowed to fall to a dangerously low level so that when Horner took over there was only one other medically qualified member of staff. As Horner later noted in a biographical note written in the third person, by 1928, 'the great journal of which he now assumed sole charge had been in a shaky condition for years

[6] For criticism of the standard of *Journal* illustration see *BMJ* Supplement, 6 May 1922, 130; 28 April 1923, 130; 23 July 1927, 33; 15 Oct. 1927, 145.

[7] BMA mss. MCCSC, Council Minutes 14 Dec. 1927, pp. 88–9. At the time of his retirement Williams's salary was £2000 p.a.

[8] *The Times*, 2 Jan. 1928.

[9] *Journal*, 13 March 1954, 648–9.

past.'[10] What was needed was a dynamic editor capable of sparking a revival in its flagging fortunes. Horner, emphatically, was not that man.

Norman Gerald Horner was born in 1882 in Tonbridge, Kent, where his father was a general practitioner and medical officer to Tonbridge School. He attended that school himself before going to Caius College, Cambridge, from where he graduated BA in the natural science tripos in 1902. Horner received his medical training at St Bartholomew's Hospital and qualified MRCS and LRCP in January 1906. He graduated from Cambridge MB and BCh in 1910, and MD in 1919. In 1911, after brief appointments in hospitals and general practice, during which time he acquired journalistic and editorial experience on the *St Bartholomew's Hospital Journal* and the *Hospital*, he was employed by Squire Sprigge as assistant editor of the *Lancet*. There he was much occupied in reporting the national insurance question. In 1915 Horner left the *Lancet* to take a temporary commission in the RAMC, seeing service as a captain on the western front. He returned to England two years later to become assistant editor of the *BMJ*, thereby commencing a 29-year association with the *Journal*, of which 19 (1928–1946) were as editor. His initial salary was £750 a year on a scale rising (by increments of £50 a year) to a maximum of £1000 a year.[11]

The manner of Horner's appointment to the *BMJ* staff says much about the man. The position was obtained for him by his wife—a dominant woman who pushed her husband beyond the limit of his professional capabilities. When it was known that Charles Taylor intended to resign, 'leaving Dawson Williams alone to conduct the journal, Mrs. Horner went of her own accord to see Dr. Williams, told him that Horner did not want to return to *The Lancet*, where he had already been replaced, and persuaded him to get Horner released from the army for the *B.M.J.*'[12]

In Squire Sprigge and Dawson Williams Horner had worked with two of the most eminent twentieth-century medical editors. His apprenticeship and long *Journal* experience made him a natural choice as Williams's successor. The BMA did not advertise the editorship and considered no candidates other than Horner. But though he may have been kindly, courteous, knowledgeable in medical matters, and the possessor of an 'incisive mind and considerable literary gifts', he was not a judicious choice.[13] Temperamentally incapable of providing leadership, distrustful of innovation, and reluctant to

[10] *BMJ* mss. Horner File, Norman Gerald Horner. Personal Memoirs, handwritten notes, pp. 8–9. This note formed the basis for Horner's obituary notice. The BMA made sure that it never again was saddled with an editor who had outlived his usefulness by introducing, with Horner's appointment, a mandatory retirement age of 65.

[11] In his final year as assistant editor, 1927, Horner's salary was £1500.

[12] R. S. Stevenson, *Goodbye Harley Street* (London: Christopher Johnson, 1954), p. 88; Author's interview with T. D. V. Swinscow, 9 Feb. 1989.

[13] *Journal*, 13 March 1954, 648–51. Hart was the last *BMJ* editor appointed in open competition. His successors have all been promoted from within the editorial office.

assume responsibility, Horner was totally unsuited to editing a periodical which, under his two immediate predecessors, had become an authoritative voice in medicine. Horner was pedantic and, like most pedants, lacked vision. Diffident, quiet, shy, and weak, he possessed little self-confidence and was extremely sensitive even to well-meant criticism. What would such a man have made of the complaint of one disgruntled BMA member who wrote: 'It is clear that the British Medical *Journal* is run on the Hitlerite policy'?

Above all, Horner considered himself unworthy of editing the *Journal*, for he had always 'worshipped at the shrine' of Williams and could not regard himself as an adequate replacement to his 'great chief'. Consequently, when he became editor he was averse to making any changes from the 'halcyon days', and the *Journal* became firmly stuck in a rut. Shortly before his death Hugh Clegg, Horner's successor as editor, described what it had been like to work under a man who 'did nothing except sit there and shift columns'. The *Journal*, he recalled, 'wasn't being edited and people were beginning to complain'. On one occasion in the early 1930s Clegg and a sub-editor, Robin Gray, confronted Horner with a request for a 'declaration of policy'. All they succeeded in doing was to reduce Horner to a state of embarrassed silence. Gray resigned shortly afterwards maintaining that Horner would drive him mad if he remained.[14]

Shortly after Horner's appointment, *The Times* suggested that, because 'the *Journal* found its way into the house of nearly every English medical practitioner throughout the world', the responsibility of running it was 'well-nigh crushing'. The sad truth is that Horner was well and truly crushed.[15] If Michael Foot had Horner in mind when he wrote of the 'powerful and opinionated editor' of the *BMJ* as an 'independent power within the innermost BMA councils', demanding and obtaining full editorial freedom, he was lamentably far from the truth.[16]

Of other editorial staff in the 1920s and 1930s there is little to say, but not because they were few; indeed, during Horner's early years they came and went with remarkable speed and regularity. For his part Horner always believed that the Association did not fully appreciate the difficulties which these repeated arrivals and departures caused him.[17] To what extent Horner contributed to the rapid turnover is a moot point. For $2\frac{1}{2}$ years between 1920 and 1923, R. Scott Stevenson was sub-editor. In a volume of reminiscences written towards the end of his life, he recalled his time on the *Journal* staff. This had commenced when Williams's death was imminently expected:

[14] *BMJ* mss. Clegg File, Transcript of Richard Smith's interview with Hugh Clegg, Jan. 1982.

[15] *Ibid.*; *BMJ* mss. JCM (1943–4) JNL. 3, I Harris to Lord Dawson of Penn, 18 Nov. 1943; *BMJ* Supplement, 28 July 1928, 34; *The Times*, 28 Feb. 1928; R. S. Stevenson, *Goodbye Harley Street*, p. 88 (note 12).

[16] Michael Foot, *Aneurin Bevan* (London: Macgibbon and Key, 1962 and 1973), Vol. II, pp. 111, 116.

[17] *Journal*, 13 March 1954, 648–51.

I was not a very good 'sub-editor' for that was the inaccurate term then given to the third man on the staff of the *Journal*. I had expected a post of some responsibility—after all, I had been in practice and on a hospital staff in Manchester and had dropped my income to one third for the sake of the opportunity of coming to London—but when the editor recovered I merely saw the callers nobody else would see, went to the functions with which nobody else could be bothered, wrote annotations and sometimes leaders on the duller or more trivial subjects, put in or took out the commas or semicolons and knocked the capitals down to 'lower case', wrote or edited the abstracts from the foreign medical journals, but never once discussed the contents of the *Journal* with the editor, or received a word of approval or of condemnation from him.[18]

The one other member of the inter-war editorial staff who should be mentioned at this stage is Hugh Clegg since he went on to succeed Horner as editor in 1947. Clegg was appointed sub-editor in April 1931 at a salary of £750 a year (on a scale rising to £1000). In 1934 he became the *Journal*'s first deputy editor.[19]

Chiefly typographical

Wartime shortages and economies had caused a marked deterioration in the appearance of the *Journal*. With the return of peace and renewed access to better paper, there was some improvement. During the 1920s, despite criticism by members on such matters as quality of illustration, few attempts were made to improve standards of design and presentation. In fact it was not until the 1930s that the *Journal* received the full 'face-lift' it needed.

During its time in the Strand the *Journal* had always employed its own compositors. Until 1923 they set by hand the type which was then sent out for printing, machining, and distribution by outside contractors. As we have seen, Odhams had undertaken these tasks since 1911. In fact, their contract was renewed for most of the inter-war period, being terminated only in 1937.[20] In 1923 the BMA Council, recognizing that the *Journal*'s type had become so dilapidated that it needed urgent replacement, authorized the purchase, at a cost of £4750, of four linotype triplex machines 'of the most modern pattern' in order to allow machine-setting.[21] Hugh Clegg later wrote that 'Linotype machines were introduced into this country in 1889, but it took the *B.M.J.* longer probally [sic], than any other periodical to realize that mechanical setting by linotype was more efficient and more economical.'[22] The change greatly affected the compositors 'who had been good servants of

[18] R. S. Stevenson, *In a Harley Street Mirror* (London: Christopher Johnson, 1951), p. 5. In the late 1930s Stevenson served on the *Journal*'s short-lived Board of Directors.

[19] *BMJ* mss. JCM (1933–4) JNL. 20, Agenda, 18 May 1934.

[20] *BMJ* Supplement, 24 April 1937, 203.

[21] *Ibid.*, 28 April 1923, 130; 3 May 1924, 186.

[22] *BMJ* mss. JCM (1951–2) JNL. 7, Publishing Sub-committee, Editor's Memorandum, 23 Aug. 1951.

British Medical Journal, October 29th, 1932

The British Medical Journal

THE JOURNAL OF THE BRITISH MEDICAL ASSOCIATION

ANNUAL PANEL CONFERENCE
See "Supplement"

Including an Epitome of Current Medical Literature
WITH SUPPLEMENT

No. 3747 SATURDAY, OCTOBER 29, 1932 Price 1/3

"Pitibulin" (Trade Mark)

Denotes Unvarying Pituitary Extract

Conforming to the requirements of the Therapeutic Substances Regulations, 1927, "Pitibulin" is prepared according to the official standards, its activity being expressed in terms of the accepted unit.

"Pitibulin" maintains the stringently high criteria of therapeutic efficiency, safety in use and stability, self-imposed by its manufacturers—qualities which have given it its high place in the esteem of physicians.

It has made a reputation among the Profession as the Pituitary Extract which can be relied on in emergency.

"Pitibulin" is supplied in boxes of 6 and 12 ampoules containing 2·5, 5 and 10 units per ampoule.

Literature giving fuller particulars of the therapeutic applications of "Pitibulin" will be sent on request.

Allen & Hanburys Ltd., London, E.2.

Telephone: Bishopsgate 3201 (10 lines) Telegrams: "Greenburys Beth London"

ISSUED WEEKLY] [COPYRIGHT] [REGISTERED AS A NEWSPAPER

BRITISH MEDICAL JOURNAL

JOURNAL OF THE

BRITISH MEDICAL ASSOCIATION

SATURDAY JANUARY 9 1937

PRINCIPAL CONTENTS

WITH SUPPLEMENT AND EPITOME

LONDON
BRITISH MEDICAL ASSOCIATION
TAVISTOCK SQUARE

REGISTERED AS A NEWSPAPER *Copyright* WEEKLY, PRICE 1/3, No. 3966

Two *BMJ* covers, before and after Morison's re-design. Source: *British Medical Journal.*

the Association for many years'. But it was achieved without falling foul of their trade union. Indeed, as the chairman of the Journal Committee ironically reported, 'the matter had been managed so well that the JOURNAL had had what was probably unique—a compliment paid to it by the general secretary of the Compositors' Union in London for the consideration shown to senior members of the printing staff.'[23]

In 1925 the BMA moved from the Strand, where it had been located for almost half a century, to its new home in Tavistock Square. The last issue of the *Journal* to be put together on the old premises was that of 30 May 1925. During the Whitsun holidays the editorial and printing departments, under Horner's supervision, moved to the new site. The four type-setting machines were dismantled and re-positioned on the fourth floor of the north-east wing, where they were shortly joined by a fifth, capable of setting display advertisements.[24] The new arrangement was less than a year old when the unthinkable occurred—the *Journal* lost an issue. The reason, of course, was the 1926 General Strike. Odhams' print workers walked out on 4 May and did not return till 17 May. The *Journal*'s type-setters were called out on 6 May and remained on strike for a week. As a result the 8 May issue failed to appear; the next number came out late bearing the double date 'May 8th and 15th 1926'.[25] This appears to have been the only time in the *Journal*'s history when it failed to make its scheduled appearance in some form or other.

Although the early 1930s were years of some strain in both the editorial and printing departments—with the exception of Horner, editorial staff changed almost completely in both 1930 and 1931—several changes aimed at improving the *Journal*'s appearance were introduced. These included improved paper, new type faces, and the adoption of a photogravure process for reproducing special plates.[26] But in 1934 two members of the Journal Committee—the chairman, Ronald Gordon, and Professor Richard Berry—acting on comments received from members of the Association, drew up a memorandum suggesting the need for further improvements.[27] This led to the appointment of a 'special sub-committee' to investigate the matter. It comprised Gordon, Berry, Clegg, Horner, and Ferris-Scott, who was then the BMA's financial secretary and the *Journal*'s business manager. Of these, the first three played the most prominent parts. Reviewing these developments in its 1935 report Council concluded that though 'improvement has been achieved and . . . many criticisms have been met, much yet remains to be done'. Hence the decision 'to take the necessary steps to bring the *Journal*

[23] *BMJ* Supplement, 28 July 1923, 54.

[24] *Ibid.*, 24 April 1926, 142.

[25] *Ibid.*, 23 April 1927, 141–2.

[26] *Ibid.*, 19 April 1930, 129; 25 April 1931, 138; 30 April 1932, 173; 21 April 1934, 170–1; *Journal*, 5 Dec. 1931, 1051–2.

[27] *BMJ* mss. JCM (1933–4) JNL. 19, 16 March 1934.

into accord with modern habits of reading and modern standards of typography'.[28]

On Horner's recommendation the sub-committee approached an 'expert in typography', Stanley Morison, who, in the mid-1930s, having recently re-designed *The Times*, was at the height of his fame.[29] Morison offered his services in preliminary discussions for no fee, after which the sub-committee recommended that the princely figure of up to £25 should be set aside to meet fees for technical advice.[30] On 12 April 1935 Morison delivered his observations on the *BMJ*'s typography. The *Journal* was, he said, 'from a typographical standpoint a reasonably good amateur production', old fashioned and inferior to the standards of the daily press certainly, but rather better than the average learned journal. Although it was arguable that a publication that aimed at keeping readers abreast of the latest developments in medicine 'should employ the most efficient typographical technique for this purpose', there was, thought Morison, no necessity to change type and layout unless there was general dissatisfaction among readers or members of the sub-committee. Having been informed that a considerable body of opinion did favour change, Morison produced a string of criticisms of the *Journal*'s existing design, and proposals for its re-design. Indeed, as is now apparent, all of the changes made in 1937 originated with Morison and had been worked out by him almost as soon as he was first approached. For these services Morison was paid one hundred guineas.[31]

The sub-committee, having accepted Morison's criticisms and recommendations, then sought to ascertain their financial implications. It reached two major conclusions. First, that 'a much better *Journal* can be produced at less cost if it were composed, machined and despatched by an outside firm of printers.' Second, that the employment of a full-time 'advertising canvasser' might increase advertising revenue by between 50 and 100 per cent. In addition, it arrived at a number of 'minor conclusions', including the need to

[28] *BMJ* Supplement, 20 April 1935, 155. See 25 April 1936, 199; *Journal*, 2 Jan. 1937, 32; R. S. Stevenson, *Goodbye Harley Street*, p. 89 (note 12).

[29] Stanley Arthur Morison (1889–1967) left school at the age of 14 and was soon a clerk with the London City Mission. In 1912 he discovered an interest in printing and typography, and there followed a number of jobs in publishing. In the 1920s he became a freelance consultant, establishing himself as 'Britain's greatest authority on letter design'. A prolific writer and designer, Morison served the Monotype Corporation, Cambridge University Press, and *The Times* for many years. In 1932 *The Times*, with which he was connected till 1960, was re-designed to his specification. At the time of his association with the BMA he was beginning the task of writing and editing *The History of The Times* (London: The Times, 1935–52). *Dictionary of National Biography 1961–1970* (Oxford: Oxford University Press, 1981). See Nicolas Barker, *Stanley Morison* (London: Macmillan, 1972).

[30] *BMJ* mss. JCM (1934–5) JNL. 21, 15 March 1935.

[31] *Ibid.*, JNL. 27, Special Sub-committee, Report by Dr. Clegg of Suggestions Put Forward by Mr. Stanley Morison, 12 April 1935; JCM (1936–7) JNL. 21, 19 March 1937.

improve the quality of paper, provide a better cover, and to achieve more publicity for the *Journal*.[32] Some years later Clegg recalled:

> When it was proposed in 1935 that the composing room should be dismantled and the machines sold there was considerable opposition to the the [sic] idea, an opposition that was manifest at many meetings of the Journal Committee and vigorously sustained in Council. It was looked upon almost as a revolutionary proposal. Yet the B.M.J. must have been the only periodical left in London which then owned its own composing room.[33]

In its inquiries relating to design and presentation, the sub-committee came across some worrying matters relating to the *Journal*'s business management. It found, for example, that there was no binding contract to print the *Journal* and, therefore, 'no absolute assurance that the work will be regularly continued'. Similarly, there was no binding contract to supply paper. It was bought from month to month from different firms without tender. An agent was employed on a 2 per cent commission to inspect and approve the *Journal*'s paper, but 'so far as can be ascertained, no existing member of either the *Journal* or Finance Committee was aware of this appointment.' The sub-committee also expressed dissatisfaction with arrangements relating to the sale of advertising space.

These discoveries led to the conclusion that the *Journal* needed 'much closer and more frequent supervision' than the Journal Committee could provide. The sub-committee therefore proposed that, while the Journal Committee should remain responsible for directing 'general policy', a board of directors should take charge of *Journal* production. Its members would be elected at three-yearly intervals, meet at least 10 times a year, and receive payment for their work.

In 1936 Council reached several decisions relating to production and management. First, a new typography and layout would be introduced from the first issue of 1937. This would include a re-designed cover incorporating Eric Gill's serpent, staff, and sash emblem, printed in red on a grey background, which would replace the medallion featuring Charles Hastings's portrait. This design was 'not the choice of the Journal Committee but the choice of a gentleman [Morison] who was regarded as a great authority on typography and who thought that the old medallion was archaic'. Gill was also responsible for the new light-faced type used on the front cover. Contents were to be set out on a front cover bereft of advertising. Second, the BMA's composing department was to be closed and the work of composition, as well as of machining and despatch, performed by Eyre and

[32] *BMJ* mss. JCM (1935–6) JNL. 13(A), Report of the Journal Special Sub-Committee (undated).

[33] *Ibid.*, JCM (1951–2) JNL. 7, Publishing Sub-committee, Editor's Memorandum, 23 Aug. 1951.

Spottiswoode, who had won a five-year contract through competitive tender. Third, a contract for paper supply had been agreed with another firm. Fourth, management of the *Journal* was to be completely re-organized with the appointment of a 'Board of Directors'. The new Board took charge of business matters, including staffing, external contracts, and advertising. One of its first acts was to appoint an experienced advertising manager, Charles Francis. Establishment of the Board left the Journal Committee with no real role. In consequence, its members, without demur from Horner, decided 'to take a closer part in considering the contents of the *Journal*'. The effect was significantly to reduce editorial independence. Ernest Hart must have turned in his grave.[34]

The *Journal* 'came out in its new dress' on 2 January 1937. The revision was far-reaching, and, indeed, went from cover to cover. For the first time, the principal contents were displayed, as they have been ever since, on a front cover from which advertising was absent. Furthermore:

> types of a new and more legible design have been composed in rightly adjusted columns, surmounted by new heading types of related design, and the whole bound up within a stronger pair of covers. The most striking change of all is that of the front cover, where the grey paper and the scarlet device present what are in fact the only revolutionary innovations.[35]

Although it had been intended that outside contractors would be responsible from the outset for producing the re-designed *Journal*, 'for technical reasons connected with the new machinery ordered by the new printers', that is, a rotary printing-press, composing continued to be 'in-house' for the first three months of 1937. Only then was the employment of the 29 compositors terminated and the printing equipment sold. The space freed by the new arrangements gave the editorial department more accommodation.[36]

The *Journal*'s long-overdue re-design met with widespread approval. In 1937 the Chairman of the Representative Body told an enthusiastic Annual Representative Meeting that 'With the changes made and in prospect he believed the *British Medical Journal* would be the outstanding medical journal of the world.'[37] Council noted in its Annual Report for 1936–7 that

[34] In 1944 the Board was re-named the Publishing Sub-Committee of the Journal Committee. As such it continued to be responsible for the *Journal*'s business management. *BMJ* mss. JCM (1943–4) JNL. 10, Minutes of Sub-Committee re. Relationship between the Journal Committee and the Board of Directors, 25 Jan. 1944; JNL. 23, Publishing Sub-Committee, Agenda, 20 April 1944; JCM (1951–2) JNL. 7, Editor's Memorandum, 23 Aug. 1951; *BMJ* Supplement, 27 June 1936, 343; 24 April 1937, 207–8; 24 July 1937, 54; *Journal*, 30 Nov. 1940, 751; R. S. Stevenson, *In a Harley Street Mirror*, pp. 34–5 (note 18).

[35] *Journal*, 2 Jan. 1937, 32–3. The *Journal* switched to the Harvard system of referencing from the same issue.

[36] *BMJ* Supplement, 24 April 1937, 207–8. Almost all these staff were immediately found employment elsewhere, most with Eyre and Spottiswoode. See *BMJ* mss. JCM (1935–6) JNL. 29, 5 June 1936; JCM (1951–2) JNL. 7, Editor's Memorandum, 23 Aug. 1951.

[37] *BMJ* Supplement, 24 July 1937, 55.

'messages of congratulation still continue to reach headquarters and criticisms have been very few.'[38] One of the 'few' was directed at the removal from the cover of the medallion bearing the portrait of Charles Hastings. At the 1937 ARM Dr G. T. Foster-Smith of the BMA's south-west Essex division, moved: 'That this meeting views with horror and amazement the sacrifice of the memory of Sir Charles Hastings and instructs the Council to surmount the alleged difficulties in the restoration of his image and superscription to the place of honour on the cover of the *British Medical Journal*.' Although Foster-Smith insisted that the change was 'a blot on the memory of the BMA's founder', his motion was lost.[39] The *Journal* later noted that Foster-Smith sounded 'the only discordant note in a chorus of praise that was as flattering as it was unexpected'. When Gill died in 1940 it observed that 'The four years that have almost passed have fixed Mr. Gill's beautiful design firmly in our affections and admiration.'[40] Charles Hastings has never (yet) regained his place on the cover; Eric Gill's motif, on the other hand, is still (1989) to be seen there, albeit not in its original colour and in a marginal position. In the context of *Journal* history, Hastings's relegation was not inappropriate for, as we have seen, he had not always been one of its champions.

Morison's typographical reforms lasted till the 1960s when further updating was thought to be necessary. Clegg again approached Morison, but Morison felt that a younger man should be entrusted with the task. Accordingly, the typographical director of Eyre and Spottiswoode was commissioned to undertake the job. In 1963, shortly after the introduction of major changes in layout, the *Journal* switched from Times New Roman print to Plantin.[41]

Family affairs

In the Victorian period the *Journal* had been part of the medical profession's virtual conspiracy of silence on the subject of contraception (see Chapter 7). In contrast, during the inter-war period artificial birth control became a widely discussed, if still controversial, subject both in society at large and in the pages of the *BMJ*. Although partly a medical issue, contraception was also inextricably linked with certain fundamental social, psychological, and moral questions, including population politics, eugenics, and changing notions of motherhood, womanhood, and sexuality. This, after all, was the

[38] *Ibid.*, 24 April 1937, 207; 24 July 1937, 54–5.
[39] *Ibid.*, 24 July 1937, 54.
[40] *Journal*, 30 Nov. 1940, 751.
[41] *BMJ* mss. JCM (1961–2) JNL. 23, Agenda, 16 May 1962; JCM (1962–3) JNL. 21, 5 June 1963.

age of Freud and Havelock Ellis, of economic depression, social Darwinism, and the rise of the European dictatorships.

Why did birth control become a big issue in the 1920s and 1930s? Undoubtedly the war was important in bringing the matter into the open, for it 'helped to break down official prejudice about contraception' and to familiarize people with the condom. Moreover, because of the human losses it entailed, the war re-opened the debate on population and the birth rate and, hence, on maternal welfare, which had been a familiar feature of the Edwardian years. In addition, by the 1920s the means existed for artificial contraception on a large scale.[42] The question was whether it was medically and socially desirable.

Eugenists were ambivalent about contraception. Some feared that, while the 'fit' and successful controlled their fertility, social and economic failures—the 'unfit'—would supply an ever-increasing proportion of the population. There was evidence that the decline in the birth rate since the 1870s was socially, if not genetically, differentiated. In 1920 a leading article in the *Journal* expressed serious concern about the decline of fertility among the middle and upper classes, and the 'fecundity of the poor and miserable', among whom 'there are likely to remain vast numbers of persons who will not place even the restraint upon their sexual impulses which the use of contraceptives involves.' The result, it feared, would be national decadence and national disaster.[43]

Among the proposed eugenist solutions for reversing this trend were voluntary sterilization of and State birth control for the 'unfit' or 'worst stocks', and action 'by such means as changes in the marriage and divorce laws' to increase the birth rate of the 'classes superior in intelligence and capacity'.[44] In Germany and some US states this sort of thinking found legislative expression, including in sterilization laws. But though such questions were regularly discussed in inter-war Britain, no action was taken.[45] Doctors formed a sizeable proportion of the membership of the Eugenics Society, and the Royal College of Physicians and other medical bodies supported the movement for voluntary sterilization, but most doctors

[42] Jeffrey Weeks, *Sex, Politics and Society. The Regulation of Sexuality Since 1800* (London: Longman, 1981), pp. 187–8; J. Peel, 'The Manufacture and Retailing of Contraceptives in England', *Population Studies* (1963) xvii, 116–20. This was less a result of technical innovation than the growing range of products and retail outlets.

[43] *Journal*, 1 May 1920, 611–12; see 30 Oct. 1920, 671-2. In fact, during the inter-war years the decline in family size was a cross-class phenomenon. J. Weeks, *Sex, Politics and Society*, p. 202 (note 42).

[44] These views were expressed by some speakers at a meeting of the London Association of the Medical Women's Federation. See *Journal*, 2 July 1921, 11–12.

[45] Greta Jones, *Social Hygiene in Twentieth Century Britain* (London: Croom Helm, 1986); see Charles Webster (ed.), *Biology Medicine and Society, 1840–1940* (Cambridge: Cambridge University Press, 1981), p. 7.

shunned the movement. Both the BMA and the *BMJ* 'showed consistent hostility to eugenics over a period of years'.[46]

The medical profession held a wide range of views about artificial contraception. Some opposed it, 'even in the poorest classes', on moral, religious, and physiological grounds, believing that, as well as causing gynaecological problems, it 'removed the fear of consequences from the husband, and hence encouraged too frequent sexual intercourse. Mankind was already oversexed ... and unbridled sex passions were likely to lead to effeminacy and degeneration, to war against self-control and self-respect.'[47] Here was the Shavian precept—that marriage combined 'the maximum of temptation with the maximum of opportunity'—gone mad. Some associated contraception with prostitution. Since Christian marriage ostensibly existed for the procreation of children, artificial contraception within marriage, it was argued, undermined a sacred institution and reduced wives to the level of prostitutes.[48]

During the 1920s the central figure in much of the discussion relating to birth control was Dr Marie Stopes (1880–1958). Stopes was not medically qualified but a Doctor of Science and a PhD. She was an academic palaeobotanist whose unhappy and unconsummated first marriage had led to her taking a deep interest in sexual relations. In London in 1921 she founded, with her second husband, Humphrey Verdon-Roe, the Mother's Clinic for Birth Control. Her book, *Married Love* (1918), was not a treatise on contraception, indeed, it 'dealt scarcely at all with birth control'.[49] Rather, it was, as the *Journal* delicately put it, 'a small work ... to meet the need of healthy young people of the educated class for information as to the sexual responsibilities of marriage'. In its review the *Journal* gave the book a cautious welcome:

> To the married and to those about to marry, provided they are normal in mind and body and not afraid of facing facts, this should prove ... most helpful. ... We therefore commend it to medical men and women, and through them to those of the general public who in their judgement are likely to profit by its teaching.[50]

[46] G. R. Searle, 'Eugenics and Class', in C. Webster (ed.), *Biology, Medicine and Society*, p. 226 (note 45); G. Jones, *Social Hygiene in Twentieth Century Britain*, pp. 89, 91, 98 (note 45).

[47] *Journal*, 2 July 1921, 11–12; 16 July 1921, 93–4. Lesley A. Hall refers to the prevalence of the view that 'excessive marital indulgence could ruin the health of both partners'. ' "Somehow Very Distasteful": Doctors, Men and Sexual Problems between the Wars', *Journal of Contemporary History* (1985) **20**: 554.

[48] See Lucy Bland, 'Purity, Motherhood, Pleasure or Threat? Definitions of Female Sexuality' in Sue Cartledge and Joanna Ryan, *Sex and Love. New Thoughts on Old Contradictions* (London: Women's Press, 1983), p. 13.

[49] *Dictionary of National Biography, 1951–1960* (London: Oxford University Press, 1971). See Ruth Hall, *Marie Stopes. A Biography* (London: André Deutsch, 1978).

[50] *Journal*, 4 May 1918, 510. The rest of the medical press was also welcoming. See L. A. Hall, ' "Somehow Very Distasteful": Doctors, Men and Sexual Problems between the Wars', p. 561 (note 47).

There was certainly no hint here of the stormy relationship which the tempestuous and self-adulatory Stopes and the *BMJ* were destined to have.[51]

The *Journal*'s birth control debate 'took off' in 1921 after it summarized a discussion of the subject by the London Association of the Medical Women's Federation. In the course of this, several speakers, but especially Mary Scharlieb, the 76-year-old author of books with such titles as *Womanhood and Race Regeneration* (1912), expressed views violently antipathetic to contraception.[52] During July and August this prompted a stream of forthright, not to say, vitriolic, correspondence, including letters from Stopes and the doctor she later sued for libel, Halliday Sutherland.[53] Opinion as to the benefits or otherwise of contraception was pretty well divided. At the end of the summer Dawson Williams called a halt, after which he declined to reopen the *Journal*'s correspondence columns for this kind of discussion.[54] However, in October he did publish a short report on the first meeting of the Medical Women's Federation. This listed contraceptive methods, and in so doing, it has been claimed, 'the *British Medical Journal* broke entirely new ground by summarizing, for the first time in a medical paper, the practical methods of contraception.'[55]

At this time the closest the *Journal* came to expressing an editorial opinion was in a review of a pamphlet, *Love—Marriage—Birth Control* (1922), written by Lord Dawson of Penn, a long-time supporter of birth control.[56] In this the *Journal* suggested that, though the time was not ripe for 'dogmatic statement', the practice of birth control was 'a matter of conscience between the two parties to a marriage . . . and . . . if they seek medical advice, for the judgement of the doctor they may consult'. The *Journal* conceded that there were circumstances in which contraception was justified, but those circumstances largely concerned cases where conception was likely to pose health risks.[57] This limited approval of contraception nevertheless contrasted starkly with a 1901 leader in which it was stated that 'The medical profession

[51] Stopes clashed not only with the *Journal* but with the medical profession at large, which she regarded with scarcely disguised contempt. Although some doctors admired Stopes, generally the profession tended to suspect her. See R. A. Soloway, *Birth Control and the Population Question in England, 1877–1930* (Chapel Hill, North Carolina: University of North Carolina University Press, 1982), pp. 266–7; Ruth Hall (ed.), *Dear Dr Stopes. Sex in the 1920s* (London: André Deutsch, 1978), pp. 9, 83.

[52] *Journal*, 2 July 1921, 11. Scharlieb was a gynaecologist and had been one of the pioneer women medical practitioners. She elaborated on her views in a letter to the *Journal*. See 16 July 1921, 93.

[53] See *Ibid.*, 23 July 1921, 131; 30 July 1921, 168–70; 6 Aug. 1921, 219–20; 13 Aug. 1921, 261–2; 20 Aug. 1921, 301–2; 27 Aug. 1921, 338–40.

[54] See R. A. Soloway, *Birth Control and the Population Question in England, 1877–1930*, pp. 258–9 (note 51).

[55] *Journal*, 29 Oct. 1921, 708; J. Peel, 'Contraception and the Medical Profession', *Population Studies* (1964–5) **xviii**: 133–45.

[56] *Ibid.*; see F. Watson, *Dawson of Penn* (London: Chatto and Windus, 1950).

[57] 21 Jan. 1922, 105–6.

as a whole has set its face against such practices, which are unnatural and degrading in their mental effect, and ofttimes injurious to both husband and wife in their physical results.'[58] Contraception, which the *Journal* scarcely distinguished from abortion, was, in 1901, regarded as unmitigated 'evil'. In other words, the *Journal* adhered to the views it had expressed in the 1870s.

The extent to which such attitudes persisted in the early post-war era is illustrated by the Ministry of Health's dismissal of a nurse, in 1922, for providing contraceptive advice at maternity clinics.[59] By 1928, when Horner became editor, the *Journal*'s line had been modified to the effect that doctors were justified in giving potential parents contraceptive advice or instruction even when the decision to avoid conception had been made on non-medical grounds.[60] However, these comparatively liberal views contrasted with attitudes behind the scenes towards the birth control movement, especially as personified by Marie Stopes.

Following publication of *Married Love* Stopes had been besieged with requests for contraceptive advice. She sought to provide this in *Wise Parenthood* (1918) and other books, including *Contraception* (1923). Although the *Journal* carried no review of *Wise Parenthood* (or any of Stopes's other books), it did advertise it on its front cover. However, in 1921 the Journal Committee considered the 'propriety' of the advertisement and resolved that 'the matter be referred too the Medical Department with a view to ascertaining the opinion of the Women Medical Practitioners on the subject.' The outcome of the consultation process was a decision that the *BMJ* should cease to accept advertising for *Wise Parenthood*; this decision was evidently extended to the rest of her books.[61]

Stopes was convinced that her exclusion from the *Journal*'s editorial and advertising pages was the product of a conspiracy whereby 'Catholic physicians had infiltrated the association's hierarchy and the editorial board of the *BMJ*.'[62] Some years later, in the course of an address on contraception to the BMA's Portsmouth division, she let it be known that she regarded the advertising ban as 'unfair' and 'invidious'. Her audience, impressed by her 'admirable' treatment of a 'difficult subject', agreed that it did appear that she had been unfairly treated and instructed their honorary secretary to

[58] *Ibid.*, 29 June 1901, 1630. In 1917 a *BMJ* contributor had lumped together contraception, masturbation, prostitution, adultery, illegitimacy, and abortion as crimes against physiological law. See 24 Feb. 1917, 280.

[59] Cited in F. Mort, *Dangerous Sexualities: Medico-Moral Politics in England since 1830* (London: Routledge and Kegan Paul, 1987), p. 250. Birth control advice was not available in Ministry of Health clinics until 1930. See R. Hall (ed.), *Dear Dr Stopes*, p. 16 (note 51). In 1917, the *Lancet* had dismissed birth control as 'a distasteful subject'. See 11 Aug. 1917, 207–8; P. Fryer, *The Birth Controllers* (London: Secker and Warburg, 1965), p. 247.

[60] *Journal*, 15 Sept. 1928, 499–500.

[61] BMA mss. MCCSC, Journal Committee, 17 Nov. 1921, 275; 5 Oct. 1922, 142.

[62] R. A. Soloway, *Birth Control and the Population Question in England, 1877–1930*, p. 266 (note 51). Both Scharlieb and Sutherland were Roman Catholics.

ascertain the reason why 'Dr. Stopes' books ... are denied in the *British Medical Journal* those advertising facilities which are readily afforded by other medical journals'.[63] Horner explained that the decision was 'based on the amount of publicity cultivated by Dr. Stopes'. Although no more precise reason was ever provided, it seems clear that the Association was

> in a quandary. It wanted to gloss over the obvious differences doctors had about birth control while at the same time staking it out as a preserve of the medical profession in the future. Marie Stopes, to its official way of thinking, was an unqualified interloper whose claims were premature and whose scientific credentials and title were misleading and troublesome.[64]

The simple truth is that the *Journal* wished 'to avoid controversy and to give no credibility to nonmedical authorities'.[65]

When, in 1926, the Journal Committee reviewed its decision, it decided to leave it unchanged. Four years later, advertisements for *Contraception*, submitted by both the publisher and Stopes's Society for Constructive Birth Control, were again turned down. On this occasion the BMA's Wandsworth division, urged on by Stopes's husband, pressed the Journal Committee for an explanation, but the committee merely obfuscated.[66] The advertisements continued to be submitted and continued to be rejected. The BMA's objection seems to have lain less in the content of the books than with how their author conducted herself. Accordingly, the Journal Committee refused an advertisement for 'Birth Control Technical Demonstrations free' on the grounds 'that it is one of the Dr. Marie Stopes Clinics, and that her name appears in the text of the advertisement'. Towards the end of 1932, by which time Stopes had passed the pinnacle of her influence, the committee decided that advertisements for her books could be accepted, but it soon found itself troubled by a Stopes advertisement (for a lecture on birth control) that did not tally with other public pronouncements describing the lecture.[67]

By the 1930s the Journal Committee was beginning to be faced with the question of how to react to the advertising not only of contraceptive literature but also of contraceptive products.[68] It agreed to appoint advisers capable of assessing the value of specific chemical preparations, as a pharmacologist had for some years been employed to do in respect of drugs,

[63] BMA mss. MCCSC, Journal Committee, 18 March 1926, 401. It has been suggested that the BMA was opposed to its divisions inviting Stopes to address them. See R. A. Soloway, *Birth Control and the Population Question in England, 1877–1930*, p. 265 (note 51).

[64] *Ibid.*

[65] *Ibid.*

[66] BMA mss. MCCSC, Journal Committee, 18 March 1926, 401. The Journal Committee had refused to review its decision when asked to do so by Stopes's husband. See *BMJ* mss. JCM (1930–1) JNL. 3, 17 Sept. 1930; JNL. 6, 8 Oct. 1930; JNL. 11, 4 Feb. 1931.

[67] *Ibid.*, (1931–2) JNL. 19, 16 March 1932; (1932–3) JNL. 7, 20 Oct. 1932; JNL. 21, 18 May 1933; (1933–4) JNL. 1, Agenda, 20 Oct. 1933.

[68] *Ibid.*, (1931–2) JNL. 4, 15 Oct. 1931; JNL. 14, 15 Oct. 1931.

but it fought shy of recommending acceptance of advertisements for contraceptives without the explicit approval of Council. This was forthcoming in June 1932,[69] and in 1933 the *Journal* began to carry such advertising. In 1936 the National Birth Control Association commended the *Journal*'s policy of accepting advertisements only for products of proved reliability, commenting that this policy 'should be very valuable to doctors throughout the country who seem frequently to be guided in their choice of the contraceptives they recommend to their patients largely by the advertisements in the medical papers.'[70] In the mid-1930s the Journal Committee co-operated closely with the NBCA on the advertising of contraceptives.

Soon after the *Journal*'s introduction of contraceptive advertising, the protests from BMA members began to arrive. For example, Dr Joseph Daniel, honorary secretary of the Irish Guild of St Luke, SS Cosmas and Damian, complained that 'These advertisements are offensive to the moral principles of Catholics, and therefore to the vast majority of members of the Medical Profession practising in Ireland.' Daniel went on to inquire whether it was BMA and *BMJ* policy 'to advocate and support the spread of the theory and practice of contraception'.[71] Other letters in a similar vein followed. Although the Association's financial secretary was not able to satisfy these correspondents with his attempt to justify publication of the advertisements, the Journal Committee saw no need to amend its policy. This refusal shows how much the attitudes of the BMA and *BMJ* had changed.[72]

Advocates of birth control were a controversial fringe group in the early 1920s. The *BMJ* was sufficiently concerned to avoid being associated with the movement to give private endorsement to Stopes's clinic in 1921 while publicly maintaining a discreet silence.[73] By the 1930s contraception had become more mainstream, and respectable enough to be discussed in women's magazines and the general press. But the *Journal*'s correspondence columns give ample evidence of the persistence of views that had been to the

[69] *Ibid.*, JNL. 31, 18 May 1932; (1932–33) JNL. 1, Agenda, 20 Oct. 1932. The *Journal*'s first adviser was C. I. B. Voge, a biochemist at Edinburgh University, who was an expert on chemical contraception. J. Peel, 'The Manufacture and Retailing of Contraceptives in England', 120 (note 42).

[70] *BMJ* mss. JCM (1936–7) JNL. 8, M. A. Pyke to A. Macrae, 10 Nov. 1936. The NBCA was formed in 1931 from the National Birth Control Council. It constituted an amalgamation of all the birth control organizations, including Stopes's (although she soon resumed her independence). In 1939 the NBCA became the Family Planning Association. See J. Weeks, *Sex, Politics and Society*, p. 195 (note 42).

[71] *BMJ* mss. Journal Committee (1933–4) JNL. 20, Agenda, 18 May 1934.

[72] *Ibid.*, (1934–5) JNL. 1, Letters from John F. Falvey and R. M. Courtauld, Agenda, 19 Oct. 1934; see (1938–39) JNL. 36, Letter from Dr Elizabeth Cameron, Agenda, 17 March 1939. However, as recently as 1960 the BMA heeded the advice of Roman Catholic members and rejected advertisements from the Family Planning Association submitted to *Getting Married* and *Family Doctor*. *J. Peel*, 'Contraception and the Medical Profession', 145 (note 55).

[73] R. A. Soloway, *Birth Control and the Population Question in England, 1877–1930*, p. 267 (note 51).

fore in the early 1920s. In 1936, when contraception was the subject of several letters, correspondents expressed their fears of 'race suicide' brought about by rampant birth control, of the desirability of larger families among the business and professional classes, and the need for 'the control of birth control' before it destroyed the Empire. One writer saw artificial contraception as part of a 'full-fronted attack ... against life ... Life is checked at its springs by birth control; escaping this, it is thwarted in its self-expression by big business and bureaucracy; and now finally, we see its almost wholesale destruction threatened by bombing aeroplanes and poison gas. If this gloomy association of ideas suggested the need for some sort of regulatory control of contraception, another Jeremiah lamented the impracticality of such a solution, '... legislation aimed at its prohibition would produce a business of "rubber running" that would put American bootleggers in the shade.'[74] During the two months over which this correspondence lasted, Horner published not one letter defending contraception. Neither can these views be dismissed as the ravings of cranks. In October 1936 Sir Henry Brackenbury, erstwhile Chairman of the BMA Council, expressed similar views in his address to the York Medical Society.[75] Even after the Second World War members of Council were opposed to 'associating the BMA with any body of people advocating contraception; it ... [is] ... outside the province of their Association'.[76]

Health, medicine, and health services

The 1920s and 1930s saw few major developments in medicine, health, and the health services. After the shake-up of the 1911 National Insurance Act, the administration of medical services continued little changed until the Second World War. At best the insurance scheme provided only partial access to medical care. With the exception of sanatorium treatment for patients with tuberculosis, who did not have to be insured workers, it supplied only a general practitioner service, of allegedly inferior quality, and free drugs. Some doctors were accused of allocating a minimal amount of their time to panel patients. Whether or not this was so, and the profession vehemently refuted such imputations, the quality of the GP service undoubtedly varied between regions, for practitioners were unevenly distributed throughout the country with the result that more affluent districts tended to have more doctors than poorer areas such as south Wales or north-east England.[77] But the greatest shortcomings of national health insurance were

[74] *Journal*, 4 Jan. 1936, 33; 11 Jan. 1936, 87; 18 Jan. 1936, 135; 1 Feb. 1936, 238; 8 Feb. 1936, 286; 15 Feb. 1936, 339; 22 Feb. 1936, 390; 29 Feb. 1936, 447–8.

[75] *Ibid.*, 24 Oct. 1936, 828–32.

[76] *BMJ* Supplement, 12 April 1947, 54.

[77] Lindsay Granshaw, 'Health for All. The Origins of the National Health Service, 1848–1948: A Fortieth Anniversary Retrospect'. Catalogue of an Exhibition held at the Wellcome Institute for the History of Medicine, 7 June to 2 Sept. 1988.

in its failure to provide hospital or specialist treatment and its coverage of only insured workers and not their dependants.[78]

The three-tier hospital system (voluntary, municipal, and Poor Law), which had been unaffected by the National Insurance Act, remained much as it had been during Queen Victoria's reign, though the funding of voluntary hospitals—through charity and subscription and patients' fees—was becoming increasingly difficult.[79] In some regions these hospitals suffered from serious shortages of consultants. Voluntary hospitals mainly treated short-term acute cases; the Poor Law institutions, in which were to be found most hospital beds, dealt mainly with the old and the chronically ill. Poor Law infirmaries were often 'dreary, unattractive' places in which 'the quality of service was flagrantly substandard'.[80] They lacked laboratories and possessed little in the way of specialist equipment or personnel. As for the 'dental picture', this has been described as 'in all respects ... gloomy'.[81] But though there were serious gaps in the inter-war medical services, there was also an impressive array of provisions that had been developed over many decades, if not centuries. The system was characterized as much by its bewildering complexities, inefficiencies, and inequalities as by its omissions. What was needed was not more piecemeal reform, but comprehensive re-organization.

However, the inter-war period saw the implementation of no new grand strategy but a succession of *ad hoc* measures which tended to confer increasing responsibility upon local authorities. It is tempting to see these developments as the outcome of a struggle between the ideal of 'root and branch' reform and the reality of there being insufficient funds to realize it in conditions of economic depression and financial retrenchment. But this is an oversimplification, because it ignores the importance of the three 'i's: ideology, inertia, and interest groups. In other words, there was no consensus on reform, but, rather, reluctance to sweep away existing arrangements and start anew. The BMA recognized the need for change but remained—as during the national health insurance crisis of 1911–12—implacably opposed to the prospect of a whole time salaried profession, which tended to loom large in many proposals for reform.

The 1920s and 1930s saw the appointment of several committees of

[78] PEP (Political and Economic Planning), *Report on the British Health Services* (London: PEP, 1937), pp. 15, 194–229.

[79] Health provision changed in its details rather than its principles e.g. a Ministry of Health was set up to administer national health insurance (1919); the State's contribution to the scheme was cut from two-ninths to one-seventh as an economy measure (1926); the proportion of general practitioners and of the workforce within the national insurance system steadily increased; administration of Poor Law infirmaries was handed over to county and borough councils (1929). See Almont Lindsey, *Socialized Medicine in England and Wales. The National Health Service, 1948–1961* (Chapel Hill, North Carolina: University of North Carolina Press, 1961), Chapter 1; D. Fraser, *The Evolution of the British Welfare State* (London: Macmillan, 1984), pp. 198–201.

[80] A. Lindsey, *Socialized Medicine in England and Wales*, p. 17 (note 79).

[81] *Ibid.*, p. 12.

Hospital Patient (one of large family in poor district, given a glass of milk): 'How far down can I drink?'

How far down can I drink?: from *Mr Punch Among the Doctors*. Source: Bodleian Library, Oxford.

inquiry, most notably Lord Dawson's Consultative Council on Medical and Allied Services and the 1926 Royal Commission on National Health Insurance, charged with examining health services and medical provision. Lord Dawson, later a BMA president, acknowledged the necessity of making health services available to all sections of society and put forward detailed proposals for primary and secondary health centres. However, the Council rejected the abolition of fees, which might have made this attainable, on the grounds that the public purse could not bear the burden and that a State medical service was undesirable. The Royal Commission favoured a more comprehensive system of health care and questioned the insurance principle as a means of finance. But it too rejected the practicality, in prevailing circumstances, of providing the necessary money from public funds.[82] Instead, it advocated mere tinkering with the insurance scheme.

The *BMJ* tended to abstain from editorial comment on these inquiries into the nation's health services. Though it was critical of the 1926 Royal

[82] *Journal*, 29 May 1920, 739–45; A. Lindsey, *Socialized Medicine in England and Wales*, pp. 26–7 (note 79); C. Webster, *The Health Services since the War*, Vol. 1. *Problems of Health Care. The National Health Service before 1957* (London: HMSO, 1988), p. 19.

Commission's timidity, it expressed neither approval nor disapproval of the Dawson Committee's proposals.[83] In retrospect, more important than the official inquiries was the Labour Party's commitment, dating from 1934, to a free and comprehensive health service provided by a full-time salaried staff.[84] This, however, was not a matter to which, at the time, the *Journal* paid any attention.

The BMA, it has been said, 'was more critically aware of the deficiencies in the medical service' than any other body in Britain.[85] In the subsequent debate over a national health service it has sometimes been portrayed as merely an obstructionist pressure group, intent on protecting its members' interests at all costs; but it also played an important part in formulating constructive proposals. Some of these were for reforms of specific aspects of health care, such as its plans for a maternity service; others were for a national medical service.

BMA reports compiled in the 1930s had 'a decisive influence upon government policy in the 1940s'.[86] The first of these, published in 1930, was presented as 'a coherent and inclusive scheme of medical service ... [which] ... would, it is believed provide the community with a service available for every class of the population, comprehensive enough to cover the whole field of preventive and curative medicine ...'.[87] It envisaged a service that provided more than mere access to a general practitioner, which was the main benefit of national health insurance. These benefits would continue to be provided on the existing contributory basis. Membership of the scheme would be compulsory for all covered by NHI and also for their dependants and the indigent, whose contributions would come from public funds. Most of the rest of the population would be eligible to join on a voluntary basis.[88] Viewed from a post-1948 perspective, the greatest defect of this plan was that it did not extend to hospital treatment.

Not surprisingly, the *Journal* welcomed proposals which had emanated from its parent body:

> The scheme is important and timely. It is becoming more generally recognized that national provision of the kind proposed is desirable, even necessary ... The State has passed beyond the stage, which occupied almost the whole of last century, in which it conceived its duties in regard to public health to be confined to general sanitation and infectious disease. It has passed beyond the stage, occupying fully the first quarter of the present century, in which it concerned itself also with the treatment of a few

[83] *Journal*, 13 March 1926, 491–2; 20 March, 1926, 535–6.

[84] C. Webster, *Problems of Health Care*, p. 24 (note 82); K. O. Morgan, *Labour in Power, 1945–1951* (Oxford: Oxford University Press, 1984), p. 152.

[85] A. Lindsey, *Socialized Medicine in England and Wales*, p. 27 (note 79).

[86] *Ibid.*; C. Webster, *Problems of Health Care*, p. 25 (note 82). The BMA published its plans for a maternity service in 1929.

[87] *BMJ* Supplement, 26 April 1930, 166.

[88] *Ibid.*, 165–82.

The Comparative Unimportance of the Human. Ramsay MacDonald and Neville Chamberlain are accused of spending too much on armaments. Cartoon by David Low, published in the *Evening Standard*,* 23 February 1934. Source: Centre for the Study of Cartoons and Caricature, University of Kent at Canterbury.

* Associated Newspapers plc,

special conditions and with limited sections of the community, or at least of that large proportion which is unable to make such provision for itself.[89]

However, the leading article in which these observations were made admitted that 'lack of funds will probably prevent the actual establishment of a comprehensive national scheme during the next few years.'[90] The prediction that nothing would be done proved accurate. In 1938 the BMA produced an updated version of its proposed General Medical Service for the Nation. This, like its predecessor, formed part of the Association's Council Report and, as such, was published in the Supplement rather than the *Journal* proper. The *Journal* did not accord it a leading article.[91]

In comparison with the 1940s and after, scientific medical research in the inter-war years existed on a modest scale. The major innovations in the drug treatment of disease were the isolation of insulin by Canadian researchers at the Toronto Medical School in 1922 and, from 1935, the development of

[89] *Journal*, 26 April 1930, 787.
[90] *Ibid.*
[91] *BMJ* Supplement, 30 April 1938, 253–66; Rosemary Stevens, *Medical Practice in Modern England. The Impact of Specialization and State Medicine* (London: Yale University Press, 1966), p. 55.

sulphonamides, which had major implications for the treatment of various diseases and were soon to prove invaluable in treating war wounds. The *Journal* published a summary of the Canadian research findings, commenting in an editorial that 'readers . . . cannot fail to draw the conclusion that a scientific advance of immense importance has already been accomplished.' These views were hotly disputed by some correspondents.[92] Penicillin, discovered by Fleming in 1928, remained in the research phase until the 1940s. The *BMJ* did not loom large in the dissemination of findings: Howard Florey *et al.* published their observations on the chemotherapeutic potential of penicillin in the *Lancet*. The use of antibiotics and chemotherapeutics for treating tuberculosis also made little impact on clinical practice until after the war. Calmette and Guérin had discovered the immunizing agent for tuberculosis (BCG) early in the century but, although extensively and safely used in Europe, it was largely ignored in Britain till after the Second World War.[93]

During the 1920s and 1930s morbidity and mortality rates maintained the downward trend that had started in the late nineteenth century. But the picture was not universally rosy. Maternal mortality may actually have worsened before improving in the late 1930s, while the gap in health standards between the social classes and different geographical regions remained. Furthermore, such standards may have declined in comparison with those of other western nations.[94] Some diseases remained a potent threat. The 1918–19 influenza epidemic accounted for some 150 000–200 000 deaths in England and Wales alone, while tuberculosis, diphtheria, and whooping cough continued to kill many thousands every year. But overall, infant and child mortality showed appreciable improvement, and the decline in deaths from infectious diseases, especially tuberculosis, was substantial. By most objective criteria, general standards of health improved during the 1920s and 1930s, though these improvements doubtless owed more to environmental and economic factors such as better diet, housing, public health, and higher incomes than to medical intervention.

The largely unspectacular development of medicine and the health services limited the scope for dynamic medical journalism. Indeed, it has been suggested that the *BMJ* was dull in the 1920s and 1930s not because of any

[92] *Journal*, 4 Nov. 1922, 833–5, 882; Michael Bliss *The Discovery of Insulin* (Basingstoke: Macmillan, 1987).

[93] F. B. Smith, *The Retreat of Tuberculosis, 1850–1950* (London: Croom Helm, 1988); Linda Bryder, *Below the Magic Mountain: A Social History of Tuberculosis in Twentieth Century Britain* (Oxford: Oxford University Press, 1988).

[94] There are 'optimist' and 'pessimist' views on British health and welfare standards between the wars. A recent statement of the optimist case is to be found in John Stevenson, *British Society 1914–1945* (Harmondsworth: Penguin, 1984), Chapter 7. The pessimist case is argued in Charles Webster, 'Health, Welfare and Unemployment during the Depression', *Past and Present* (1985) **109**: 204–30. See also the same author's 'Healthy or Hungry Thirties?' *History Workshop* (1982) **XIII**: 110–29, and his introduction to *Biology, Medicine and Society, 1840–1940*, pp. 12–13 (note 45).

inherent defect in its editors but because their scope was limited by circumstances. By the same token, it is claimed that Horner was criticized not so much because he was an unsatisfactory editor but more because, unlike his predecessors, he did not fight back against the critics who had always been ready to attack incumbents of his office.[95] This, however, is an overly charitable view. Social conditions between the wars, at least in some regions of the country, were such as to give much scope for bold socio-medical journalism. Horner's journalism was seldom bold; instead he tended to prevaricate, to avoid giving offence, and to shun controversy. If he had a vision for the *Journal* it was, in the words of one who knew him, to publish the average article for the average practitioner.[96] As a result he made the *Journal* inoffensive and bland; indeed, simply average.

It is widely accepted that a high proportion of ill-health in the 1920s and 1930s, as in previous decades, was caused by dietary deficiency. In the inter-war years 'the dietary standards . . . of the many rose' so that 'the "average" diet of the 1930s was "better" than ever before'. But at the same time, about one-third of the population had insufficient calories and protein, while perhaps more than half was deficient in vitamins.[97] Great impetus had been given to the study of nutrition by food shortages during the First World War, and during the inter-war period the subject became much debated in medical circles and, indeed, more widely.[98] It is instructive to examine how Horner's *Journal* handled this debate, and to ponder how this differed from the way in which socio-medical questions had been treated by it in the past.

In the late nineteenth and early twentieth centuries great strides were taken towards understanding the principles of diet and nutrition. In 1912 Frederick Gowland Hopkins (1861–1947) demonstrated conclusively that animals fed sufficient protein, fat, carbohydrate, and mineral salts would decline in health if not also supplied with 'accessory food factors'—that is, vitamins, as these substances later became known.[99] Although the chemical composition of vitamins remained uncertain for some years, it soon became accepted that they were vital to good health, that they could be obtained through a diet in which fresh food formed a substantial part, and that their absence retarded growth, impaired healing, and led to diseases such as rickets, scurvy, beri-beri, and pellagra. If all this seems obvious now, it should be noted that in the nineteenth century rickets was supposed by some to be an infective disease of unknown origin.

95 Author's interview with John Thwaites, retired Deputy Editor of the *BMJ*, 18 Feb. 1989.

96 Author's interview with T. D. V. Swinscow, retired Deputy Editor of the *BMJ*, 9 Feb. 1989.

97 J. Burnett, *Plenty and Want. A Social History of Diet in England from 1815 to the Present Day* (London: Scolar Press, 1979), pp. 298–9.

98 See e.g. *Journal*, 26 May 1923, 905–6; 20 Sept. 1924, 504–8; 21 Feb. 1925, 358–9.

99 J. C. Drummond and Anne Wilbrahim, *The Englishman's Food. A History of Five Centuries of English Diet* (London: Cape, 1957 edn), pp. 361–2, 421–4; W. M. Frazer, *The History of English Public Health* (London: Baillière, 1950), pp. 263–4.

In 1919 and subsequently *Journal* editorials emphasized the need for major research on nutrition.[100] During the 1920s much was discovered by researchers such as J. C. Drummond and R. H. A. Plimmer. A good deal of this work was published in the *BMJ*, including Green and Mellanby's finding that vitamin A could increase resistance to infection and sepsis. On the basis of Plimmer's research the *Journal* argued that 'every possible endeavour should be made to induce our population to change its habits and once more eat wholemeal bread' instead of the vitamin-deficient white bread. In 1926, however, it still believed that sunlight offered the best means of preventing rickets.[101]

During the 1920s the debate on nutrition was primarily medical and scientific; in the early 1930s, as the nation plumbed the depths of economic depression, it was politicized as the focus of attention shifted to include the level of family expenditure on food necessary to maintain health and fitness. Several investigations, including one by the BMA, were undertaken. In 1933 the BMA Council appointed a Nutrition Committee 'to determine the minimum weekly expenditure on foodstuffs which must be incurred by families ... if health and working capacity are to be maintained and to construct specimen diets'. In November the *Journal* published the findings as a special supplement, but provided little editorial comment.[102] The BMA Committee found that 5s 10d was the minimum weekly amount that an adult male should spend on food. It has been calculated that on this basis nearly eight million people were living below the BMA minimum.[103]

Further inquiries followed. In 1936 two powerful and influential reports were published: John Boyd Orr's *Food, Health and Income* and *Poverty and Public Health* by G. C. M. M'Gonigle, medical officer of health for Stockton-on-Tees, and J. Kirby. M'Gonigle and Kirby showed how suburban re-housing could lead to an increase in dietary deficiency as a greater proportion of income went in paying higher rent and transport costs.[104] The Orr report, said *The Times*, showed that 'half of the population is living on a diet insufficient or ill-designed to maintain health.'[105] Indeed, Orr's study showed that only 10 per cent of the population, that with an income of over 45s a head, as against the average of 30s, had a surplus of all necessary dietary ingredients.[106] The *Journal* devoted a leading article to Orr's findings, but did little beyond summarizing them, concluding, rather lamely: 'This report,

[100] *Journal*, 22 March 1919, 349–50; see 26 May 1923, 905–6; 6 Feb. 1926, 250.

[101] *Ibid.*, 6 Feb. 1926, 250; 2 Oct. 1926, 607; 20 Oct. 1928, 691–6; 1 June 1929, 984–6. See also Edward Mellanby's papers, 'Diet and Disease', *ibid.*, 20 March 1926, 515–18; 'The Relation of Diet to Health and Disease', *ibid.*, 12 April 1930, 677–81, and his book review 15 Feb. 1930, 289; G. Jones, *Social Hygiene in Twentieth Century Britain*, p. 75 (note 45).

[102] *Journal*, 25 Nov. 1933, 980.

[103] J. Burnett, *Plenty and Want*, pp. 304–5, 316 (note 97).

[104] Reviewed in *Journal*, 18 July 1936, 125.

[105] Quoted in J. Burnett, *Plenty and Want*, p. 304 (note 103).

[106] J. C. Drummond and Anne Wilbrahim, *The Englishman's Food*, p. 447 (note 99).

while admittedly based in some respects on scanty data, deals with the problem of national nutrition on such a large scale and yet in such detail that it will prove of great value to workers in very many fields, and deserves study by all.'[107] This response is a typical example of how Horner's *Journal* temporized, not only on the relationship between nutrition and health but also on socio-medical questions as a whole and, indeed, most topics of controversy.

[107] *Journal*, 21 March 1936, 587–8.

10
War and reconstruction

The *Journal* in wartime

In August 1914 war had come as a bombshell for which the BMA was ill-prepared. Twenty-five years later things were very different. The rise of the fascist dictatorships, international tensions in Europe, the Japanese invasion of Manchuria, German re-armament, the Abyssinian crisis, the Anschluss, civil war in Spain, Munich and its aftermath: all of these brought war and the threat of war into the pages of the *BMJ* and before the committees of the BMA long before 3 September 1939.[1] Thus the *Journal*'s index for July–December 1936 includes numerous entries on air raid precautions and gas attacks. In February of the same year one correspondent wrote gloomily, 'if the present drift continues war is going to come almost immediately, and there is no doubt that the super-bomb has been specially designed for the destruction of the super-city.'[2] He was at least more accurate than Colonel Fuller of the Staff College, Camberley, whose predictions the *Journal* had carried in 1923. Fuller's scenario of the future conflict envisaged 500 enemy aeroplanes dropping anaesthetizing gas on the sleeping citizens of London preparatory to enemy police landing to gain control of the capital pending Britain's surrender.[3]

Most *Journal* items on war-related subjects were summaries of parliamentary business or reports of official committees, though from about 1937 an increasing number of original articles and letters were published, particularly on the possible role of the medical profession in the event of hostilities. The *Journal*'s index for its first volume of 1939 lists entries for a large number of topics under the headings of 'air raid precautions', 'war wounds and air raid casualties', and 'war—national defence'. These included articles on anti-gas helmets for infants, evacuation schemes, anaesthesia in wartime, gas masks in the operating theatre, blood transfusion, and the prevention and treatment of shock. A series of signed articles entitled 'War Wounds and Air-Raid Casualties', which commenced in April 1939, was published in book form in the following October. The *Journal* also carried advice to housewives on what materials to store for use if and when war came. This item elicited praise

1 *Journal*, 9 Sept. 1939, 571–2.
2 *Ibid.*, 8 Feb. 1936, 286.
3 *Ibid.*, 17 March 1923, 480–1.

at the 1939 ARM and the information was subsequently published as a 2d pamphlet, 'How to Stock Your Larder', which sold over 100 000 copies.[4]

Behind the scenes, in the committee rooms of BMA House, the prospect of war was also being taken seriously. From 1935 the Ministry of Health and the BMA collaborated closely in framing measures for the organization of the medical profession in war.[5] In the late 1930s it was widely expected, after events in Abyssinia and Spain, that the onset of hostilities would trigger bombing on a massive scale. The government's Imperial Defence Committee predicted as many as 1.2m casualties in the first two months.[6] In the light of these fears, the prospects for being able to continue to publish the *Journal* in London looked bleak. With Hitler threatening Czechoslovakia, the *Journal*'s Board of Directors called a meeting for 30 September 1938 to discuss publishing arrangements in the event of war. The meeting was cancelled when the international situation eased (Chamberlain and Hitler signed the Munich Agreement on the previous night), but the matter re-surfaced in the following year. In January the Board of Directors took several decisions aimed at safeguarding publication in the event of the destruction of either BMA House or Eyre and Spottiswoode's London printing works. They decided that publication in London would continue 'at least until such time as the Government administrative offices are moved out', though later that year serious consideration was given to a proposal for transferring the printing operation to Derbyshire (the BMA had taken the lease on a house in Buxton) or elsewhere.[7] As soon as war broke out a reserve stock of paper was moved to the Midlands and arrangements made for printing to be carried out there if necessary.[8]

In other words, the coming of war was as widely anticipated in the pages of the 1930s *Journal* as it had been overlooked in 1914. It was not, however, the subject of editorial comment until 9 September, the *Journal*'s first issue after the outbreak of war, when a leader tackled the subject of 'War and the Medical Profession'. This dealt largely with the BMA's long-term co-operation with government in organizing medical services for the emergency. It included a passing condemnation of Hitler, who was seen as having duped the German people, and the observation that in the coming struggle 'the

[4] *BMJ* Supplement, 29 July 1939, 64; 20 April 1940, 58.

[5] Sir Arthur MacNalty (ed. in chief), *History of the Second World War. United Kingdom Medical Series*. F. A. E. Crew, *The Army Medical Services. Administration* (2 vols. 1953, 1955), Vol. I, pp. 10, 16. The BMA had fought for much of the inter-war period to improve terms and conditions of service in the RAMC.

[6] Harry Eckstein, *The English Health Service. Its Origins Structure and Achievements* (Cambridge, Massachusetts: Harvard University Press, 1964), pp. 86–7.

[7] *BMJ* mss. JCM (1938–9) JNL.8, 14 Oct. 1938; JCM (1938–9) JNL.35, Agenda, 20 Oct. 1939; JNL.41, 19 May 1939; Board of Directors' Signed Minutes (1937–44) 20 Jan. 1939; Elston Grey-Turner and F. M. Sutherland, *History of the British Medical Association 1932–1981* (London: British Medical Association, 1982), p. 27.

[8] *BMJ* mss. JCM (1942–3) JNL.3, Board of Directors' Report, 31 Dec. 1942.

British doctor has this advantage over his German Colleague—he works among a free people."[9]

In common with the First World War, that of 1939–45 imposed considerable pressure on the uninterrupted production of a high-quality *Journal*. With the surrender of the Netherlands and Belgium, the imminent collapse of France, the British Expeditionary Force penned in around Dunkirk, and the onset of the German bombing of England, May 1940 has been described as Britain's darkest hour.[10] In these circumstances the prospects for the *Journal*'s continued publication in London were again discussed by Horner, Hugh Clegg, and Ronald Gordon, Chairman of the Board of Directors. Again it was decided that, since the editorial department had to remain in close contact with the printers, publication should remain at BMA House. It was agreed that this decision would be reviewed only if Tavistock House or Eyre and Spottiswoode's printing works became untenable owing to bomb damage, if the staff became too depleted to carry on, or if the general situation became so bad as to render the *Journal*'s postal distribution impossible. In such circumstances efforts would be made to re-assemble staff in the Midlands so that the *Journal* might be re-started.[11]

London was the main target of enemy bombers; almost half of all British civilian war deaths occurred in or around the capital. Raids were at their most frequent between September 1940 and May 1941; as Horner later noted, this was a period of intense anxiety and personal danger: 'conditions of life and work . . . imposed a severe strain upon all engaged in producing the *Journal*.'[12] In April 1941 BMA House was severely damaged by a bomb, though this disrupted *Journal* production comparatively little. Worse was to come. On 10 May the Norwich Street works in which the *Journal* was printed were totally destroyed. The made-up type for the *Journal*'s 17 May issue was lost in the devastation. Clegg later called this 'the most dramatic event' in the *BMJ*'s history. The rotary machine specially purchased to print the *Journal* was 'almost the only piece of apparatus that survived'.[13] Even so, Eyre and Spottiswoode could no longer fulfil their obligation to print the *Journal*; their contract with the BMA was therefore deemed to have terminated. Temporary arrangements were made for printing to be transferred to the Bowling Green Lane works of the Temple Press, where the 17 May edition, the so-

[9] *Journal*, 9 Sept. 1939, 571–2.

[10] W. N. Medlicott, *Contemporary England, 1914–1964* (London: Longmans, 1967), p. 428.

[11] *BMJ* mss. Board of Directors' Signed Minutes (1937–1944) 24 May 1940. As it turned out, of course, Midland cities, notably Coventry, were also heavily bombed. The *Lancet* moved its offices out of London at the beginning of the war. JCM (1951–2) JNL.7, Editor's Memorandum, 23 Aug. 1951.

[12] *Ibid.*, JCM (1942–3) JNL.4, Editor's Report, 24 Dec. 1942.

[13] *Ibid.*, JNL.3, Board of Directors' Report, 31 Dec. 1942; *Journal*, 17 May 1941, 755; 31 May 1941, 824.

called 'phoenix number', was hastily re-set and despatched on schedule. Nine issues of the *Journal* (17 May to 10 July 1941 inclusive) were printed here.[14]

But the Board of Directors and senior BMA officers were keen that printing should be transferred to a safer, though accessible, site outside London. Accordingly, arrangements were made for Fisher, Knight and Co of the Gainsborough Press to perform the work in St Albans. Horner had reservations about the 'lengthening of the line of communication' and switching from rotary to the slower flat-bed printing method.[15] He was concerned that these changes would necessitate advancing the date of going to press and make the introduction of last minute changes more difficult.[16] However, the Board of Directors was persuaded to help overcome one of these objections by agreeing that the editor could hire a car to take him to St Albans when the occasion arose. In any case at the time there was no real alternative to Fisher, Knight and Co. The term of the initial contract was three years or 12 months after the end of the war, whichever was longer.[17] In the event the firm was still printing the *Journal* at the end of 1965.

During this period of emergency, 'when things were at their worst in London' as Horner put it, the *Journal* celebrated its centenary.[18] A 'Centennial Number' appeared on 5 October 1940. It included a leading article on the centenary and another on 'change of thought in medicine, 1840–1940'. There was also an article by Sir D'Arcy Power, who had known every *Journal* editor as far back as Jonathan Hutchinson, facsimile reproduction of the *PMSJ*'s first page, and messages of congratulation from the great and the good. But generally the centenary was a low key affair, for this was more a time for looking to present and future concerns than reflecting upon past glories. Apart from the threat from the air, continuing problems included lack of staff (as both BMA staff and print workers joined the armed services), scarcity of paper (and that at inflated prices), higher postal and printing costs, and loss of advertising.

In fact, while the bulk of advertising declined during the war, revenue increased significantly because of the higher charges imposed. Growing circulation meant that some advertisements had to be rejected because of lack of paper on which to print them. But such was the growth of the Association that advertisers were prepared to pay substantially more for space in the *Journal*. Thus, although its editorial, administrative, and

[14] The Temple Press and Eyre and Spottiswoode had made an informal agreement to help each other out in the event of one of them suffering bomb damage. *BMJ* mss. JCM (1951–2) JNL.7, Editor's Memorandum, 23 Aug. 1951.

[15] *Ibid.*, Board of Directors' Signed Minutes (1937–1944), 6 June 1941; JCM (1942–3) JNL.3, Board of Directors' Report, 31 Dec. 1942.

[16] *Ibid.*, JNL.4, Editor's Report, 24 Dec. 1942.

[17] *Ibid.*, JNL.3, *BMJ* Board of Directors' Report, 31 Dec. 1942. Fisher, Knight had tendered for the *Journal*;'s printing in 1936. *Ibid.*, JCM (1951–2) JNL.7, Editor's Memorandum, 23 Aug. 1951.

[18] *Ibid.*, JCM (1942–3) JNL.4, Editor's Report, 24 Dec. 1942; *Lancet*, 19 Oct. 1940, 493.

production expenses rose, its financial health was better than ever. In 1940 the *Journal*'s income amounted to £69 200, while expenditure was £73 300, leaving a deficit of £4100. By 1945 income had risen to £116 600, but expenditure only to £96 400. As a result the *Journal* showed a profit of £20 200. By 1943 finances were healthy enough for the *Journal* Committee to sanction an increase in the scale of payments to contributors for the first time since 1920.[19]

Paper was in short supply throughout the war and consequently was expensive and subject to rationing, which became particularly strict after the fall of Norway in April 1940. In general, publishers were restricted to 60 per cent, later 40 per cent, of their pre-war consumption.[20] The paper problem was exacerbated by the rapid growth in BMA membership and hence of *Journal* circulation. By 1945 membership of the Association exceeded 51 500, an increase of some 12 000 on 1939; in May of that year the *Journal*'s print run was almost 53 000. During the First World War, it will be recalled, BMA membership and *Journal* circulation had fallen. If the *Journal* had been published as a commercial venture it would have been possible to conserve scarce paper by reducing the print-run. But there was limited scope to do this because of the constitutional obligation to supply the *Journal* to each BMA member. From early 1942 circulation outside the Association was substantially reduced in an effort to conserve paper. Applications for non-member subscriptions were refused, and in 1944 the *Journal* published appeals to readers who did not wish to keep their copies to return them so that they could be passed on to those whose direct subscriptions could not be accepted.[21]

The main economy measure was to reduce the *Journal*'s size. The weekly eight-page 'Key to Current Medical Literature' was axed as early as 9 September 1939, while the number of photogravure insets was cut by about 50 per cent at around the same time. The annual educational number of the *Journal* was not published in 1940 or for the rest of the war. During the first six months of 1940 the average size of each issue fell to around 100 pages of advertising and text, as against the 144 of 1938. By 1944 each issue contained between 60 and 64 pages, of which no more than 40 contained editorial matter. Apart from turning down advertising, other economy measures included reducing the size of margins and printing on paper of less weight.[22]

[19] *BMJ* Supplement, 10 July 1943, 6; 13 May 1944, 107, 4 Aug. 1945, 27; *BMJ* mss. Board of Directors' Signed Minutes (1937–1944), 22 June 1943; JCM (1942–3) JNL.9, 19 May 1943. The new payments were (per thousand words) 3 guineas for leaders, annotations, and reviews, 4 guineas for 'scale A leaders', and 45s for all other solicited contributions. The previous rate had been 30s per thousand words.

[20] On the paper problem generally see Angus Calder, *The People's War. Britain 1939–1945* (London: Cape, 1969), p. 590.

[21] *BMJ* mss. JCM (1943–4) JNL.53, Memorandum, 11 Oct. 1944; *Journal*, 21 March 1942, 393.

[22] *BMJ* Supplement, 10 July 1943, 6; 13 May 1944, 107; 23 Dec. 1944, 170; 12 May 1945, 83.

Efforts to obtain a larger ration of paper continued throughout the war. Although deemed of sufficient national importance to merit a priority allocation, the *Journal* struggled to acquire enough to supply its needs. In 1944 the BMA's president, Lord Dawson, personally appealed to the Minister of Supply for the *Journal* to be given further preference. Meanwhile Horner, Clegg, and the publishing manager made similar representations to the government's Raw Materials Department. At first the requests were unavailing, though at the end of the year the *Journal* was granted a 5 per cent increase, provided that this was used to print additional copies rather than to enlarge its dimensions.[23]

Problems were not eased by the increasing demands made on *Journal* space by contributors. After a temporary decline the number of articles submitted for publication remained more or less constant, while the volume of correspondence received grew very substantially. With fewer pages available, an abnormally high proportion of submissions had to be rejected. From 1944, with the publication of the government's White Paper on the National Health Service, pressure on space was further increased. To obviate this, some sections of the *Journal*, including, correspondence, book reviews, obituaries, and annotations were printed in smaller type. By 1945, 36 pages of text contained as much type as 44.75 pre-war pages.[24] Once again Morison's typeface showed its worth, for it proved to be easily legible in even the smallest sizes.[25] Despite all its problems, the *Journal* appeared punctually throughout the war—even when VE Day celebrations coincided with the day of going to press.[26]

Precisely who was running the *Journal* and determining its policy during the war is unclear. Certainly at some stage Clegg acquired much more responsibility and authority. Towards the end of 1940 and during the first months of 1941 Horner was absent from his office suffering from detached retinas.[27] In his absence Clegg, assisted by a sub-editor, Marjorie Hollowell (who had joined the staff in the early 1930s), took charge. Even after Horner's return it seems likely that Clegg continued to shoulder the main burden of producing the *Journal*. One of its wartime innovations, the long-running 'Any Questions' column, was planned and executed by Clegg from 1943.[28]

In spite of the difficulties under which it laboured, the *Journal* prospered during the Second World War, not only financially but qualitatively. In 1944

[23] *BMJ* mss. JCM (1943–4) JNL.51, Editor's Report, 29 Sept. 1944; JCM (1944–5) JNL.10, Publishing Sub-committee, 14 Dec. 1944.

[24] *Ibid.*, (1945–6) JNL.12, Publishing Sub-committee, 25 Oct. 1945.

[25] *BMJ* Supplement, 20 April 1940, 58; 17 May 1941, 63; 13 May 1944, 107.

[26] *Ibid.*, 4 Aug. 1945, 27.

[27] *Ibid.*, 3 May 1941, 53.

[28] *BMJ* mss. JCM (1942–3) JNL.8, Editor's Report, 4 May 1943.

the distinguished physician and historian Professor Charles Singer congratulated the editorial staff on their achievement:

War conditions are difficult for us all and the results are obvious enough. There has certainly been a fall in the quality of British journalism. But the B.M.J. has kept the flag flying really wonderfully, and I can perceive no deterioration whatever, but rather the reverse .... You really have done something—and a big something—to maintain civilisation and I congratulate you most sincerely. More power to your elbow.[29]

In 1948 *Medical Research in War. Report of the Medical Research Council for the Years 1939–45* listed 174 important papers published in the *BMJ*.[30] This brings us to the question of the *Journal*'s content.

War in the *Journal*

Early in the war the editors decided to give priority when selecting papers, to 'those of topical value relating to military medicine, surgery, hygiene, and administration, etc.' Their object was 'to afford medical men and women information and guidance which will increase their ability to serve the country'. The Supplement carried information from the BMA's Central Medical War Committee and much material on the Association's work, medical planning, and the future of medical practice.[31]

The *Journal* provided no treatment of general or military news until May 1945, when a leader briefly dealt with 'Victory in the West'.[32] Thus, the first volume of 1940 carries no mention of such pivotal events as Dunkirk and the fall of France, presumably because they were deemed to be outside its legitimate sphere of interest, even though they had implications for health, surgery, and medicine. As in 1914–18 the *BMJ* largely avoided condemnation of enemy actions and maintained its admiration for the achievements of German science and medicine, merely condemning the 'intellectual blackout' imposed by the Nazis. Only after the end of the war in Europe and the discovery of concentration camps in which German doctors had participated in the slaughter of Jews did it express unreserved condemnation, publishing an article by one of the first senior British medical officers to enter Belsen, and a leader on the 'horror camp':

What is peculiarly distressing is the knowledge that German doctors ... should so completely deny the humane tradition of their calling ... we should be doing a profound injustice to the thousands upon thousands of tortured Europeans if we too easily forget what has happened. It will be some time before we can look upon

[29] *Ibid.*, JCM (1942–5) JNL.5, 14 Dec. 1944, 5.

[30] Sir Arthur MacNalty (ed. in chief), *History of the Second World War. United Kingdom Medical Series*. F. H. K. Green and Major General Sir Gordon Covell (eds.), *Medical Research* (London, 1953); *Journal*, 15 May 1948, 942.

[31] *BMJ* mss. JCM (1942–3) JNL.4, Editor's Report, 24 Dec. 1942.

[32] *Journal*, 12 May 1945, 667.

German doctors as men imbued with the ideals of medicine common to civilized countries . . . .[33]

In 1946 the *Journal* published E. E. Dunlop's harrowing account of 'Medical Experiences in Japanese Captivity' with its stark conclusion that the 'treatment of sick prisoners by the Japanese left almost all civilized behaviour to be desired'.[34]

In terms of coverage, the *Journal* paid rather more attention to health and medicine on the home front than in the armed forces overseas. Only after the surrenders did it publish a number of papers describing the accumulated experiences of surgeons, prisoners of war, statisticians, and others. Between 1939 and 1941 it was preoccupied with evacuation, health and safety implications of the 'black-out', civilian diet, the work demands made of industrial workers, air raids, and conditions in air raid shelters. The more prosaic problems of head lice, scabies, and venereal disease were also prominent. From 1942 questions of reconstruction came to the fore. All this was in contrast to the First World War when attention had focused mainly upon events on the western front.

In earlier wars the *Journal* had had a reporter on the spot. Hart and Cormack had covered the Franco-Prussian War, Frederick Treves the Boer, and Guy Stephen the Great War. During the Second World War the *Journal* had no correspondent reporting from the front. But then this war was very different from those earlier conflicts. There were many theatres of combat, it was a war of movement rather than attrition, and a war in which the British civilian was, to an unparalleled extent, in the front line of the fighting. Civilian health care—scarcely adequate for most of the population in peacetime conditions—became a matter of great concern with the advent of 'total war'.

A leading article in 1942 summarized the differences in the challenge which faced medicine then as opposed to a quarter of a century earlier:

The medical problems of the last war were obviously medical problems, and the Medical Research Council found itself in their solution. Trench fever, trench mouth, trench nephritis, spirochaetal jaundice, gas poisoning, enteric, and dysentery—all these clearly belonged to medicine and were susceptible to attack by the familiar methods of clinical investigation, pathology, and bacteriology. The obviously medical problems of the present war have been equally well handled. We have due cause for pride in the treatment of war casualties, the application of the sulphonamide drugs to war wounds and epidemics, the improvement in the transfusion of blood and blood substitutes . . . .[35]

[33] *Ibid.*, 9 June 1945, 813–16; see 5 Jan. 1946, 4–8, 'Observations on Cases of Starvation at Belsen'; 25 Jan. 1947, 143, 148–50, 'Medical Experiments on Human Beings in Concentration Camps in Nazi Germany'.

[34] *Ibid.*, 5 Oct. 1946, 481–6; see 19 Oct. 1946, 585–6.

[35] *Ibid.*, 21 Feb. 1942, 262–3.

After detailing other medical successes, the article went on to argue that the profession had fared less well in its efforts to tackle 'new problems with a medical aspect' such as broken homes, life in air-raid shelters, evacuation, work strain, the black-out, transport dislocation, and the employment of married women with young children. These problems of the home front had become only too clear during the blitz.

In retrospect many of those who lived through the London blitz came to view the experience with nostalgia. It was a time of danger, privation, and anxiety, but also of camaraderie and fellowship. There is, however, little sense of the fun and pleasures of community to be detected in the *Journal*'s coverage of air raid shelters. Its centennial number included an article on hygiene in the shelters. This began: 'Air-raid shelters were at first regarded with indifference, but as daylight raiding developed they became places of refuge for an hour. With the onset of all-night raiding, however, they have become dormitories, and the health problems they create have become urgent.'[36] The solitude, discomfort, and cold of domestic Anderson shelters encouraged up to one-third of the London population to frequent communal shelters, including underground railway stations. The resulting 'nightly scenes . . . with their sprawling multitudes on every kind of rough upholstery, have to be seen to be believed'. Ill-ventilated and lacking lavatories, some underground stations were grossly overcrowded, dirty, and insanitary: 'Until the rush hour is over and the staff are free to clean up, the stench of the platforms and passages . . . is overpowering. 'Tube (or shelter) sore throat' is said to be already a common complaint.' The *Journal* feared the onset of serious epidemics as winter advanced, and called for provision of proper sitting, sleeping, and sanitary facilities, as well as for light, warmth, ventilation, first-aid, and medical provision. If doctors were organized on a rota they would be able to weed out cases of infectious disease and encourage improved personal hygiene. The alternative was 'a state of affairs in respect of infectious and contagious diseases which may prove more devastating than the *Blitzkrieg*'.[37]

These views elicited considerable response from correspondents, most of whom were supportive, though one accused the *Journal* of 'smug self-complacency' and of toeing the government's propaganda line, concluding:

> If you must write on shelters, go out and live there for a few nights; wake up in the morning with aches and stiffness in all your joints; learn to know the people, don't just visit them like a being from another planet surrounded by photographers and reporters; and then come back and write a fresh article on shelters.[38]

The *Journal*'s main objective was to influence the committee, chaired by Lord

[36] *Ibid.*, 5 Oct. 1940, 457.
[37] *Ibid.*; see 12 Oct. 1940, 495–6.
[38] *Ibid.*, 19 Oct. 1940, 537. Letter from E. Cronin.

Horder, which had been appointed in September 1940 to consider health conditions in shelters.[39] In October a member of the *Journal* staff interviewed Horder and obtained inside information on the committee's deliberations. When, in the next month, the report was published and government action taken, they were found largely to accord with *Journal* forecasts and recommendations.[40]

Although the *Journal* was well pleased with the outcome of the Horder inquiry, it refused to let matters rest but sent a 'representative' to investigate shelter conditions throughout London. His brief was to visit typical shelters and find out how far the Horder recommendations had been implemented. Outside the East End he found some improvements, with heating, ventilation, lavatories, first aid posts, medical attention, and even canteens being provided in some deep shelters. In the East End, however, the position was found to be much less satisfactory. Poor lighting, damp, inadequate sleeping arrangements, deplorable sanitation, and absence of medical facilities remained the order of the day. The findings of its representative prompted the *Journal* to press for the appointment of a 'supreme co-ordinator', preferably a medical practitioner, with power to rectify conditions in shelters. It denied any political motivation:

> . . . the speedy winning of the war depends to an incalculable degree upon the health, security and serenity of the mass of civilian workers and their families . . . the health of whole communities [is] gravely menaced—a menace the graver because the epidemic months of January and February are upon us. More than a hundred nights of sheltering under conditions resembling in certain respects . . . those of seige have created in certain quarters an Augean stable, and some swift, bold, Herculean strokes are demanded for its cleansing.[41]

This was powerful stuff in a war in which the press was subject to censorship and the wrath of government if it stepped out of line. Since June 1940 it had been a punishable offence to circulate reports or statements 'likely to cause alarm or despondency'.[42] Significantly, the *Journal* voiced its strongest criticisms when Horner was incapacitated and Clegg in charge. But shelter

[39] 'Recommendations and Further Recommendations of Lord Horder's Committee regarding the Conditions in Air-Raid Shelters with Special Reference to Health; and a Brief Statement of Action taken by the Government thereon'. Cmds. 6234 & 6235 (London, 1940).

[40] *Journal*, 23 Nov. 1940, 709; 30 Nov. 1940, 747–8.

[41] *Ibid.*, 7 Dec. 1940, 796–7; 14 Dec. 1940, 841; 21 Dec. 1940, 873–5; 11 Jan. 1941, 57–8. The *Journal* subsequently undertook a survey of the feeding of the London shelter population. See 8 Feb. 1941, 203–6.

[42] A. Calder, *The People's War*, pp. 155, 583–6 (note 20). In addition, newspapers could make no reference to troop movements, identify bombed localities, publish weather forecasts, or even refer to recent weather conditions lest the enemy be assisted. The *Daily Worker* was suppressed for opposing the war during the period of the Nazi–Soviet pact. The *Daily Mirror* was warned over its conduct and in March 1942 came close to suffering the *Daily Worker*'s fate over Zec's notorious 'price of petrol' cartoon. E. R. Chamberlin, *Life in Wartime Britain* (London: Batsford, 1972), pp. 169–70. The *Journal* had to delay mention of the bomb damage to BMA House until several weeks after the raid in question. *Journal*, 31 May 1941, 824.

conditions continued to be one of the *Journal*'s prime concerns throughout the early part of the war. At a Council meeting in December 1940 the *Journal*'s treatment of the 'shelter problem' received warm praise.[43]

In September 1941 the shelter survey was repeated to ascertain what improvements had been effected and what problems remained. On this occasion the *Journal* also investigated conditions in the shelters of seven provincial cities: Bristol, Cardiff, Birmingham, Manchester, Liverpool, Glasgow, and Newcastle.[44] Although it criticized conditions outside the capital, it believed that some of the provincial cities 'have quite a lot to teach the London authorities'. The overall verdict was that, though considerable improvements had been made, some shelters remained most unsatisfactory: 'The shelter problem is by no means solved. Perhaps when the solution is reached and the perfect shelter makes its appearance the need for it will have passed away.'[45] This was prophetic, for by September 1941 the heaviest bombing of London was already over. Thereafter the shelter problem eased and the *Journal*'s concentration on it declined. Against expectation, no serious outbreaks of disease affected the shelter population, though, as the official history states, 'it is not easy to say with certainty why this was so.'[46]

Towards the NHS

The war is often seen as having been crucial in the genesis of a national health service, but, though it undoubtedly exerted 'an important catalytic influence', it did not need a war to establish the inadequacies of the existing 'system' or to generate a mass of ideas for comprehensive and coherent reform. The BMA was as committed to change as anyone, if only because of its concern about the future of general practice, which was being 'squeezed' by expanding public health services and hospital contributory schemes.[47] Consequently, it is absurd to suppose, as Michael Foot and others have, that the organized profession was implacably opposed to a comprehensive national health service.[48] But it did take the war to create the will to convert existing ideas and dissatisfactions into the reality of the National Health Service. The first step towards it was the establishment of the Emergency Medical Service (EMS) in 1939.

The EMS, or Emergency Hospital Scheme as it was also, more accurately,

43 *BMJ* Supplement, 4 Jan. 1941, 3.

44 *Journal*, 20 Sept. 1941, 411, 414–15; 27 Sept. 1941, 443–4, 451–3.

45 *Ibid.*, 444.

46 Sir A. MacNalty (ed. in chief), *History of the Second World War. United Kingdom Medical Series*: Sir A. S. MacNalty, *The Civilian Health and Medical Services* (London, 1953, 1955), Vol. I, p. 213.

47 C. Webster, *The Health Services since the War.* Vol. 1, *Problems of Health Care. The National Health Service before 1957* (London, HMSO, 1988), p. 16.

48 Michael Foot, *Aneurin Bevan* (London: Macgibbon and Key, 1962 and 1973), Vol. II, p. 102.

known, was born of the expectation that if war came it would produce vast numbers of casualties in need of urgent treatment. How the medical services would cope was a difficult question, for there was no reliable information even on the number of hospital beds in England and Wales. In 1938 a government survey showed that in institutions of all types there were almost 400 000 beds—a figure well short of that which it was thought would be needed to cope with the expected number of bombing victims. Armed with this information, the Ministry of Health embarked upon a programme of improving and expanding existing facilities, allocating hospitals to wartime functions, accumulating supplies, recruiting staff, and organizing a system for evacuating patients so that a pool of empty beds would always be available in urban areas. While the existing authorities would continue to run hospitals, a substantial degree of central direction was introduced, with some staff recruited and directly employed by the ministry.[49]

The BMA negotiated with the Ministry on the EMS, particularly over the terms and conditions of service for the employment of doctors. The *Journal* kept its readers abreast of developments while they were in the planning phase, but refrained from editorial comment.[50] When war broke out it congratulated its parent body and the government for establishing such an efficient medical organization for the emergency. Before long, however, with Hitler failing to unleash his bombers on Britain, the *Journal* was bemoaning the waste of staff, beds, and expertise implicit in the EMS.[51] The scheme, it thought, needed modifying if civilian sickness were to be dealt with and medical staff adequately remunerated and efficiently utilized. In response to changing circumstances the BMA and government co-operated in reforming the scheme. As a result it 'became almost a national service, covering the sick of all kinds .... In the end, what emerged was a single integrated regionalised hospital service under close central supervision .... A greater contrast with the pre-war hospital scene could scarcely be imagined.' It was a change which the *Journal* was happy to endorse.[52] The reformed EMS signposted the more comprehensive changes in medical provision, not all of which did the *Journal* welcome so heartily.

After establishment of the EMS, it is easy to see, in the succession of political and administrative steps that followed, an inexorable progress towards creation of the NHS. In 1940 the BMA, anxious 'to update its image and seize the initiative', set up a Medical Planning Commission 'to study wartime developments and their effects on the country's medical services

[49] For a comprehensive treatment of this subject see Sir A. MacNalty (ed. in chief), *History of the Second World War. United Kingdom Medical Series*, C. L. Dunn (ed.), *The Emergency Medical Services* (London, 1952–3).

[50] *Journal*, 18 Feb. 1939, 335.

[51] *Ibid.*, 9 Sept. 1939, 571–2; 25 Nov. 1939, 1045–6.

[52] John E. Pater, *The Making of the National Health Service* (London: King's Fund, 1981), pp. 21–2; *Journal*, 25 Nov. 1939, 1045–6.

both present and future'.[53] This was an unwieldy body, comprising over 70 members drawn not only from the BMA but from various other institutions such as the royal colleges. It was chaired by the BMA's Chairman of Council, Henry Souttar, who emphasized that 'it was the profession's desire that every individual should have at his service, whatever his economic status, all necessary medical resources.' Accordingly, the 'problem of the first magnitude' which the committee faced was how to provide a 'complete medical service' for 95 per cent of the population.[54]

The *Journal* foresaw problems for such a large committee in achieving any agreements that were more than feeble compromises. But it had no doubt about the need for its appointment, even though a later correspondent termed its leader on the subject 'grandfatherly':

> War has thrown up into sharp relief the deficiencies of our peacetime system of administering relief to the sick and of promoting and maintaining the health of the people. These deficiencies were, of course, plain enough to many medical men before the war, and the B.M.A. had formulated a series of constructive proposals to deal with them .... It now proposes to prepare for the return of peace so that Medicine may be ready to meet its responsibilities in a world in which many values will be changed, fresh conceptions of society will be formed, and in which new stresses and strains will appear in the moral, material, and economic fabric of the democracy we hold to be our rightful heritage.[55]

Winston Churchill's reaction to the Commission's appointment was, on the other hand, distinctly lukewarm. While many believed that reconstruction planning was a vital aspect of waging war, in that it generated enthusiasm and raised morale, Churchill regarded it as a distraction from the main business in hand, namely, winning the war. Consequently, he regarded the BMA's initiative as likely merely to 'afford a useful addition to the abundant material available in the reports of Commissions and elsewhere, when the opportunity of reconstruction comes'. Many *Journal* correspondents were also critical of the Commission, though for different reasons, namely, its relatively old, undemocratic, and unrepresentative membership.[56]

The Medical Planning Commission produced its interim (and only) report in June 1942. This has recently been described as 'radical' and 'liberal'. Michael Foot, whose biography of Aneurin Bevan presents a less than adoring portrait of the BMA, goes so far as to term it 'an imaginative breakthrough ... the boldest document ever issued by the BMA which went beyond anything previously conceived by the doctors outside the Socialist

[53] *BMJ* Supplement, 4 Jan. 1941, 1–2; C. Webster, *Problems of Health Care*, p. 25 (note 47).
[54] *Journal*, 17 May 1941, 759.
[55] *Ibid.*, 4 Jan. 1941, 19; 22 Feb. 1941, 296.
[56] *Ibid.*, 25 Jan. 1941, 142; 5 *Hansard* 368 (21 Jan. 1941) col. 71; J. E. Pater, *The Making of the National Health Service*, p. 35 (note 52).

Medical Association'.[57] The report emphasized two principles: first, the need for an integrated health service which aimed at preventing as well as relieving sickness; second, the availability to every individual, regardless of means or place of residence, of all necessary health services, whether general or specialist, domiciliary or institutional.[58] The *Journal* accepted the need for change along the lines indicated by the Commission even if it meant some loss of independence, group practice, an end to the buying and selling of practices, and salaried service.[59] Neither was the *Journal* at odds with the rest of the BMA in welcoming such change. Later in the year, for example, the Annual Representative Meeting gave a positive response.

The MPC report and its reception by the Association has sometimes been contrasted with the BMA's post-1942 negativism towards changes similar to those previously proposed within BMA House. If, as has been suggested, the MPC report 'propounded many of the features eventually embodied in the National Health Service', why did the Association come into such violent collision with those planning the service in the mid-1940s?[60] Michael Foot and others have tried to resolve the paradox by arguing that, though the Association was happy to make plans on an untimetabled basis, it rejected similar plans when the intention was to implement them in the foreseeable future.[61] To agree with this is to accept that hypocrisy and deceit prevailed on a grand scale within the BMA. There is a far simpler explanation. The MPC plan envisaged a key role for the medical profession in management and administration. The *Journal* approved that plan on condition that the profession acquired such a role, thereby enabling it to maintain its status and dignity. Its leading article on the report made it clear that:

> While it is appreciated that administration raises questions of governmental policy which are not purely medical, it cannot be too strongly emphasised that the majority of the profession would view with grave apprehension the sacrifice of individual independence entailed by an organized service unless some such reforms in management as have been outlined were embodied in the scheme.[62]

What really concerned the Association and the *Journal* was that administrative responsibility would rest not with the profession but with politicians and bureaucrats, who would then be free to dictate to medical practitioners. This concern reflected the profession's distrust of the Ministry of Health, which in its two decades of existence had done little to win doctors' respect:

[57] C. Webster, *Problems of Health Care*, p. 25 (note 47); J. E. Pater, *The Making of the National Health Service*, p. 39 (note 52); M. Foot, *Aneurin Bevan*, Vol. II, pp. 107, 109 (note 48).

[58] *Journal*, 20 June 1942, 743–53.

[59] *Ibid.*, 20 June 1942, 764–5; J. E. Pater, *The Making of the National Health Service*, p. 40 (note 52).

[60] E. Grey-Turner and F. M. Sutherland, *History of the British Medical Association 1932–1981*, p. 38 (note 7).

[61] M. Foot, *Aneurin Bevan*, Vol. II, pp. 109–10 (note 48); see A. Calder, *The People's War*, p. 622 (note 20).

[62] *Journal*, 20 June 1942, 765.

> ... the Ministry ... since 1920 had shown little or no interest in a comprehensive health service, or even in extending NHI. Nor had it campaigned as had the BMA, for improved nutrition for the lower income groups .... To general practitioners particularly, the Ministry was the unsympathetic skinflint which had fought them over the level of the NHI capitation fee no less than seven times since 1920. The Ministry also had the reputation of ignoring the advice of its medical advisory bodies (beginning with the Dawson Report of 1920) and, in general, of subordinating its medical and other professional staff to a dominant lay administration.[63]

While the Medical Planning Commission presented a bold vision of the future, it believed that implementing its principles would be a lengthy process. For the short term, it recommended extending national health insurance to provide a fuller service for a larger proportion of the population. But publication of the Beveridge Report, on 1 December 1942, called all this into question, for it was predicated on three assumptions, one of which (Assumption B) was that a national health service would be established.

The Beveridge Committee had been appointed in June 1941 with a brief to examine social insurance and allied services. It was not directly concerned with medical provision except in so far as national health insurance provided for medical benefit to be paid to the sick. This was merely one of the social security benefits that Beveridge wished to incorporate into a fairer and more rational social insurance plan. However, because of its assumption that a health service would be established, and the rapturous public reception accorded it, the Beveridge Report carried important implications for medical planning.

The report, much publicized by the press, was eagerly awaited and avidly read by a population hungry for good news. It appeared at a critical moment in the war. The eighth army's recent victory over Rommel at El Alamein was virtually the first good military news in more than three years of combat. At last the enemy had proved vulnerable; few could doubt that much tough fighting lay ahead, but at the same time there seemed some point in considering plans for the peace. As the *Daily Herald* put it: 'The prospect of winning the war growing even clearer, has sharpened the appetite of the British people for news of its Government's plans for "winning the peace".' So high were public expectations that critics of Beveridge were likely to be dubbed 'enemies of the people'.[64] Accordingly, the government was under pressure to announce immediate acceptance of the Beveridge plan and a commitment to legislation. In February 1943 the Lord President of the Council, Sir John Anderson, told Parliament that the plan, including Assumption B, would be implemented. In these circumstances health service

[63] J. E. Pater, *The Making of the National Health Service*, p. 61 (note 52); see H. Eckstein, *The English Health Service*, p. 132 (note 6); Paul Addison, *Now the War is Over* (London: BBC and Cape, 1985), Chapter 4; Frank Honigsbaum, *The Division in British Medicine* (London: Kogan Page, 1979), especially Chapter 21.

[64] *Daily Herald*, 4 Dec. 1942; *Statist*, 5 Dec. 1942; see C. Webster, *Problems of Health Care*, p. 35 (note 47).

planning became a more immediate priority. This then was the context in which the *Journal* gave editorial consideration to the Beveridge plan.

The *Journal*'s reaction was neither hostile nor enthusiastic. Its main concern was with the report's implications for medical practice. It accepted, as had the MPC, the need for thorough investigation of the finance and organization of a national health service. It also stressed that all 'details and arrangements must be worked out with the full consent of those who provide the service.'[65] In February 1943 the BMA Council decided to recommend to the Representative Body that the Association should express willingness to co-operate in the planning of a national health service, provided that the conditions of service were agreed with the profession and that private practice was not outlawed. In reporting this the *Journal* expressed its opposition to the notion of whole-time salaried service on the basis that the doctor should be the servant of his patient, not of the State. Although this observation drew criticism from several correspondents, who complained that doctors were already too much the servants of patients, the prospect of a State medical service in which doctors were salaried civil servants was one of the points that the profession remained determined to oppose to the end.[66]

From white paper to Bevan

In March 1943 confidential and non-committal discussions between the profession and the Minister of Health in the Coalition government (Ernest Brown) commenced. A Representative Committee, dominated by the BMA, spoke for the profession.[67] However, the progress of these talks was interrupted when a press leak appeared to show that the government was leaning towards whole-time salaried service. This was the signal for Charles Hill, then the Association's deputy secretary, to convene a mass meeting of the BMA's metropolitan counties branch for the purpose of condemning the Brown plan. The *Journal*'s reaction to the alleged proposals was one of dismay. It hastened to publish a leader, described as sounding a 'shrill note of warning', which, contrasting sharply with the 'calm and objective tone' of its earlier pronouncements, opined that if whole time salaried service commenced 'doctors will no longer constitute an independent, learned, and liberal profession, but will instead form a service of technicians controlled by central bureaucrats and by local men and women entirely ignorant of medical matters.'[68] 'Why the hurry?' asked Charles Hill, who favoured the

[65] *Journal*, 12 Dec. 1942, 700.

[66] *Ibid.*, 13 Feb. 1943, 193–4; 27 Feb. 1943, 266. *BMJ* Supplement, 13 Feb. 1943, 23–4.

[67] *Journal*, 20 March 1943, 359; *BMJ* Supplement, 10 April 1943, 41–3; E. Grey-Turner and F. M. Sutherland, *History of the British Medical Association 1932 1981*, pp. 40 1 (note 7); H. Eckstein, *The English Health Service*, pp. 140–1 (note 6).

[68] B. Abel-Smith, *The Hospitals 1800–1948. A Study in Social Administration in England and Wales* (London: Heinemann, 1964), p. 459; *Journal*, 29 May 1943, 670–1. For the profession's long-standing opposition to salaries see F. Honigsbaum, *The Division in British Medicine*, part 2 (note 63).

appointment of a royal commission. In the face of such forthright opposition, Brown, observing that he was not committed to any timetable in producing a white paper, agreed to think again and to put his leaked proposals 'in the discard'. This phrase, the *Journal* noted darkly, 'is a term used in the game of poker. It is well to remember that cards in the discard are re-shuffled and find their way back into subsequent games'.[69]

Government planning and negotiations with interested parties continued until February 1944 when Brown's successor as Minister of Health, Henry Willink, published the white paper which 'provided the first detailed public statement of the government's intentions' for a national health service.[70] The main principles enshrined in the document were uncontroversial, as were the goals of 'the reduction of ill- health and the promotion of good health among all citizens'. There was, furthermore, a large degree of consensus regarding the means of achieving them, that is, a comprehensive service of prevention and cure of the highest possible quality, which would be free at the point of delivery (with the possible exception of charges for appliances) for anyone who wished to make use of it. The only controversial item was whether all or most of the population should be included (this was the so-called 100 per cent issue). Until mid-1945 BMA leaders favoured 90 per cent inclusion, thereby leaving the wealthiest one-tenth of the population to receive their medical care by way of private practice. This would have had the effect not only of enhancing medical incomes but of freeing practitioners from total dependence on public funds. It was, however, the questions of finance, organization, and administration that gave rise to the fiercest and most enduring conflict.

Central responsibility was to rest with the Minister of Health, who would be advised by a Health Services Council (a professional statutory body) and Central Medical Board. The board, which would employ and allocate general practitioners, would consist mainly of medically qualified members. Local organization of clinics, health visiting, home nursing, etc. was to be the responsibility of the county and county borough councils. These local authorities, assisted by professional consultative bodies, would, where necessary, combine (as Joint Hospital Authorities) to provide hospital services. Voluntary hospitals could remain autonomous but were to be financially encouraged to enter the public scheme. Consultants, whether part-time or full-time, would be salaried. General practitioners would also be free to choose whether to enter the scheme. If they worked in health centres they would come under the jurisdiction of local authorities and be paid a salary;

[69] *Journal*, 29 May 1943, 670–1; *BMJ* Supplement, 22 May 1943, 61–2; J. E. Pater, *The Making of the National Health Service*, pp. 61–3 (note 52); H. Eckstein, *The English Health Service*, pp. 140–3 (note 6); E. Grey-Turner and F. M. Sutherland, *History of the British Medical Association 1932–1981*, pp. 41–2 (note 7).

[70] C. Webster, *Problems of Health Care*, p. 55 (note 47). For details of the negotiations see Frank Honigsbaum, *Health Happiness and Security: the Creation of the National Health Service* (London: Routledge, 1989).

But do you think it will cure the patient? Cartoon by David Low, published in the *Evening Standard*,* 19 May 1944. Source: Centre for the Study of Cartoons and Caricature, University of Kent at Canterbury.

otherwise they would normally be remunerated by capitation fee. There was to be compensation for the loss of the selling value of practices.[71] All these proposals were put forward as a basis for discussion. The white paper was not, therefore, a blueprint for legislation, as white papers later became, but performed the function of a green paper. In this sense there could be no complaint when the medical profession availed itself of the right to discuss.

Parliamentary reaction to the white paper was generally enthusiastic; indeed, it has been suggested that 'very few announcements of policy have had a more enthusiastic parliamentary reception.'[72] Of course, we know now that it was the jumping off point for over four years of struggle between the BMA and three governments (Coalition, Caretaker, and Labour). But how did the *Journal* react to the white paper and subsequent developments? In fact its opposition was comparatively hard line. Its first leader summarized the contents of the white paper and outlined the substantial area of agreement which existed between the government and the BMA. It then went

[71] *Parliamentary Papers* **VIII** (1943–4), pp. 315–99.

[72] H. Eckstein, *The English Health Service*, p. 139 (note 52). Webster's verdict is that the Commons was only 'reasonably positive'. *Problems of Health Care*, p. 59 (note 47).

on to express reservations about some of the proposals; for example, it feared that the voluntary in hospitals would perish and that the proposed system was over-bureaucratic. But the *Journal*'s main concern was with the future of general practice.

If, as seemed probable, private practice declined owing to patients' refusing to pay twice for the same service (once over the counter and once through taxation), GPs would not only suffer loss of income but would find themselves entirely dependent on public money. Consequently, though the white paper did not directly threaten introduction of a State medical service, and, indeed, explicitly ruled this out, the *Journal* feared that such would be the outcome. 'It is important to recognize in the white paper the unmistakeable direction in which the mind of the Government is moving—and that is towards the institution of a whole-time salaried medical service.' This was a direction in which, the *Journal* cautioned, 'the profession refuses and will refuse to follow . . . If this interpretation is correct, it is useless to deny that there is trouble ahead.'[73] In contrast, the lay press was largely welcoming. The *Lancet* saw the white paper as an acceptable compromise, while the *Medical Press and Circular* regarded it as 'a good basis for negotiation'. Even the BMA's initial reaction was one of 'cautious welcome', though this was not to last.[74]

During the rest of 1944 the BMA attempted to gauge the mood of its members by means of a 'questionary' and representative meetings, as well as proceeding with informal discussions on the white paper with the Minister. Formal negotiations were suspended until the ARM had had its say in December. Throughout this time the *Journal* was relatively quiescent. Its second volume for 1944 carried only one leader on the white paper (on the ARM verdict). All correspondence on the matter was published in the Supplement, which traditionally reported Association business, rather than in the *Journal* proper. Most correspondents expressed hostility to the white paper in whole or in part. Specific criticisms varied, but underlying virtually all the letters was the dread, verging on paranoia, of State control and lay interference in professional affairs. In itself, of course, the tenor of published letters proves nothing, even about editorial sympathies. Slightly more revealing are the results of the questionary conducted by the British Institute of Public Opinion, which showed the BMA leadership to be considerably more militant than, if not completely out of step with, the membership.[75]

[73] *Journal*, 26 Feb. 1944, 293–5; see 13 May 1944, 663–4.

[74] *Lancet*, 26 Feb. 1944, 279–80; 4 March 1944, 313–14; *Medical Press and Circular*, 12 April 1944, 226; C. Webster, *Problems of Health Care*, pp. 57, 60 (note 47).

[75] *BMJ* Supplement, 5 Aug. 1944, 25–30. The results of the questionary have been variously interpreted. H. Eckstein, *The English Health Service*, p. 147 (note 6), suggests that they constituted a 'repudiation' of the leadership. C. Webster, *Problems of Health Care*, p. 61 (note 47), feels that they 'generally supported' the BMA. If there was a lesson for the Association in the events of 1911–12 it was that the membership did not always act in accordance with its articulated beliefs.

The obvious danger was that the mistakes of 1911–13 were about to be repeated, with the Association advocating policies which the rank and file would not support. The parallels were obvious, and in July the *BMJ* Supplement carried an article entitled '1911 and 1944'. The anonymous author hypothesized that

> ... as the doctors in 1911 fought against the introduction of the National Health Insurance system which, after it came into operation, they learnt to approve, they may now once more be about to fight a Government proposal which, in another thirty years' time, they will come to acknowledge is to their own and the public's advantage.[76]

In the event this proved prophetic. The author, however, went on to argue that, despite appearances, 1944 actually bore few similarities to 1911. The profession, he concluded, was in duty bound 'to endeavour to deter the Government from the extreme socialistic step of making State provision for all, including those who do not need or want it'.[77]

While the questionary, of which so much had been hoped, provided less than a ringing endorsement of BMA headquarters, the Annual Representative Meeting which met in London in December 1944 showed more heart for a fight. In the course of four days some 270 members considered over 370 motions on the white paper. The net result was a decision to negotiate with the government on the white paper only if it were 'altered in essentials'. Guy Dain's (Chairman of Council) motion was carried unanimously:

> That it be an instruction to the Association's representatives on the Negotiating Committee that, without prejudice to other issues, including the 100% question, remuneration and compensation, consideration of administrative structure, central and local, should precede consideration of all other questions, and that agreement on this subject is an essential prerequisite to discussion of other subjects.[78]

The results of the questionary were to be ignored; Dain dismissed them curtly. The ARM, which the *Journal* felt was more truly representative of rank and file opinion, 'would determine the Association policy'.[79] Elsewhere there was more doubt. *The Times* warned that 'the conference has willed almost all the ends and rejected almost all the means'. The *Lancet*, unburdened by a constitutional link with a professional body, was able to take a more dispassionate view than the *Journal*. It accepted that some of the arguments within the ARM had been reasonable and constructive, but it

[76] *BMJ* Supplement, 1 July 1944, 1–3.

[77] *Ibid.*, 3.

[78] *Journal*, 16 Dec. 1944, 794; *BMJ* Supplement, 16 Dec. 1944, 147–65.

[79] *Ibid.*, 165; *Journal*, 16 Dec. 1944, 794; B. Abel-Smith, *The Hospitals*, p. 469 (note 68). See H. Eckstein, *The English Health Service*, pp. 150–5 (note 6), who questions the representativeness of the Association's Representative Body.

feared that the zealots who had orchestrated opposition to the white paper laid the profession open to ridicule with their absurd demands.[80]

Within a few weeks of the ARM another organization held a conference in London. This too had the white paper high on its agenda. One speaker, paraphrasing Woodrow Wilson, referred to the ARM decision as 'an attempt to make the world safe for hypocrisy'. 'Harley Street,' he continued, had 'developed a new definition of the concept of democracy: "Government of the people by the doctors for the doctors".' The subsequent vote showed unanimity on the need for full implementation of the government's proposals. The body in conference was the Labour Party.[81] It was clear that a Labour government would not be prepared to dilute the white paper. But for the moment the Labour Party had no power and apparently little prospect of achieving it. What were its resolutions but so much hot air? In the meantime, armed with the endorsement of the ARM, the profession could resume negotiations with the minister.

During the first months of 1945 the Negotiating Committee, on which the BMA had a majority, won several important concessions. These included abandonment of the notion of full-time salaried service, acceptance that private practice could continue, and changes in the administrative machinery which placed the profession more centre stage. In return the profession conceded the 100 per cent issue by agreeing that the new service should be available to the entire population. This was a concession which the *Journal*, mindful of the support expressed for a 100 per cent scheme through the questionary, viewed with equanimity.[82] The Minister produced interim proposals which were submitted to a Special Representative Meeting of the BMA in May.[83] But with the end of the war in Europe (9 May), the fall of Churchill's Coalition (23 May), and a General Election scheduled for 5 July, everything came to a halt.

The *Journal*, consistent with its policy of ignoring party politics, carried no reference to the General Election result or Aneurin Bevan's appointment as Minister of Health. Only some months later, after Bevan had visited BMA House to meet members of Council, did it publish a pen portrait of the man. He was, in the words of one member, 'obviously clever and charming with the cherubic outlook and manner of a boy'. The adjective 'cherubic' has also been used to describe Charles Hill, the BMA's chief negotiator. The image arises of two cherubs battling it out over the future of the nation's health services. But Bevan was far more than a personable 'boyo from the valleys'. For all his charm he could be tough and uncompromising; moreover, he

[80] *The Times*, 9 Dec. 1944; *Lancet*, 16 Dec. 1944, 790; J. E. Pater, *The Making of the National Health Service*, p. 90 (note 52).

[81] *BMJ* Supplement, 6 Jan. 1945, 3.

[82] *Journal*, 12 May 1945, 668–9.

[83] C. Webster, *Problems of Health Care*, pp. 67–71 (note 47).

possessed an intellect and caustic wit which made him a consummate debater and fearsome negotiator. According to the *Journal*, 'There is something disarming about the way in which the new Minister confesses his ignorance and his willingness to learn .... At the same time, behind this disarming front there is probably a very combative spirit.'[84] 'Disarming' and 'combative'; such were the qualities that the new Minister of Health relied on in his dealings with the medical profession. It was to prove a powerful combination.

At the time of Bevan's visit to BMA House there was great uncertainty about precisely what he had in mind. Labour had accused Willink of leaving health service planning in a 'muddle'; consequently preparation of its detailed proposals would take some time.[85] Meanwhile the ARM carried on as though nothing had happened, even passing a resolution that any compulsorily insured person should be entitled to opt out and receive a financial grant towards the cost of private medical care. The *Journal* was wise enough to recognize that 'in view of the upsetting of the chessboard owing to the new political situation these debates seemed a little unreal.'[86]

The situation was indeed unreal. Thirty months of almost ceaseless activity were suddenly followed by deafening silence from the Ministry of Health. The doctors' Negotiating Committee had nothing to do but kick its heels. In 1944 the profession had kept the politicians waiting; now the roles were reversed. It was the 'phoney war' all over again. The rumours started in November, with the lay press reporting that voluntary hospitals would be nationalized, that large independent hospital regions (instead of the Joint Authorities) were to be created, and that Bevan had no intention of consulting the BMA over the form of the service, as against terms and conditions for doctors. The *Journal* could only reflect that 'no useful comment can be made' until the profession heard from the Minister himself. Council decided to take the initiative by reminding Bevan of the Negotiating Committee's existence. For his part, Bevan coolly intimated that the Committee would not be denied an opportunity to express its views.[87]

In December 1945 Bevan informed the Commons that, though his proposals had yet to be finalized, they would definitely prohibit the sale of practices and include steps for ensuring 'a proper distribution of doctors to fit the public need'. Willink termed the statement 'vague and menacing'. The Negotiating Committee wanted more details before deciding whether

[84] *BMJ* Supplement, 1 Dec. 1945, 119. As Morgan points out, Bevan was not quite the tyro he claimed to be. K. O. Morgan, *Labour in Power 1945–1951* (Oxford: Oxford University Press, 1984), p. 152. For a more balanced 'Life' of Bevan than the Michael Foot biography see John John Campbell, *Nye Bevan and the Mirage of British Socialism* (London: Weidenfeld and Nicolson, 1987).

[85] *Journal*, 25 Aug. 1945, 269.

[86] *Ibid.*, 4 Aug. 1945, 159; *BMJ* Supplement, 4 Aug. 1945, 30–1.

[87] *Ibid.*, 10 Nov. 1945, 101; 17 Nov. 1945, 106; 24 Nov. 1945, 112–13. See H. Eckstein, *The English Health Service*, pp. 159–60 (note 6).

Bevan's plans were tolerable. In the meantime it regarded them as 'fraught with danger to public and professional freedom'. The *Journal* reacted with yet more hostility, speculating that Bevan was likely to end up with precisely what he wished to avoid: a new health service run by discontented men with 'a sense of grievance'.

The real difficulty felt by medical men who are not partisan Socialists—and they comprise the majority of the profession—is that they see themselves being called on to fashion a service in co-operation with a Government which has rigid doctrinaire views on the ordering of society. If the Government does not recognize this fact and has not the strength of mind to model the new service on the basis of fact and not theory, then the evolution of medical practice may turn out to be retrograde ... the medical profession ... has read the writing on the wall, and does not pretend to like it.[88]

Inevitable conflict

The National Health Service bill and an explanatory white paper were published on 20 March 1946. Their appearance heralded the beginning of the final phase in the protracted process of creating the National Health Service. In many ways it was also the most acrimonious phase, with the BMA becoming ever more strident in its opposition. As for the *Journal*, in contrast to its more dispassionate approach of the early 1940s, it too, in editorials that were published more or less weekly, became far more vocal in its opposition to government plans.

The detailed proposals have been summarized by many authors in the past, so here it is necessary to provide only a brief outline. The bill offered a publicly funded medical service, free at the point of delivery, and comprehensive except for the industrial and school medical services. All hospitals, including the voluntary ones, were to be incorporated in a State network. General practitioners who joined the scheme would be remunerated partly by salary and partly by capitation fee. Overall responsibility for the service was to rest with the Minister, who would be advised by a Health Services Council on which medical representatives would be in a majority. Local administration would be effected through Regional Hospital Boards and Local Hospital Management Committees; County and County Borough Councils were to be responsible for certain domiciliary and clinic services (e.g. ambulances, home nursing, maternity, and child welfare), while Local Executive Councils would have responsibility for general practitioners and dentists.[89]

The BMA Council was 'opposed, on grounds of public interest, to certain important features of the Government's proposals'. The *Journal*'s leader on

[88] 5 *Hansard* 416 (6 Dec. 1945) col. 2512; *Journal*, 15 Dec. 1945, 834, 851–2.

[89] *Parliamentary Papers* 1945–6 III National Health Service Bill, p. 67 *et seq*; *Parliamentary Papers* 1945–6 XX Summary of the Proposed New Service, pp. 511–46; see *Journal*, 30 March 1946, 461–74, 489–91.

Old Low's Almanack. Cartoon by David Low, published in the *Evening Standard*,* 17 December 1946. Source: Centre for the Study of Cartoons and Caricature, University of Kent at Canterbury.

* Associated Newspapers plc,

the bill shows that it shared Council's misgivings. It particularly regretted the lack of administrative co-ordination, the growth of a centralized bureaucracy ('a committee can't heal a sick man'), the demise of the voluntary hospitals from which 'doctors have for centuries received their nourishment and inspiration', and the potential loss of independence for general practitioners: 'Will the kind of regimented medical service contemplated give the right setting and stimulus to the Jenners, Hunters, Budds, Snows and James Mackenzies of the future?' The profession, the *Journal* suggested, had to consider its position.[90]

Once again, the *Lancet*, though not blind to the bill's shortcomings, was far more welcoming than the *Journal*.[91] It was not, however, the views of its 'esteemed contemporary' which upset the *Journal*, but those of 'the most powerful organ of public opinion in the country', *The Times*, which had followed the *Lancet* line while ignoring 'the different expression of opinion

[90] *Ibid.*, 490; see 13 April 1946, 575–6.
[91] *Lancet*, 23 March 1946, 421–4; 6 April 1946, 503–4.

voiced in these columns on the Bill as a whole and on the hospital question in particular'. In consequence, 'the non-medical and informed public which looks to *The Times* for a balanced presentation of majority medical opinion on an important issue is not, we think, provided with it.' Instead it found attacks on the BMA. At a later stage in the NHS controversy the *Journal* accused *The Times* of pursuing an 'unrelenting course of opposition' to the BMA.[92]

Of course, the *Journal*'s main concern was less with the perceived iniquities and inequities of one newspaper, however influential, than with the tenor of Bevan's proposals. But favourable press reaction to the bill served to harden the *Journal*'s attitudes. Its first response had been to encourage the profession to question whether the bill would lead to a State service, frustrate medicine, and run counter to the public interest. It urged doctors to define their priorities and consider whether the bill would compromise them, but it desisted from urging outright opposition to the government's plans.[93] Within three weeks, however, it was complaining that civil servants would run the hospital service, that 'medical men working in it will be wholly or partly State employees working under Civil Service direction', and that general practitioners would soon be in a similar relationship. Its correspondence columns, one leader claimed, showed that medical men 'dislike the general tenour [sic] of the Bill'. Further negotiations were required.[94] By this time, however, what the *Journal* called 'two of the most important discussions since 1911 affecting the future of medicine' were little more than a week away.[95] These were the debate on the second reading of the government bill and the BMA's Special Representative Meeting.

The BMA meeting resolved itself overwhelmingly in favour of the right to buy and sell practices and freedom for doctors to practise where they wished. Representatives conclusively rejected salaried service and the nationalization of hospitals. They also decided that there should be a plebiscite on whether the Negotiating Committee should meet the government to discuss terms and conditions of service. In the Commons the government had little difficulty in piloting the bill through its second reading, but the *Journal* considered that the profession should 'press hard for those amendments which it considers to be essential to an ordered evolution of the medical services of this country . . . it must do all it reasonably can to stop at its source a stream that threatens to become an inundation.' This the BMA continued to do, though in the remaining stages of the parliamentary process few important concessions were won in the face of Bevan's affable but determined resistance to what he

92 *Journal*, 20 April 1946, 612–13; 24 Jan. 1948, 155–6; *The Times*, 22 March 1946.

93 *Journal*, 30 March 1946, 489–91.

94 *Ibid.*, 20 April 1946, 612–13; 27 April, 1946, 653–5.

95 *Ibid.*, 4 May 1946, 686–7.

saw as vested interests.[96] A government with an assured majority in the Commons was under little pressure to compromise. It would have to do so only if it chose to avoid having the NHS implemented by disaffected and demoralized doctors, or was forced to do so by the intransigence of a unified profession refusing service. The controversy was rapidly approaching a crisis.

By July, with the bill passing smoothly through Parliament, the *Journal* realized that there was only one question of overriding importance which could not be settled by politicians at Westminster. The time would come when this would have to be answered by doctors, who, knowing the exact terms of the Act, would have to decide whether to accept service. 'Until the Bill has become an Act it will not be possible to ascertain the fully considered views of the medical profession on the Government's main proposals for a National Health Service. We shall not attempt to forecast what the reaction of the majority of doctors will be.'[97] A few days later Guy Dain, the diminutive Birmingham GP who was Chairman of Council throughout the NHS crisis, told the BMA's Annual Representative Meeting much the same thing: 'we have come to the time when one side or the other has to give way. A conflict is inevitable.'

The ARM took up the recommendation of the recent SRM that the profession should be balloted on whether to negotiate terms and conditions of service or to break off all negotiations with the government.[98] The wording of the question, which went out soon after the NHS bill had received the Royal Assent (November 1946), was: 'Do you desire the Negotiating Committee to enter into discussions with the Minister on the Regulations authorized by the National Health Service Act?' Respondents were required to answer yes or no. Although organized by the BMA, the plebiscite question was sent to every individual on the *Medical Register*. Ostensibly the profession was to be given a free hand to decide the question undirected by the BMA leadership. In reality it was subjected to considerable influence on how it should vote by the materials that were despatched along with the voting slips, namely, a letter from Charles Hill and the report of the Negotiating Committee. As for the *Journal*, it was as intransigent as ever. By quoting Dain's hostile assessment of the new Act in an editorial, it indicated that only by voting 'no' could BMA members avoid betraying their elected representatives. The *Lancet*, on the other hand, recommended a 'yes' vote.[99]

When the results of the plebiscite were revealed they showed that 37 per cent of all civilian doctors had voted yes, 44 per cent no, and 19 per cent had

[96] *BMJ* Supplement, 11 May 1946, 119–35; *Journal*, 11 May 1946, 725–7; 20 July 1946, 91–2; C. Webster, *Problems of Health Care*, pp. 97–103 (note 47).

[97] *Journal*, 20 July 1946, 92.

[98] *Ibid.*, 3 Aug. 1946, 163–4, 168–9; *BMJ* Supplement, 3 Aug. 1946, 36–46.

[99] *Journal*, 9 Nov. 1946, 697; 16 Nov. 1946, 739; *BMJ* Supplement, 16 Nov. 1946, 123–30; *Lancet*, 16 Nov. 1946, 719–20; J. E. Pater, *The Making of the National Health Service*, p. 136 (note 52); K. O. Morgan, *Labour in Power 1945–1951*, p. 158 (note 84).

not responded. Of all those who voted, including service doctors, 46 per cent said yes and 54 per cent no. This was hardly a decisive statement; the main thing it showed was the deep division within the profession. The *Lancet* thought that one of the reasons for the 'no' vote was the 'partial picture' of the scheme presented by BMA leaders, that is, a picture in which imperfections and risks were highlighted while opportunities were played down. 'For our part,' it continued, 'we see in the new service a chance of realising great aims.' It believed that the narrowness of the majority 'does not justify non-cooperation with the Government of the day'. However, the BMA Council concluded that it had no mandate to continue negotiating. Accordingly, it recommended to the Association's policy-making arm, the Representative Body, which was to meet on 28 January 1947, that it should vote against further negotiations.[100] The Act was on the Statute Book, but would the profession agree to operate it? An impasse appeared to have been reached.

The last lap

An impasse was prevented by the presidents of the three English royal colleges who, on 2 January, wrote to Bevan asking for clarification of certain points and an assurance that the Minister would endeavour to meet professional objections. Bevan's reply was conciliatory. He emphasized, for example, that capitation fees would be the main method of remunerating general practitioners, that he would have no power 'to direct a doctor to go anywhere or do anything', and that he had no plans for a full-time salaried service. More generally, he wanted the profession to have the opportunity to influence the final form of the service before individual doctors exercised their right to decide on whether to enter it. All this was enough to convince Council that its advice to the Representative Body should be changed; it therefore recommended that negotiations should be entered into, and 'that after the conclusion of these discussions a second plebiscite of the profession be taken on the issue of entering the Service'.[101]

As usual the *Journal*, which since the beginning of the year had been edited by Hugh Clegg, endorsed the Council decision. That decision, it suggested, showed 'neither appeasement nor weakness' but a willingness 'to meet the Minister half way if he himself will meet them half way'. The *Journal* then went rather further than Council, calling on the Minister to negotiate on the clauses of the Act as well as the regulations to be drawn up under its terms.[102] When the Special Representative Meeting convened on 22 January it

[100] *Journal*, 21 Dec. 1946, 947–8; 11 Jan. 1947, 64–5; *BMJ* Supplement, 21 Dec. 1946, 161–2, 164; *Lancet*, 21 Dec. 1946, 909.

[101] *Journal*, 11 Jan. 1947, 57, 66–7.

[102] *Ibid.*, 25 Jan. 1947, 141; *BMJ* Supplement, 25 Jan. 1947, 10–11.

Operation Sabotage. Cartoon by David Low, published in the *Evening Standard*,* 15 January 1948. Source: Centre for the Study of Cartoons and Caricature, University of Kent at Canterbury.

accepted that negotiations should commence.[103] The remainder of 1947 was a period of intense and detailed negotiations between representatives of the profession and the Ministry of Health. But there was little for the *Journal* to report or comment on, for the negotiations took place behind closed doors and with the minimum of publicity.

It was not until December 1947 that the *Journal* was able to consider their outcome. Its verdict was unfavourable. Bevan, it opined, 'has refused to amend the Act in any one particular and has in effect done little to remove those grave doubts on certain aspects of the Act which unsettle the majority of the profession in this country.'[104] Its main concerns continued to be, as ever, with State control and loss of professional independence. It was soon known that the second plebiscite was to be held in January 1948, only five months before the 'appointed day' when the Act, along with the new social security legislation, would come into operation. On this occasion the *Journal* made it clear how it expected the profession to vote:

[103] *Journal*, 1 Feb. 1947, 185; 8 Feb. 1947, 227; 15 Feb. 1947, 258; *BMJ* Supplement, 1 Feb. 1947, 15–19; 8 Feb. 1947, 21–2.

[104] *Journal*, 20 Dec. 1947, 1002–4.

> The National Health Service is the first and most important step towards denying the medical profession . . . freedom. If the medical profession does not hold this to be an absolute good necessary to its fruitful evolution, or if it does not believe that its real freedom is threatened by the Health Service Act, then it will presumably accept Mr. Bevan's invitation to co-operate with him in starting the new Service next July. If, however, the medical profession, after deep reflection upon 'the essence' of Mr. Bevan's proposals, concludes that this Act is the first and irrevocable step towards a whole time State medical service, then it must have the courage and integrity of mind to refuse to serve under the Act until it has been amended in those particulars which the profession holds to be essential to its continued existence as a body of free men.[105]

The priority was for continued professional unity, notwithstanding that the Minister had sought to create division by offering consultants 'the bait' of pay beds in State hospitals. It was not, the *Journal* suggested, money that was at stake, but principle. The BMA Council was also explicit in advocating opposition to service under the existing arrangements.[106]

In the first six months of 1948 the *Journal* played its most important part in the protracted debate over the NHS. Throughout the 'struggle' it had been an opinion-former, disseminator of information, and forum for discussion. It continued to be all of these, but in a far more sustained and forceful manner. Its leaders, almost all of which were written by Hugh Clegg, became more hard-hitting, persuasive, and, ultimately, decisive in influencing grass roots opinion and thereby determining BMA policy. The rest of its pages became ever more dominated by health service business. Correspondence on the subject, only a small proportion of which could be published, came flooding in at a rate of some 30 000 words a week.[107] In the early weeks of the year the *Journal* concentrated on raising the morale of the troops: 'We believe . . . that the plebiscite . . . will show that the majority of the medical men and women of this country will refuse to take service under the Act in its present form.' If this were to happen Bevan would be forced to amend the Act or 'put the health services of this country into jeopardy, embitter the relationship between the doctor and the State, and sow among doctors themselves discords that will echo for years to come'.[108]

Plebiscite forms were sent out to all medical practitioners on 31 January. They asked three questions: do you approve or disapprove of the NHS Act; do you favour or oppose acceptance of service under the Act in its present form; and will you abide by the decision of the majority if it is against accepting service? The result was an overwhelming rejection of the Act and service under it. O. C. Carter, chairman of the Journal Committee, judged that 'the quality of argument advanced in the *Journal* . . . played a large part

[105] *Ibid.*, 27 Dec. 1947, 1037–8; see 20 Dec. 1947, 1004.
[106] *Ibid.*, 3 Jan. 1948, 18; 31 Jan. 1948, 207.
[107] *Ibid.*, 6 March 1948, 454.
[108] *Ibid.*, 10 Jan. 1948, 63–4.

in enabling the members of the profession to come to a decision on how they should vote in the [second] plebiscite.'[109]

The *Journal* regarded the outcome, along with the bellicose reaction of the Representative Body and other BMA groups, as a clear message that the government had to make concessions.[110] A similar conclusion was evidently drawn by Bevan, for on 7 April, on the advice of the President of the Royal College of Physicians, Lord Moran, he undertook to make it statutorily clear that he did not intend introducing full- time salaried service. He also offered to modify the of proposals on remuneration so that, after a fixed element of salary for three years, payment would be entirely by capitation fee.

It later became a matter of dispute among BMA members as to whether these concessions were significant. Clegg believed that they were. In two letters to Lord Moran he wrote with relief of the 'deadlock' being broken and of the termination of 'a fight which, if continued to the end, would have been disastrous'. Bevan's concessions, he wrote, 'represent a great "victory" for the Plebiscite'. By influencing the Minister, Clegg felt, Moran had 'done a very great service to the medical profession . . . when the shouting has died down medical men will recognize this.' His one regret was that it had not been the BMA who had made the first move.[111]

Clegg realized that these views, which he proposed to express in an editorial, would be unpopular and provoke a hullabaloo in the *Journal*'s correspondence columns. In the hope of discouraging letter writers he 'would try to put the matter in perspective' in his leader. But he recognized that some 'will have to be allowed to blow off steam—the correspondence columns provide a useful safety valve'.[112] In a leader headed 'Mr. Bevan's Gesture' Clegg expressed the view that Bevan had made 'a big concession'. He urged that Bevan's 'temperate and conciliatory words' should meet with a like response. As Clegg had anticipated, the editorial drew much critical comment. One correspondent wrote: 'Our net gains from these "conciliatory" assurances would seem to be *nil*, and we are likely to lose from their possible weakening effect on some in our ranks.' Council, too hastily, as some of its critics later argued, decided that there should be a third plebiscite.[113]

Plebiscite forms, which carried the same wording as those issued in January, went out on 19 April. As before, they were sent to all registered practitioners. Each form notified the recipient that, if there was a majority against accepting service, and that majority included 'approximately' 13 000 GPs (out of a national total of 20 500), then the BMA would continue to advise against acceptance of service. Accompanying the forms was a Council

[109] *BMJ* Supplement, 27 March 1948, 49.

[110] *Journal*, 21 Feb. 1948, 347–8; 20 March 1948, 550–1; 27 March 1948, 604–5.

[111] Royal College of Physicians, NHS Papers, Box 1, Item 81. Hugh Clegg to Lord Moran, 13 and 21 April 1948. Reproduced in F. Honigsbaum, *Health Happiness and Security*, pp. 219–21 (note 70), see also pp. 150–1.

[112] *Ibid.*

[113] *Journal*, 17 April 1948, 737–8; 24 April 1948, 791–3.

statement outlining what it had and had not achieved. This suggested that Council advised continued opposition: 'Bearing in mind that what we have secured falls short of what we have sought, the Council's view is that while progress has been made to that end, the freedoms of the profession are not sufficiently safeguarded.' In a 'fighting speech' at Shrewsbury, Guy Dain, the Chairman of Council, urged rejection; but on 24 April a *Journal* leader hinted that the vote should be for acceptance.

We must take note of the fact that public opinion, as expressed by those who represent their constituents in Parliament and by responsible daily and weekly newspapers, considers that Mr Bevan has made a conciliatory move towards a solution of present difficulties. It is recognized that this move has been made as the direct result of the enormous vote of no confidence in the present Act given in the plebiscite earlier this year. The Government had to take this into account and has in consequence modified its policy. Doctors must now ask themselves whether the modifications go far enough to remove their underlying fears of the Act in its modified form.

At the same time, Clegg refrained from reporting Dain's Shrewsbury speech. Thus, unusually, there was a clear difference between the opinions of Council and *BMJ*.[114]

The plebiscite form went to 54 667 voters, 74 per cent of whom voted. Of those who voted over 60 per cent expressed disapproval of the Act, though this was less than half of all those eligible to vote. On the question of accepting service, slightly more than half of those entitled to vote were against acceptance but, crucially, only 9588 general practitioners voted against, that is, substantially fewer than the 13 000 required to satisfy Council that it should maintain the BMA's policy. As a result Council recommended to the Representative Body that it should co-operate with the Minister in establishing the new service. In a leading article entitled 'What we have gained', the *Journal* observed that the profession, and the BMA in particular, had won many important improvements in the five years since Ernest Brown had first published his plans. Bevan, it maintained, had compromised,

and compromises are the traditional English way of settling disputes. For the medical profession to reject the compromise and to be intransigent would cost it the support of public opinion .... During the past months the medical profession has shown its strength and has shown, too, that it can use it with wisdom.

The *Journal* recognized that many of its correspondents rejected the idea of a comprehensive medical service, but observed that while 'this is a tenable position ... it is not the policy of the British Medical Association'. At the end of May a Special Representative Meeting accepted the Council recommenda-

114 *Ibid.*; *BMJ* Supplement, 24 April 1948, 105–6; F. Honigsbaum, *Health Happiness and Security*, pp. 150–1 (note 70).

tion and thereby 'brought to an end a debate which has lasted nearly six years'.[115]

Had the BMA achieved a victory? Had all the years of negotiation, dispute, and acrimony been worth while? As in 1911–13 opinion was divided. What seems certain is that the *Journal*, and especially its leading articles of 17 and 24 April, had played a decisive part in bringing matters to a conclusion. BMA members differed as to whether it had been a laudable or treacherous part. As the 'What we have gained' leader stated, 'some correspondents have taken this *Journal* to task because of the content and tone of the leading articles that have appeared' since Bevan's statement of 7 April. Among these was Dr Simpson of Burnley who wrote:

> To anybody who has followed the editorials of the *B.M.J.* during the past two months those of the last three issues must be a subject of derision .... No impartial reader could say that these were 'well balanced'. The words may be this or that, but the horrid smell of appeasement comes up from all those three articles. The *B.M.J.* is dividing the doctors, and it is doing so deliberately. On the eve of battle no general could maintain the morale of his troops by making a well-balanced statement which reflected the indecision and revolt of a minority of the high-ranking officers.[116]

Simpson went on to accuse the *Journal* of conditioning doctors to betray their own freedom:

> Will you be good enough, Sir, to tell the doctors—you who have prated so much about freedom and independence—what of these things you have achieved for them. You know very well that you have achieved little worth while. The doctors will be just as much the servants of the State machine as if the BMA's campaign had never started.

Other letters were equally full of outraged accusations: 'I am horrified and most disappointed by the tone of your leader in the *Journal* of April 17'; 'In all my life and experience I have never known such deplorable lack of decisive generalship at the moment of crisis.' But the *Journal* was not without support. The BMA's Holland division unanimously resolved that their honorary secretary should convey their congratulations to the *BMJ* for its 'extremely fair and lucid' editorials; 'they have shown a realistic and common-sense attitude throughout and have enhanced the value of the *Journal* considerably in the eyes of those who are neither "die-hards" nor "eviscerates".'[117]

The *Journal*'s role was debated at a Special Representative Meeting on 28 May when Simpson, complaining of 'the disastrous effect on the plebiscite of the *BMJ* leaders of April 17 and 24', tabled a motion calling for Clegg's dismissal. Simpson was supported by Dr Hale-White of Marylebone, who

[115] *Journal*, 8 May 1948, 894; 15 May 1948, 936–7; 5 June 1948, 1086.
[116] *Ibid.*, 15 May 1948, 950.
[117] *Ibid.*, 951; 22 May 1948, 1005; 29 May 1948, 1047, 1049.

said that 'nothing could have been further removed from the policy of the Representative Body as expressed at its last meeting [i.e. of 17 March 1948] than the articles now questioned. They expressed a complete reversal of policy without any consultation with this Body.' But Clegg and the *Journal* were supported by members of Council and others. R. W. Cockshut, for example, said the leaders were 'a noteworthy example of editorial comment at its best'. He felt that Simpson's motion reflected disappointment at not finding 'flaming propaganda' in the leaders. When a vote was taken fewer than half a dozen of those present voted in favour.[118]

This is not the place to undertake a detailed assessment of either the BMA's behaviour or its success in the NHS question. However, several conclusions are inescapable. First, when the NHS came into operation it proved a boon to the profession, not least in eliminating that bane of general practice, the bad debt. Second, it should not be forgotten that its general scope and many of its features were similar to BMA proposals dating back to the 1930s. Third, many of the so-called concessions which eventually caused the Association to pull back from the brink in 1948 had either been already conceded by Bevan or concerned threats to professional freedom which were more imagined than real.[119] For these reasons it is hard to understand why the BMA exhibited 'quite extraordinary negativism' towards the plan and battled against it for almost as long as Britain battled against Hitler.[120] But with the advent of the Labour government in 1945 the whole question acquired a 'subtext' in which the profession saw itself as upholding 'freedom', 'democracy', and 'independence' against the threats of 'bureaucracy', 'nationalisation', 'regimentation', and 'socialism'. Amid rhetoric like this the details of the health service became of secondary importance.

Our concern is with the role of the *Journal*. Until the spring of 1948 the *BMJ* had been very much to the fore in encouraging BMA opposition not simply to details but also to some of the principles of the NHS plan. Its *volte-face*, which clearly was crucial in defusing professional opposition, is not satisfactorily explained by Bevan's alleged concessions, for the Minister offered little that he had not offered before.[121] Even the concession on salaries—in favour of payment by capitation fee, on which so much store was set—was of strictly limited significance. As one *Journal* correspondent wrote: 'Capitation rates are only a salary in a disguised form.'[122] To say that the *Journal* recognized that the dispute was one which could not be won begs the question of why it reached such a conclusion only in April 1948. Perhaps it

[118] *Ibid.*, 5 June 1948, 1086–7; F. Honigsbaum, *Health Happiness and Security*, p. 152 (note 70).

[119] See M. Foot, *Aneurin Bevan*, Vol. II, pp. 207–8 (note 48); J. Campbell, *Nye Bevan and the Mirage of British Socialism*, p. 177 (note 84).

[120] K. O. Morgan, *Labour in Power, 1945–1951*, p. 159 (note 84).

[121] *Ibid.*, p. 160.

[122] *Journal*, 22 May 1948, 1005.

recognized Bevan's determination to implement the service on 5 July come what may and that, as in 1913, no matter how doctors expressed themselves in words and votes, economic necessity would compel them to register, thereby undermining the resistance of all others. This was what Bevan believed would happen.[123] Certainly, Clegg realized that if doctors did not enter service willingly then they would suffer grievously, for the NHS would be established anyway, chaos would follow, and 'the disorder of the Service will be laid at their door'.[124] While BMA leaders remained drunk on their own oratory, Clegg was brought to his senses by a sharp attack of realism.

Thereafter, Clegg's leaders exercised a vital role. In retrospect, it may be observed that, by encouraging the profession to settle, they helped it to avoid inevitable defeat and humiliation. In 1946–8 the medical profession gave up more than in 1911–13, but, though the NHI dispute was widely perceived as a defeat, the NHS fight is generally felt to have ended in victory. As two recent studies conclude: 'In contrast to the 1913 fiasco, BMA leaders came through with flying colours' and 'The BMA had won its spurs as the standard-bearer of the middle classes.'[125]

[123] See J. Campbell, *Nye Bevan and the Mirage of British Socialism*, pp. 175–6 (note 84); J. E. Pater, *The Making of the National Health Service*, p. 179 (note 52).

[124] Clegg to Moran, 13 and 21 April 1948 in F. Honigsbaum, *Health Happiness and Security*, pp. 219–21 (note 70).

[125] *Ibid.*, p. 152; E. Grey-Turner and F. M. Sutherland, *History of the British Medical Association 1932–1981*, p. 76 (note 7).

11
The post-war world

Clegg and others

When Hugh Clegg joined the *Journal* as a sub-editor in April 1931, he was starting a 34-year stint on the editorial staff. He became the first deputy editor in 1934 and, at the beginning of 1947, succeeded Horner as editor. Clegg assumed the editorship at a potentially difficult time, for negotiations over the NHS were entering their final phase. In truth, however, he had been shouldering editorial responsibility for some years before 1947 owing to Horner's ill-health and general lack of capacity. He had, for example, conducted the negotiations with Stanley Morison over the *Journal*'s redesign. He had also been in sole charge during Horner's prolonged wartime absence through illness and had written most of the editorials dealing with the Beveridge Report and the NHS. It has been suggested that he had *de facto* control of the *Journal* from as early as 1939.[1] Clearly, Clegg already possessed a wealth of experience, including in the exercise of authority, when he became editor.

Hugh Anthony Clegg was born in June 1900 at St Ives, Huntingdonshire. He was one of seven children (the third son) born to the Rev. John Clegg, the headmaster of a local school, and his wife, Gertrude. As a clever child of a far from wealthy family Clegg was, from an early age, under pressure to finance his education by winning scholarships.[2] His father's tutoring in the classics helped him to win a King's scholarship to Westminster School. He then went to Trinity College, Cambridge, as a Westminster exhibitioner, gaining, in 1922, a first class honours degree in the natural science tripos. His medical training took place at St Bartholomew's Hospital, where he qualified with the conjoint diploma in 1925. After junior hospital appointments at Barts and the Brompton Hospital for Diseases of the Chest, he graduated MB BChir in 1928. He gained the MRCP in 1929 (FRCP in 1944) while assistant medical officer to the Metropolitan Asylums Board in charge of a tuberculosis unit. He then became resident medical registrar to Charing Cross Hospital. Private practice and hospital consultancy might have followed, but Clegg

[1] T. D. V. Swinscow, *Reap a Destiny* (Cambridge: Cambridge University Press, 1989), p. 131; *Dictionary of National Biography, 1981–90* (Oxford: Oxford University Press forthcoming); *The Times*, 7 July 1983; *BMJ* Supplement, 2 Aug. 1947, 40.

[2] In later life Clegg felt a sense of grievance that his parents had always required him to succeed. The overriding need to do so was a constant theme in Clegg's career. *BMJ* mss. Clegg File, Clegg interview; author's interview with T. D. V. Swinscow, 9 Feb. 1989; author's interview with John Thwaites, 14 Feb. 1989.

lacked the financial means to launch himself in this direction. Keen to marry (which he did in 1932), he gave up clinical work and opted for a regular salary on the editorial staff of the *BMJ*. He remained with the *Journal* without a break until his retirement at the end of 1965.[3]

In some ways Clegg's family and educational background were similar to Horner's. Both had grown up in scholastic settings in the English provinces; both had attended leading public schools before proceeding to Cambridge where they studied the natural sciences. Both trained at St Bartholomew's. But in terms of temperament they could hardly have been more different. Where Horner was timid, emollient, and indecisive, Clegg was pugnacious, unpredictable, candid, energetic, and mercurial. His could be an overbearing, irascible, and daunting presence; Horner, on the other hand, hardly possessed a presence at all. Those who worked with Clegg refer to difficulties in dealing with him. Thus, Stephen Lock, his next but one successor as *Journal* editor, has written: 'Clegg was not an easy man—to get to know or to retain as a friend.'[4] Though an admirer of Clegg, Lock suggests he could be a trying boss:

> His staff tended to pass through sine waves of personal relationships: successively extreme approval, disapproval and withdrawal of work, and renewal of esteem. Whole issues of the *BMJ* already ready for Tuesday press might be torn apart and reassembled on a Monday afternoon . . . . Articles that a subordinate had already accepted might be rejected (usually with good reason) and the junior left to explain matters.[5]

Easily bored, he sometimes 'courted trouble' and tormented subordinates merely to keep himself amused.[6] Like the Wakleys, Clegg had been a useful boxer in his youth; sometimes he conducted the *Journal* as though he was still wearing the gloves.

A revealing pen portrait of Clegg is provided by Douglas Swinscow, who for 18 years served under him as a member of the *BMJ* editorial staff. His first impression of Clegg was of an amiable, avuncular figure. 'Never', he writes, 'can a first impression have been more misleading':

> A more typical appearance was his challenging expression and stance. Of muscular build and a little below average height, with a broad intellectual forehead below thinning grey hair, his brown eyes gazed steadily ahead, while the set of his features and especially his firm mouth and jaw expressed determination . . . . Combative by nature, sceptical by outlook, he enjoyed the excitement of finding an issue on which to

[3] Clegg's biographical details have been culled from *Munk's Roll* vii (London: Royal College of Physicians, 1985), pp. 103–6; *Dictionary of National Biography 1981–90* (note 1); T. D. V. Swinscow, *Reap a Destiny*, especially Chapter 11 (note 1); see *Who's Who*; *The Times*, 7 July 1983; *Journal*, 16 July 1983, 166, 220; *Lancet*, 16 July 1983, 175; *BMJ* mss. Clegg interview; notes for Clegg obituary.

[4] *Dictionary of National Biography, 1981–90* (note 1).

[5] *Munk's Roll* vii, pp. 104–5 (note 3).

[6] *BMJ* mss. Clegg File, Sir Austin Bradford Hill to Martin Ware, 20 Feb. 1972; author's interview with Stephen Lock, 27 June 1989.

pick a quarrel, revelled in the fight that usually followed, and could rarely rest content with mere victory unless he could drive the lesson home to the end.[7]

'Hyper-suspicious ... with an abnormal temperament ... he could make himself extremely unpleasant'. These are other memories Swinscow has of Clegg. On the other hand, he rarely lost his temper, and could be amusing and entertaining company. Yet even Clegg's more attractive personality traits such as frankness could cause offence, for some felt that he carried this to the point of rudeness.[8]

Whatever Clegg's deficiencies of character, there can be no doubt that his achievements as an editor were considerable, particularly in rescuing the *BMJ* from the dullness of the 1930s, re-establishing its scientific reputation, and asserting some degree of editorial and financial independence from the BMA—so far as this was possible given that the *Journal* remained 'the organ of the Association'. In sum, Clegg transformed the *BMJ* 'from a parish pump magazine to a great international journal. That was his achievement.'[9] This achievement owed much to his personal dynamism. Horner's *BMJ*, chameleon-like, had taken on the editor's colourless personality. Whatever Clegg's faults, he could not in justice be accused of lacking colour. Under his leadership the *Journal* was re-energized.

What of other post-war editorial staff? During the war the *Journal* had been produced by a 'skeleton' staff. It is only a slight exaggeration to suggest that Clegg and his secretary had run it by themselves. Horner, apart from one long absence, remained at his post for the duration and the first 18 months of peace. But he drifted further and further into the background, mainly occupying himself with writing obituaries.[10] There was also Marjorie Hollowell, a lay sub-editor appointed in the early 1930s.[11] Harvey Flack, recruited as an assistant editor in the 1930s, had joined the RAMC in 1939. He spent most of the war as a medical officer in Cairo, where a motor accident caused him permanent facial disfigurement. He rejoined the *Journal* in 1944. Swinscow provides a sympathetic picture of Flack 'whose warmth of temperament made the newcomer feel at ease and made Flack himself a welcome guest in any company'. Clegg, however, did not share these opinions. He considered Flack, with his bent for popular journalism, to be unsuited to work on the *BMJ*, and managed to have him shunted off into the editorship of the BMA's new popular health magazine, *Family Doctor*, which was launched in 1951.[12]

In 1946 two new sub-editors (this grade was abolished in 1947) were

[7] T. D. V. Swinscow, *Reap a Destiny*, 134, 137–8 (note 1).

[8] *Ibid.*; Swinscow interview, 9 Feb. 1989.

[9] *Ibid.*

[10] T. D. V. Swinscow, *Reap a Destiny*, p. 135 (note 1).

[11] She subsequently worked as a sub-editor on *Abstracts of World Medicine*, from which she retired at the end of 1965.

[12] T. D. V. Swinscow, *Reap a Destiny*, p. 136; see also Chapter 14 (note 1).

recruited. They were Drs T. D. V. Swinscow and E. G. Murphy. Swinscow was to remain for 31 years, rising to the position of deputy editor. Murphy had the temerity to disagree with Clegg over the direction of the *Journal* and other matters. As a result, his appointment was not confirmed at the end of his probationary period. His replacement was John Thompson, who before his appointment was Dorset County Medical Officer. He too became a deputy editor and for a time seemed Clegg's likely successor. But Clegg, who was in a position to recommend his successor, doubted whether Thompson's uncertain state of health could bear the strain. He also felt that Thompson was too pliant and accommodating and lacked the strength of character to say no. Accordingly, and to Thompson's intense disappointment, Clegg decided to recommend Martin Ware, who had joined the *BMJ* from the Medical Research Council in May 1950. In 1963 Thompson, who had suffered from depression for many years, took his own life.[13] Ware, who succeeded Clegg in 1965, remained as editor for a decade. His successor was Stephen Lock, who had been appointed Medical Assistant Editor following Thompson's death.

Of other post-war staff brief mention should be made of Gordon Ostlere (1949–50), who, as Richard Gordon, went on to write successful popular fiction, including *Doctor in the House*, *Doctor at Sea*, etc. He claimed, perhaps not wholly facetiously, that writing *Journal* obituaries had been the training ground for his fictional writing. John Rowan Wilson (1962–65), a more serious writer than Gordon, supposedly made use of his time at the *BMJ* to gather material for his novel, *The Side of the Angels*, in which the director of a Siberian research centre is said to bear more than a passing resemblance to Hugh Clegg. John Crammer, a biochemist, joined the *Journal* at the same time as Ware but stayed only till 1952 when he left to pursue a career in psychiatry. His successor, John Thwaites, on the other hand, had a long stay as assistant, later deputy, editor (1952–70). As a general practitioner in Brighton, he had served on the BMA Council and various committees, including the Journal Committee, before, during, and after the war. Throughout his time on the *Journal* he was responsible for editing the *BMJ* Supplement, which he took over from Swinscow. This was an unenviable task as the Supplement, with its concentration on medical politics and BMA affairs, was never short of critics.[14]

In comparison with earlier periods, we lack detailed information on *Journal* personnel and salaries for the post-war years. However, in June 1951, as part of a management economy exercise, the Publishing Sub-committee compiled a full list of staff in the editorial department along with dates of

[13] *Ibid.*, pp. 175–6, 179-81; *BMJ* mss. JCM (1946–7) JNL.44, 13 March 1947, p. 10.

[14] T. D. V. Swinscow, *Reap a Destiny* pp. 153–4, 163–4 (note 1); *Munk's Roll* vii, p. 106 (note 3). Printed information on staff and other matters has been supplemented by interviews with Drs John Thwaites and Douglas Swinscow. Thwaites remained on the staff in a part-time capacity till 1980.

appointment, previous positions, and salaries. This shows that there were then 23 staff in post including the editor (salary, £3750 a year), John Thompson, his deputy (£2200), and three assistant editors—Swinscow, Ware, and Crammer—whose salaries ranged from £1800 to £1500 a year. Other staff consisted of an information officer, clerks, 'copy preparers', secretaries, and typists. The total annual wage bill for all 23 employees was £19 932 12s. In addition, retaining fees were paid to six advisers to the editor and a reporter, Harry Cooper, who had first worked for the *Journal* as long ago as 1907. He remained in post till the end of 1955 when serious illness compelled his retirement. The *Journal* and other BMA periodicals were supported by a publishing department and an advertising department. The advertising manager, C. W. Francis, was the best remunerated of all the staff included in the Journal Committee's survey. His salary was £1250 a year, but in 1950 commission had taken his earnings to £4284.[15]

Austerity years

When Labour won the 1945 General Election it came to power with big plans, which included nationalization of key industries, creation of a planned economy, implementation of a comprehensive scheme of social insurance, establishment of a national health service, and a massive programme of house-building. With a huge Commons majority it had the mandate to proceed with its plans. Public expectation knew no bounds: the good times had arrived. Plentiful jobs paying good wages; abundant food and housing; free health care, medicine, dentistry, and spectacles; and 'cradle to grave' social security to prevent anyone from falling by the wayside—such were the aspirations that loomed large in the popular imagination. However, the Labour government inherited not only a wealth of expectation but profound economic problems which were a legacy of six years' total war. It has been estimated that the Second World War consumed about 25 per cent of Britain's total national wealth. Foreign trade and investment, which were indispensable to national prosperity, had been devastated. When, in August 1945, the United States abruptly terminated the lend-lease, 'the financial situation confronting Attlee and his new colleagues was frightening in the extreme.'[16] Labour's health and welfare proposals would have been unrealizable had not a US loan been secured in 1946.

Given the unpromising circumstances, 1946 proved an extremely successful year for the Attlee government. The economy boomed as exports and capital investment in industry grew impressively. Outside a few blackspots such as south Wales there was little unemployment. Labour's ambitious

[15] *BMJ* mss. JCM (1950–51) JNL.84, Publishing Sub-committee, 6 June 1951; (1955–6) JNL.14, 8 Dec. 1955.

[16] K. O. Morgan, *Labour in Power, 1945–51* (Oxford: Oxford University Press, 1984), p. 144.

'A youth who bore mid snow and ice . . .'. The winter of 1947 was hard and long. Cartoon by David Low, published in the *Evening Standard*,* 12 March 1947. Source: Centre for the Study of Cartoons and Caricature, University of Kent at Canterbury.

* Associated Newspapers plc,

legislative programme went ahead apace and its popularity remained high. In contrast, 1947 'was a year of almost unrelieved disaster'.[17] One problem at least was not of the government's making. Between late January and the end of March the winter was the coldest since 1880–1; such a prolonged freeze was not to be experienced again till 1962–3. In February there were 10 days of unremitting frost, a sequence which broke a record dating from 1841. These were conditions which caused rivers, canals, and even the sea to freeze; ice-fields were spotted in the North Sea. Snowfalls exceeded anything experienced in living memory. Many villages were isolated and could be supplied with food and medicine only by air. All of this meant that the fuel crisis, which would have occurred anyway owing to coal shortages caused by a lack of manpower, became severe. Demand for power soared as temperatures plunged; coal stocks dwindled while weather conditions hampered transportation of those supplies that were available. Industries vital to the

[17] *Ibid.*, p. 330.

restoration of the economy shuddered to a halt; unemployment rose alarmingly.

On 7 February Emmanuel Shinwell, Minister of Fuel and Power, told the Commons that many power stations had already had to close down, and that, in consequence, both business and domestic electricity consumers would lose their supply. Sir Stafford Cripps, President of the Board of Trade, drew up a plan for allocating fuel supplies which gave power stations priority and required other users to suffer intermittent power cuts. But the plan was based on forecasts of demand which turned out to be considerably underestimated. As a result, it failed.

What did all this have to do with the *BMJ*? In common with households, offices, and factories, the *Journal* was affected by the fuel crisis and power cuts. Office temperatures fell below freezing point and staff were obliged to work by candlelight, encased in overcoats, scarves, and gloves. Whether the *Journal* could continue to appear as normal depended on whether its printers could obtain a constant electricity supply. For a time the issue of 15 February appeared to be in doubt:

> The printers of the *British Medical Journal* on Monday this week had no electricity to turn over the machines, and by 7 p.m. on Monday night the Editor was still unable to learn from the Ministry of Fuel and Power whether it would be possible to produce this week's *Journal*. On Tuesday permission was granted to go to press this week, but the printers were still short of electrical power . . . .
>
> At the time of going to press we understand that we shall not be able to publish the next two issues of the *Journal*, which during the two recent world wars was regarded as indispensable to the national effort. On May 10, 1941, the *Journal*'s printers were destroyed by German bombs, the production of the *Journal* continued uninterrupted. We regret that this time it looks as if it will be impossible to repeat 'Operation Phoenix'.[18]

The problem was that the government had not only decided that the weekly press should be suspended for two weeks in order to conserve scarce fuel, but had reached agreement on observation of the interdict with the Periodical Trade Press and Weekly Newspaper Proprietors' Association (PPA). Some of the weeklies, including the *Spectator* and the *Economist*, made arrangements for national dailies, which were not covered by the suspension order, to carry some of their material.[19] This was permissible, though it was not a realistic option for a scientific journal. What was not permissible, the government decided after further consultations with the PPA, was to issue duplicated substitutes. Neither could there be any exceptions to a blanket ban. Indeed, the government also ruled that the

[18] *Journal*, 15 Feb. 1947, 258; *BMJ* mss. JCM (1946–7) JNL.41, Editor's Report, n.d.

[19] *The Times*, 11, 15, 18 Feb. 1947. When the *Journal*'s 15 February issue was in doubt inquiries were made to see whether printing could be undertaken by various national papers, including *The Times*, *Daily Telegraph*, and *Daily Express*, or by printers in Bristol or York. *BMJ* mss. JCM (1946–7) JNL.41, Editor's Report, n.d.

suspension 'applies irrespective of ... what type of power is used' in the production process.[20] These remarkable rulings could be justified only on the grounds that the ban should not enable one periodical to gain an advantage over a rival. They prompted Clegg to obtain a legal opinion from the BMA's solicitors. This stated that neither the agreement between the Ministry and the PPA nor the ban on a duplicated periodical had any force in law.[21]

The Times was ambivalent about suspension. It felt that the government was in a hole of its own making and could not understand 'why, if electricity is not consumed in the process, are duplicated substitutes for suspended periodicals not to be tolerated?' It also complained that the government had failed to show that it would save enough electricity to compensate for the damage done. In short, the ban constituted a 'shocking exhibition of indifference to the social necessity of the printed word', and 'deprivation of an essential freedom of the public which even in time of war was not so curtailed'. But, while urging no repetition of the ban and restoration of the weeklies as a matter of 'the highest priority', *The Times* acknowledged that it 'must be accepted under protest'.[22]

The *BMJ* was not a member of the PPA, having been refused membership in 1938 on the grounds that it was not an independent publication. Clegg, in any case, was not inclined to bow to a government decree of doubtful legality. He determined that come what may, even if it was impossible to print the *Journal* by the usual means, its almost unblemished record of weekly publication would not be interrupted. Doubtless the fact that the government issuing the orders was also the government that was perceived to be trying to force an unacceptable national health service on the doctors did nothing to diminish this determination. Accordingly, *BMJ* staff set to work on compiling the 22 February issue.

The possibility of printing in a part of the country not covered by the fuel ban was investigated. But no printer would proceed unless granted permission by the Ministry, and Clegg could not obtain such permission. The only alternative was to produce a *Journal* consisting of a single foolscap sheet, 'printed' on both sides of the page. The *Journal* tried to hire electrical duplicators from the Roneo Company, but the company wanted no part in a scheme designed to circumvent the government ban.[23] Clegg, who sought the views of the Ministry and the Central Office of Information, was told that there was no objection to a duplicated *BMJ* produced without power. But this did not seem feasible since the *Journal* possessed only one suitable machine. However, Charles Hill, no friend of the Attlee government, agreed to make BMA staff and equipment available for duplicating and despatch.

20 *The Times*, 17 Feb. 1947.
21 *BMJ* mss. JCM (1946–7) JNL.41, Editor's Report, n.d.
22 *The Times*, leading articles of 18 and 22 Feb. 1947.
23 *BMJ* mss. JCM (1946–7) JNL.41, Editor's Report, n.d.

The whole production process was to be undertaken by hand (or foot in the case of the treadle-operated addressograph machines), and 'without the consumption of a watt of electricity'.[24] The exercise was then repeated for the following week. In both weeks it proved possible to produce and circulate a full print-run of 62 000 copies of what were known as the 'pemmican issues'—pemmican being highly condensed information or reading matter as well as a dried meat preparation used by North American Indians for emergency food. Slight improvement in fuel supplies meant that a normal issue was possible for 8 March.

Although the pemmican issues could include little news or information, most of the *Journal*'s regular features were present. There were, for example, summaries of letters, short news items, 'any questions', obituaries—and situations vacant, which generated advertising revenue of £315. There were even two leading articles, one of which explained that the issue had been produced 'by permission' of the Ministry and COI—a phrase those departments later disowned, claiming that lack of objection was quite different from a grant of permission. The single leader in the second 'pemmican', entitled 'Freedom to Print', attacked those who, in 'a pernicious abuse of power' would 'introduce restrictive practices under cover of a national crisis'. To the *Journal* Committee Clegg reported that 'All our contacts with this Ministry [of Fuel and Power], direct and indirect, provided a deadening demonstration of the paralysing effect of the bureaucrat in control.'[25]

The only other weeklies to appear during the course of the ban were *Isis*, *Science To-day*, and *Liberal News*, though none of these possessed the circulation or standing of the *BMJ*.[26] Of the first 'pemmican' *The Times* said that 'the medical profession must congratulate the *BMJ* on its editorial ingenuity and refusal to give in.' The profession needed no such prompting; letters of congratulation came flooding into the *BMJ* office.[27] Many contained the same message: do not allow ministerial tyrants to crush initiative, undermine liberty, and impose their will.

After all the high-flown rhetoric had died down, what had the *BMJ* achieved with its two 'pemmican' issues? Did their appearance have any lasting significance? It is hard to agree that they signified defiance of government by a free and independent press as Clegg had done nothing to which the Ministry or COI objected. He would have done this only if, acting on the belief that the ban had no legal authority, he had found the means to come out as normal. The episode really had a dual significance. First, the *Journal* maintained its continuity of publication in which so much pride was

[24] *Journal*, 8 March 1947, 300; *The Times*, letter from Clegg, 26 Feb. 1947. On one occasion the ink in the addressograph machines froze.

[25] *Journal*, 1 March 1947, 1; *The Times*, 26 Feb. 1947; *BMJ* mss. JCM (1946–7) JNL.41, Editor's Report, n.d.

[26] *Journal*, 8 March 1947, 300.

[27] *The Times*, 21 Feb. 1947; *Journal*, 8 March 1947, 307.

taken. Second, Clegg, newly-appointed to the editorship, had succeeded in making a gesture demonstrative of his determination, ingenuity, and independence of thought. This was particularly significant given the BMA's continuing struggle with another Ministry over the NHS, but it also enabled Clegg to impress upon the BMA that he would not take kindly to their interfering with the *Journal.* Together, what these amounted to was a contribution to *BMJ* mythology as 'the paper they could not gag'.[28] Therein lies the true importance of the 'pemmican' episode.

The gold-headed cane

It has been suggested that Clegg was at his 'combative best' in his handling of the *Journal* at the time of the government's suspension of periodicals.[29] Certainly, he served notice that his style of editorship was likely to be very different from his predecessor's, for it is inconceivable that Horner would have questioned the ban or tried to circumvent it. The BMA was pleased with Clegg's achievement; headquarters staff helped to facilitate it, and the membership applauded it. In its Annual Report for 1947 Council congratulated the *Journal* on being 'the only weekly journal of any size and standing not to be deceived by the Government's bluff and by what was nothing more or less than arbitrary censorship through temporary suspension of publication'. The sentiments were echoed by the Journal Committee.[30] However, within a decade Clegg was to show another aspect of his combativeness, and this was to prove much less appealing to the BMA Council.

In April 1956 Clegg published a leader, which he himself had written, entitled 'The Gold-Headed Cane'.[31] This was a trenchant critique of the Royal College of Physicians (RCP). The occasion of the attack was the election of Sir Russell Brain to a seventh year as President of the College. But its main purpose was to describe an archaic, degenerate, confused, and rudderless institution which was out of touch with its Fellows and Members, unsure of how to react towards the NHS and Welfare State, and generally incapable of occupying that role in the medical world which its history had conferred upon it. Brain's extended period in the presidency, following, as it did, Lord Moran's nine years in office, was presented as a symbol of the College's plight.

Much of the article was couched in general terms, but a specific criticism related to the refusal of the RCP to accept the BMA's invitation to cooperate with it in considering some of the outstanding problems of medical education. In raising this point it appeared to some that the BMA was a

[28] See *BMJ* Supplement, 2 Aug. 1947, 41.

[29] T. D. V. Swinscow, *Reap a Destiny*, p. 140 (note 1).

[30] *BMJ* Supplement, 26 April 1947, 76; see 2 Aug. 1947, 41.

[31] *Journal*, 7 April 1956, 791–3. The gold-headed cane is a symbol of the authority of the President of the Royal College of Physicians.

party to the *Journal*'s strictures. This, however, was not the case; indeed, the Association was actively seeking to develop a closer relationship with the College. Clegg's leader seemed likely to damage, if not sabotage, this process. As a result Clegg laid himself open to criticism from two powerful factions: the leaders of the RCP, who felt personally affronted by his onslaught, and, more importantly, from his employers within the BMA.

Sure enough, as soon as the *Journal* appeared the Chairman of Council, E. A. Gregg, who was a London GP, and several other Council members contacted Clegg to express their outrage at the editorial.[32] Meanwhile Brain, in a letter to the *Journal*, accused Clegg not only of misrepresenting the work and constitution of the RCP but also of using the *Journal* as a propaganda organ to further the designs of the Association: '... the main trend of the leader is the clear implication ... that the B.M.A. should occupy a position of exclusive privilege and power in medicine.' At the same time Brain grasped the opportunity to let fly a few barbed arrows of his own in respect of BMA conduct and management, not the least of which was to point out that Gregg had been the Association's Chairman of Council since 1949.[33]

The BMA's deputy chairman, T. Rowland Hill, in another letter published by the *Journal* totally rejected Clegg's 'grotesque picture of the Royal College'. The views expressed in the 'Gold-Headed Cane' leader, he emphasized, in no way reflected BMA thinking:

> I am distressed at the lack of useful purpose to be served by so ill-judged a tirade in the editorial columns of the *British Medical Journal.* One might imagine that the object was to destroy what has been a steadily increasing friendship and co-operation. The one small comfort that I can give myself is that I am sure—and I hope Sir Russell Brain will take this from me—in spite of the *British Medical Journal* being called the 'Journal of the British Medical Association' and its being naturally thereby assumed by those not in the know that its unsigned editorials are pronouncements of the Association itself, that the leading article in question must have been published without either the authority or the knowledge of the B.M.A. Council.[34]

Council discussed the matter at its May meeting. Clegg was summoned to the Council Chamber where, as he later recalled, '[they] had me on the mat. The attack which I had the pleasure of listening to was an object lesson in organized mischief-making.'[35] Council tried to persuade Clegg to agree to publish no leading articles, except on clinical or scientific medicine, which had not been approved by BMA officers. When he refused, Council passed a motion dissociating 'itself from the publication of the leading article "The Gold-headed Cane" ... of which article the Council had no prior knowledge,

[32] T. D. V. Swinscow, *Reap a Destiny*, p. 168 (note 1).
[33] *Journal*, 14 April 1956, 857.
[34] *Ibid.*, 21 April 1956, 919.
[35] *BMJ* mss. Clegg File, Clegg interview.

the article being entirely the responsibility of the Editor, according to the usual practice'.[36]

That such a point needed to be made is evidence of the degree to which the *Journal* was perceived as lacking an independent voice and regarded as simply the official mouthpiece of the BMA. Of course, the *Journal* had always been dependent on the Association by which, in most years, it was financially subsidized. Also its editors had always known that they might incur the wrath of the BMA if they published material deemed to be contrary to BMA interests or policy. The classic example of this was the Morrell Mackenzie affair when Ernest Hart had aroused the displeasure of his employers by publishing the 'dying Emperor's words' criticizing his German physicians. Hart, a dominant personality with a strong position in the BMA hierarchy, had ridden out the storm. But the mid-twentieth century Association was a very different organization from that of the 1880s. Its emphasis was no longer 'scientific and social' but heavily medico-political. In Hart's day the *Journal* had led the Association in matters of medical politics, but the reverse had long since been the case. The Association did not want a maverick editor of the *Journal* undermining agreed policy. Horner had allowed the Association to have a say in editorial matters through the Journal Committee. He avoided controversy and never flouted BMA policy, but under his editorship (and that of Dawson Williams), a large proportion of the *Journal* was supplied 'by the Presidents of the various sections of the British Medical Association at the Annual Meeting and this was an enormous convenience for an inert editor because the responsibility of choosing those people was completely outside his hands ... and this was, of course, what ruined the *BMJ*.'[37] Thus, the Association played an important role in the conduct of the *Journal*. During the NHS crisis all political leaders were submitted for approval by the BMA secretariat. The yardstick for approval was whether the views expressed clashed with BMA policy. As we have seen, when, in 1948, Clegg was deemed to have published a leader inconsistent with BMA policy, demands for his dismissal were debated.

Clegg survived those demands. He did so not only because the Special Representative Meeting concluded that he had not breached BMA policy, but also because there was ambivalence about whether editorial freedom should be entirely destroyed. There nevertheless remained an unspoken assumption that an editor who disagreed in print with the Association was likely to find himself in trouble. In publishing his 'Gold-Headed Cane' leader Clegg did not go against BMA policy for there was no policy proscribing criticism of the Royal Colleges. But, unwittingly, he compromised BMA

[36] *Ibid.*; *BMJ* Supplement, 12 May 1956, 277. Article 46 of the BMA constitution specified that 'the *Journal* shall be conducted by a paid editor who shall be responsible for all that appears therein ...'.

[37] *BMJ* mss. Clegg file, Clegg interview.

interests. Whether his criticisms of Brain and the RCP were valid was of little, or at least secondary, importance. The major question was, could the *Journal*, on this or any other issue, take a line which was unpalatable to the BMA? In other words, was its editor a free agent or merely the operator of part of the propaganda machine?

Since such a question raised matters of BMA policy it could only be decided by the Annual Representative Meeting. In 1956 this was due to take place at Brighton. The Winchester division, a BMA branch which contained members who were out of sympathy with Clegg, moved the following motion: 'That this Representative Body instructs the Council to take steps to ensure that leading articles in the *BMJ* reflect the policy of the Association.'[38] Clegg had decided that if it were approved, he would have no alternative but to resign, continued service under such conditions being impossible.

After outlining the background to his motion and making polite references to the eminence of the *Journal* and its editor, the Winchester delegate, H. H. Langston, succinctly stated his case.[39] He argued that the *BMJ* was the organ of the Association and 'there was no doubt that the vast majority of the medical profession regarded the *Journal* and its articles as the mouthpiece of the Association and its policy.' It was therefore highly embarrassing for the Council to have to dissociate itself from a leading article, and highly inconvenient for the Association to have its friendly relations with the Royal College of Physicians disrupted. Langston found a seconder and one other speaker to support his motion, but seven speakers spoke against it. They stressed that the leader in question was legitimate comment on a topical issue, that it did not breach Association policy, and, perhaps most importantly, that editorial freedom was vital if the *Journal* was to remain at the 'top level in world approbation'. When a vote was taken, the motion was defeated by an 'overwhelming majority'. The matter was closed. It seemed that an important principle had been settled in Clegg's favour and in favour of press freedom. The *BMJ*'s status was safe; it need not degenerate into what Clegg scathingly called a 'parish pump magazine'. Clegg and the rest of the editorial staff were able to remain in post. But was the incident anything more than a petty quarrel of purely local significance?

The 'Gold-Headed Cane' controversy has entered *Journal* mythology in the same way as the 'pemmican' episode has. Fundamentally they were similar incidents in that both centred upon the right to publish. In one case the question was whether publication would occur at all; in the other it was a matter of whether comment which powerful voices might find offensive or unwelcome could find a place in the *Journal*. In both instances the *Journal* seemingly upheld its right to speak out and its refusal to be intimidated. But

[38] *Ibid.*, 14 July 1956, 12; T. D. V. Swinscow, *Reap a Destiny*, pp. 172–3 (note 1).

[39] Langston would have known Clegg well for he had served on the *Journal* Committee since 1953.

beyond vindicating Clegg's actions in a particular instance, what was the longer term significance of the Brighton vote? Swinscow argues that it 'brought greater definition, stability, and authority to the journal, and to the association a sharper awareness of its democratic conscience and its corporate power'. Lock takes a similar line. He argues that Clegg's leader established the *BMJ*'s editorial freedom and persuaded the Association to recognize the *Journal* as its conscience.[40] Are these inflated claims?

One of the points that emerged clearly in the course of the Brighton debate was that Clegg's leader had not contradicted any decision of the BMA's policy-making body, the ARM. This was of great importance in getting Clegg off the hook. If he had attacked a BMA policy it is doubtful whether he would have escaped censure or more serious consequences. The ARM accepted that the editor was not under the control of Council. But the chairman of the *Journal* Committee observed, and nobody contradicted him, that the editor was in duty bound not to criticize BMA policy as laid down by the Representative Body:

> The editor, like any other official, like all other persons in the Association, was expected to work, and had done nothing else than work, within the framework of the policy laid down by the Representative Body. That was a positive statement with a negative side, in that the editor, like the other officials, *must not advocate a policy which was contrary to that which had been laid down by the Representative Body*, and the editor had not done so [my emphasis].[41]

So the Brighton debate established that, although the 'Gold-Headed Cane' leader had not been contrary to BMA policy, the editor of the *Journal* was bound to desist from criticizing BMA policy.

Did such a restriction imply loss of editorial freedom? Clearly it did in so far as it established that the editor was not in an entirely autonomous position. This had not always been accepted in the past. In 1950 a Glasgow representative had moved 'that the Representative Body deprecates the practice of the *Journal* in publishing the estates of deceased doctors'. The ARM carried the motion but the chairman of the *Journal* Committee 'pointed out that the meeting could not instruct the Editor what he was to publish, it could only express its view'.[42] If this were so, the editor was not bound to act in accordance with ARM decisions. Indeed, the BMA's Articles of Association specified that the editor alone was responsible for everything (apart from Council notices) published in the *Journal*. Hence, only unwritten convention obliged him to refrain from opposing BMA policy.

In practice, given that the policy-making body met comparatively rarely—

[40] T. D. V. Swinscow, *Reap a Destiny*, pp. 166–7 (note 1); S. P. Lock, 'The Gold-Headed Cane'. Unpublished Lecture delivered at the Wellcome Institute, 3 March 1988.

[41] *BMJ* Supplement, 14 July 1956, 14.

[42] *Ibid.*, 7 Oct. 1950, 149.

usually annually—the likelihood was that on any specific issue the BMA would have no clear and detailed policy. So, even if the editor was bound to comply with ARM decisions, his day-to-day independence would be considerable. In this sense it is doubtful whether the editor of the *BMJ* actually had and has less independence than any newspaper editor (medical or otherwise) answerable to proprietors. His position is precisely that outlined by a member of Council (W. Wooley) in the Brighton debate: '. . . the editor of any journal, any newspaper, was the king-pin; he had complete freedom to print what he liked or to reject what he liked from his journal or newspaper so long as what he did fitted in with the policy of his employers.'[43] Clegg accepted this proposition throughout his editorship. In 1949 he said, coincidentally in a talk given to the Winchester division, that the editor of an official journal (such as the *BMJ*) had his hands

> very much tied. I do not say this in a spirit of complaint, but to state a fact which is so obvious that some people seem to miss it.
>
> First of all, critical comment on Association policy is out of the question, as much as the Editor would like 'to have a go'.[44]

Eleven years later, he wrote: 'If the British Medical Association's policy is opposed to a full-time salaried service, then I should not feel I had a right to advocate a contrary policy.'[45] The 'Gold-Headed Cane' leader changed nothing.

Boom, bust, and recovery

The *Journal* emerged from the Second World War in excellent financial shape. In the course of hostilities BMA membership had risen by some 12 000. *Journal* circulation had increased correspondingly and, while this did not in itself make the *BMJ* more profitable, it brought it more prestige and made it more attractive to advertisers. The space available for advertising shrank owing to paper shortages, but those pages that were available could be sold at a premium. In 1937 a standard display page had cost £20 whereas by the end of the war the price had risen to £120 with the best pages, such as the back cover, going for £160.[46] Consequently, one week's advertising revenue could exceed £2000.

Production costs rose steeply during the war, but not at the same rate as income. For most of its existence the *Journal* had not been self-financing, but was subsidized out of BMA subscription income. In 1943, however, its accounts showed a surplus. Although the 1944 figures showed another

[43] *Ibid.*, 14 July 1956, 13.

[44] *BMJ* mss. Clegg file, copy of Clegg's Address to the BMA's Winchester division, 24 Nov., 1949, p. 11.

[45] Hugh Clegg, 'Some Principles and Problems of Medical Editing', *International Record of Medicine* (1960) **173**: 421.

[46] *BMJ* mss. JCM (1950–1) JNL.62, Publishing Sub-committee, 28 March 1951.

deficit, there followed an unparalleled sequence of financial success (Table 11.1). Dr O. C. Carter, chairman of the *Journal* Committee, told the 1946 ARM that 'never before had the *Journal* been in such a sound position both scientifically and financially.'[47]

Table 11.1 Gross financial results of the *BMJ* 1943–50

Year	Surplus (£)
1943	5 987
1944	−3 119
1945	18 204
1946	12 857
1947	31 519
1948	25 734
1949	56 836
1950	40 897

In this post-war period the only blot on a landscape otherwise bathed in a rosy glow of success was the continuation of paper controls which prevented profits from rising as rapidly as the BMA would have liked. Indeed, in the late 1940s, with circulation increasing apace, the paper problem became more severe than ever.[48] But on balance the atmosphere was distinctly 'bullish' and hence somewhat at odds with the prevailing note of national austerity. Between 1944 and 1947 nine new quarterly periodicals were established in the *Journal* department, while in 1951 a mass circulation popular health journal, *Family Doctor*, was launched with the help of a cinema advertising campaign. By 1951, with *Abstracts of World Surgery* and *Abstracts of World Medicine*, both launched in 1947, the department was publishing a total of 17 periodicals, for all of which Clegg had overall responsibility.

At the end of 1947, the year of the big freeze, fuel shortages, and pemmican issues, serious consideration was given to producing the *Journal* in French, German, Italian, and Spanish. The idea was that English proofs would be sent out free of charge to foreign publishers, who would translate the articles and publish them in their own language. Clegg gained an introduction to the French *Presse Universitaire* by way of Dr Paul Dubs, a French representative on the World Medical Association, but this and other possibilities, including that of a monthly English language version of the *Journal* for overseas

[47] *BMJ* Supplement, 3 Aug. 1946, 54.

[48] See e.g. ibid., 4 Aug. 1945, 27; 3 Aug. 1946, 55; 26 April 1947, 75; 10 April 1948, 83; 2 April 1949, 189.

consumption, came to nothing.[49] Nevertheless, these plans indicate the confidence that was running through the *Journal* in the late 1940s.

Towards the end of 1950, however, the bubble burst and the regular surpluses turned into deficits. Ironically, in view of the fact that paper rationing had caused the *Journal* so much difficulty, the main cause of this downturn was the dramatic increase in the price of paper after de-rationing in February 1950. At first it was estimated that return to a free market in paper would raise the *Journal*'s annual paper bill by about £25 000. This would have been serious enough, but what actually happened was an increase from £69 269 in 1950 to £144 667 in 1951. Paper which had cost 5½d per lb in January 1950 had risen to 1s 2d by May of the following year.[50] From showing a healthy profit the *Journal*—in fact the entire BMA publishing operation, believed to be the largest in the world for medical publications—faced the prospect of substantial deficits. The Publishing Sub-committee had hoped that BMA publications would show a surplus of £100 000 for 1951. In August Clegg estimated that the *Journal* deficit could be as high as £50 000 (it turned out to be £30 578) (see Table 11.2).[51]

Table 11.2 Gross financial results of the *BMJ* 1951–65

Date	Surplus (£)	
1951	−30 578	
1952	14 491	
1953	71 852	
1954	42 458	
1955	32 574	
1956	3 175	
1957	3 492	
1958	33 701	
1959	56 178	
1960	48 101	
1961	−13 600	
1962	13 053	
1963	62 656	
1964	63 040	
1965	62 600	(estimated)

[49] *BMJ* mss. JCM (1947–8) JNL.52, Journal Committee, 15 April 1948. In the early 1960s negotiations to produce a monthly version of the *Journal* in Spanish came close to fruition. They ultimately foundered because the one Spanish publisher prepared to proceed on a sufficiently large scale for the project to be viable was deemed unsuitable because of its links with the pharmaceutical industry. Around the same time, there were also discussions about a Japanese language version. At the time of Clegg's retirement discussions were in train for other foreign language editions and an Australian version of the *Journal*. See (1962–3) JNL.16, 6 March 1963.

[50] *Ibid.*, JCM (1950–1) JNL.30, Publishing Sub-committee, 16 Nov. 1950; (1951–2), JNL.23, Editor's Report, 11 Oct. 1951. *BMJ* Supplement, 12 May 1951, 195.

[51] *BMJ* mss. JCM (1951–2) JNL.7, Editor's Memorandum, 23 Aug. 1951; JNL.24, 11 Oct. 1951; JNL.72, 6 March 1952.

Of course, these developments did not harm the *BMJ* alone; they affected all BMA publications, indeed, all publishing ventures in the United Kingdom. It has been estimated that in 1951 over 50 British periodicals were forced out of existence by rising costs.[52] In one sense what spiralling paper costs meant to the *Journal* was a return to the pre-war norm when it had regularly 'lost' several thousand pounds each year or, to put it another way, had been a net consumer of BMA funds rather than a contributor to its coffers. In 1938 the *BMJ* deficit was over £19 000, yet this had generated little sense of crisis. In any case, even with a deficit running at £30 000 p.a. the *Journal* represented good value to the Association and its 66 000 members (1951). In 1951 the BMA membership fee stood at 4 guineas; less than 10s of each subscription, a fairly modest proportion, was needed to fund the *Journal* for the year.[53] However, after a period of sustained profitability the return to losses was viewed with alarm. Traditionally the *Journal* had derived a degree of protection from the full force of a harsh economic climate by virtue of its link with the Association, which absorbed its deficits. But during the 1940s the Association had begun to rely heavily upon the *Journal* to help finance its other activities. Because the *Journal* was performing so well, membership subscriptions were not raised. Hence when *Journal* income fell the BMA faced financial difficulties. In these circumstances the Association became desperately keen for its publishing arm to generate more revenue and reduce its costs.

Because the *Journal*'s circulation was principally to BMA members, it was difficult for it to increase its income or effect economies simply by raising its price or reducing its print-run. Indeed, its financial problems were exacerbated by the fact that additional circulation, if it came through growing BMA membership rather than non-member subscriptions, increased costs without increasing income. By the same token, falling circulation could make the *Journal* more profitable. When, in 1962, the BMA faced the secession of its Australian branches and the resignation of a large proportion of its Australian members, the *Journal* could contemplate a considerable fall in its costs. For the Association, on the other hand, secession meant a large loss of income.[54]

In 1951, notwithstanding howls of protest from the pharmaceutical companies, advertising rates were raised 10 per cent; it was also decided that more could be done to increase *Journal* sales abroad. But even with the new rates, and even if higher sales targets were achieved, deficits looked certain to continue. In any case the state of the *Journal*'s finances was not the only problem. Indeed, for Clegg it was a relatively minor one, though he was

[52] *BMJ* Supplement, 19 April 1952, 172.

[53] *BMJ* mss. JCM (1951–2) JNL.48, Supplementary Agenda, Editor's Memorandum, 10 Jan. 1952.

[54] *Ibid.*, (1961–2) JNL.13, Business Manager's Notes on the Draft Budget for 1962, 13 Dec. 1961.

concerned that economies could affect the quality of the *Journal*'s content if they entailed appreciable page reductions. But his main worry was the *Journal*'s business management and, specifically, the extent to which he had become embroiled in it. Even before the post-war growth in BMA publishing Clegg had found himself sharing, with the Board of Directors' secretary, many of the *Journal*'s business decisions. Because there was no adequate business management structure, Clegg had become, to his increasing disgruntlement, 'more and more involved in the business side of the work'; in fact, not only 'the Editor of a weekly journal but the executive head of a publishing house'. In these circumstances both he and the Publishing Sub-committee recommended to Council that there should be a thorough and 'urgent' re-organization of business management. Council agreed.[55]

Although there was unanimity on the need for change, there were many contrasting views about what should be done. One set of suggestions focused on cost-cutting. O. C. Carter, who was chairman of both the *Journal* Committee and the Publishing Sub-committee, and no friend of Clegg, felt that the *Journal* could save money if its average size were reduced by four pages an issue.[56] Another suggestion was to ascertain how many BMA members actually wanted the *Journal* so that circulation might be trimmed accordingly. The *Journal* Committee resolved in favour of investigating the financial implications of a circulation cut of 20 000–30 000. As for management, Carter favoured far closer supervision of *Journal* affairs by officials of the Association.

Most of these ideas, especially for closer supervision by the BMA, were anathema to Clegg, though he was willing to follow the example of the Swedish Medical Association and discontinue supplying the *Journal* as an automatic benefit of Association membership. This would mean that it would go only to those who specifically subscribed to it. Clegg always believed that people did not appreciate a benefit received free of charge. By making the *Journal* a subscription periodical he felt he would gain release from many of those who complained about it. But in general Clegg held very different ideas from the *Journal* Committee. He preferred to save paper not by trimming every issue, which would inevitably lead to the loss of much valuable material, but by jettisoning the annual educational number (which dated from Ernest Hart's day and had recently returned after its wartime suspension). A more revolutionary suggestion came in the resurrection of an idea which had been floated in 1948, but had then come to nothing. This was for a fixed percentage of BMA subscription income to be allocated to the *Journal*. This, Clegg believed, would exercise an important psychological

[55] *Ibid.*, (1950–1) JNL.23, Editor's Report, 11 Oct. 1951; (1951–2) JNL.7, Editor's Memorandum, 23 Aug. 1951; JNL.28, Joint Meeting of Journal Committee and Publishing Sub-Committee, 24 Oct. 1951.

[56] T. D. V. Swinscow, *Reap a Destiny*, p. 156 (note 1).

function in that it would end the perception of the *Journal* as a loss-making branch of the BMA.[57] As for the running of the publishing business, he thought that the time had come to take it out of the hands of part-time medical men acting as amateur businessmen and place it in professional hands. At first Clegg favoured the appointment of a full-time business manager, though he had second thoughts when he learnt what this could cost.[58]

The opinions of outside experts, notably from Oxford University Press, were canvassed but the *Journal* and the Association were thought to be in a unique position and therefore unable to benefit from the example of publishing houses. Faced with several differences of opinion, Council decided to appoint management consultants (Harold Whitehead and Partners) to investigate the organization of the BMA's publishing activities 'with a view to improving efficiency and effecting economy'; they also decided to reduce the number of pages in the *Journal*, but threw out the idea of exploring wholesale circulation cuts.[59]

Whitehead and Partners reported to Council in early 1952. They made several recommendations for economy, such as use of cheaper paper. They also expressed astonishment that the *Journal* had no annual budget and recommended the introduction of budgetary discipline (which could allow for deficits as well as surpluses) as a priority. In addition, instead of having two committees responsible for the *Journal*—the Journal Committee and the Publishing Sub-committee—the consultants suggested there should be but one. Finally, they proposed the appointment of a full-time business manager to perform all those tasks previously undertaken by the Publishing Sub-Committee and (till 1943) the Board of Directors.

Council accepted all these suggestions, though the *Journal*'s budget remained a fiction in so far as no portion of subscription income was actually earmarked for its expenses.[60] In 1951 Clegg had complained that 'Without any allocation from the members' subscription or without separate subscription to the *Journal* it is impossible . . . to manage on proper business lines a publishing activity of our size, which involves a turnover of between £400 000 and £500 000 a year.'[61] But the complaint fell on deaf ears. Six years later he

[57] *BMJ* mss. JCM (1950–1) JNL.23, Editor's Report, 11 Oct. 1951; (1951–2) JNL.46, Agenda, 10 Jan. 1952; JNL.50, 10 Jan. 1952.

[58] *Ibid.*, JNL.7, Editor's Memorandum, 23 Aug. 1951; JNL.18, Publishing Sub-committee, 3 Oct. 1951; JNL.24, 11 Oct. 1951; JNL.28, Editor's Memorandum, 24 Oct. 1951.

[59] *Ibid.*, (1950–1) JNL.71, Publishing Sub-committee, Editor's Report, 26 April 1951; JNL.74, Publishing Sub-committee, O. C. Carter's memorandum, 17 May 1951; (1951–2) JNL.11, Publishing Sub-committee, 23 Aug. 1951; JNL.23, Editor's Report, 11 Oct. 1951; JNL.48, Editor's Memorandum; 10 Jan. 1952; JNL.57, Agenda, 14 Feb. 1952; JNL.70, Publishing Sub-committee, 14 Feb. 1952; *BMJ* Supplement, 12 May 1951, 195; 4 April 1953, 114–15.

[60] *BMJ* mss. JCM (1951–2) JNL.86, Agenda, 8 May 1952; JNL.89, Supplementary Agenda, 8 May 1952; (1952–53) JNL.19, 11 Sept. 1952; (1957–8) JNL.7, Financial Policy, 24 Oct. 1957; *BMJ* Supplement, 4 April 1953, 114–15.

[61] *BMJ* mss. JCM (1950–1) JNL.23, Editor's Report, 11 Oct. 1951.

told the Journal Committee that, 'members would be shocked if they knew that no part of their subscription went to the *Journal* funds and that, in addition, the *Journal* was expected to contribute to the Association funds.' He always felt that if the *Journal* surpluses of 1943–50 had been paid into a reserve fund, 'the publications would not have been in such an unfavourable position when costs were rocketing in 1951.'[62] One of the Journal Committee members agreed, observing 'that members were unaware of this position and probably thought half the subscription went to the *Journal*'.[63]

In 1952 the *Journal*'s financial position began to improve, though whether this was due to the re-organization or merely to the fall in the price of paper and improvement in general economic conditions is a moot point, for business re-organization had made comparatively little progress by that time. The business manager, for example, did not take up his position till 1953.[64] The appointment of the manager—Maurice Webb, recruited from the BBC, was the first incumbent—did have the effect, however, of relieving the editor of much of the responsibility for financial management. In 1958 Webb resigned to return to the BBC as head of its advertising department. On his departure Clegg stated that he had 'no doubt' that Webb had been responsible for a marked improvement in the *Journal*'s financial position. He managed to head off suggestions that no successor should be appointed. In July the position was filled by R. H. L. Russell, an employee of Whitehead and Partners, who had recommended the creation of the post of business manager. Russell, who had been chiefly responsible for conducting Whitehead's investigation, had been an unsuccessful applicant for the post when Webb was appointed.[65]

Journal income, for 1952, rose by some £25 500, mainly because of higher advertising charges and a fall in the price of paper of over £15 000. Other costs rose, but the *Journal* was still able to show a surplus of over £14 000.[66] The price of paper declined further in 1953, during the course of which the *Journal* showed a surplus of £71 852. Both advertising revenue and the surplus on the year, at the beginning of which the annual subscription was raised to 6 guineas (within the British Isles), were the highest ever. The Journal Committee could consider restoring the lost pages.[67] The crisis was over. There remained, however, the question of defining the *Journal*'s relationship with the BMA.

After 1951, for the remainder of Clegg's editorship the *Journal* remained in generally sound financial health, even when potential disaster such as labour

[62] *Ibid.*, (1957–8) JNL.4, 29 Aug. 1957.
[63] *Ibid.*, (1956–7) JNL.15, 22 Jan. 1957.
[64] *Ibid.*, (1952–3) JNL.25, Publishing Sub-committee, 30 Oct. 1952.
[65] *Ibid.*, (1957–8) JNL.27, 26 June 1958; (1961–2) JNL.5, 27 July 1961.
[66] *Ibid.*, (1952–3) JNL.47, Income and Expenditure Account, 23 April 1953.
[67] *Ibid.*, (1953–4) JNL.14, 19 Nov. 1953; JNL.16, Realisation Statements, 25 Feb. 1954; *Journal*, 31 Jan. 1953, 262; *BMJ* Supplement, 10 July 1954, 44.

disputes in the printing trade (especially in 1956 and 1959) or increased postal charge—as in 1957, for example—threatened to upset both publishing continuity and solvency (see Table 11.2). By the early 1950s the Association was again relying upon the *Journal* to make an appreciable contribution to its overall income, thereby allowing it to hold down the price of membership subscriptions. Consequently, when costs rose and surpluses fell, as they did in 1956 with the introduction of higher postal charges, the Association expected the *Journal* to economize or find ways of generating more revenue in order to save it from possible financial embarrassment. This rankled with Clegg, who felt that if the Secretariat's income was inadequate it should raise subscriptions rather than impose upon the *Journal*:

> . . . journal surpluses over the years had concealed from the Association the real state of its finances. The membership subscription should have been raised in 1945 but journal surpluses were available and were used to spend money in all sorts of directions. The Journal Committee foresaw the present position in 1942 but failed to convince the then Chairman of Council and Treasurer.[68]

In 1957 Clegg pushed hard for the *Journal* to retain its surpluses and/or to receive an allocation from subscription income in order to establish a 'reserve fund' to protect the *Journal* during hard times and to provide for its future development. The position was complicated by doubts concerning taxation. However, in December, swayed by Clegg's persuasive advocacy, and contrary to the advice of the BMA's finance officers, the Journal Committee agreed to recommend to Council that surpluses on publications should be paid into a reserve fund for the use of the publications.[69] The question rumbled through the BMA's bureaucratic maze for several years before Council and the General Purposes Committee resolved, in 1962, that 'the disposal of any surpluses from the *Journal* should be determined by the Council from year to year.'[70] Both Clegg and members of the Journal Committee considered this to be a most unsatisfactory compromise. Journal Committee minutes report the reaction of one of its number, Sir Arthur Thompson, as follows: 'it was complete folly that the Journal should not have a reserve out of their own resources with which the Journal Committee could deal. He was entirely opposed to the policy that Council should regard the *Journal* as an enterprise from which they could expect profit.'[71] Clegg observed that the *Journal* department wanted 'to get straight with the

[68] *BMJ* mss. JCM (1957–8) JNL.15, 12 Dec. 1957. For a similar assessment see *BMJ* Supplement, 5 April 1952, 140.

[69] *BMJ* mss. JCM (1956–7) JNL.15, 22 Jan. 1957; (1957–8) JNL.9, 24 Oct. 1957; JNL.13, Accounting and Taxation Considerations in Connection with Financial Policy in Relation to Publications (Memorandum by the Financial Comptroller and the Accountant), 12 Dec. 1957; JNL.15, 12 Dec. 1957; JNL.17, Financial Policy in Relation to the Publications. Memorandum from the Journal Committee, 6 March 1958.

[70] *Ibid.*, (1961–2) JNL.23, Agenda, 16 May 1962.

[71] *Ibid.*

Association . . . that the period of plundering *Journal* money should come to an end'.[72] The Journal Committee drew up a response to the resolution which emphasized the importance attached to establishing a £100 000 reserve. Later that year Council agreed to the creation of such a fund. An important victory in establishing a degree of financial autonomy had been won.[73]

In 1960, a year which produced a *Journal* surplus in excess of £48 000, income from advertisements amounted to nearly £611 000. These figures underline the commercial success achieved by the *Journal.* The only worrying aspect about the statistics for income was that they showed how heavy was the dependence upon advertising revenue. In 1960 this provided about 92.5 per cent of the *Journal*'s income. Some considered this to be dangerously high as it left the *Journal* vulnerable in the event of a sudden decline in demand for space from advertisers. The validity of the fears concerning the *Journal*'s vulnerability was shown in 1961 and 1962 when advertising revenue fell away badly, allegedly because of uncertainty over Britain's application to join the Common Market. In 1961 it was down £47 000 on the previous year, leaving the *Journal* with its first deficit for a decade.[74]

In these circumstances the Journal Committee recommended strenuous efforts to boost non-member subscriptions. To this end numerous promotional exercises were undertaken. In 1963, for example, the manager, Charles Parker (who had replaced Russell in December 1961), made an extensive tour of Canada and the USA. In 1965 he embarked upon a world tour. By 1965 these efforts were beginning to pay dividends; non-member subscriptions for that year were 11 737, as against 7173 in 1958. Most of this increase was accounted for by overseas subscriptions. In reality, however, there was little likelihood of advertising income ever ceasing to provide the vast bulk of revenue unless a proportion of membership fees was earmarked for the *Journal.* This practice, long adopted by the American Medical Association, had always been rejected by the BMA on the grounds that subscription income should be exclusively at the disposal of Council. With the *Journal* producing healthy annual surpluses it became a complete 'non-starter'. For the *Journal* this has been, perhaps, a blessing in disguise, for it is likely that, if it ever had been adopted, editorial independence, fragile flower that it has always been, would have come under increased pressure.

In terms of its circulation and surpluses the *Journal* made solid advances in the two decades following the Second World War. Circulation made steady upward progress, interrupted only by secession of the BMA's Australian branches in 1962. The criticism raised by members at many annual meetings during its first 100 years, that the *Journal* should be self-supporting or profitable, could no longer be made. Advertising revenue increased substan-

[72] *Ibid.*

[73] *Ibid.*, (1962–3) JNL.6, 24 Oct. 1962.

[74] *Ibid.*, (1961–2) JNL.12, Business Manager's Report for 1961.

tially. Rates were regularly raised during the 1950s and 1960s and by 1965, the end of Clegg's editorship, the basic page rate for advertisers ranged from £198 to £480 for four colours printed on art paper (colour, incidentally, was still almost entirely missing from the editorial pages in 1965). In 1964 annual revenue from advertising amounted to £539 000. *Journal* sales to non-members, though at an all time peak, yielded only some £70 000.[75] The operating surplus for 1965 was over £62 000 for the third year in a row.

Revival

Circulation growth and profitability are two criteria by which the success of a newspaper or periodical may be judged, and in regard to these Clegg's *Journal* was eminently successful. But neither provides an adequate yardstick by which to assess the *BMJ*. Its circulation is largely a function of BMA membership; in 1965 only some 14 per cent of its circulation went to non-member subscribers. Moreover, as that membership increases, so advertising revenue and profitability should also increase as the pages of the *Journal* become more attractive to prospective advertisers. Hence, revenue has little to do with the quality of the content. On the basis of circulation growth the *Journal* of the 1920s and 1930s was also highly successful, though its content in those decades is often considered to have been dull.

Clegg is usually perceived as a highly successful editor. On his retirement his achievements were formally recognized in several ways, including the award of the CBE and the BMA's gold medal. His *Munk's Roll* entry praises him as an 'innovator as well as an upholder of standards' who changed the course of post-war British medicine and produced a *Journal* of international standing. His *Journal* obituary refers to him as an editor of 'genius'.[76] Such recognition was not based on the *Journal*'s circulation growth or profitability, but on its content, and it is to that content that we should now turn.

Clegg was a committed internationalist, active in the World Medical Association (founded in 1947) and a vice-president of the International Union of the Medical Press (1953). In 1956 he presided over the first international congress on medical editing to be held in Britain. He also organized the first world congress on medical education.[77] From the moment he became the *Journal*'s official as well as *de facto* editor, he placed a high priority on re-establishing its overseas reputation. This had been a goal that Ernest Hart—like Clegg, an indefatigable traveller—had achieved three-quarters of a century earlier, but the wider world had slipped very much into the background during Horner's editorship. Clegg and other editorial staff began to travel widely on the *Journal*'s behalf, spreading its name, acquiring

[75] *Ibid.*, (1965–6) JNL.13, Supplementary Agenda, 10 Nov. 1965.

[76] *Munk's Roll* vii, pp. 104–6 (note 3); *Journal*, 16 July 1983, 220; see also *Dictionary of National Biography, 1981–90* (note 1).

[77] *Journal*, 21 Sept. 1957, 690; *Dictionary of National Biography, 1981–90* (note 1).

Table 11.3 *BMJ* circulation 1945–65

Year	Circulation	Year	Circulation
1945	53 000	1956	79 000
1946	57 750	1957	80 000
1947	62 500	1958	80 700
1948	67 000	1959	83 300
1949	70 000	1960	86 200
1950	72 500	1961	88 300
1951	72 400	1962	79 700
1952	76 000	1963	80 000
1953	76 400	1964	81 400
1954	75 000	1965	82 800
1955	76 600		

Circulation, always a complicated matter, has become all the more so in recent years with different versions of the *Journal* going to different categories of subscriber. The *BMJ* has never kept full and consistent circulation records. The main objects of keeping any record are to attract potential advertisers and to justify scales of charges. During the 1960s the advertisement manager notified advertisers of print-runs; since these included copies sent to store they provided an exaggerated guide. I am advised by the present advertisement manager that this is no longer current practice. Current figures also exclude, among other things, student subscriptions and copies sent to retired practitioners, since such readers are of little interest to advertisers. Circulation figures presented here are drawn from the records of the BMA's Journal Committee. Wherever possible they are based on copies posted (as opposed to print-run) during the month of September in any year. As always, circulation varied from week to week owing to deaths, resignations, and lapsed memberships and subscriptions.

contacts, and keeping a finger on the pulse of overseas developments. For, when Clegg expressed his determination to make the *BMJ* something other than a 'parish pump magazine' (a favourite phrase), he was thinking not only of its relationship with the Association but of its position and responsibilities in the context of world medicine. His aim was to publish 'all that is best in British medicine' (another favourite phrase) and to project it to an overseas market hungry for medical knowledge—hence his vigorous though largely unavailing pursuit of opportunities to produce international and foreign language editions of the *Journal*. He began to print regular reports of international conferences—something the *Lancet* had been doing for several years. In 1949 he produced a special issue on the World Health Organization, 500 copies of which were purchased by the WHO for distribution to delegates at the UN General Assembly. In 1950 the *Journal* carried many of the papers read at the First International Conference on Internal Medicine in Paris.[78]

All of this made for a *Journal* far removed in character from Horner's.

[78] *BMJ* mss. JCM (1950–1) JNL.23, Editor's Report, 11 Oct. 1951.

Where Horner had aspired to publish the 'average article for the average practitioner', Clegg was 'determined to make the *B.M.J.* a first class journal through original publications'.[79] He knew he had much ground to make up on the *Journal*'s great rival, the *Lancet*, and embarked upon a relentless pursuit of excellence. He was not above accepting articles on his own initiative, but generally relied on the system of peer review which he established. What he refused to countenance was continuation of the practice of publishing papers simply because they had been read at a BMA meeting. Under his editorship these too had to compete against other submissions and win publication on merit. This change, which had a major impact on the *Journal*'s content, alienated many people in the BMA. In adhering to it Clegg did more to uphold the *Journal*'s independence from the Association than ever he did through his 'Gold-Headed Cane' leader.[80]

The type of material carried by the *Journal* also changed dramatically. Statistics began to make a regular appearance, while great attention was devoted to the large-scale clinical trials and epidemiological research which flourished after the war:

> ... he accepted long and heavily statistical papers ... at a time when statistics were still suspect and disliked. The attitude of the profession was changing but it wasn't all that in love with statistics or epidemiology .... It is easy to swallow the spate of it *now* ... It was quite another matter to put ... in the forefront of the B.M.J. ... trials of treatment in t.b. and rheumatism, trials of whooping cough vaccines, retrospective inquiries into smoking, and so on.[81]

As for leading articles, these began to be written by authorities on their subjects rather than, as hitherto, generalists with felicitous pens. To this end editorial staff combed specialist journals to find prospective leader writers.[82] Of course, Clegg's endeavours were facilitated by the exciting developments in medicine that occurred during his editorship, but he deserves credit for seizing upon them and recognizing the need to transform the *Journal*.

Realization of his goals was no easy matter, for many BMA members, particularly GPs, had no desire to receive in their weekly magazine a rich diet of scientific papers in which they had no real interest and which they could not understand anyway. From these people Clegg, usually through Council or at ARMs, received frequent complaints and regular demands for blander, more readily digestible, fare. For example, at the 1949 ARM Dr C. P. Wallace argued that the *Journal* should be made 'more easily readable' and presented 'in a more popular form. ... Too often the scientific articles which appeared were more suitable to specialist journals, and others were produced

[79] *Ibid.* Clegg file, Hill to Ware, 20 Feb. 1972.
[80] *Ibid.*; Clegg interview; Lock interview 27 June 1989.
[81] *Ibid.*, Austin Bradford Hill to Martin Ware, 20 Feb. 1972; see *Munk's Roll* vii, p. 104 (note 3); *BMJ* Supplement, 27 March 1954, 101.
[82] Swinscow interview, 9 Feb. 1989.

by intellectual snobs.'[83] Clegg always responded in the same way: that nobody should expect to read the *Journal* from cover to cover and find everything uniformly interesting and comprehensible. They should read it selectively, in the same way that they read their daily newspapers, picking out appealing items. If they did this, he argued, they ought to find something that would inform, instruct, stimulate, or amuse them. For those who could not, he had no sympathy. Clegg was no compromiser and never allowed himself to be deflected by his critics. While recognizing that the BMA, and consequently the *Journal*'s readership, was a 'broad church' for which he had to cater, he adhered rigidly to his task of returning the *Journal* to the forefront of serious medical journalism. He believed that there was only one way of achieving this: 'There is no doubt in my mind that the reputation of the *BRITISH MEDICAL JOURNAL* . . . depends largely upon the standard of the original communications published in the opening pages each week.'[84]

Aware that the *Lancet* was the *Journal*'s chief rival, he paid close attention to what it was doing, not only what it was publishing but also how many literary pages it carried and at what price. On several occasions he resisted proposed increases in non-member subscriptions and cuts in the *BMJ*'s dimensions on the grounds that they would make it uncompetitive in relation to the *Lancet*:

At the last meeting of the Publishing Subcommittee attention was drawn to the fact that there were more literary pages in the *Journal* than in *THE LANCET* and suggestion arose that the size of the *Journal* should be cut down. It seems to me that this is an unfortunate and unjustifiable comparison. I would like to suggest that we do not sink to the level of *THE LANCET* . . . it is of the utmost importance that we should do all we can to increase non-member subscriptions, and in competition with *THE LANCET* in this field we are persuading non-members to pay four guineas a year for the *BRITISH MEDICAL JOURNAL* as against *THE LANCET*'s two guineas. We have to try to persuade non-member subscribers that they are getting their money's worth. . . . This is, of course, not to suggest that we should just make a bigger journal for the sake of making a bigger joural, but if we are to compete successfully with *THE LANCET* then we have to make sure that we are at least covering as much ground.[85]

By 1951 Clegg felt that he had done much to restore the *Journal*'s reputation and close the gap on the *Lancet*. '*THE LANCET*', he wrote in October of that year,

used to have a bigger reputation abroad than the *BRITISH MEDICAL JOURNAL*. I think we can say that this picture is now being changed . . . If one is to believe what

[83] *BMJ* Supplement, 9 July 1949, 34.

[84] *BMJ* mss. JCM (1951–2) JNL.23, Editor's Report, 11 Oct. 1951; Clegg file, Address to Winchester division, 7–10; *Journal*, 28 Feb. 1953, 496-7; 14 March 1953, 620; 21 March 1953, 673; 28 March 1953, 730–1; H. Clegg, 'Some Principles and Problems of Medical Editing', 419–25 (note 45).

[85] *BMJ* mss. JCM (1951–2) JNL.23, Editor's Report, 11 Oct. 1951.

one hears from medical men not only in this country but in other countries, the standard of the *BRITISH MEDICAL JOURNAL* has improved ... and is held in high repute.[86]

This view was upheld by Walsh McDermott, Professor of Public Health at Cornell University Medical College, New York (and editor of the *American Review of Respiratory Diseases*). On the occasion of Clegg's retirement, he wrote:

When you started with the BMJ it really had relatively little influence on this side of the Atlantic, but under your leadership it has become a 'must' for all of us here. And, I know it has been so throughout the rest of the English-reading world. It is no small feat to do that in any situation, but to do it with so distinguished a competitor as the Lancet was truly a remarkable feat.[87]

During Clegg's editorship the *Journal* provided coverage of all the myriad changes occurring in medicine. As we have seen, the establishment of the NHS was of major concern in 1947 and 1948. Thereafter, the health service became a prime feature of the *BMJ*'s contents in any and every year. During periods of perceived crisis it could become a dominant preoccupation; in the first six months of 1957, for example, it was the subject of 19 leading articles. Other major developments in health and medicine were given the 'Clegg treatment'.

In his first summer as editor there occurred 'the worst epidemic of poliomyelitis yet encountered in Great Britain'.[88] Thereafter, for more than a decade the disease took a grip on the popular imagination which far outstripped its importance in terms of morbidity and mortality. The alleged dangers of public swimming baths, flies, unwashed fruit and vegetables, and over-exertion provided the basis for much tabloid sensationalism though, as a *Journal* leader pointed out in 1950, the 'risk of contracting poliomyelitis in its paralytic form is, even in a sharp epidemic, far less than it is popularly imagined to be.'[89] The *Journal* provided regular epidemiological reports on the disease, information on treatment, and exhaustive coverage of the vaccination debate.[90] In 1956 the Ministry of Health announced its scheme for the mass vaccination of children born between 1947 and 1954, the operation of which turned the *Journal* into a trenchant critic of government policy. Leading articles headed, 'Another Ministry Blunder', 'Polio Fantasies', and 'Cheap Propaganda on Polio' show that the *Journal* could be as fierce a critic of a Conservative as of a Labour government.[91]

As well as renewing the *Journal*'s emphasis on international affairs and

[86] *Ibid.*

[87] *Ibid.*, (1965–6) JNL.21, Agenda, 30 March 1966.

[88] *Journal*, 30 Aug. 1947, 338.

[89] *Ibid.*, 16 Sept. 1950, 664–5; 16 Aug. 1952, 379–80; 5 Dec. 1953, 1258–9.

[90] *BMJ* Supplement, 10 April 1948, 82.

[91] *Journal*, 14 May 1955, 1204; 21 Jan. 1956, 157–8; 28 Jan. 1956, 220; 20 Oct. 1956, 929–30; 9 March 1957, 571–2.

scientific medicine, Clegg paid close attention to the broad social and political context of medicine, another aspect of the *Journal* which had waned during the 1920s and 1930s. Thus, in the 1950s and 1960s the *Journal* concerned itself with the end of rationing, 'Teddy' boys, glue-sniffing, drugs in athletics, motor-cycle crash helmets, food irradiation, drunken driving, space travel, the nuclear threat, child abuse, the Common Market (as it was then called), changing sexual morality, the ethics of human experimentation (a particular interest of Clegg's), family planning, toxic pesticides, boxing and brain damage, the televising of surgical operations, abortion law, and so on.[92] One topic that merits closer examination is the series of papers by Doll and Bradford Hill on smoking and lung cancer, which made such an impact in the 1950s and early 1960s. Their research, much of which was published in the *BMJ*, played a large part in establishing an incontrovertible link between tobacco smoking and lung cancer. In consequence, the *Journal* came to the forefront of the movement to publicize the dangers and reduce the incidence of smoking.

Smoking and lung cancer

Suggestions of a link between smoking and lung cancer date back at least as far as Adler in 1912, while during the 1930s and 1940s Ochsner and DeBakey expressed a 'definite conviction that the increase in the incidence of pulmonary carcinoma is due largely to the increase in smoking'.[93] Such views, however, seem to have exerted little influence on the *BMJ*'s contributors. During the nineteenth century the *Journal* had taken a tolerant view of tobacco smoking (see Chapter 7). In 1938, referring to Professor Pearl's finding that non-smokers lived longer than smokers, a leader writer had commented that, although Pearl had shown a correlation between smoking and reduced longevity, 'some little distance must be travelled before one can be sure that non-smokers live longer than smokers because they do not smoke.'[94]

In January 1947 the *Journal* carried an 'Any Questions' item inquiring whether 'tobacco smoke contain[s] any injurious products, and has it any demonstrable carcinogenic activity?' The inquirer went on to ask whether there was evidence linking tobacco abuse with cancer or other diseases. For smokers the answer was more reassuring than otherwise:

> Tars are formed when tobacco is heated, but these are only weakly, if at all, carcinogenic when painted on the skin of mice. It is difficult to assess the extent to which tobacco can be blamed for the disorders mentioned. Publications on the subject

[92] See *Dictionary of National Biography, 1981–90* (note 1) for Clegg's involvement in medical ethics.

[93] *Journal*, 29 June 1957, 1519.

[94] *Ibid.*, 9 April 1938, 791.

Couldn't we tell 'em that we've discovered *clean* tobacco . . .? Charles Hill, Harold Macmillan, R. A. Butler, and Peter Thorneycroft reflect on the possible consequences for government revenue of the MRC's condemnation of cigarette smoking. Cartoon by Vicky, published in the *New Statesman*, 6 July 1957. Source: Centre for the Study of Cartoons and Caricature, University of Kent at Canterbury.

often have a partisan flavour . . . there is no reason to suspect that it [tobacco smoke] has any permanent effect on the heart . . . . There is no evidence for believing that carcinoma of the stomach or bronchus can be attributed to tobacco.[95]

Such an answer might well have been given 70 years earlier. Later in 1947 a leading article published at the time of Hugh Dalton's budget, which imposed large increases in tobacco duty, expressed uncertainty as to whether 'the social and psychological benefits of smoking outweigh the disadvantages.' The tone of this leader and of some of the correspondence which followed it continued to be one of amused tolerance.[96]

Within a few years, however, research conducted in the United States had suggested a definite link between smoking and cancer of the lung.[97] When the findings of Wynder and Graham and of Levin, Goldstein, and Gerhardt were reported in the *Journal* they elicited the editorial comment that 'strong support has been given to the existing financial reason for not smoking.' The *Journal* carried little correspondence on the subject, though one writer suggested that the increase in motor exhaust fumes and road tar dust should not be overlooked when seeking to explain the increasing incidence of lung cancer.[98] It was against this background that Richard Doll and Austin

[95] *Ibid.*, 25 Jan. 1947, 166.

[96] *Ibid.*, 26 April 1947, 570; 17 May 1947, 696; 7 June 1947, 827; 28 June 1947, 950

[97] *JAMA*, 27 May 1950, **143**, 329–36, 336–8.

[98] *Journal*, 24 June 1950, 1477; 8 July 1950, 107. These factors had been frequently linked with lung cancer in the 1920s and 1930s.

Bradford Hill published in the *Journal* their ground-breaking preliminary report on 'Smoking and Carcinoma of the Lung'.[99]

Doll and Bradford Hill had begun their investigation in 1947. Their starting point was a phenomenon observed by many other writers, namely, the huge increase in deaths attributed to lung cancer in Western nations since 1900 (in England and Wales the increase was approximately 15-fold in the period 1922–47). Having dismissed improved diagnosis as an adequate explanation of the development, they hypothesized that there were two possibilities: increased atmospheric pollution or tobacco smoking. Doll and Bradford Hill undertook a complex and large-scale statistical inquiry into 2475 notified cases of cancer in 20 London hospitals over an 18-month period in 1948–9. Their conclusion was that 'there is a real association between carcinoma of the lung and smoking.' Moreover, 'smoking is . . . an important factor, in the production of carcinoma of the lung' and 'the risk seems to vary in approximately simple proportion with the amount smoked.' There was, however, insufficient evidence to show 'a simple time relationship between the increased consumption of tobacco [which had risen from just over 2 lbs per person per year in 1901 to almost 4 lbs in 1947] and the increased number of deaths attributed to cancer of the lung'. Finally, they speculated that those aged over 45 who smoked more than 25 cigarettes a day ran 50 times the risk of non-smokers of developing the disease. This paper was the first published in the United Kingdom to present compelling evidence of a link between tobacco smoking and lung cancer.

In a leading article the *Journal* observed that Doll and Bradford Hill's findings 'have very serious implications'. It also noted, however, the absence of 'convincing experimental evidence about tobacco as a cause of cancer'. The writer recognized that 'the practical question which the doctor in practice has to answer is whether any of his patients—for instance, those with smoker's cough—should be advised to give up smoking.' But in the absence of evidence concerning the degree of risk, he was prepared to say only that the likelihood of contracting cancer 'does apparently increase in direct proportion to the amount smoked daily and to the total duration of the habit'. The internal evidence suggests that this leader may have been written by Ronald Bodley Scott, who later contributed to the *Journal* an article entitled 'Some Medical Aspects of Tobacco-Smoking'. In this, after reviewing the effects of smoking upon the respiratory system, he reached a similarly ambivalent conclusion: 'The moral we should draw is obscure: perhaps we should caution all young men and women not to smoke more than 20 cigarettes a day.'[100]

Meanwhile the number of deaths from cancer of the bronchus and lung

[99] *Ibid.*, 30 Sept. 1950, 739–48. On Doll and Bradford Hill's researches see Joan Austoker, *A History of the Imperial Cancer Research Fund, 1902–1986* (Oxford: Oxford University Press, 1988), pp. 194–7.

[100] *Journal*, 30 Sept. 1950, 767–8; 29 March 1952, 671–4.

continued to rise. In 1951, for the first time, it exceeded that of deaths from respiratory tuberculosis (13 233 as against 12 036 for England and Wales).[101] In that year Doll and Bradford Hill launched the second phase of their work. This consisted of a questionnaire, sent to all doctors on the *Medical Register*, inquiring about their smoking habits. The intention was to divide the profession into four broad categories: heavy, moderate, light, and non-smokers, and then, over a period of years, to measure the mortality of each group in relation to the certified causes of death. Bradford Hill, who was a personal friend and near neighbour of Clegg—they often travelled by train into London together—used the *Journal* to publicize the questionnaire and to appeal for a high response rate.[102] While this study was in its early stages Doll and Bradford Hill published their second major paper in the *Journal.*

The paper—a very long one by *Journal* standards—was essentially an extension of their 1950 report. It used the same methods but was based on more detailed investigation of smoking habits and on the experience of patients from the provinces as well as those from London and the Home Counties, and took account of the possible effects of atmospheric pollution in and out of the home. The finding, however, was unchanged: 'it is concluded that the association between smoking and carcinoma of the lung is real.'[103] It is hard to overestimate the importance of this paper and its predecessor of 1950. They were often challenged, but never refuted. They provided the inspiration for a wealth of further research which confirmed and extended their findings. They opened up the medical, ultimately the public and political, debate that was to lead to fundamental changes in attitudes towards smoking.

The *Journal*'s immediate response to Doll and Bradford Hill's second report marked the beginning of this change. In an editorial entitled 'Smoking and Lung Cancer' it expressed an opinion far more forthright than it had ever offered before:

Statistics it is said cannot prove causation. . . . All that these things can do is to show that probability of a causative connexion between an agent and a disease is so great that we are bound to take what preventive action we can, accepting the theory as though the proof were absolute until further research leads to some modification. It would seem that such a position has now been reached with lung carcinoma, in that

[101] *Ibid.*, 13 Dec. 1952, 1316. By the early 1960s the annual number of deaths from lung cancer had risen to around 22 000.

[102] *Ibid.*, 10 Nov. 1951, 1157, 1163; 15 Dec. 1951, 1460. The BMA despatched Doll and Bradford Hill's questionnaires and letters. *Ibid.*, 26 June 1954, 1455; *BMJ* mss. Clegg file, Hill to Ware, 20 Feb. 1972. In the USA Wynder and Graham were engaged in a broadly similar study of the relationship between physicians, smoking, and lung cancer. By making use of *JAMA* obituaries, which, unlike *BMJ* practice, then recorded cause of death, they were able to identify cancer victims and direct questionnaires to deceased doctors' estates. They found a 'highly significant association between the use of tobacco and the development of pulmonary cancer'. See *New England Journal of Medicine* (1953) **248**: 441; *Journal*, 2 May 1953, 986.

[103] *Ibid.*, 13 Dec. 1952, 1271–86.

tobacco has been incriminated as the vehicle conveying an agent responsible for a large proportion of the cases.[104]

The writer went on to call for intensive research on the chemical constituents of tobacco with a view to isolating the carcinogenic agent(s). He assumed that the tobacco companies would undertake this in the expectation that isolation would be followed by removal, thereby rendering smoking 'a less dangerous occupation than it appears to be now'. Meanwhile, 'the younger generation will have to decide, each for himself or herself, whether the additional risk of contracting lung carcinoma is worth taking.'

Publication of Doll and Bradford Hill's second report and the *Journal*'s leader thereon brought forth many letters from *BMJ* readers. The opinions they expressed ranged from demands for the immediate banning of tobacco products, to frank scepticism that smoking had been shown to be a cause of lung cancer.[105] But in 1954 the Minister of Health, Iain Macleod, advised by a committee which had reviewed the Doll and Bradford Hill research, conceded that there was a 'strong presumption' of a causal link between smoking and lung cancer. He was unwilling to issue public health warnings but suggested that 'young people should be warned of the risks apparently attendant on excessive smoking'. By this time the *Journal* was ready to 'go further' than this and advise medical men to 'tell patients that there is probably an increased risk, to greater or less degree, associated with any amount of smoking, especially of cigarettes'.[106]

Notwithstanding the available evidence, both tobacco consumption and death from lung cancer continued to increase during the 1950s. In these circumstances Clegg came to believe that the *Journal* could play an important part in furthering GPs' understanding of the link between smoking and lung cancer, thereby helping them to deter their patients, especially the young, from smoking. He felt that much of the evidence on smoking and lung cancer had been 'embodied in long and technical articles'; there was little in the way of 'a clear guide to the facts'. But such a thing was urgently needed, for Clegg thought that it was 'imperative for all concerned to see that the public is repeatedly informed of the possible dangers to health and life from smoking cigarettes'. He therefore commissioned Doll and Bradford Hill to supply simple and concise answers to 31 questions on 'Lung Cancer and Tobacco'. Their response was published in place of the regular 'Refresher Course for General Practitioners'.[107]

In 1954 Doll and Bradford Hill published in the *Journal* the first of their

[104] *Ibid.*, 13 Dec. 1952, 1299–301.

[105] *Ibid.*, 27 Dec. 1952, 1417; 17 Jan. 1953, 161; 7 Feb. 1953, 338; 14 Feb. 1953, 399; 28 Feb. 1953, 505–7; 7 March 1953, 564; 14 March 1953, 618; 21 March 1953, 677–8; 11 April 1953, 833; 18 April 1953, 888; 16 May 1953, 1105; 6 June 1953, 1281; 13 June 1953, 1335.

[106] *Ibid.*, 20 Feb. 1954, 445, 465.

[107] *Ibid.*, 19 May 1956, 1157, 116–63; see 10 Nov. 1956, 1104–5.

three reports on 'The Mortality of Doctors in Relation to their Smoking Habits', the second of which appeared in November 1956 and the third in 1964, by which time Bradford Hill had retired. Their importance lay less in the generation of new conclusions than in the confirmation they gave, by using a different method, of previous findings. However, the additional data also suggested a causal link between smoking and chronic bronchitis and coronary thrombosis.[108] These papers gave rise to questions in the House and a flood of comment in the general press. During the time of their appearance the *BMJ*, along with other general and specialist medical journals, was publishing a steady stream of papers and leaders on the links between cancer, other medical conditions, smoking, and atmospheric pollution.[109] In 1957 the *Journal* carried a paper by another doyen of smoking and lung cancer research, Ernest Wynder of the Sloan–Kettering Institute in the USA.[110] By this time, the *Journal* opined, there could be little doubt that the statisticians and clinicians 'have closed every loophole of escape for tobacco as the villain in the piece'.[111]

By 1957, with the MRC advising the government that 'a major part of the increase' in lung cancer was 'associated with tobacco smoking, particularly in the form of cigarettes', the *Journal* was ready to contemplate something more than public education. A leader published in that year suggested that there was 'something to be said for prohibiting smoking in such public places as cinemas and theatres'. By the early 1960s, with deaths from lung cancer and chronic bronchitis continuing their upward trend, it had come to the conclusion that health education alone would not succeed in deterring juvenile smoking. It would 'need to be combined with some measure of public control'.[112]

For much of the time that all this was going on, however, the *Journal* continued to carry advertising for cigarettes. This apparent hypocrisy was reminiscent of what had occurred at the time of the 'secret remedies' campaign, when some proprietary medicines had been condemned in the *Journal*'s editorial pages while others were being advertised elsewhere within its covers. Then, *JAMA* had set a standard that the *Journal* had found difficult to follow. Mortality from lung cancer in the United States was far lower than in Britain, but in 1954 *JAMA* had ceased to accept advertisements for tobacco products. Once again it, rather than the *BMJ*, seemed to be setting the example. Struck by the inconsistency between the *Journal*'s

[108] *Ibid.*, 26 June 1954, 1451–5, 1480–1; 10 Nov. 1956, 1071–81, 1104–5; 30 May 1964, 1399–1410. The data generated by the questionnaire led Doll and Bradford Hill to conclude that medical men between the ages of 25 and 45 were at special risk of dying of poliomyelitis. See *ibid.*, 16 Feb. 1957, 372, 394.

[109] *Ibid.*, 26 June 1954, 1473–4; 8 Jan. 1955, 91–2; 15 Oct. 1955, 923–9; 15 Oct. 1955, 954–5; 3 Dec. 1955, 1345–51; 12 May 1956, 1092–4. See indexes for many further references.

[110] *Ibid.*, 5 Jan. 1957, 1–3.

[111] *Ibid.*, 29 June 1957, 1518–20.

[112] *Ibid.*, 1520; 16 Dec. 1961, 1625–6.

editorial and advertising policies, a BMA member, J. P. Anderson, sought an explanation. The Journal Committee replied merely that it remained ready 'to take advertisements for cigarettes provided the "copy" is acceptable'. Disgusted by 'the *Journal*'s refusal to practise what it preaches', Anderson resigned from the Association.[113] However, in the same year—1957—the *BMJ* carried its last advertisement for cigarettes (du Maurier). Advertising for pipe tobacco ceased to be accepted in 1958.

During the 1950s and 1960s the subject of tobacco smoking and lung cancer gained a grip on the consciousness of medical writers, researchers, and practitioners akin to that which had prevailed in respect of venereal diseases in the 1870s or was to apply in the case of AIDS in the 1980s. The *Journal* played a critical part in the process by virtue of its unique ability to perform two functions. First, it published some of the most important original research, most notably that of Doll and Bradford Hill, establishing the importance of smoking as a cause of lung cancer and other diseases. Second, it disseminated this, along with more readily digestible notes and comments, to the great majority of British doctors. It was thereby able to play a role as both initiator and orchestrator of the debate on smoking. During the high points of its history the *Journal* has accomplished this dual role to stunning effect. Ernest Hart was the master of the art. It says much of Clegg's editorship that it can be compared with that of the great man.

Of course, the *Journal*'s role in the debate on lung cancer and smoking was not an unqualified triumph. It certainly persisted for too long in carrying advertising for cigarettes. It also miscalculated in other ways: it underestimated the power of the tobacco companies to defend themselves and overestimated the readiness of the public to heed research findings and shun tobacco products. Towards the end of Clegg's editorship it was gradually dawning that 14 years after Doll and Bradford Hill's first paper, with the incidence of deaths from lung cancer continuing to increase, there was still a long hard road to be travelled before the 'deadly cigarette' went the way of other conquered health hazards.[114]

Conclusions

In the sense that the *BMJ* remains a flourishing publication there is no conclusion to this history, or rather, the conclusion is that, unlike most pre-Victorian and Victorian medical journals, it has survived for 150 years. During those years there have been successes and failures, peaks and troughs, triumphs and disasters. Existence has not always been smooth, or progress always onward and upward. But in general the *Journal* should be viewed as a success; how else could it have lasted for so long?

[113] *Ibid.*, 2 Feb. 1957, 285.
[114] See e.g. *Journal*, 18 Jan. 1964, 133–4.

In terms of editorial tenures, the *Journal* may be seen as having passed through two distinct periods. The first lasted from its foundation to 1870. In those 30 years there were nine editorial regimes: Green and Streeten, Streeten, Ranking and Walsh, Walsh, Cormack, Wynter, Markham, Hart, and Hutchinson. Between 1870 and 1990 there have been only six more: Hart, Williams, Horner, Clegg, Ware, and Lock. The change from rapid turnover to stability symptomizes the *Journal*'s transformation from struggling infancy to mature adulthood. It is unrealistic to attribute responsibility for effecting the change to any one individual. But if one man is to be singled out, it is Ernest Hart, who, flawed genius though he may have been, is the towering figure in the *Journal*'s history. By establishing the *Journal* as a flourishing and influential periodical, he laid the basis for the BMA's twentieth-century emergence as an institution of major national importance.

It has been suggested that until the mid-1930s the British Medical Association amounted to little more than a 'gentleman's club'. Although this is, perhaps, to understate its earlier importance—it had after all contributed notably to the national health insurance debates in 1911–12 and, more creatively, to the conduct of medical services in the First World War—there can be little doubt that it became a very different body after the reform of its constitution in 1902. Before that time the *Journal* rather than the Association had sought to represent medical opinion. Its success brought the Association members, money, and authority, thereby providing the launching-pad for its emergence as a powerful interest group. 'Fancy,' said R. Scott Stevenson when first shown the BMA's new premises in Tavistock Square, 'all this built out of a weekly newspaper.' His guide, the Association's financial secretary, demurred, pointing out that BMA House was the headquarters of a great association. Stevenson replied: 'Between you and me . . . don't let's deceive ourselves.'[115] His opinion echoed one expressed many years earlier by the *Jewish Chronicle*. 'The growth of the Association', it had said at the time of Hart's death, 'has largely been due to the success of the Journal.' It went on to point out that 'the history of the Journal is the history of Ernest Hart.'[116]

Hart's influence lived after him. Under the guidance of his protégé, Dawson Williams, the *Journal* continued to flourish, at least for his first two decades in control. In the years before the First World War important scientific papers were published at an unparalleled rate; moreover, crusading journalism, the hallmark of the Hart regime, was well represented in the campaign against secret remedies. But in the post-war years Williams's powers declined and the *Journal* entered a lean period, for a large part of which it was edited by Gerald Horner. For two decades it was characterized by dullness, timidity, and parochialism; its principal concerns were those of the 'parish pump'. The *Journal* has always been strongest when run by an

[115] R. Scott Stevenson, *Goodbye Harley Street* (London: Christopher Johnson, 1954), p. 83.
[116] 14 Jan. 1898.

independent editor whose horizons extended beyond the Association's interests. Of course, the *Journal*'s link with the BMA is at once a strength and a weakness. It benefits by being part of a large professional body with a large guaranteed readership that attracts lucrative advertising. On the other hand, it will always be suspected of lacking independence and 'toeing the party line'. Clegg appreciated that its standing was diminished if it allowed the Association to dominate it. His success was to assert some degree of autonomy, to drag the *Journal* out of its moribund state, and project it towards what may, in the future, come to be regarded as its second 'golden age'.

His triumph in these respects was not total. From the perspective of the late twentieth century the *Journal* of the 1950s and 1960s, with its lack of humour, celebration of Royal anniversaries, and absence of colour seems not only 'dated' but somewhat narrow and severe. Shortly before his death in 1983 Clegg, while expressing reservations about some of the changes, particularly the advent of signed leaders, that had occurred since his retirement, expressed his admiration for the breadth of its coverage.[117] This certainly became more extensive in the 1970s and 1980s. Like some of his predecessors Clegg stayed on as editor for too long; by the time he retired medicine bore little resemblance to its state when he had qualified. It is a measure of his achievement that this did not obscure his earlier successes.

[117] *BMJ* mss. Clegg file, Clegg interview.

Postscript

STEPHEN LOCK, EDITOR, *BMJ*

Any history must stop some years before the date of its publication, and I would not attempt to close the gap between Peter Bartrip's penetrating account of the BMJ up to 1965 and the present day. The events are too close for assessment and I have been concerned in too many of them to judge the light and the shade. So I have listed these in a chronology, and will instead look forward at the role of the general medical journal and its development. For, surprisingly, over the past century, whatever their circumstances, most general journals have shown a consistency—in shape, practice, and evolution. This reflects, I believe, what both the medical profession and society need. It is not too fanciful even to believe that if Ernest Hart or Hugh Clegg returned today he could resume the editorial chair of the *BMJ*.

The contents of general medical journals, it seems to me, are dictated by their four traditional roles: informing (reports of original work); instructing (putting work into perspective); commenting (editorial and outside); and 'amusing' (a broad term that reflects the wider perspective of medicine in society). Whatever philosopher one follows, knowledge arises out of a hypothesis, which is either supported by observation or experiment, or refuted and replaced by another hypothesis. But scientific work is not an end in itself: it has to be exposed to criticism and replication or modification by colleagues in the wider world. Such a process was one reason for founding the *Philosophical Transactions of the Royal Society*. Before 1665, when both the *Journal de Scavans* and the *Transactions* appeared, scientists had to communicate their results in a book or in letters to fellow scientists. The result was inefficient, might deny the discoverers their priority, and might even lead to piracy or plagiarism of results (the 'philosophicall robbery' of Robert Boyle, one of the Royal Society's founder fellows). Moreover, such work had not been evaluated by peer review.

Publication in journals overcame these objections: by publishing the scientist's name and the date on which the article had been received it gave him priority, evaluation gave the work authenticity, and afterwards publication disseminated it to critical readers—who could then replicate, modify, or refute it. Hence the pivotal role of publication, reinforced by statements by later scientists, such as Faraday's 'Work, finish, publish' or John Ziman's 'the object of science is publication'.

Ultimately much scientific work is superseded or shown to be false.

Perhaps no more than 10 per cent turns out to be valid and important and is incorporated into standard databases such as textbooks and review articles, a process that in medicine may take 10–15 years or longer. But on this base much of contemporary medical practice is founded—and practice often also affects public policy. Take cigarette smoking and lung cancer as an example. As Bartrip shows in his last chapter, the simple idea that one caused the other was put forward by two Americans before the Second World War. The hypothesis was shown to be statistically valid by a large case-control study in Britain in the 1940s and 1950s, published in the *BMJ* in 1954. These findings were then validated by other formal epidemiological studies, including one by the U.S. Surgeon-general, with the result that physicians pressed both individual patients and governments for action. Such efforts are continuing, but we've come a long way in 35 years: doctors in Britain and the US have largely given up smoking; virtually every citizen in the developed world knows of the dangers; and some countries have swingeing taxes on tobacco, ban advertisements, and legislate for smoke-free air.

All this has arisen out of publication—of the hypothesis, the epidemiological studies, the comments in the editorials and correspondence columns, and the journal campaigns to influence both medical and public opinion. And the same could be said for other topics, for example, nuclear weapons. Certainly those who work where the health services are organized know that much of medicine becomes political: government treasuries will not shift funds or allocate new money to fresh developments without validated data. An example only 20 years ago was the introduction of expensive drugs such as levodopa, and today it applies to newer, even more expensive agents such as erythropoietin and thrombolytics and to developments such as magnetic resonance imaging, pancreas transplantation, and even hospice care for the terminally ill.

This pivotal role is why the general journal has been described as a 'mirror of medicine'—and it might be asked whether the editor has a part at all. Surely the job could be done largely by computer, together with the help of outside expert advisers? But this is to regard a mirror as passive; even to look at a dictionary of symbols in art is to be assured that this isn't so. True a mirror is one symbol for pride, vanity, and even lust, but it is also a symbol of prudence, perception, and truth. A mirror can merely reflect, but it can also be used to focus on a particular issue; the type of glass is important for the image, and so on. But, let us shift the comparison to the impresario. In Paris just before the First World War there was a group of brilliant individuals: Igor Stravinsky, Tamara Karsarvina, and Leon Bakst. Somebody quite different was needed to bring composer, dancer, and designer together and create a marvel, *The Fire Bird.* This somebody was Diaghilev, the great impresario and a creative genius in his own right.

Without Diaghilev, much of Western art this century would not have evolved as it has. Much the same can be said about how some medical editors have influenced medicine over the past 180 years. So, besides running highly useful journals providing information, instruction, comment, and amusement, they have adjusted the mix according to their philosophies. And the great editors have added something that only the great impresarios can. They have balanced their journals and have campaigned for matters dear to their hearts and their consciences: Thomas Wakley of the *Lancet* for medical reform, Ernest Hart of the *BMJ* against infanticide, and, latterly, Robbie Fox of the *Lancet* for the recognition of the 'greater medical profession', and Arnold Relman of the *New England Journal* for an organized health service in the USA.

So the great editor must hold profound and informed convictions and possess the technical competence to deal with them. But he or she must also take care not to run a one-man band; he has to develop a strong team within and outside the office. Even if, like Ernest Hart, the editor is a compulsive traveller, his journal will still have a consistent strength whether he is actually around or not. All this must be done, moreover, against a background of stability, meaning editorial freedom and a healthy bank balance. The two last are indissolubly linked and, though they can never be absolute, they are rarely obtained without fighting; not for nothing did Hart say: 'An editor needs, and must have, many enemies: he cannot do without them. Woe be unto the journalist of whom all men say good things.' But when the editor has surrendered editorial freedom the journal has rapidly become tawdry, as occurred when Gerald Horner succeeded Dawson Williams and handed editorial control of the *BMJ* over to the medical politicians; Sir Douglas Black has described how in the 1930s one professor at St Andrews told every new class of students that one of the weekly medical journals should be put into the wastepaper basket still in its wrapper.

In 1946, then, Hugh Clegg had a difficult task in regaining editorial independence, but he was fortunate in two ways. First, he was able to forgo any subsidy by increasing the journal's income. This was the era of the drug revolution, initiated by the antibiotics and followed by the antihypertensives and the neuroleptics. Pharmaceutical manufacturers wanted to promote this spate of new drugs and where better than in the *BMJ* with a bright new editor? Equally valuable was the surge in 'classified' advertisements for jobs in the new National Health Service, with its myriad of fresh posts in both the hospitals and general practice.

Second, Clegg was fortunate in his powerful position on the medico-political scene; his journal often filled a vacuum by creating BMA policy, particularly during the NHS negotiations. He was well placed to argue with his titular masters, who might otherwise have told him what to write—but he was also one of them, and often his ideas were better thought out than theirs. And his trenchant writing was now done against a background of journal profitability, so that an opponent could not criticize the journal's views and remind its editor that the BMA was paying for these.

Clegg's successors have been preoccupied with balance sheets ever since—more so than with fighting for editorial freedom, an issue that has rarely arisen since the 'Gold-headed Cane' editorial (p. 288), and more than it did after Hart had won the battle over publishing the handwriting of the dying Emperor Frederick (p. 83). In fact relations with the BMA have consistently improved since 1965 and it is difficult to think of the gap that used to exist between the different sides of the courtyard at BMA House.

Another way of increasing revenue has been by diversifying its sources. At the time, one of Clegg's innovations was heavily criticized, since it then lost money, but his successors have blessed his foresight. The new source was the group of special journals, initiated by either the *BMJ* or a society, edited by a specialist with an independent editorial board, and published by the *BMJ*. The first of these, the *Archives of Disease in Childhood*, had been started by the *BMJ* as long ago as 1926, and the *British Heart Journal* followed in 1939, with the *Abstracts of World Medicine* in 1947. Clegg was active in promoting new titles during and just after the Second World War and by the time he retired they totalled 16, with an overall circulation of 34 500. Now there are 14, with a total circulation of 45 000, and there is also an active book publishing programme (with a list of 90 titles, publishing 10–12 new ones every year).

I have emphasized our publishing activities because profitability is the backdrop for much of the fun of the job—editing the *BMJ*. The revenue from these diversified activities has enabled us to survive post-war inflation, including the 30 per cent hyperinflation in the late 1970s. For added to all these problems is the burden placed on the *BMJ* by the (otherwise) welcome rise in BMA membership. Ever since the war the *Journal* has been produced at no cost to its members, receiving no subvention from BMA subscriptions. Often, despite the difficulties, the *BMJ* has made a surplus, even after every BMA member has been supplied with a free copy every week. And overall the group has been consistently profitable, currently with an annual turnover of £15m, more than £3m in earmarked reserves, and a staff of over 100.

Such a strategy has enabled the *BMJ* to survive and to change its appearance, presentation, and content. The new look of 1988 did not merely continue the tradition of good design started by Clegg and Stanley Morison in the 1930s: besides economies from using a standard size paper and a flexible layout, it enabled us to introduce fresh sections such as six pages of News, a full list of contents, and an Editor's Choice for that week. 'This Week in the *BMJ*' explains the reason for publishing any individual article; if one seems too recondite for the general reader the authors can point out implications for practice.

Such 'user-friendliness' is a characteristic of general journals that my colleagues and I admire, and it is no secret that we based the revised *BMJ* on *The Economist*, *The Listener*, *Nature*, and *Science*. Such changes were in line with the policy of making the articles themselves more readable. We placed much more emphasis on authors shortening their articles before acceptance, and then on creative sub-editing—rewriting for easy comprehension, particularly by non-native English readers.

Authors don't always like having their articles changed, but, provided that the meaning isn't altered, and authors can check this on a proof, the readers' interests come first. For years editors have rewritten the leading articles—with few complaints from their authors, who are often grateful for the increased clarity—while any article by a staff member is scrutinized by two or three colleagues. And the frequent gibe that this results in uniform mediocrity can be refuted by the variety of styles in the articles. Radical creative editing is well illustrated by the 'ABC' series, of which we have now published 15 since the 'ABC of Ophthalmology' in 1979. The authors provide a draft, which they know will be totally rewritten and married to relevant illustrations. They then have an opportunity to check this for accuracy and emphasis. Not every subject is suitable for such treatment, and conventionally styled articles still have a valuable role. Nevertheless, with the right subject, such as child abuse or resuscitation, a short and pithy text with high-quality illustrations is a powerful combination.

Shortening original articles and introducing Short Reports have enabled the *Journal* to continue its important informative function; we still publish as many papers as previously but in less space. The pages released have been used for developing the sections for instruction, comment, and amusement—including Regular Reviews, a larger correspondence column, and two new sections, one called at first Medical Practice and then Middles, the other Practice Observed, devoted to family medicine. But more important, I hope, has been a change in attitude. To a reader today the *Journal* of 1965 seems not only ponderous but pompous. There are numerous verbatim lectures by the good and the great (even in Clegg's time one of the first articles was the President's address to the BMA's Annual Representative Meeting); an extraordinary number of pages is devoted to reporting the political debates and the scientific seminars at BMA meetings; anybody with an FRS always has it printed after his name; dinners are reported at length; the leading articles are anonymous and often sit on a fence made of waffle; though much space is devoted to medical policies, all are BMA events (or whinges about pay); and, as for news of the world outside or campaigning series of articles, Ernest Hart might never have reported on conditions in Europe or in the Colonies or attacked infanticide or the lack of an Armed Forces medical service.

Somebody reading today's *BMJ* in 2115 will have as many adverse comments, and this is not to criticize Clegg—his place is secure in the pantheon of great medical editors—but to give the background to some of the latter day changes. Few speeches or lectures are worth putting into print: if they are good then they have been correctly tailored for a different occasion. Again, anonymity largely belongs to the past. So many assertions have implications for public policy that the non-specialist must know the evidence and who is putting these forward, particularly in editorials—a trend that is world-wide. (But anonymity may still have a place; after checking the facts, the editor may avoid a libel action by making a complaint general rather than specific, or protect the identity of a junior doctor, civil servant, or employee whose job might be in jeopardy.) And, like many other medical organizations, the BMA has started to publish a medico-political newspaper, thus taking the load off the *BMJ* of publishing the mass of day to day medico-political events.

Another change has been the increased rigour in vetting original articles for publication, for analysis has shown how many poor ones have been published. Initially this means good, unprejudiced, and quick peer review, followed by discussion by an editorial committee and statistical assessment, with the authors being required to make the agreed changes if the article is accepted. Editors should also be ready to admit that they may have been wrong, particularly allowing appeals from the authors of rejected articles and seeking fresh peer review. And they should audit their own practices.

Most editors work in isolation and they have much to learn, from each other and from referees, statisticians, authors, and publishers—nationally and internationally. Hence the rage for truth has continued with forming editors' organizations—such as the Council of Biology Editors (1957) and the European Association of Science Editors (1967), both of which publish regular bulletins and occasional manuals on editing, style, illustrations, economics, and so on. *BMJ* editors have participated in both of these, and in helping other national or regional organizations, such as in Australasia, India, and South-East Asia. In 1979 the *Journal* was also a founder member of the 'Vancouver Group', the International Committee of Medical *Journal* Editors, made up of the editors of the 13 principal general journals in the world. This has produced recommendations on reference format, definition of authorship, duplicate publication, and editorial responsibility in cases of medical misconduct.

All of these 'journalogical' developments, however, would be mere piety unless the contents of the *BMJ* justified the effort. So in the past 25 years has it reflected the changes in society in general and in medicine in particular? To do this has not been as easy as it sounds. For many editors of major general journals share my perspective that something has happened to clinical research; possibly the papers reporting high quality work of general interest are being submitted straight to special journals rather than to general ones; possibly today's advances are less intelligible to the non-specialist, are more fragmented, or are dotting small i's and crossing small t's; or possibly clinical as opposed to basic research is over the top, having peaked in the 1950s and early 1960s. Certainly the proportion of good scientific papers by British workers has been falling and the *BMJ* has relied increasingly on contributions from elsewhere, particularly the Nordic countries. And we see few clinical papers published in other journals, general or specialist, that invoke envy. To be cynical, it is difficult to see how general journals would have got sufficient high-quality original work without the appearance of AIDS, although we continue to publish good articles on well-established subjects such as diabetes, hypertension, and asthma.

So the supply would have altered the contents of general journals anyway, but there was also a considerable demand for radical changes. For all over the world the post-war era has been one of disenchantment with the professions; no longer will society accept their omniscience and unchallenged authority. In particular, health has come under attack, for its costs, ethics, and relationships. And in Britain, with the first universal State health service in the world, there are particular problems. Socially the country has the hallmarks of an ancient regime; general industry is underfunded and decaying; and we spend much less on capital investment, education, and infrastructure than our counterparts.

To some extent, however, health has been fortunate: though Britain spends less of its gross national product than other countries, the National Health Service has been strikingly cost-effective. Administrative costs are small and general practice (where 90 per cent of patient contacts occur) is not only now of a high standard but also an effective barrier to unnecessary hospital care. Moreover, power within the profession has been diffused: whereas in 1945 it rested with two or three medical royal colleges, today there are no fewer than 16 colleges and faculties. This plurality makes it difficult for doctors to speak with one voice, but it has enabled individual sections of the profession to develop without interference. Finally doctors have realized that medicine is not the whole answer to medical problems: adverse social factors also have an important role in causing disease, especially deprivation, alcoholism, and unemployment.

The development of general practice is a good example of how these changes have been reflected in the *BMJ*. Since the Lloyd George bill of 1911 family doctors have been powerful negotiators, as documented in the *Journal* reports of the various committees and argued about in its Letters to the Editor. The intellectual basis of general practice was much less obvious—in fact, many hospital doctors probably agreed privately with Lord Moran's inept aside that general practitioners had fallen off the ladder of achievement and esteem. So when a college of general practitioners was incorporated in 1952 the *BMJ* warmly welcomed the idea, publishing the report of its steering committee and commenting in a further editorial three years later that 'here we seem to see a veritable renaissance of general practice which has behind it men of vision, energy, and courage who, like the men who founded quite a different kind of society in the seventeenth century, eschew politics and seek to add to knowledge as well as take part in its organisation.'

Not everybody approved of a college of general practitioners, however, and there was occasional opposition in the correspondence columns; yet before it started its own journal the college's activities were fully recorded in the *BMJ* and commended in further editorials. Despite this, general practice was still in the doldrums, and it was difficult to achieve high standards in service work let alone academia. The problem was not only esteem; the discipline was starved of resources, and a popular phrase of the time described it as a 'cottage industry'. In the early 1960s the agitation by the BMA for the formation of group practices with proper premises and ancillary staff came to a head. Much of the arguments raged in the *BMJ*, in editorials, letters to the editor, and reports of the committee debates, and the *Journal* defied BMA policy to run a series comparing the advantages and disadvantages of health centres with those of group practices.

All this resulted in the Family Doctor Charter of 1965, and the *Journal* then reflected rapid improvements in standards by introducing the heading 'The New General Practice', with the articles later being collected into a book. Finally the development of vocational training and academic units resulted in enough original and other material to have a completely new section 'Practice Observed', giving to family medicine the prominence it deserved.

Other important developments for the whole profession in the 1960s and 1970s included the postgraduate educational centres and professional audit and both were reflected in commissioned articles and reports of progress. Interestingly it was then that views about the National Health Service began to change. When I arrived at the *BMJ* in 1964 the attitudes of my colleagues, as also reflected in the *Journal*, were those of White Russians expecting the Tsar to come back—disillusion with the new regime, with the return of the pre-war system just around the corner. Gradually opinions altered: reports showed that other health services were more expensive and less effective, and that the British one was ideal for treating serious disease and rotten for other conditions—with a second-rate hotel service (poor manners and decrepit premises) and long waiting lists. Three reorganizations of the NHS failed to overcome the drawbacks and the *BMJ* correspondence and editorials started to argue that we needed to retain its structure and improve the details—spending proportionately as much on health as other developed countries.

All this culminated in an emotional support of the status quo when in 1989 Kenneth Clarke published radical proposals for yet another reform of the National Health Service. Many people thought that he had produced only some vapid principles without giving the all important details; in editorials and commissioned articles the *BMJ* explored some of the implications of the proposals, showing how complex the issues were. The conclusions were that, though the profession welcomed some of the proposals—money following the patient and medical audit (which doctors had started some years before)—the others were far too vague to introduce without blueprints, pilot studies, and modern information systems in place.

These arguments are still far too near to be able to assess what part, if any, the *BMJ* will have played in the outcome. But a general journal is valuable in being able to disseminate such proposals widely and accurately, to allow both editorial and external comment on them, and to document their evolution as it occurs. To look back at the *BMJ* in the 1930s and 1940s is to be reminded of its similar role in moulding and reflecting opinion over the original National Health Service. If politicians had done this they would not have recently repeated the inaccurate gibe that the BMA was against the NHS; in fact, from the establishment of a planning committee in 1936 the Association had always supported the principle of a health service, with the later arguments centring on details.

Another important change in attitude has been the emphasis on how important social factors are in causing many diseases. Probably no publication since Seebohm Rowntree's pre-war survey *Poverty and Progress* has shown this as cogently as the Black Report of 1984: Disraeli's 'two nations' were still present 150 years later. Yet there was a clear attempt by the government to suppress it. Only a few copies of a duplicated text were produced, the launch occurred in the dead period of the summer parliamentary recess and there was only a last minute press conference. As did other journals and newspapers, the *BMJ* could bring all this out into the open, summarizing and commenting on the report's principal findings and conclusions, as well as the reasons for censorship. Even more importantly, it could extend some of these in series of commissioned articles: what are the effects of unemployment, alcohol, or bad housing on health, and why does Britain find it necessary proportionately to have twice as many of its citizens locked up in prisons as the Netherlands? Campaigning journalism this might be (and this phrase was to be used as a term of abuse by the establishment old-boy network who objected privately to similar series on research policy and the General Medical Council) but, scrupulously checked, the facts were accurate and the opinions those of an identifiable writer—while the correspondence columns were open to those who wanted to object. It was an attitude, I hope, that Hart would have supported and, to my mind, such series were just as valuable as an equivalent number of original articles.

Yet this does illustrate the tension inherent in any general journal, between its 'newspaper' and its 'recorder' functions (to use Sir Theodore Fox's terms), and between letting too many subjective views intrude into objectivity. But it is out of this that the fun arises, and I can think of few jobs that could offer such satisfaction, particularly given the close-knit and expert editorial and managerial team the *BMJ* has had over the past 25 years. It was this that made essential the fights for editorial freedom, the financial manoeuvrings, and the time devoted in the early 1970s to contesting a libel action that threatened the right to print scientific findings that had undergone rigorous evaluation. It is this also, I believe, that should make the history of the *BMJ* of interest to other people. And, though there can be no objective measures of reader satisfaction with the journal, one can quote the words of Robbie Fox's successor at the *Lancet*, Ian Douglas-Wilson: 'An editor should aim to please himself; if he does not do that, he will certainly please nobody else.'

Anniversaries tend to be smug and self-satisfied occasions, but I would hate anybody to think that the *BMJ*'s editorial team is unaware of many unanswered questions. Why are so many original articles in journals so substandard after so much work on them? Why do possibly only a 10th of those published in any journal end up as valid after only 10 years? Is far too much time spent on being fair to indifferent papers that stand no chance of being published? Could we do better if we dismantled our ponderous, and expensive, peer review mechanism—or do we need more? How many important happenings in medicine are totally ignored by the *Journal*, for one reason or another? These questions are not peculiar to the *BMJ* but I wonder whether our decline in the citation figures, and our lowish position compared with other contemporaries, means that we have been wrong in our choice of articles or have been seduced by the attractions of documenting social evils—or that authors still dislike journals which are attached, however loosely, to powerful political organizations. Further, why, compared with Hart, have we found it so difficult to rebuild after the war regular reports by foreign contributors? Moreover, to my mind one of the most interesting sections of the *BMJ* contains the book reviews—yet most are indifferently written and it is the least read part of the whole journal. Why?

Above all, I envy Wakley and Hart their radical journals, relatively unfettered by the libel laws; what medicine needs today perhaps more than anything else is its own *Private Eye*, or, possibly more attainably, the return of *World Medicine* under Michael O'Donnell. All professions need to be reminded of 'how things really are'—the deceits, the shabby compromises, and the true reasons for particular decisions. Yet a truly radical approach is, I suspect, incompatible with the essential contents of a general journal, and perhaps too much self-criticism may make a profession excessively inward looking. In any case when Peter Bartrip's book comes to be revised for the 200th anniversary, I hope that it will be able to report a sustained evolution. The journal group will be larger and equally profitable and the *BMJ* will be continuing to reveal, criticize, stimulate, and shock, acting as a conscience to the medical profession and goading it to act, without any close identification with the medical establishment.

Developments since 1965: A chronological framework

STEPHEN LOCK, EDITOR, *BMJ*

1965 (December)	Hugh Clegg retires as editor. Circulation of *BMJ* 82 800. Total of 16 special journals published, with overall circulation of 34 500. Four publications on book list.
1966	Martin Ware, editor. Publishes original article 'Porphyria: a Royal Malady' by Ida Macalpine and Richard Hunter (later expanded into a book). A classic work, even if there are doubts about its verisimilitude; rejected by Clegg but retained by Ware for publication under his editorship—an important symbolic gesture away from Clegg's preoccupation with hard science and dislike of 'soft' papers (particularly social medicine).
1967	Australian edition (ended 1968).
1968	New cover design—not universal contents on cover. First 'Personal View' (Lord Platt).
1971	'Medical Practice' section introduced (collecting Middle Articles, Current Practice, and Book Reviews, together with new features).
1972	Libel action. Action discontinued after 35 days of hearing in the High Court of case brought by Mr. S. L. Drummond-Jackson alleging libel in an Original Article published in *BMJ* (May 1969). First of many medical writing courses world-wide in Helsinki by *BMJ* team. Professional and Scientific Publications established to publish journals belonging to other societies.
1974	'Short Reports' introduced. Signed meeting reports introduced.
1975	Martin Ware retires (July). Journal circulation 84 000 (16 800 to non-members). 17 special journals published, overall circulation 51 000. Stephen Lock, editor. Materia non Medica and twice-yearly Book Supplements introduced.
1976	Co-ownership of six special journals established, with those specialist societies that had played a major part with the BMA in establish-

ing them. Introduction of 'Hanging Committee'—a changing group composed of two medically qualified members of the *BMJ* staff, two of the four associate editors (consultants), and a statistician. Having read all the dozen or so original articles under consideration and the referee's report on them, they discuss every week which should be accepted. They also hear appeals on decisions and discuss general policy.
Introduction of Minerva and Medicine and the Media.

1977 Statistical assessment of Original Articles introduced.

1979 First 'ABC' (Ophthalmology, by P. A. Gardner).

1980 First cottage technical editor appointed (freelance, working largely from home).

1981 'Split run': introduction of three separate but editorially identical editions—Clinical Research, Overseas, and Practice Observed. These used miniprint, in the first two for the Practice Observed section and in the third for the Clinical Research section (a hand lens was provided, but many subscribers could read the miniprint with the naked eye). The advertisements were different for the three editions, and so revenue was increased—but more importantly it enabled the journal to develop a new section devoted to academic as well as service general practice. Subsequently miniprint was abandoned because of insufficient regular contributions from general practice. Signed editorials introduced.

1982 Special issue for 150th Anniversary of BMA.
First Christmas issue with special articles and cover design by a young artist (on this occasion Paul Cox).

1983 Hugh Clegg dies.
Keynes Press introduced.

1987 *BMJ* presents special tapestry by Marta Rogoyska to BMA Library for 100th anniversary.
Hugh Clegg scholarship for medical students to spend three months at *BMJ*.
Memoir Club books introduced.

1988 New design by Eiichi Kono, realized by Ray Fishwick, the *BMJ's* designer since 1975. A4 format, five column grid; new sections (News, Editor's Choice, This Week in the *BMJ*, Opinion). This won the Charlesworth Award for Typographical Excellence in 1989.

1989 Registrar in medical journalism: appointment of an additional, junior doctor to serve on the staff for one year.

1990	'Audit in Practice' section started. Celebrations of the 150th anniversary of the *BMJ*. Plans include publication of history, special issue of *BMJ*, and *Apollo*, a Keynes's Press anthology of poems by doctors, edited by Professor Edward Lowbury; two-day Wellcome/*BMJ* conference on history of scientific journals at Royal Institution; exhibition at BMA House; anniversary banquet in Banqueting House.
1990 (April)	Circulation of *BMJ* 105 000 (20 000 to non-members). 14 special journals printed (seven co-owned, seven owned by *BMJ* group); total circulation 45 000. Nine PSP journals published. Book list shows 63 *BMJ* books published since 1984, 13 Memoir Club titles, and 13 Keynes Press editions (three having sold out). Total turnover for financial year 1989–90 £14 million; surplus £400,000; revenues earmarked in journal's name £3½ million. Total staff 100.

Chairman of Journal Committee

1965–6	J. G. M. Hamilton
1967	Sir Alan Moncrieff
1968–9	Sir Thomas Holmes Sellors
1970–2	L. P. Garrod
1973–82	Sir James Howie
1983–7	Barry O'Donnell
1988	R. A. Keable Elliott

Index

The letter '*n*' immediately following a page number refers to footnotes.